The Emperor Who Never Was

THE EMPEROR
WHO NEVER WAS

Dara Shukoh in Mughal India

S U P R I Y A   G A N D H I

THE BELKNAP PRESS OF
HARVARD UNIVERSITY PRESS
Cambridge, Massachusetts
London, England
2020

First printing

Library of Congress Cataloging-in-Publication Data

Names: Gandhi, Supriya, 1977– author.
Title: The emperor who never was : Dara Shukoh in Mughal India /
Supriya Gandhi.
Description: Cambridge, Massachusetts : The Belknap Press of Harvard University
Press, 2020. | Includes bibliographical references and index. |
Identifiers: LCCN 2019032493 | ISBN 9780674987296 (cloth)
Subjects: LCSH: Dārā Shikūh, Prince, son of Shahjahan, Emperor of India,
1615–1659. | Princes—India—Biography. | Philosopher-kings. |
India—History—1526–1765.
Classification: LCC DS461.9.D3 G36 2020 | DDC 954.02/57092 [B]—dc23
LC record available at https://lccn.loc.gov/2019032493

CONTENTS

NOTE ON TRANSLITERATIONS
AND CONVENTIONS

For ease and elegance, I have eschewed the use of technical diacritical marks for proper names and for Persian, Arabic, Hindi, Urdu, and Sanskrit words. In most cases, I transliterate these in a manner approximating their pronunciation in South Asia. For specialists, the relevant terms and phrases can be reconstructed generally with little ambiguity. Today, Dara Shukoh's name is most commonly transliterated and pronounced as "Dara Shikoh." However, "Dara Shukoh," which I employ here, more accurately reflects the name in seventeenth-century usage during the prince's lifetime. I do retain "Mughal" for the dynasty to which Dara Shukoh belonged. Though anachronistic, the term for the great Indian dynasty is enmeshed in our historical vocabulary for the period.

The Emperor Who Never Was

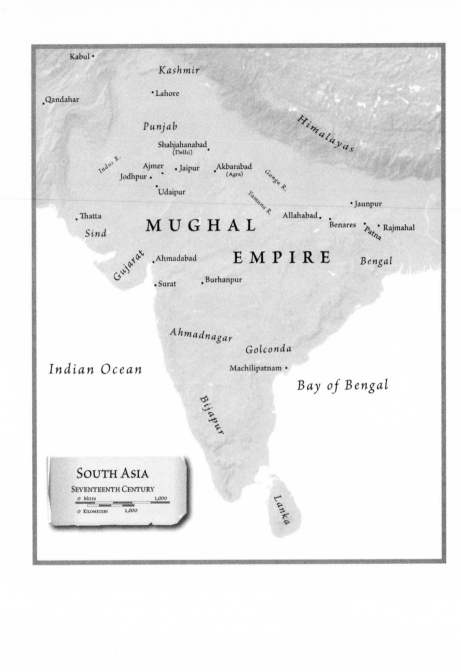

Kabul •

Kashmir

• Qandahar

• Lahore

Himalayas

Punjab

Shahjahanabad •
(Delhi)

Indus R.

Ajmer
• • Jaipur
Jodhpur •

Akbarabad •
(Agra)

Ganga R.

• Udaipur

Yamuna R.

• Jaunpur

• Thatta

Sind

Allahabad •

Benares •
• Patna
• Rajmahal

M U G H A L

E M P I R E

Bengal

• Ahmadabad

Gujarat

• Surat

• Burhanpur

Ahmadnagar

Golconda

Indian Ocean

Machilipatnam •

Bay of Bengal

Bijapur

Lanka

SOUTH ASIA

SEVENTEENTH CENTURY

0 MILES   1,000

0 KILOMETERS   1,000

INTRODUCTION

August 29, 1659

A judge takes his seat in the private audience hall of Delhi's red sandstone fort. Only days ago Aurangzeb, the new emperor, had proclaimed himself ruler of Hindustan, choosing the title Alamgir, or "world-seizer." The emperor is not physically present in the room, but his authority is palpable. Shadows flicker behind a latticed marble partition, through which imperial women listen to the proceedings, unseen. The trial is about to begin. A prisoner is dragged in, his hands and feet shackled. Dara Shukoh, elder brother of Aurangzeb, stands charged with apostasy.

The prosecutor is unrelenting in his cross-examination. "Dara Shukoh, tell us, are you a secret Sikh?" And then, "So you believe, frankly, Prince, that the Hindu faith is as valid as the Muslim faith?" Dara Shukoh eloquently defends his ideas. "Who cares which door you open to come into the light?" he asks. Finally, the prosecutor orders Dara to present his ring. Damning evidence. It is engraved with "Allah" on one side and "Prabhu," a Hindu word for the divine, on the other. He snaps, "Prince Dara, it is unpalatably clear . . . that you strayed, long, long ago, from the pure path of Islam." Shortly after the trial, Aurangzeb orders armed slaves to snuff out his brother's life.

Dara Shukoh and Aurangzeb were real historical figures. They were Muslim princes of an Indian dynasty founded in 1526 by their forefather, Babur. Toward the end of his life, Dara initiated a large project of engaging with what we might today call Hindu thought. The prince himself made a comparative study of Hindu and Islamic religious concepts and had the Upanishads, a collection of Hindu sacred texts, translated into Persian. He was killed in a struggle for succession that he lost to his younger brother, Aurangzeb. But there probably never was a trial. At least, the historical chronicles of the time do not speak of one. The scene described above comes from a 2015 theater performance staged in London, adapted by Tanya Ronder from a play written and directed in Lahore by Shahid Nadeem.[1]

Yet the trial has been so integral to the modern story of these two brothers. Mohsin Hamid's *Moth Smoke,* published in 2000, uses the trial of Dara Shukoh as an allegorical frame for his gritty novel about contemporary Pakistan. Akbar Ahmed's 2007 play dramatizes the prince's trial by drawing on the author's earlier experience as a magistrate in Pakistan. Many historical novels about the Mughal Empire feature the trial. Even Ishtiaq Husain Qureshi, historian of independent Pakistan, refers to a "political trial," of Dara Shukoh, arguing that it "was meant to demonstrate to the orthodox that the empire had been saved from a revival of heresy."[2]

The trial is a powerful motif because it transforms a story about seventeenth-century India into a narrative about today. It creates a dialectic between two opposing visions of Islam: Islam as zealous extremism, immediately familiar in our present context, and its counterpoint—Islam as Sufi antinomianism. But even without the supposed trial, the brothers' clash is a story that addresses the deepest questions of who we are and how we got here.

The battle for succession between Dara Shukoh and Aurangzeb is an origin myth of the subcontinent's present, seen as a crucial turning point in the progression of South Asian history. But it is not a stable myth. Its tellings and retellings shift and settle into the subcontinent's fault lines of nation and ideology.

According to one version, Aurangzeb's victory over Dara Shukoh cleared the way for Muslim political assertion in the subcontinent. In his 1918 collection of Persian verse, *Rumuz-i bekhudi,* the poet-philosopher Muhammad Iqbal, who also outlined an early vision for the state of Pakistan, pronounces judgment on the two brothers. For him, Dara Shukoh represented a dangerous shoot of heresy in the Mughal dynasty that needed to be uprooted: "When the seed of heresy that Akbar nourished / Once again sprang up in Dara's essential nature / The heart's candle was snuffed out in every breast / Our nation was not secure from corruption.[3]

Iqbal speaks glowingly of Aurangzeb, sent by God to save the Muslim community: "Divine Truth chose Alamgir from India / That ascetic, that swordmaster/To revive religion He commissioned him/To renew belief He commissioned him." Aurangzeb here takes on an almost prophetic role. In fact, later in the same poem, Iqbal compares him to Abraham, a foundational prophet of Islam, who smashed stone idols in the Kaaba in order to foster monotheism.[4]

Later, after the new nation-state of Pakistan was born, Ishtiaq Husain Qureshi wove Dara Shukoh and Aurangzeb into his story of the subcontinent's Muslims. Like Iqbal's account, Qureshi's is teleological. Historical events lead inexorably to the present, all linked by a single thread. Aurangzeb's victory over Dara becomes a crucial turning point in the march to a separate Muslim homeland. Qureshi says approvingly of Aurangzeb, "Character and ability overcame resources and numbers. . . . This was the hour of triumph for orthodoxy."[5]

In a contrasting version, this fratricidal war is a tragedy. Its outcome becomes the reason South Asia's nation-states now bristle with mutual hostility and its societies suffer from religious violence. The columnist Ashok Malik expresses this view in his remarks on Dara's killing, saying, "It was the partition before Partition . . . Dara Shukoh was killed on an August night 350 years ago, and with him died hopes of a lasting Hindu-Muslim compact."[6]

Well before Malik and others who share his perspective, secular nationalists in the early twentieth century mourned the result of this seventeenth-century succession struggle. They saw Dara Shukoh as a premodern seeker of harmony between Hindus and Muslims. In 1910, the twenty-three-year-old future nationalist leader Maulana Abul Kalam Azad defended Dara. The Sufi prince, he argued, was a "master of direct spiritual experience" for "in quest of the goal, he lifted away the distinction between the dervish monastery and the Meccan sanctuary." In Azad's view, Aurangzeb valorized reason over mysticism and set the stage for future discord between Hindus and Muslims.[7]

This origin story sometimes takes on another twist. In this version, Dara Shukoh is the singular exception in centuries of oppression under Muslim rule. We see this, for instance, in the case of the nineteenth-century Hindu reformer in the Punjab, Kanhaiyalal Alakhdhari. Alakhdhari denounced the Mughals and the Delhi Sultans, pronouncing, "for the last eight hundred years, the fate of India was as dark as the reflection in a mirror."[8] Yet, ironically, he relied heavily on Dara Shukoh's Persian translations of Hindu texts to educate the Hindus of his time about their own traditions.[9]

This nineteenth-century attitude toward the prince continues to reverberate. In 1990, the journalist Saeed Naqvi interviewed the Hindu nationalist leader Bhaurao Deoras. Naqvi pressed Deoras to acknowledge that, throughout history, Muslims had embraced or admired aspects of Hindu thought. He gave the example of Dara Shukoh: "Someone like Dara Shikoh. Now Hindus must accept him as a hero."

"He is a hero," Deoras acquiesced. "But the Muslim community did not permit him to live."[10] Ironically, for someone like Deoras, Dara is only redeemed by his untimely death. Had Dara lived to rule, like Akbar, no doubt he too would have been vilified.

In their multiple guises, Mughal royals like Aurangzeb and Dara Shukoh still inhabit today's South Asia. Their names (particularly Aurangzeb's) are regularly invoked in the public realm. Their personalities seem luminously transparent even when the details of their historical contexts remain shadowy. Dara Shukoh and Aurangzeb are mythical characters. They were, of course, also historical figures. But they are mythical because they seem familiar enough to have always existed and because their story animates modern ideologies. If in myth, as Roland Barthes once said, "history evaporates," myth also clads ideological structures in a narrative form.[11]

What we know of the two brothers is lodged in countless layers of accumulated historical memory. In Dara Shukoh's case, although the prince prolifically documented his spiritual and intellectual explorations, the accounts and anecdotes related by others—his contemporaries and those after him—have been more influential in shaping his later image. Chronicles, from a victor's viewpoint, written by Aurangzeb's courtiers and partisans, list Dara's heresies. Whisperings and tidbits of gossip make their way from oral tradition into colorful eighteenth-century writings. Early memoirs of European visitors to the Mughal court inform later, colonial narratives. Other colonial accounts often paint Aurangzeb as a brutal despot, in an effort to show that Indians could not effectively rule themselves.

The two brothers, together with their supporters, emerge as polar opposites: Dara as idealistic, naive, leading a motley band of wayward Sufis, naked ascetics, and Hindu pandits; Aurangzeb as austere, shrewd, ruthless, flanked by Muslim clerics, and helming a powerful army of the nation's nobility. Needless to say, these images fail to capture the complexity and nuance of their lives and contexts.

Despite these oversimplified, anachronistic portraits of Dara Shukoh and his younger brother, often what is at stake is whether Dara Shukoh is remembered at all. Aurangzeb's legacy persists far more vividly. In India, a politician breaks with his father's party, and his opponents mockingly call him Aurangzeb. The connotations of this dog-whistle are immediately apparent. Nobody needs to explain that it signals both the politician's lack of filial respect and his support among Muslim voters. Another politician demands to change the name of Delhi's Aurangzeb Road, because this reminder of the Mughal emperor inflames a festering wound over his temple destructions, both real and alleged. Aurangzeb's looming presence in modern South Asia overshadows that of his elder brother.

Remembering Dara Shukoh today—or erasing his memory—is a political act. In Pakistan, laments Shahid Nadeem, "Dara . . . has almost been wiped out from the history books."[12] In today's India, the prince receives only inconsistent, sporadic commemoration. In 2017, the Hindu-nationalist-dominated municipal corporation of Delhi voted to rename a road, named for the British governor general Lord Dalhousie, after Dara Shukoh.[13] This renaming served only to complete the erasure of Aurangzeb from Delhi's public spaces. But when the four-hundredth anniversary of Dara Shukoh's birth fell in March 2015, there had been no official recognition of the event by the ruling Hindu nationalist party. This was the sort of occasion, in a different age, where scholars and politicians would have feted the late prince as an early harbinger of secularism and pluralism.

In 2014, with the late storyteller Ankit Chadha, I began work on the script for a performance on Dara Shukoh's life. It contained the incipient seeds of this book. When faculty at Ambedkar University put on a festival commemorating Dara Shukoh's birth anniversary, Ankit performed the story as a dastan, a traditional form of Urdu storytelling, on the steps of a hybrid Mughal-British mansion where the prince himself had once lived.

For my collaboration with Ankit, I sifted ingredients for a story out of a polyphony of Persian and Hindi sources—a poem here, an anecdote there. I was keen that we avoid romanticizing the prince as a hapless do-gooder. Ankit advised me that a dastan should not sound like a history lesson. Together, we worked on developing a narrative arc that built up dramatic tension and condensed in miniature the complexities of Dara Shukoh's life and times.

Before working on the dastan, I had already started another, longer, story. At first, I resisted writing a biography of Dara Shukoh, though I had earlier closely studied several of his writings. I had no wish to promote an outdated and flawed idea of history that privileges "great men." Neither did I seek to step inside Dara Shukoh's mind and try to ascertain his inner motivations. But I did want to explore his context in the court, along with the Mughal state's workings, and the ideas surrounding him. I also wanted to investigate the other people—women and men, famous and forgotten—whose paths crossed his, and the material conditions that allowed him to rule and write his books. History is often too messy to enclose in the storyline of a single person. What follows is not a biography in a narrow sense of the word, though it follows closely the life and times of a single figure. Dara Shukoh and his writings are at the story's center, but its focus is wider.

I use narrative to craft this book, because stories like Dara Shukoh's that are constantly told and retold are never complete. They are always in need of new tellings. The tale's barest contours are indisputable: Dara Shukoh was a Mughal prince in seventeenth-century India. Like most princes, he studied and wrote; but he threw himself into these activities more deeply than did most other royals. As was the case for princes in early modern empires, his succession to the throne was by no means assured. He had to stake his claim to the throne, and in the process he was killed.

But the argument is in the details. The particulars of Dara's times and his own trajectory are so crucial to the story's texture. The strands of Dara's story are tightly woven into many others. We see this, for instance, in the ways the Mughal state negotiated its place among its Hindu-majority subjects; in how the court cultivated the support of a diverse and powerful nobility that bridged religious and ethnic fissures; in the patterns of Muslim learning and piety in circles associated with the court, which did not reflect the stark divisions between Sufis and ulama seen in the modern day; and in the very vision of kingship that Mughal sovereigns and courtiers infused with so much wonder, awe, and mystery that few subjects would dare even conceive of their world without a supreme ruler. This was the context in which Dara Shukoh came of age and expected to rule.

The last biography of Dara Shukoh in English was first published in 1935. It was one of two important books on the prince to appear in India during the first half of the twentieth century.[14] These were serious, weighty studies. Kalika Ranjan Qanungo, author of the biography, combed through historical chronicles to detail Dara Shukoh's public life and military campaigns. Bikrama Jit Hasrat's book, not a biography, as such, but a study of the prince's writings, collates and describes the many works that Dara composed or sponsored. For Hasrat and Qanungo, Dara Shukoh symbolized a lost possibility of Hindu-Muslim concord that needed to be recovered. Qanungo writes, "It is hardly an exaggeration to say that anyone who intends to take up the solution of the problem of religious peace in India, must begin the work where Dara had left it." The two make their sympathies plain. Hasrat calls Aurangzeb "a stern puritan."[15] Qanungo declares, "The world has not become richer in any way by the long reign of Aurangzib; but it would have been certainly poorer without a Dara Shukoh."[16]

The division of focus that these two books display is telling. One reconstructs Dara's political life and the other examines his writings. Each, in its own way, suspects that for all Dara Shukoh's talents and interests, the prince would not have been a capable ruler. He was too deeply immersed in spiritual affairs, they suggest. As this narrative goes, it was almost inevitable that, for the sake of the empire's continuity, Dara would succumb to Aurangzeb's ruthless ambition and political acumen. Bikrama Jit Hasrat ascribes purely transcendent motives to Dara's "burning passion for knowledge," and rejects any attribution of "political forethought" to the prince's "theosophist" inclinations.[17]

But Dara Shukoh's life story, set in the religious and political landscape of seventeenth-century India, is a far more intricate and complex mosaic. Dara's spiritual journey was integrally linked to his role as ruler. He was a prince brought up to think of himself as a future emperor; indeed, he might very well have become one. Dara Shukoh developed sustained religious and intellectual interests, perhaps to a greater degree than any other Mughal prince before him, though his elder sister Jahanara accompanied him in exploring Sufi devotional practice. He very consciously sought to advance spiritually, first under the tutelage of his Qadiri Sufi teachers and later by engaging with a range of religious figures and books. However, his foremost concern was how to weld the life of a prince, enmeshed in the material world, with the cultivation of his inner self. His writings show that he viewed his spiritual activities as inextricably linked to his role as a royal. For him, these two goals did not clash; indeed, they were inseparably connected.

Dara Shukoh was not a misfit in the Mughal court. He tapped ingredients of political authority—asceticism and piety—that sovereigns in the subcontinent had long used. For example, both his great-grandfather Akbar and his grandfather Jahangir made public decisions to abstain from animal flesh. They each made barefoot pilgrimages to the shrine of the twelfth-century Iraqi Sufi Muin-ud-Din Chishti in Ajmer. They also met with non-Muslim religious figures, including Hindus and Christians, and had artists memorialize these encounters. Of course, Mughal emperors were not primarily humble devotees. They were seen foremost as divine sovereigns. A distinctive notion of divine kingship arose in Mughal India, gathering up a profusion of symbols and idioms of power from Greco-Persian, Central Asian, and Indic traditions.[18] Dara Shukoh engaged with these ideas and practices. Instead of rejecting rulership, he sought to define Mughal sovereignty in his own way.

The prince's interest in Indic religions continued a legacy fostered by Muslim rulers before him. Dara Shukoh was never a liberal, nor did he promote interfaith harmony in the modern senses of these terms. Yet he oversaw an extraordinary exercise in cross-cultural understanding, particularly during the last few years of his short life. The intellectual fruits of this period form his most enduring bequest.

The courts of Muslim rulers the world over had long nurtured a tradition of translation. In Baghdad, the Abbasid caliphs ordered masses of

Greek works to be translated into Arabic. Even before the Mughal conquest of Hindustan, at the time of the Delhi Sultans, Muslim rulers and aristocrats in the subcontinent fueled a hugely generative encounter between Sanskrit and Persian knowledge systems. They mined Sanskrit learning for manuals on topics such as music, astronomy, and the care of domestic animals, which they rendered into Persian. This process gained a new momentum when, under Akbar, in the 1570s, the Mughal court started to commission Persian translations of several Sanskrit works, including the Ramayana and the Mahabharata. Akbar's court also produced writings such as the *Ain-i Akbari,* which surveys the subcontinent's terrain, peoples, and practices.[19]

Through the works he authored or sponsored, Dara Shukoh gradually went beyond many of these previous projects to advocate a notion of religious universalism. He came to believe that a common core of truth underlay traditions as different as Islam and Hinduism. Non-Muslims too, embraced various means to contemplate and grasp God's oneness or even the oneness of all existence. Indeed, some of their texts and techniques, he felt, were even more effective than abstruse discussions of Islamic theology and mysticism. Like other Muslims of the time who were intrigued by Hindu thought, Dara never renounced Islam. His universalist position allowed him to embrace ideas from other traditions while remaining a Muslim.

The prince was not alone in advocating the idea of a universal font of monotheism. By the time Dara Shukoh began his own study of Indic religions, the court, which still supported Sanskrit scholars, was no longer driving the projects of interpretation and translation that had once thrived under its canopy. Other Muslim and Hindu scholars, on the fringes of the court, or far removed from court patronage, composed Persian works based on Sanskrit or Hindavi texts. For instance, one Shaikh Sufi produced at least six renditions of Indic treatises on subjects such as yogic breath control, and techniques of liberation from the material world.[20] Like Dara Shukoh, such writers and translators often treated their Indic sources as repositories of an esoteric wisdom, equivalent to the truth revealed in Sufi works. These short tracts traversed the subcontinent. Their paths were carved by the increasing numbers of people, Hindus as well as Muslims, who could read Persian. Dara Shukoh's studies were thus part of a larger conversation spanning time and geography. He popularized an idea that was by no means uniquely his. After his death, the texts that he composed and sponsored continued to find readers.

Dara Shukoh's life also offers an intimate glimpse into his father's reign. Many historians understand the period of Shah Jahan's rule (1627–1658) as a time of creeping conservatism. They often view it as a transition from the rule of his more liberal predecessors, Akbar and Jahangir, to that of Shah Jahan's successor Alamgir, regarded as a bastion of orthodoxy. On the one hand, Shah Jahan is known for the glittering perfection of his miniature paintings as well as for the luxurious artifacts and opulent architecture he commissioned. On the other hand, Shah Jahan underwent periods of abstinence, kept a beard, and abolished the full prostration from his court ceremonies. In Qanungo's words, "The character of Shah Jahan partook of a double nature, a combination of Muslim orthodoxy and the profane tradition of the age of Akbar."[21]

This assessment is problematic, because the polarized categories of orthodoxy and profanity do not accurately reflect the attitudes that prevailed during Shah Jahan's reign. These labels stem from decades of colonial historiography that privileges the study of the lives and larger-than-life personalities of Mughal rulers. However, Shah Jahan, too, is responsible for shaping his later memory. The emperor became renowned for the tight control he exerted over his image. For instance, he carefully supervised the work of his painting ateliers. He had the official histories of his reign revised when they did not meet his satisfaction.

Today Shah Jahan is not known for his mystical proclivities or deep ties to Sufi personages beyond the routine patronage expected of a ruler. His public image did not appear to have much room for displays of devotion to Sufis. But what is often ignored in histories of Shah Jahan is how closely the lives of the emperor and his two eldest children, Jahanara and Dara, were aligned. The three lived and traveled with each other throughout almost the entirety of Shah Jahan's reign. It was Shah Jahan who first introduced Dara Shukoh to the Qadiri Sufi Miyan Mir, a figure who would have a lasting impact on the prince's trajectory. Later, the emperor, of his own accord, maintained close relations with Miyan Mir's order, and his successor, Mulla Shah. Indeed, with her father's blessings, Jahanara kept up her relationship and patronage to Mulla Shah over the years. Though Dara Shukoh remained Mulla Shah's disciple, he would later turn his attention to other Sufi teachers and to Hindu religious figures. For a better understanding of Dara Shukoh's project of rulership, we must study, in tandem, Shah Jahan's intellectual and spiritual activities and those of his favorite son and heir. And to fathom the story of succession in which Dara was entangled, we must look also at the rocky path by which his own father, Khurram, became the "king of the world."

A close look at Dara Shukoh's life and times—for our own times—is overdue. It is impossible to escape its implications for the present. But we can still choose to situate the prince in his own context, exploring the diverse voices and perspectives from the period. And we can step away from the shadow of Dara's tragic end, approaching his story without assuming that his fate was predetermined. When we evaluate Dara primarily as a failed statesman, we overlook his contribution to ideas of Mughal kingship. The institution of kingship in Mughal India was not static. It was constantly being remade. This more generous view no longer dismisses his activities as beyond the permissible bounds of behavior for a Mughal royal. It allows us to then gain a deeper perspective on Mughal sovereignty.

I

EMPIRE

1615–1622

J AHANGIR, THE "WORLD CONQUEROR," had barely finished moving his court from Agra to Ajmer when he decided to go hunting. It was the end of November 1613. The forty-five-year-old emperor mounted his horse and rode with his entourage to a large water reservoir some seven miles away at Pushkar, which was surrounded by sandy, undulating plains. They crossed two ridges of the Aravalli foothills before the sacred lake, rimmed with temples both recent and old, came into view. The settlement at Pushkar was small, populated mainly by Brahmin households. Throngs of pilgrims flocked to visit its temples and holy men. The emperor's servants set up camp on the lake's shore.

As a rule, nobody thought to hunt in the lake's inviolate precincts, but the emperor spent a couple of days shooting waterfowl. He also inspected a particularly magnificent temple, which, he was informed, had cost a hundred thousand rupees to build. Its patron was a certain Rana Shankar, the uncle of the neighboring kingdom's ruler Rana Amar Singh (d. 1620). Upon seeing the statue of black stone venerated there, Jahangir shuddered in revulsion. That "loathsome statue," he wrote later in his memoirs, "had the shape of a pig's head, while the rest of it resembled the body of a man." This was, of course, the Hindu deity Vishnu in the form of Varaha, the Grand Boar. Jahangir remarked that devotion to the statue was a "deficient creed of the Hindus." Before returning to Ajmer, Jahangir ordered that it be smashed and thrown into the sacred lake. For good measure, he also drove away a yogi who frequented a nearby shrine and had the idol held there destroyed.[1]

Jahangir did not usually go about desecrating temples, but this was an exceptional situation. The province to which Ajmer lent its name was a frontier of sorts. Though the empire's borders extended much farther north and west—sweeping up Qandahar, Kabul, and Swat—Ajmer adjoined Mewar, the last Rajput state to stubbornly hold out against Mughal annexation. Crushing the Varaha idol served as both a threatening provocation and a warning to Rana Amar Singh. It inaugurated the final phase of a long drawn-out war between the Mughals and the Mewar Rajputs.

Jahangir then headed back for Ajmer. Upon returning, the emperor and his entourage ascended a hill alongside the fourteenth-century Taragarh Fort perched on Ajmer's southwestern edge. Nestled in a valley between two parallel hilltops, Ajmer was further fortified by a rampart with an adjoining moat installed by the emperor's late father, Akbar. Known as the Daulat-khana, "fortune's abode," Akbar's red sandstone fortress edged the northeast portion of the walled enclosure. The fortress where Jahangir now stayed faced the city with an enormous gate, where the emperor made daily public appearances at a latticed balcony called a *jharoka*. Inside, the fort concealed a lofty, airy, pillared audience hall in a walled garden. Farther north, behind the ridge, the town bordered the expansive Anasagar reservoir with lapping waves. On its shore was a landscaped garden, where Jahangir spent candlelit evenings with the women of his household.[2] But the city's real hub was in its southwest, on the banks of the Jhalra spring—the well-tended *dargah* of Khwaja Muin-ud-Din, an Iraqi Sufi who, four centuries earlier, established the Chishti order in the subcontinent. Jahangir's own father, Akbar, had walked here all the way from Agra to pray for an heir. Visitors would cross three large paved courtyards to pay their respects at the saint's shimmering marble tomb inlaid with gold and mother of pearl.[3]

A fortnight or so after arriving in Ajmer, the emperor dispatched his third son, the twenty-one-year-old Khurram, to Udaipur so that the prince could conclude the ongoing military campaign against Rana Amar Singh. Khurram pitched camp at Lake Pichola with his armies, sending a steady stream of soldiers to chase the Mewar rana out from his capital Udaipur, farther and farther into the hills.

With his kingdom ravaged after more than a year of grueling warfare, the rana finally capitulated in February 1615. Arriving to meet Khurram with whatever gifts he could muster, Amar Singh grasped the prince's ankle in an extravagant performance of surrender. Khurram, in turn, reportedly lifted the rana's head and pressed it to his breast, in order to console him—a

Submission of Rana Amar Singh to Prince Khurram.

gesture both benevolent and patronizing.[4] Mewar was now a vassal of the Mughal state. The contract between them spared the rana the further humiliation of submitting before Jahangir. Instead, Amar Singh sent his son Karan as his envoy to accompany Khurram back to the court at Ajmer.

On the first of March, Khurram headed a victory march through the city. He then made a grand entry into the Daulat-khana's audience hall, bringing with him the rana's gifts as well as charitable offerings, including a thousand gold coins for the shrine of Khwaja Muin-ud-Din Chishti. In his memoirs, Jahangir writes of the pride that he felt upon seeing his victorious son. He was so overjoyed to see Khurram, he broke with protocol to hug him and shower him with kisses. The emperor's immediate task, though, was to win over Karan. It was not enough to crush Mewar. Karan Singh, its next ruler, Jahangir writes, "had a savage disposition and had never seen a royal assembly, having grown up in the mountains." The Rajput prince had to be groomed in Mughal etiquette, tastes, and ways so that he could become a trustworthy ally.[5]

Over the next several days, Jahangir treated Karan lavishly. Both he and his favorite wife, Nur Mahal, bestowed the Rajput prince with elephants, jeweled daggers, rich textiles, falcons, and gemstone prayer beads. These gifts not only showcased the emperor's wealth and magnanimity; they also burdened Karan with obligations to the emperor. Before Karan returned home, Jahangir took the Rajput hunting. The emperor explains in his memoirs that he wanted to show off his skill in shooting with a gun. Since the time of Akbar, the hunt also had a symbolic value as a Mughal practice of taming recalcitrant nobles.[6]

The emperor's men had spotted a lioness, and though Jahangir preferred to shoot only male lions, he decided to go ahead with the pursuit. Despite gusts of wind that could have interfered with his bullet's course and an elephant who took fright upon seeing the fierce animal, Jahangir shot the beast straight between the eyes. Karan Singh was impressed. The emperor celebrated his success by chronicling the event in his memoirs.[7] Jahangir also thought the event important enough to be illustrated. A miniature painting survives from the time; in it, the emperor appears in the upper left center, sitting cross-legged atop an elephant with his rifle poised upward. He turns to face Karan who is following behind on another elephant, his right arm crooked at the elbow, lifted behind his head in amazement. Flanked by others on elephants and a horse, the two face a clearing in the midst of which the dead lioness lies, belly exposed, by a stream. The viewer's line of sight is directed to the emperor, as nearly all the men portrayed look up at him, pointing or gesturing in wondrous awe toward his prey.[8]

ON THE THIRTIETH OF MARCH, around the same time of the month as Jahangir and Karan Singh's hunting expedition, Khurram's second wife Arjumand Bano went into labor. The twenty-two-year-old princess was of Iranian origin, the daughter of Asaf Khan, brother of Jahangir's wife Nur Mahal. She was thus Jahangir's niece through marriage as well as his daughter-in-law. Arjumand and Khurram were betrothed in 1607. His father, the emperor, placed the ring on her finger himself.[9] Five years later, in 1612, the couple celebrated with a glittering wedding.

Dara Shukoh was Arjumand's third child in as many years. The first child was born a year after their marriage—a girl named Hur-un-Nisa, "Houri among women." Arjumand gave birth to their second-born child, also a girl, almost exactly a year later in March 1614, and called her Jahanara, "Ornament of the world." This time, she delivered a boy after the second of the night's four watches had passed. Soon after the birth, the emperor himself named the baby Dara Shukoh, meaning "Majestic as Darius," after the legendary ruler of ancient, pre-Islamic Persia.[10]

In his memoir, Jahangir mentions visits to Khurram's house in Ajmer during this time. This indicates that at the period of Dara's birth, Arjumand must have been staying there and not in one of the elaborate tents in which Mughal elites often led their migratory lives. She would have had with her some senior women of the household. A certain Huri Khanum, wet nurse to her daughter Jahanara, may have been among them.[11] To breastfeed the newborn prince soon after his birth, there were other noblewomen too, as it was customary for Mughal princes and princesses to have wet nurses. Sometimes more than one would be employed, chosen from among the wives of high-ranking noblemen. Arjumand could thus regain her fertility early and focus on producing more children. But apart from being a means of nourishing the baby, this practice stemmed from the idea, present in the Quran and early biographical accounts of the Prophet, that milk and blood were parallel ways of creating kinship ties.[12] Through one act of suckling, the newborn Dara Shukoh could instantly acquire a whole other "milk" family. The infants of the royal Mughal family were linked through ties of milk to the children of their nurses, who were considered to be their foster siblings. In fact, one should not imagine that in the Mughal imperial household, blood generated a comparable emotional bond. Princes vied with their own brothers and half-brothers for the throne, while their foster families very rarely posed such a threat. As a result, milk brothers became crucial members of a grown prince's entourage and occupied positions of power and responsibility. Wet-nursing also gave the foster mothers a way to gather wealth and political influence.

Though family relations between siblings and co-wives were potentially fraught, it is not unheard of to see expressions of love and loyalty for a spouse. It would not be an overstatement to say that anyone growing up in Jahangir's India would be familiar with the idea of romantic love, *ishq*, in Persian lyric poetry. Passionate and unrequited, ishq is frequently likened to a malady. It is also a central metaphor conveying the soul's yearning for divine union. But there was also room for another understanding of love as the companionship and intimacy of a married couple. Jahangir writes that he did not think anyone in the whole world was fonder of him than his wife, Nur Jahan.[13] Later chroniclers would celebrate the deep bond between Arjumand and her husband. At the time of Dara Shukoh's birth, Khurram and Arjumand had not spent time apart since their marriage; indeed, they never did. Their "mutual friendship and rapport," remarked the court historian Mirza Amin Qazwini (fl. 1645), "reached such a height as was never found between any husband and wife in all the classes of sultans or other people." Their love was not based merely on "carnal desire," but on their "inner and outer good qualities," as well as on "physical and spiritual harmony."[14]

Such conjugal attachments, though, were not predicated on monogamy. Mughal royal men not only had access to concubines, but they also married multiple times, a practice sanctioned by the Quran and the Prophet's personal example as well as by the courtly cultures of India, Central Asia, Iran, and beyond.

Indeed, while still betrothed to Arjumand, in November 1610, Khurram first wed the daughter of another Iranian nobleman, Mirza Husain Safavi.[15] The wedding was celebrated with pomp. Qazwini later described the festivities as rivaling the beauty of the famous gardens of Eram in ancient Iran.[16] The bride's father was a descendant of Shah Ismail (d. 1524), the founder of the Safavid dynasty in Iran. Most marriages in the royal family were to some measure informed by political expediency, and this was no exception. There is good reason to suspect that Jahangir arranged this match after Arjumand's paternal uncle, Muhammad Sharif, was implicated in a conspiracy to assassinate Jahangir and was subsequently executed.[17] The plot's mastermind was Jahangir's eldest son Khusrau, who harbored hopes of the throne.

In August 1611, ten months after their wedding, Khurram's wife, who was known as Qandahari Mahal in the chronicles, gave birth to a daughter named Purhunar Bano.[18] Had she delivered a son, she would probably have had a more prominent role in Khurram's life. By now, the young prince was already making arrangements for his marriage to Arjumand, which would take place early the next year.

The fortunes of Arjumand's family had brightened dramatically. In the same year, 1611, Jahangir married her paternal aunt Mehr-un-Nisa, "Sun among Women," a recently widowed thirty-four-year-old. After Mehr-un-Nisa's husband Sher Afgan, the "Lion Tosser," was in 1607, she had attached herself as attendant to Ruqaiya Begam, Jahangir's elderly stepmother, who, being childless, had raised the future emperor. Mehr-un-Nisa won the emperor's heart four years after the death of her husband, when he spotted her at a court bazaar to celebrate the Persian new year.[19] He renamed her Nur Mahal, "Light of the Palace," after his own given name Nur-ud-Din, "Light of the Faith." Later, in 1616, he would give her the more grandiose appellation, Nur Jahan, "Light of the World."[20] Shortly after their wedding, her father Itimad-ud-Daula, who was Arjumand's grandfather, was brought out of house arrest and appointed minister in charge of the kingdom's finances. Arjumand's father, Abu-l-Hasan, became the *Khan-i saman,* the head chamberlain responsible for the imperial household's intricate workings, a position that required great managerial finesse. Jahangir later granted him the title Asaf Khan. With all these pieces in place, it was only fitting that Arjumand and Khurram's wedding soon be finalized.[21]

Three years after the wedding, celebrations were warranted once more with the birth of Dara Shukoh, Khurram's firstborn son. As the first son of a third son, Dara was merely one of several male children in the extended Mughal family. Yet, after fathering a son with Nur Jahan's niece, and winning a splendid victory in Mewar, Khurram's status soared even higher, especially in contrast to that of his brothers. The eldest of his half-brothers, Khusrau, born of the Rajput Raja Mansingh's daughter, had disgraced himself years earlier by scheming against his father, in a bid for the throne even before the death of his grandfather, Akbar. During the end of his life Akbar favored his grandson Khusrau as the heir apparent in direct opposition to his son Jahangir, who had him all but imprisoned. Sensing a potential threat from Khusrau, Jahangir had already made his second son, Parwez, the heir apparent. Parwez was half-brother to both Khurram and Khusrau. His mother, Sahib Jamal, was herself a cousin of Akbar's foster-brother Zain Khan, who bore the Turkish sobriquet Koka, indicating his status as a brother through milk-kinship.

Dispatched by his father, Jahangir, at the age of sixteen, Parwez set out on an ill-fated expedition to Mewar. Khusrau, resentful, was upset that Jahangir did not install him as governor in Bengal, where he would have had a measure of independence. So the elder prince surreptitiously left Agra for the Punjab with his men. Meanwhile, Jahangir had Khusrau followed in hot pursuit, instructing that he be captured, and killed if necessary. While recounting this episode in his memoirs, Jahangir quotes a line of verse: "Sovereignty brooks no bonds between fathers and sons; an emperor has no relatives."[22]

Though the emperor does not tell his readers, the line is taken directly from the *Iskandar-nama*, a famous Persian narrative poem celebrating the heroic exploits of Alexander the Great, by the renowned Persian poet Nizami Ganjawi (d. 1209). Written as a *masnawi*, a poetic form used, above all, for epics, mystical allegories, and romances, the poem chronicles how Alexander fused his quest for mystical knowledge with his vast ambitions to rule the entire world. Alexander, styled here as a pious conqueror and the quintessential philosopher-king, had long been a model for Muslim royal authority even before the storied days of the Abbasid caliphs. The verses from this particular passage reflect the sublime and terrifying power of kings. They conclude with the charged observation that "toward his own son a king shows no love."[23] Jahangir's vast collection of illuminated manuscripts included a prized copy of Nizami's quintet, in which the tale of Alexander can be found. This text, he notes, contained exquisite miniatures executed by the "great masters."[24]

Khusrau was eventually defeated in Lahore and was apprehended while trying to ford the Chenab River. Jahangir, reluctant to put him to death, had him blinded instead. Over the next few decades, several European visitors to Mughal India reported different versions of the gory punishment. An anonymous Persian source, evidently witness to the events, mentions that Khusrau was blinded with a sharp wire. This is reminiscent of an episode in which Jahangir's grandfather Humayun had the eyes of his brother Kamran Mirza scratched out with a needle. The emperor reportedly later softened toward his son, sending physicians to attempt to partially reverse the damage to his vision. Jahangir also met Khusrau in Agra before the move to Ajmer, after being encouraged to do so by his wives and daughters. The disabled prince was compelled to accompany the emperor's retinue as a hostage wherever they went, though he did not fully abandon his own imperial ambitions.[25]

It was impossible to predict at Dara Shukoh's birth what his future might hold, though the victory against Mewar had solidified his father's position now as the favored prince. At the time of Khurram's campaign in Mewar, his elder brother Parwez headed the Mughal armies in the Deccan. Stationed on the banks of the Tapti River in Burhanpur, the capital city of a region in central India dotted with Chishti Sufi shrines, Parwez supervised the war against the neighboring sultanate of Ahmadnagar. Before the emperor Akbar's death in 1605, it had looked as though Ahmadnagar might slip easily into Mughal hands. But just two years later, a powerful former slave and military officer from Abyssinia, Malik Ambar (d. 1626), had propped up the reigning Nizamshahi dynasty of Ahmadnagar, resisting a Mughal take-over. Nevertheless, years later when Parwez reached Burhanpur, he had a good opportunity to make a name for himself as an administrator and military commander. Though the emperor was in his prime, the question of succession could come up at any moment. With no established rule determining who would succeed the throne, it behooved a prince to rack up military experience and consolidate his power and influence.

DARA SHUKOH WAS STILL AN INFANT in Ajmer with his family, when in the third week of December 1615, two Englishmen residing in the city made their way south. They were a rather oddly matched pair. One, William Edwards, was a merchant adventurer who had been serving as the East India Company's agent at the Mughal court since February of that year and had styled himself as King James's envoy.[26] The other, Thomas Coryate, was a traveler who had walked all the way from Jerusalem to Agra and then had turned around and gone to Ajmer when he discovered that the court of the "most mighty Monarch, the Great Mogul" had shifted base.[27] There he fell in with a group of nine compatriots, all affiliated with the newly formed trading company.[28]

The loquacious Coryate wore the garb of the places he lived in, and had acquired a smattering of languages, including Arabic, Turkish, Hindi, and Persian. He published two detailed accounts of his journeys while abroad. The travels were as much for the benefit of an audience back home as for his own pleasure.[29] He was ever eager to hobnob with distinguished people from his country. In a letter from the Ajmer court, Coryate addresses his "fraternity," a salon of regular drinking partners who frequented the Mermaid Tavern in London and whose members included the likes of the English bard William Shakespeare. Coryate mentions that he and Edwards were en route to receive "a very generous and worthy English Knight," whom Coryate described as a "deare friend."[30] News of the arrival uplifted Coryate, who was already enjoying the most "pancraticall and athleticall" of health in Ajmer.

Coryate's guest was none other than Sir Thomas Roe (d. 1644), the first ambassador from England to the Mughal court. Roe had landed in September at the western port city of Surat, where four years earlier Jahangir had allowed the English to establish a trading factory.[31] From this toehold, English merchants battled the Portuguese to cut into their trading monopoly over large sections of India's western coast.[32] Roe's predecessor, Edwards, had recently obtained a formal, if temporary, *farman*, an imperial decree that secured the East India Company's trade at Surat. This move was designed to protect English trading interests against competing interference from the Portuguese and the Dutch. Traveling north via Burhanpur, where he met Parwez, Khurram's elder brother, Roe hoped to prevail upon Jahangir to grant more permanent trading privileges and autonomy to the English to pursue their mercantile interests.

The ambassador arrived, ill and exhausted, accompanied by a group of English attendants. He was in his mid-thirties, and bearded. While in India, Roe always wore the full dress of an English aristocrat, complete with starched ruffled collar and cuffs. Coryate immediately welcomed him with an "eloquent oration." For Roe, Coryate would cut an eccentric figure, not entirely flattering to English interests before the Mughal emperor. The men spent the night in tents pitched in a field before proceeding to Ajmer. Once there, Roe collapsed and took to his bed, where he remained for several days.[33]

Roe's journey from Surat had been trying. He felt harassed by the governor of Surat, Zulfiqar Khan, who confiscated gifts meant for the emperor and sought payment for their return. Importantly for Roe's relations with the court, Zulfiqar Khan served as Khurram's deputy. The prince had recently been granted control over Gujarat. Khurram maintained investments in the Indian Ocean and the Red Sea, as did the Queen Mother, known as Maryam Zamani, "Mary of the Age," and the powerful Nur Mahal, soon to be titled Nur Jahan.[34] Throughout his dealings at the court, Roe would meet the most resistance from Khurram, his aunt Nur Mahal, and her brother Asaf Khan. The English ambassador set out for the Mughal court, aiming not only to secure trading rights for the East India Company but also to redress his humiliations at the hands of the local governor.[35]

The town that murmured and bustled beyond Roe's walls in Ajmer had swelled considerably since the emperor's arrival two years earlier. While there were the several noblemen and women who accompanied Jahangir, there were also the thousands of others, seldom mentioned in histories, who provided the elite with services needed to maintain their lavish lifestyles. Tent-pitchers, horse-groomers, camel-drivers, torch-bearers, palanquin-lifters, and elephant-mahauts toiled along with water-carriers, maidservants, and cooks. Messengers, with bells on their belts announcing themselves, ran miles every day, many fueled with stimulants and soothed by opium. Jugglers, musicians, and dancers entertained; among them were Persian-crooning *lolonis* and *domnis* who sang in Hindavi. Petty shopkeepers sold provisions, often at the mercy of government overseers who extracted their commissions.[36] But the soldiers and those responsible for feeding and housing them would have been the most numerous of all Ajmer's temporary residents. And we can assume that those whom we would today call sex workers, though marginalized and vilified, plied their trade to locals and outsiders alike.

In many respects, Ajmer was a microcosm of the kingdom. The entire population of the subcontinent was nearly one hundred and fifty million according to one estimate, second only to China. European travelers frequently commented on both the opulence of the Indian elite and on the immense population of Indian cities. Exaggerated accounts of population size could act as metonyms for the subcontinent's wealth and fecundity; yet they also point to the sheer magnitude of a thriving society that flowed with people.[37] The ranks of the Mughal ruling elite, however, were much smaller. Akbar had over seventy five thousand nobles at the very lowest ranks of the aristocracy. At the highest echelons, there were about one thousand, while, during Jahangir's reign, that number expanded to roughly fifteen hundred.[38]

Each nobleman commanded a fixed number of horsemen according to his *mansab*, or rank, in a formalized hierarchy. Depending on his pay grade, which was granted by the emperor, a nobleman drew income from the taxes on lands allocated to him. He used these funds for his own expenses and to support an army placed at the emperor's disposal. Many émigrés and local elites sought to enrich themselves through the *mansabdari* system, which reached its classic form during the bureaucratic reforms of Akbar's reign.[39]

The Mughal nobility did not hail from a single group or clan. It was an ethnically diverse aristocracy, claiming members with Indian Muslim, Rajput, Maratha, Afghan, Iranian, and Turani (i.e., Central Asian) backgrounds. From the late sixteenth to the mid-seventeenth century, immigrants from Iran or their descendants came to take an increasing share of these positions.[40] Apart from the Mughal nobility, there were elites affiliated with other Indian kingdoms, vassals to the Mughal court. Other powerful figures included religious authorities, such as ulama and Sufis, some of whom presided over large endowments, as well as wealthy merchants and bankers. Nevertheless, their numbers, too, were relatively small compared with the masses who populated the subcontinent. Like other urban centers in India, Ajmer also had a thriving population that was neither destitute nor exceedingly wealthy. "Middle class," however, is perhaps too homogenizing and anachronistic to refer to the myriad professional groups of scribes, accountants, revenue collectors, and other employees of the vast and expanding Mughal bureaucracy, as well as the merchants, money changers, physicians, and others whose means of sustenance were "independent of feudal property."[41]

Jahangir's kingdom was a busy crossroads for overseas and domestic traders traveling by land and sea. The imperial family had financed their own trading ventures with ships ferrying pilgrims and merchants across the Indian Ocean for the annual pilgrimage to Mecca. Though the English agents—called "factors" after the factories they established for trade—were conspicuous by their dress, they were by no means the only "firangis" to visit Ajmer. Portuguese merchants and Jesuit missionaries had been frequenting the Mughal court since the days of Akbar.[42]

The emperor's lengthy halt in Ajmer attracted sellers of rare and luxury goods. Jahangir praises the delectable pomegranates of Yazd and the melons of Kariz that Iranian merchants brought to Ajmer, remarking that "it was as though I never tasted a melon or pomegranate before."[43] These foods arrived in such abundance that the courtiers and nobles got a share of them too. Oftentimes melons made the long journey from Badakhshan, while pomegranates and other fruits and nuts, like apples, pears, quinces, almonds, dates, raisins, hazelnuts, and pistachios, came from Qandahar or Kabul.[44] Packed snow and crushed ice were brought in from the steeps of the Himalayas, while porters lugged Jahangir's drinking water all the way from the banks of the Ganges on their shoulders in large sealed copper pots suspended on poles. Hindu royalty, too, regularly imbibed this holy water that the less privileged carefully hoarded for end-of-life rituals. From Akbar's time onward, it became an imperial custom to import drinking water from the sacred river, which was referred to in Persian as *ab-i hayat,* the "elixir of life."[45]

But even without the influx of aristocrats with their servants and soldiers, Ajmer had its own local economy centered around Khwaja Muin-ud-Din Chishti's shrine. Pilgrims visited regularly; their numbers rose during the annual *urs,* the celebration of a saint's death anniversary when he was thought to be united with the divine. The infirm, the needy, couples wishing for children—people of all sects and persuasions—jostled with magicians and acrobats, ascetics and paramours. Vendors moved through the crowds on foot, peddling their sweets, toys, and sundry trinkets; as a contemporary Dutch merchant observed, no one who visited these shrines returned without having bought something for their children.[46]

Coryate, who was sharing quarters with Roe, made himself quite at home, studying Persian and busying himself with his travelogue of curiosities. Never one to miss an opportunity for virtuosic displays of showmanship, Coryate once stood below Jahangir's jharoka window, wearing a mendicant's garb. There, he delivered a Persian oration to the emperor. Coryate called himself a *faqir darvesh* (poor dervish) and a *jahangashta* (globe-trotter) who had come from a faraway kingdom (*wilayat*). Over time, this Persian term for dominion, or region, would become synonymous with Europe in general and England in particular. Coryate's reasons for coming to India were to see His Majesty's "blessed face," His Majesty's elephants, and the Ganges River, and, lastly, to obtain a letter of recommendation from His Majesty to visit Timur's tomb in Samarqand. The emperor, much amused, tossed him a hundred silver rupees and warned him that as a Christian, he would not be safe in Samarqand. The impecunious Coryate was well pleased to receive the money, to Roe's consternation. Roe deemed the gift a humiliation, as though Coryate were a beggar. Always the hero of his own stories, Coryate retorts that he ordered the ambassador to "cease nibling" at him.[47] In his journal of the embassy, Roe describes life at the Mughal court as a continual performance, sharing "soe much affinitye with a Theatre" particularly in "the manner of the king in his gallery, the great men lifted on a stage as actors, the vulgar below gazing on."[48]

On another occasion, the Company chaplain Edward Terry witnessed Coryate climb up onto a platform during the call to prayer. He answered the muezzin with a garbled twist on the Arabic formula: "*La alla illa alla, Hasaret Easa Ben-alla*," which Terry translates to "There is no God but one God, and the Lord Christ is the Son of God." Coryate added in Hindi, "Mahomet was an impostor," speaking loudly so that all would understand. To the chaplain's relief, the locals ignored the entire provocation as the rant of a madman.[49] Coryate felt comfortable enough in Mughal India to behave this way. Describing an earlier disputation with a Muslim in Multan, he pronounces "in the Mogol Dominions a Christian may speake much more freely than hee can in any other Mahometan Country in the World."[50]

Modern European ideals of religious tolerance were still in their infancy when Coryate and his compatriots traveled to India. But these English visitors were struck by the religious diversity fostered by the Mughal state. Back in Europe, devastating sectarian wars still raged, ignited by the Protestant Reformation.[51] The Englishmen would comment on Jahangir's respect for their messiah, whom they heard the emperor call *Hazrat Isa,* "Lord Jesus." They also repeated among themselves the rumor that Jahangir, son of a Rajput princess, was uncircumcised, like his non-Muslim subjects. In their view, the emperor embraced "no certain religion," as he showed equal affection for Christians and for "Mahometans and Gentiles." The English commonly referred to the "heathens of India," their other appellation for Hindus, as Gentiles.[52] Roe recounts a drinking session with the "good King," where Jahangir, in the warmth of wine, crooned that "Christians, Moores, Jewes" were all welcome and that he did not meddle in their faith: "they came all in loue, and he would protect them from wrong, they liued under his safety, and none should opresse them."[53] In contrast to Jahangir, Prince Khurram greeted Roe with complaints of the "abuses and drunckeness" of his factors in Surat.[54]

There was no way to foretell, in 1615, that the East India Company would come to rule large portions of India less than a century and a half later. Jahangir did not find it worth his while to even mention the English ambassador in his journal. Yet Roe's anxiety about upholding his status as an ambassador of King James percolates throughout his writings on India.[55] In Ajmer, though, Roe enjoyed several favorable audiences with the emperor. In his telling, Jahangir took him as a boon-companion, with frequent drinking sessions that lasted well into the night. The English ambassador nurtured his budding relations with the ruler through a gift-giving spree of gem-encrusted gold goblets, strong wine, and dainty feathered hats for the harem. Along with the chaplain and Coryate, Roe had with him a band of musicians and merchants, seeking to dazzle the court with their looking glasses and strange maps of the world. But no matter how close he got to Jahangir, Roe was repeatedly frustrated in his efforts to better secure the East India Company's interests. Khurram, Nur Mahal, and Asaf Khan enjoyed the wonders on display, but they were less sanguine about committing themselves to exclusive trading relations with the English.[56]

Roe's journals record sumptuous meetings in a pleasure palace outside Ajmer with the erudite Mir Jamal-ud-Din Husain Inju (d. 1626). An émigré from Shiraz, Jamal-ud-Din served as an ambassador for Akbar and a governor of Bengal for Jahangir. Like Roe, the Iranian aristocrat in the Mughal service kept a personal journal with a daily record of memorable events. And, just the year before, he had finished compiling a massive Persian dictionary dedicated to the emperor.[57]

At this palace, which was lavishly decorated with murals, Roe saw panels painted with "copyes of the French kings and other Christian Princes." In a mirror image of Roe and his compatriots, who sought the East's wonders and packaged them as books and illustrations, the Mughal artists conjured up images of *firangi*s in their native attire.[58] These murals, unfortunately, have not survived. But we might imagine that they were similar in ideological weight to the splendid wall paintings adorning the *Chihil Sutun*, the forty-pillared palace in Iran's Isfahan. There, the portraits of other rulers, aristocrats, foreign diplomats, and merchants serve only to underscore Safavid might and glory.[59]

If he so wished, the émigré nobleman Jamal-ud-Din could have talked with Roe about Socrates, Plato, and Aristotle, or about Euclid, Hippocrates, Galen, and Ptolemy, all of whom he addresses in his massive lexicon as well-known figures in Persian and Arabic learning. He could converse on the Greek origins of the words for *geography, astronomy,* and *theology;* wax eloquent about Hindavi poetics; engage in religious polemic by claiming that Muhammad appears foretold in the Psalms; or explain how an astrolabe worked, tracing its origin to Greek learning and citing from the astronomer Nasir-ud-Din Tusi (d. 1274) on its proper use. He could turn to zoology and ponder the *pairuj,* that giant fowl, also known as the "elephant chicken," which changed color annually and, he explains, lives in the "jungles of the Portuguese" and at the "edge of the west," by which he meant *peru,* the Portuguese word for the South American turkey.[60] He could also present Roe with an entire word list of ancient Persian terms used in the *Zand* and *Pazand,* the Zoroastrian commentarial tradition on the *Avesta,* which he knew was still very alive among Parsi merchants of Gujarat.[61]

But of the many areas of knowledge shared between the two ambassadors, one of the more meaningful for the Indian context was their equal grasp of the story of Alexander the Great, which offered them a basic template for imperial rule. Jamal-ud-Din knew the story of Iskandar Zu-l-Qarnain well, foremost through the Persian poetry of Firdausi and Nizami. In the Persian romances, we encounter Alexander as the son of a royal Persian princess who, in a dramatic turn, discovers that he is the half-brother of Darius, the ruler of ancient Persia. Iskandar and Dara, as they are known in Persian, were familiar figures in the Mughal court. Since the time of the Delhi Sultans, Muslim potentates in India sought to emulate Iskandar's glory. In letters and paintings, Jahangir's father, Akbar, very consciously styled the world-conqueror in his likeness.[62] In his famed quintet, Nizami sings of Iskandar as a world-traveling king (*shah-i jahan-gard*) who captured the throne of Khusrau and battled darkness with light the globe over, from the Chinese and the Zanj to "the black Hindus and the yellow Rus." In the Mughal court, Iskandar came to represent the model of a sage-king who set his aspirations beyond earthly glory toward the lofty heights of heavenly wisdom and divine knowledge.[63]

Our European travelers also brought with them their own stories of Alexander's conquests of India. From the beginning of their journeys, they saw in the Indian landscape traces of Alexander's feats. Coryate himself even claims to have seen a pillar in Delhi with Greek inscriptions. The pillar, he explains, was a column erected by Alexander to commemorate his victory over India. This story, which features throughout early European accounts of the subcontinent, likely drew inspiration from one of the pillars on display in Delhi that Ashoka, the ancient emperor, had originally erected across his vast domains some hundred years after Alexander's demise.[64] The firangis also shared with their Muslim hosts the story of Alexander's philosophical correspondence with the Brahmans. The imperial image of the emperor Alexander, as a philosopher-king in dialogue with Indian ascetics, was similarly well known in the Mughal court.

By the spring of 1616, Dara Shukoh was now a toddler, with his elder sisters, three-year-old Hur-un-Nisa and two-year-old Jahanara, to keep him company. Their new sibling was due to arrive soon as Arjumand's pregnancy advanced. On the last day of May that year, little Hur-un-Nisa came down with a fever. This, in itself, should not have been cause for concern, except that within three days her skin also broke out in pustules, perhaps from smallpox. She died on a Wednesday in the middle of June.

For Arjumand and Khurram, the loss of their firstborn was devastating. Jahangir was inconsolable. Unable to write in his journal, he commanded Itimad-ud-Daula to record the tragedy. Wednesday, the day of the week on which the little girl's soul fled its earthly cage to settle in paradise, was to be renamed the "Day of Loss." On the third day after her death, Jahangir went to Khurram's house where he stayed for some days. He departed from there to Asaf Khan's residence and then to the Chashma-i Nur palace gardens. During this time, he was easily moved to tears. Itimad-ud-Daula, Hur-un-Nisa's great-grandfather, hints that the other members of the family were affected as much or even more: "If the soul of the world is treated such by her custodian, then what would befall those other servants whose lives depend on that possessor of sacred attributes and the knowledge of inner states?"[65]

After a fortnight, Arjumand delivered a "precious, noble pearl into the world of being"—a baby boy.[66] The emperor was overjoyed and promptly named his grandson Shah Shuja, "the brave king." Jahangir took a special liking to the infant, and Nur Jahan, it seems, took over his care. It was not uncommon for small children to be given to the care of women who had finished rearing their own, as was the case with Nur Jahan, or to those who did not have children. We have no record of what Arjumand felt about giving her baby Shuja over to her aunt and the emperor. Jahangir came to love this grandchild deeply, writing that the boy was dearer to him than life itself. Later, in 1618, when Shuja was two and a half, the boy would fall violently ill. In a vow that he kept for some time, the emperor swore to stop hunting, his favorite pastime, should Shuja recover.[67] Meanwhile, with Hur-un-Nisa no more and Shuja now being raised in the emperor's apartments, the young Dara Shukoh and his older sister Jahanara had all the more opportunity to form a close bond, one that would endure throughout their lives.

Back in Ajmer, Jahangir recalled Parwez from Burhanpur and sent Khurram to take over the campaign against Ahmadnagar in his stead. The

court would be stationed in Mandu, north of Burhanpur, to oversee the operation. The disgruntled Parwez left for Allahabad, where he had been sent
to keep watch while the imperial court was occupied in the south.[68] Sir
Thomas Roe, who accompanied the emperor to the Deccan, reports that
the emperor had been warned by one of his "Khans" that removing Parwez
would lead to discord between the brothers. According to Roe, Jahangir
retorted, "[L]ett them fight: I am well content; and he that prooues him-
selfe the better Captaine shall pursue the war."[69] The ambassador, who did
not know Persian, relied on multiple levels of hearsay and translation.
Whether or not these were Jahangir's own thoughts, this statement speaks
to an emerging Mughal attitude toward succession.

As the imperial entourage wound its way toward Mandu in February 1617, Jahangir decided to visit Chidrup, a Hindu holy man who
lived near the ancient pilgrimage town of Ujjain. Jahangir had heard of Chidrup from his father and had desired to meet him for a while, but he hesitated to call him over to the court in Agra. It would have been too much
trouble to expect from the ascetic, who was getting on in years, and moreover, there was always the danger that he would rebuff the emperor. People
who had truly renounced the world often did not pay heed to those with
power and wealth.

The emperor halted a short distance from Ujjain, at a garden palace in
Kaliyada, which had been constructed in the fifteenth century for the sultan
of Mandu before Akbar had annexed the kingdom. As it was built into a
river, the edifice rose out of the water, making it a cool summer retreat. From
here, Jahangir took a boat to visit the ascetic. After disembarking, the emperor made the last part of the journey on foot, out of respect for the holy
man.

With a keen eye for detail, Jahangir records the astonishingly tiny dimensions of the hollow, set into a hillside, in which Chidrup lived. He spent
over two hours with the ascetic, noting the fine points of Chidrup's austere
habits in food and clothing. The two likely conversed in Hindavi. In the
emperor's telling, they enjoyed each other's company. Jahangir describes
Chidrup as occupied in worship of the divine reality (*haqiqat*), immediately
identifying the ascetic as a monotheist and not an idolater. The emperor reports that Chidrup was well versed in the "science of Vedanta." He explains
to his reader that this is the same as "the science of *tasawwuf.*" Here, Jahangir probably means that Chidrup believed in an ultimate reality that, at
some level, was identical with the individual soul—an idea familiar to those
steeped in Sufi metaphysics.[70] In a later account of the exchange, Jahangir's close courtier, Mutamad Khan (d. 1639), elaborates that Chidrup
"equated the vocabulary of the *tasawwuf* of the people of Islam with the

practice of his own *tasawwuf."* That is to say, the ascetic explained concepts from his own tradition by likening them to the Islamic mystical ideas with which Jahangir was conversant. Mutamad Khan also remarks that "these days the science of Vedanta is taken to mean *tasawwuf,"* suggesting that this equivalence was, for him, a fairly new concept.[71] Clearly, there was quite a bit of oversimplification involved in equating an Indic philosophical system of intricate complexity with the variegated discourse of Islamic mystical thought and practice. But such efforts to draw equivalences filtered away the clouded waters of difference and allowed Chidrup and Jahangir to find common ground.

The emperor was so impressed with the Hindu ascetic that two days later he made another trip to meet him and spent a couple of hours. He also ordered that his encounter with Chidrup be illustrated.[72] In its most famous version, the image has two distinct parts. The bottom half is crowded with portraits of several members of Jahangir's retinue, in the midst of which is the emperor's riderless horse. The top half has more open space. It separates the bustle below from the contemplative exchange above. Here, Jahangir sits facing Chidrup in an archway forming the entrance to the sanyasi's cave. The emperor, on the left, is larger and bejeweled, wearing a halo representing kingship's radiant glory *(farr)*. But he sits in a deferential posture with his feet tucked under him, at the same level as the ascetic. Indeed, a Mughal emperor was hardly ever portrayed sitting alongside someone else, unless he happened to be a holy man. Chidrup, with a shaved head and clad only in a loincloth, gesticulates while speaking. In the far left, the domes and gates of a city emerge faintly from the horizon.[73]

The painting is more than just an unmediated visual record of the encounter. It also contains several symbolic references. The motif of a ruler meeting an ascetic in the wilderness is itself an old one, well established in Persian miniature paintings and seen in images from fourteenth-century Mongol Iran. It gains masterful expression in the sixteenth-century paintings of Kamal-ud-Din Bihzad (d. 1535/6), the renowned artist from Herat. Jahangir had in his collection a portrait attributed to Bihzad of Alexander in the audience of a hermit. In the Persian pictorial tradition, such encounters often took place in a cave, which was seen as a place of spiritual enlightenment and also associated with the Prophet's first revelation on Mount Hira. Mughal artists and patrons used a sophisticated visual vocabulary that imbued miniature paintings with allegorical import. For instance, the horse often connoted the carnal body. The distant palatine city served as a reminder of the temporal world. For now, both were left behind. Though in his memoirs Jahangir mentions taking a boat to visit Chidrup—not riding—the horse here helps construct a larger allegory of kingship.[74] The

Jahangir converses with Chidrup.

painting projects an image of Jahangir as a philosopher-king, wearing the
trappings of royalty lightly as he journeys on his spiritual quest. It also offers a glimpse of Jahangir's almost ethnographic interest in capturing what,
to him, seemed curious and memorable, whether through writing, collecting
precious objects and rare animals, or commissioning paintings.[75] Jahangir
also had his father Akbar's visit to Chidrup memorialized in a painting.[76]

Here Chidrup also evokes earlier Mughal courtly depictions of the legendary Hindu sage, Vasishtha, a figure well known to Jahangir. While still
a prince, Jahangir had commissioned a Persian translation of an abridged
Sanskrit text called the *Yogavasishtha,* in which the guru Vasishtha tells the
divine prince Rama a series of interconnected stories. Through these teachings, the prince transforms from being weary of the world to being a spiritually liberated ruler.[77] Jahangir also had in his possession a gorgeously illustrated *Yogavasishtha,* that had been translated for his father in 1602.
The Chidrup of Jahangir's atelier strongly resembles the paintings featuring
Vasishta in this manuscript.[78] Dara Shukoh would have been too young
to know directly of his grandfather's dialogues with Chidrup, but he no
doubt eventually saw the paintings, which survived to reinforce the Mughal ideal of the ruler who cultivates himself by associating with high-
minded ascetics.

On the military front, by the middle of 1617, Khurram had made significant headway in his Deccan campaigns. Building on Parwez's prior work,
Khurram captured the fort at Ahmadnagar and secured the allegiance of
the neighboring state of Bijapur. Jahangir received him warmly at Mandu,
swooping from his throne to embrace his victorious son. He granted
Khurram a significant raise in rank: the prince would now command the
equivalent of thirty thousand foot soldiers and twenty thousand cavalry.
Khurram also gained the right to sit on a chair by his father's throne during
court assemblies—an unprecedented privilege for a Mughal prince. In
addition, he would henceforth be known by the title "Shah Jahan," or
"world ruler."[79]

Khurram, however, was not content to rely solely on his father's favor.
Thinking ahead to secure his future, he appointed the venerable Abd-ur-
Rahim, "Khan of Khans," as his deputy in the Deccan. Abd-ur-Rahim was
not only an experienced military general who had served in the region since
the time of Khurram's grandfather Akbar; he was also a polymath and an
ardent patron of the arts and poetry; he even composed his own verse in
Hindavi.[80]

To further bond the alliance, the following September Khurram wedded
his third wife, Abd-ur-Rahim's granddaughter and daughter of Shahnawaz
Khan. Arjumand had only recently given birth to her fifth child, a daughter,

Roshanara. With this new familial tie sealing his relationship with Abd-ur-Rahim, Khurram aimed to solidify his network of support in the Deccan. His later chronicler Qazwini, however, insists that this marriage, as was that with Qandahari Mahal, was a union in name only, lacking the intimacy that Shah Jahan shared in abundance with Arjumand. According to Qazwini, the marriage to Shahnawaz Khan's daughter was contracted on Jahangir's orders. It resulted in one offspring, a son named Jahan Afroz or "World-Illuminating." The infant was handed over to the care of his relative, Janan Begam, but he died when he was just one year and nine months.[81] Again, Jahangir's memoirs record the emotional toll that the high incidence of child mortality took on the ruling elite.

Soon the imperial family set off for the north. Jahangir's entourage followed a meandering route to Agra via Gujarat, as the emperor had expressed a wish to hunt elephants there and to see the coast. It is also likely that Jahangir and Khurram sought to strengthen trading interests in the face of competing Portuguese and English mercantile activity.[82] Meanwhile, from afar, Khurram planned his next campaign. He took control of the imperial effort to defeat the small hill state of Kangra in the western Himalayan foothills—another territory that had stubbornly eluded Mughal control. For this pursuit, the prince sent his trustworthy courtier Raja Bikramjit to lead the new Kangra expedition.

During the following year, in October 1618, Arjumand bore another son in the province of Dohad. Jahangir recorded his name in his diary as "Aurangzeb," meaning "adorner of the throne," along with the conventional good wish: "It is hoped that his imprint on this dynasty conjoined with eternity will be blessed and fortunate."[83]

Before Jahangir returned to his court in Agra, after an absence of half a decade, he had at least two other meetings with Chidrup, both in late 1618. A year later, he again met him twice, this time at Mathura, the northern Indian temple town, where the ascetic had moved from Ujjain. Jahangir's diary entries record his delight in Chidrup's lofty words and his marvel at the ascetic's abstemious habits. Other chroniclers, though, hint that Chidrup was roped into playing a more political role. Mutamad Khan, a chronicler from Jahangir's court, reports that Khan Azam Koka, who was both late emperor Akbar's foster brother and Khusrau's father-in-law, paid a visit to the ascetic with an agenda in mind. Khan Azam had a tense history with Jahangir after Khusrau's rebellion in 1606 and thus had every reason to scheme against the emperor. Prince Khusrau had been imprisoned for too long, Khan Azam told Chidrup. Would the ascetic persuade Jahangir to release his son? In Mutamad Khan's account, Khan Azam apparently had to overcome his own "religious bigotry" (*taassub-i dindari*) to approach Chidrup.

The ascetic complied, successfully arousing in the emperor sympathy for his son. The emperor, records Mutamad Khan, "washed the marks of that ignorant dimwit's crimes with the pure water of forgiveness."[84] Jahangir's next diary entry, mentioning his meeting with the sage, announces that he has decided to pardon his son Khusrau and free him from prison.[85] In reality, though, the prince was kept in the custody of the nobleman Abu-l-Hasan Turbati, known as Rukn-us-Saltanat or "Pillar of the empire."[86]

What implications did Khusrau's release have for Khurram? The elder prince was still a threat despite his near total blinding, as long as he had backers. Khusrau's son Dawar Bakhsh, who was now a grown man of seventeen, was another potential contender for the throne. Nur Jahan must have been perturbed as well. Of late, Khusrau had been imprisoned in the custody of her own brother Asaf Khan. As the emperor aged, she sought to secure her own position under the next ruler. Nur Jahan had a daughter from her first marriage who was referred to by the affectionate name Ladli Begam, through whom she could potentially influence the next ruler. She had earlier been unsuccessful in arranging a marriage alliance between her daughter Ladli and the hapless Khusrau. The empress now set her sights on Shahryar, Jahangir's youngest son, for Ladli. Both Khusrau and Khurram increasingly appeared to be obstacles to Nur Jahan's plans, as she turned her favor to Shahryar.

AMID THIS THICK WEB OF COURT INTRIGUES and the inner workings of statecraft, glimpses of the lives and experiences of Mughal children are few. Visual representations of Mughal children were also fairly uncommon, though there were a number of them made at Jahangir's court. Three paintings made during this period stand out for their depiction of Khurram's sons. We have already heard of Jahangir's deep attachment to Shuja. In the spring of 1620, the emperor writes, that to his immense relief, his four-year-old grandson survived a dangerous fall from an upper-level open door. This episode may have spurred him to commision a portrait of the boy.[87] Shuja, with his childlike proportions, stands in three-fourths profile, holding a flower, with a nimbus glowing gently around his head. Pearls adorn his neck, wrists, and ankles, and drop from his earlobes. A gold string of talismanic amulets hangs across his torso, visible under his fine, translucent upper garment. He wears a turban with a feathered ornament and gilded slippers. His bearing and posture are like those of an adult of the imperial family, and the contrast with his juvenile features would seem incongruous were it not for a softness that suffuses the entire portrait.

Another painting survives of Khurram with a young Dara Shukoh.[88] A gilded divan with an enormous gold brocade bolster leaps out against a

Portrait of Shuja as a child.

turquoise background. On it sits Khurram with his eldest son facing him, nestled close. Like his father, Jahangir, Khurram is clean-shaven, except for a curved mustache. The elder prince lifts a tray of jewels from which he picks out a splendid ruby to admire. Dara, perhaps four years old here, is a miniature version of his father in dress and posture, down to the tiny sword wedged into his sash. He grips peacock feathers in one hand and a turban ornament in the other. The rich gemstones that both father and son hold are at once symbols of power and sparkling playthings. Below, an inscription in Jahangir's distinctive hand records the artist's name—Nanha. This painting was in Jahangir's collection, either gifted to him or commissioned by him, at a time when, we may surmise, he enjoyed a better relationship with his son.

Shortly after this painting was completed, Khurram's appearance changed. He grew a beard, which neither his father nor his grandfather ever sported. In a painting with a toddler, likely Aurangzeb, the prince sits in a tented pergola; the beard strikingly frames his profile. With his right arm, he clasps his little son tenderly to his side, dandling him on his knee. The child's arms embrace his father's neck. Khurram points with his left hand at a vase of flowers brought by a female attendant. Two other women fuss over the royal duo.[89]

Khurram's new style of facial grooming may seem like an insignificant change. However, many historians have argued that it reflected his growing orthodoxy, in which he followed the Prophet Muhammad who was said to have kept a beard. They read this gesture along with his abstention from alcohol, as a move toward religiosity. In contrast to Jahangir, who himself frequently admitted to his weakness for wine, Khurram long remained a teetotaler. Early in 1616, on his twenty-fourth birthday, a cup of wine touched his lips for the first time. On that occasion, Jahangir repeatedly urged his son to drink, citing Ibn Sina, the famed Iranian physician and philosopher, on the health benefits of wine.[90]

Beards, however, signified more than just religiosity, just as shaving a beard, in the Mughal context, did not necessarily indicate the abandonment of religion. In neighboring Safavid Iran and within the broader zone of Persian speakers and readers, beards connoted masculinity, a way of distinguishing oneself from young boys and eunuchs.[91] And, for Jahangir's father Akbar, shaving the beard was a means to identify with the Rajputs he wished to absorb into his empire. The clean-shaven look then became a way to signal allegiance to the emperor.[92] Khurram began cultivating his beard at a time when subtle rifts with his father and Nur Jahan began to emerge. Jahangir's memoirs hint at a cooling relationship with his son, for in the summer of 1619, the emperor began referring to him as Khurram instead

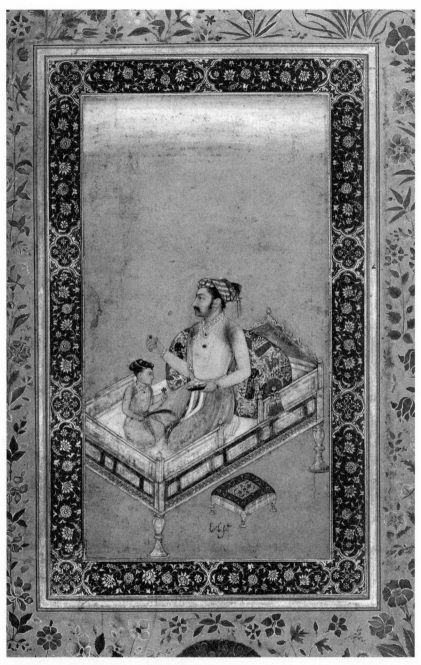

Khurram with young Dara Shukoh.

Khurram with young son and attendants.

of Shah Jahan. Khurram's beard is a visual marker that he was beginning more and more to assert his independence from his father.

As far as Jahangir's own piety was concerned, two encounters with influential Islamic scholars stand out during this period. On a trip to Delhi in late 1619, Jahangir made time for a short audience with Shaikh Abd-ul-Haqq, a distinguished religious scholar and Sufi. The emperor squeezed this meeting between several official and personal duties, including a visit with his sons and the harem ladies to the tombs of his grandfather Humayun and the Chishti saint Nizam-ud-Din, where he circumambulated the shrine of the holy man.[93] Abd-ul-Haqq of Delhi was in his late sixties, born into a family of scholars with ancestors from Bukhara. When he was only nine, his father, Saif-ud-Din, a Qadiri Sufi adept, initiated him into the order.[94] At twenty-seven, Abd-ul-Haqq had already been teaching for some years in his father's madrasa when Saif-ud-Din introduced him to Shaikh Musa, another Qadiri teacher. Shaikh Musa had connections at Akbar's court in Agra and, at some point, Abd-ul-Haqq gained an entry into imperial service.

We do not know much about Abd-ul-Haqq's time in Agra, as he later became reticent about this period of his life. It seems to have been an unhappy, even humiliating, experience. Abd-ul-Haqq's oblique allusions in an autobiographical sketch suggest that he felt deeply alienated by the atmosphere of intrigue and competition at court.[95] Eventually, he left the way a man in his circumstances could without burning bridges: by making the slow, arduous pilgrimage to Mecca. There, in his mid-thirties, he met a mentor, Shaikh Abd-ul-Wahhab Muttaqi from Burhanpur. Under him, Abd-ul-Haqq not only acquired profound expertise in the study of hadith, the reports of the Prophet Muhammad's words and deeds, but he also deepened his knowledge of Qadiri practice.

After returning to India, Abd-ul-Haqq emphasized a more sober form of mystical piety, one circumscribed by scholarship in the traditional Islamic sciences. He wrote prolifically and, upon hearing that Jahangir was in Delhi, decided to present him with a work that he considered to be one of his finest: the *Akhbar-ul-akhyar* (Reports on the Righteous). This large compendium evenhandedly assembles short biographies of Indian Sufis from all the major orders. By ascribing Chishti lineages to important Qadiris, the collection situates the Qadiri order very much within the mainstream of Sufi practice in the subcontinent.[96] Jahangir rewarded Abd-ul-Haqq suitably and remarked on the significant labor that the Sufi scholar had devoted to the task, cloistered away in solitude, while relying on God for sustenance.[97] The *Akhbar-ul-akhyar* became an influential model for many subsequent Sufi biographies. Abd-ul-Haqq would also become so renowned for his hadith studies that when one spoke of Delhi's *muhaddis* or hadith scholar, it could only mean him.

Though Abd-ul-Haqq abjured the court, he hoped to influence the emperor by directing his attention to the lives of pious Muslims.[98] Years earlier, when Jahangir ascended the throne, Abd-ul-Haqq had written a treatise on governance, directly addressed to the emperor, entitled *Risala-i Nuriya-i Sultaniya* (Epistle on Splendid Sovereignty). In another history on kings, Abd-ul-Haqq had declared, "When recalling those who have passed, the aim of those with insight/is to edify with life's lessons both pauper and emperor."⁹⁹ The muhaddis also maintained a habit of writing letters to various notables of his era, including the empress Nur Jahan.

With Abd-ul-Haqq, Jahangir discharged a ruler's duty toward the religious scholars he was meant to nurture, but Shaikh Ahmad of Sirhind (d. 1624), another prominent Sufi with a similar background, made him bristle. Born in 1564, thirteen years after the Muhaddis of Delhi, Shaikh Ahmad Sirhindi also studied under his father first and then spent some time at the court in Agra where, like Abd-ul-Haqq earlier, he met the court poet Faizi (d. 1595) and his brother Abu-l-Fazl (d. 1602), Akbar's historian and confidante. Sirhindi also left, disillusioned, though in his case he was probably more clearly uneasy with the generously eclectic religious atmosphere at Akbar's court. Returning to his father, he received Chishti and Qadiri initiation and then also eventually set out for Mecca. He did not have to go far to find a spiritual guide. Stopping in Delhi, on his way, he met the Afghan master Baqi-billah who was working to establish the Naqshbandi order in India. Sirhindi swiftly became his chief disciple, branching out independently to recruit other Naqshbandi followers in and around Sirhind.

Shaikh Ahmad Sirhindi wrote letter after letter to his deputies, instructing them in contemplative practices. He also corresponded with Mughal nobles, to whom he liberally dished out advice on the correct interpretations of God's *shariat* (divine law), and the Prophet's *sunnat* (legal precedent). The second millennium of the Islamic calendar had begun, and some, like the philosopher Abd-ul-Hakim Siyalkoti (d. 1656), thought that Shaikh Ahmad was the divinely appointed "Mujaddid," the revitalizer of the age.¹⁰⁰

In mid-1619, a collected volume of his letters reached Jahangir, who was already perturbed about Sirhindi's growing and well-organized following fanning out from Sirhind across the country. He scathingly describes the book as an "anthology of drivel (*jung-i l-muhmalat*)" which would "lead to infidelity and apostasy." Jahangir took particular exception to one letter. In his reading of it, Sirhindi dares to recount a celestial journey past the sun and the moon. There, he paused at discrimination, truth, and love to reach a level even higher than the abode of God's caliphs, Abu Bakr and Umar. Then he witnessed the highest level of gnosis obtained by Muhammad, the seal of the prophets. Jahangir cites this specific passage as proof that Shaikh Ahmad Sirhindi was guilty of *ridda* or apostasy, evoking the "Wars of Apostasy" after the death of the Prophet Muhammad, when Arab tribes who had once converted to Islam, turned back and rejected the rule of Abu Bakr, the Prophet's successor. Sirhindi's celestial vision was dangerous, as it could appear to impugn Jahangir's universal authority as emperor and God's caliph. Sirhindi composed his missives in extraordi-narily difficult Persian prose, and in this letter to his teacher Baqi-billah, he discusses spiritual states in a coded vocabulary that only initiates would understand well.[101]

The emperor summoned Sirhindi to court and interrogated him. Finding him to be arrogant and unrepentant, he had him imprisoned in the Gwalior fort, where prisoners of rank had been sent since the time of Akbar's reign. Jahangir was concerned about the charismatic shaikh's popularity. Within a year, though, Jahangir released the shaikh and gifted him one thousand rupees. Thereupon, Sirhindi remained in Jahangir's entourage, chastened, until he died in 1624.

In late 1620, Khurram and the Mughal forces finally secured the Kangra fortress. Shortly afterward, the emperor celebrated the marriage of Nur Ja-han's daughter Ladli with his own son Shahryar.[102] All the while, it was becoming clearer that Nur Jahan, at least, would not back Khurram's bid for the throne.

Almost immediately after the wedding, Jahangir dispatched Khurram to deal with a crisis in the Deccan. Malik Ambar, reneging on his earlier agree-ment, had joined forces with the states of Bijapur and Golconda to reclaim several of the territories he had earlier been forced to cede, and was now marching into Mughal territory with an army of sixty thousand men. Khurram, with his prior Deccan experience and several military victories, was the most qualified of all the princes to deal with the threat. Before leaving, however, Khurram imposed a condition. He would bring Khusrau along with him in his entourage. The elder prince now became his brother's prisoner. Jahangir, who leaves this incident out of his memoirs, had little choice but to acquiesce.

Before the battle began, Khurram staged a spectacular public act, one that chroniclers and poets would eventually celebrate. It was his thirty-first lunar birthday. Arriving at the banks of the Chambal River, he prostrated him-self in repentance (*tauba*). Then he ordered for all the wine casks that he had brought with him to be emptied into the river. He also had the royal wares of feasts crushed to pieces, including silver and gold wine pitchers and goblets, some of which were encrusted with gems. This pulverized metal was then distributed to the needy.[103]

Years later, the imperial poet laureate Kalim Kashani penned several lines commemorating Khurram's "act of repentance," as he termed it. The prince only ever drank on special occasions, at his father's insistence, remarks the poet. Yet, Kalim argues, Khurram's renunciation of wine, when he was at the height of his youth and vigor, had a special significance. Abstinence in old age did not carry the same weight: "The old man withdraws the hand of desire from wine/Not because of repentance, but out of shame for his white hair."[104]

Kalim explicitly recalls a similar act that Babur, the progenitor of the Mughal empire, had carried out, before his battle against Rana Sanga. At the Chambal River, Khurram powerfully evoked Babur's deed. But, says Kalim, there was a significant difference between the two events, in that Babur was forty-five and Khurram only thirty (he takes a modicum of poetic license with the prince's age). For Kalim, Khurram surpasses even Babur. The poet also vividly describes the river's turbulence once it mixed with the wine. All of its waves became "spears of war." Such a fire arose from the ignited alcohol that when the fish washed up on shore, they were already charred into kababs.[105] In Kalim's account, the prince would achieve a stunning victory.

2

DYNASTY

1622–1628

D ARA SHUKOH, THE ELDEST SON of seven living siblings, was almost
seven years old when his uncle died. One winter day, early in 1622,
Khusrau Mirza's body was discovered in the Burhanpur palace.[1] He was
thirty-four years old. Dara's father, Khurram (who was Khusrau's younger
brother and, lately, his custodian), had been out hunting. Nobody could
tell for sure what happened in that closed bedchamber, but it was impossible to put a lock on people's tongues. The winds of gossip blew and the
contents of hushed conversations wafted into letters and journals. Business
slowed down as merchants and government officials treaded cautiously.[2]

But the emperor, inveterate memoirist though he was, mentioned his eldest son's death so casually and briefly, he might have been recording the
weather or a banal administrative detail. On the twenty-third of February,
a letter from Khurram had reached Jahangir while he was at the outskirts
of Kashmir. The seals of all the Mughal noblemen stationed in Burhanpur
adorned it, to prove its veracity. The emperor remarked "a report was received from Khurram containing the news that Khusrau had died on the
eighth of the month after an attack of colic pain."[3]

Did Jahangir's reticence reflect a suspicion that he wished, for now, to
keep private, in order to let his sons battle out the matter of succession
themselves? Or did he have plans for dealing with Khurram that he wanted
to keep up his sleeve? Did he regret handing over Khusrau while in a state
of what Muhammad Salih Kamboh, a later chronicler, refers to as "wine's

world of oblivion," knowing full well that the younger son desired to eliminate all competition for the throne?[4]

Others, notably European traders, had no compunctions about calling
Khusrau's death a murder. William Methwold, Matthew Duke, and Francis
Futter, writing in March from far-away Masulipatnam, inform the English
factory in Surat that the "newest newes here is that Sultan Caroone hath
slayne his brother, but after what maner wee know as little as of what." By
the middle of the year they called Khusrau's death an "unnaturall fratri-
cide" and predicted that divine punishment would "fall heavey uppon the
bloody abettres," even though the crime might have been hidden "from thatt
vicekinge Mogall, per the distance of place and connivency of freinds."[5]

The rumor of Khurram's involvement would have traveled to Jahangir.
A Dutch merchant based in Agra reports that, upon hearing the news of
Khusrau's death, the emperor angrily demanded the truth in a letter that
he dashed off to the noblemen serving Khurram. Jahangir might even have
heard some of the lurid details in the Dutch merchant's account: that a slave
named Raza, dispatched to carry out the deed, went to Khusrau's room with
a group of accomplices; that Khusrau, wary, refused to open the door; that
Raza and company eventually forced their way into the room and surrounded the hapless prince, who flung at them the only weapon he could
lay his hands on—a chamber pot; that they knocked him down and
strangled him with a cord and then placed him on the bed as though he
had died in his sleep; and then, that Khusrau's first wife, the daughter of
Khan Azam Koka, was utterly distraught when she found him lifeless in
the morning.[6]

Khusrau's death caused a public stir. Khurram had judged that it would
be better to make his brother's demise known rather than try to cover it
up. The historian Kamboh would later report that, in order to avert suspicion, Khurram made sure that Khusrau had a stately funeral procession
accompanied by nobles and religious men offering prayers. Two days after
his death, he was buried in nearby Alamganj, and masses of grieving men
and women visited his grave every Friday.[7] A prince whom people believed
to have been unjustly killed could posthumously attract a large following.

Jahangir intervened by having Khusrau's body exhumed and moved up
north. In June 1622, the British merchant Robert Hughes reported to the
Surat factory that the body had reached Agra.[8] From there it was carried
to Allahabad to be buried next to the late prince's mother. The weather,
which would have been searingly hot, must have necessitated special measures to protect the prince's remains from decomposition. Embalming techniques in the seventeenth century were sufficiently developed for the dead
wife of the Italian traveler Pietro della Valle to accompany him throughout

his journeys across India in the 1620s.[9] Though Hanafi jurists generally frowned upon transferring corpses over long distances, the Mughals had a precedent in their ancestor Timur, whose body, embalmed with camphor and musk among other substances, was carried over three hundred miles to its burial place in Samarkand.[10]

After Khusrau's bier moved to Allahabad, replica tombs were made in each part of Burhanpur, and people would visit them every Thursday to pay their respects and sometimes stay the night.[11] His tomb in Allahabad then became a shrine. Jahangir also made sure that Khusrau's son, Dawar Bakhsh, was brought under his and Nur Jahan's watch.

The young Dara Shukoh and his siblings could not have escaped the commotion. For more than a year, after the constant upheaval of long journeys, Khurram's children had managed to achieve some measure of stability in the Burhanpur palace. But even before Khusrau's death, the relative calm was abruptly shattered. Little Umid Bakhsh died, at just over two years old, his passing unnoticed in the emperor's memoirs.[12] Jahanara and Dara Shukoh now had their second experience with the loss of a sibling, and Shuja, Roshanara, Aurangzeb, and the infant Surayya their first. Their mother, Mumtaz Mahal, pregnant again and grieving for Umid Bakhsh, still had to carry the additional burden of supervising her children's care and upbringing while living with their uncertain future.. What would their fate be, as the intrigues and struggles for the succession to Jahangir moved swiftly along? Khurram's other wives, Qandahari Begam and Shahnawaz Mirza's daughter, also staying in the Burhanpur Fort's women's quarters, no doubt wondered the same.

At age seven, Dara Shukoh was more or less halfway toward becoming a man. Like his father, and other male descendants of Timur in India, the prince would have had a lavish celebration marking his circumcision when he was four years, four months, and four days old.[13] Though Akbar had ordered that boys should only be circumcised at age twelve, with their full consent, this decree turned out to be too impractical for most of the elite. Around the same time, at four years or so, children had their *maktab* ceremony, marking the beginning of their formal education. The small prince Dara would have traced an *alif* on a slate, the first letter of the Arabic and Persian alphabets. Then, touching the Quran to his forehead, he would have recited the fatiha, the Quran's opening chapter.[14] As he matured in Burhanpur, Dara would have been gradually initiated into the ritual practices of Islam and those of Mughal princeship, including the five daily prayers, Quran-reading, horse-riding, and hunting.[15] During this period, he may well have begun to study calligraphic writing, Persian grammar and literature, and even Chaghatai Turkish, the ancestral language of the

Timurids, useful for communicating with Central Asian army officers. Soon, however, his life, and those of his siblings, would be rudely disrupted.

Khusrau's death had removed one obstacle on Khurram's way to the throne, yet the prince's position was hardly secure. His real threats were Parwez and Shahryar, as both were jostling to be Jahangir's heir. These days Parwez assiduously showed concern for their ailing father's health, edging closer into the emperor's good graces.[16] Shahryar, married to Nur Jahan's daughter Ladli Begam, was coming into his own under the empress's wing. Nur Jahan's already considerable wealth and authority had recently soared. Her father, Itimad-ud-Daula, had died earlier that year. In an unprecedented step, Jahangir allowed all his properties to go to her rather than revert to him as was the norm for a deceased nobleman's estate. He also granted her the right to have her own drums and orchestra played after his.[17]

Khurram soon had his first major confrontation with his father, though it was not directly linked to Khusrau's killing. On the twenty-seventh of March 1622, Jahangir, who with Nur Jahan and Shahryar was on his way to summer in Kashmir, got wind that the Safavid emperor Shah Abbas was about to besiege Qandahar, a fortress town on the western frontier of the Mughal empire.[18] Shah Abbas, whom Jahangir had earlier referred to as his brother, always had his eye set on recapturing Qandahar, ever since Akbar seized it from him in 1595. Perturbed by Khurram's recent victories over the Shii kingdoms of the Deccan, the Iranian ruler saw an opportunity to divert Mughal military resources from the southern to the northwestern frontier. Jahangir dispatched a messenger ordering Khurram to come posthaste with as large an army he could muster.[19] The emperor made plans to leave for Lahore, along with Nur Jahan, to more closely supervise the operation. He sent his senior nobleman Mahabat Khan to guard Kabul as governor of the city.[20]

The young Dara Shukoh and the rest of his family set off with Khurram, who proceeded as though he were complying with the emperor's demand. Stopping only a couple of hundred kilometers north of Burhanpur, at the hill fortress of Mandu, Khurram sent his father a list of conditions: He would remain in Mandu for several months until the muddy monsoon season ended. He required the governorship of Punjab, ostensibly to provide his army with provisions along the way. He also requested that the Ranthambor Fort be given to him for his family's use while he led the campaign in Qandahar. The tone of Khurram's letter was firm and direct.[21] Though the dispatch did not proclaim outright rebellion, the emperor construed it as such.[22] Yet, from Khurram's perspective, he was only trying to leverage his way out of a trap. The other options open to him were equally risky: He could obey his father and abandon his secure position in the

Deccan to brave the formidable Safavid army. Or, he could even try to negotiate some sort of collaboration with Shah Abbas, whose trustworthiness, or lack thereof, was all too apparent.

Nonetheless, Jahangir was deeply hurt by the insubordination of his once favorite son: "Of the patronage and favors I showered upon him I can say that until now no monarch has ever showered upon any son." He commanded that the prince be referred to not as Khurram, let alone Shah Jahan, but as *be-daulat*, which literally means both "bereft of good fortune" and "stateless," and, here, simply connotes "wretch." The emperor's health also multiplied his distress. Though sometimes he could muster the strength to mount a horse and go hunting, he felt out of sorts more often than not. Khurram's recent behavior only added to his list of woes, and the hot weather he was suffering at the time did not help.[23] A severe illness, possibly a stroke, that befell him two years earlier, would ultimately leave him unable to write his journal. Mutamad Khan soon took over the task of recording noteworthy events, though we are left to understand that Jahangir still closely supervised the project.[24]

The emperor appears to have made an effort to reach out to Khurram. A letter in Jahangir's name severely admonishes the prince, calling him an "evil-dispositioned son" who had "obliterated the filial obligations of obedience." But Jahangir also opened the door of reconciliation just a crack, by urging Khurram to fasten the "ring of servitude" onto the "earlobe of obedience." This was a metaphor for submission, as such earrings used to be worn by slaves. The prince could make amends by sending the noblemen who were with him to assist in the Qandahar campaign, his father urged.[25]

The letter, if indeed penned by Jahangir, had no effect on the rapidly worsening relationship with his son. In mid-1622, the emperor received word that Khurram had forcibly seized territories assigned to Nur Jahan and Shahryar, including the subdistrict of Dholpur, close to Agra.[26] Jahangir retaliated by confiscating the district of Hissar Firoza, part of Khurram's land allotment, which he then transferred to Shahryar, the prince's brother. The emperor then put Shahryar in charge of the Qandahar expedition.[27] This turned out to be a futile effort, as Shah Abbas eventually captured the garrison town. The Iranian sovereign wrote a letter of faint apology to his "brother" Jahangir, asking him not to be perturbed by such "trivial" matters.[28]

By March 1623, with Jahangir in Lahore, Khurram stealthily moved forward to attack the imperial stronghold of Agra. But his armies arrived to find the gates of the fort impenetrably shut, thanks to the resourceful Itibar Khan, eunuch superintendent of the women's quarters. Moreover, Nur Jahan had already sent her brother Asaf Khan to retrieve the wealth stored in its treasuries.[29] After sacking the surrounding areas, Khurram's army came face to face with the imperial army at Baluchpur, near Delhi. Here Khurram lost his finest general, Raja Bikramaditya. His army, demoralized, scattered ranks, even though the imperial general Abdullah Khan had defected to join them. They suffered a crushing defeat and were forced to flee west, with Parwez and Jahangir's commander, Mahabat Khan, chasing after them.[30]

Throughout this turmoil, Khurram's family accompanied him. In the difficult months that followed, Dara Shukoh, his siblings, and their pregnant mother endured countless upheavals and ongoing discomfort. Constant journeying was, of course, how Mughal royals lived and ruled.[31] But a fugitive's travels were of a different order. While planning his next course of action, Khurram had to also make arrangements for his household. Apart from his soldiers and those who provided for their needs, Khurram's entourage would have also included a host of maids, cooks, wet nurses, eunuchs, and other servants. The women and young children customarily traveled at the rear, at a slower pace. They endured the journey's jolts in narrow, closed palanquins, which were carried either by bearers traversing briskly on foot or by being laid across two camels. Sometimes they rode in covered litters atop elephants. As later reports witness, Arjumand was also closely involved in tactical planning and decision-making. Throughout it all, Arjumand and her cowives maintained the traditional practice of seclusion, and would have had to manage a network of informants to get news of the day's events.

For now, though, the family had a brief respite in Udaipur, where Rana Karan Singh, the son of Khurram's former foe, treated them to his hospitality. Several Rajput sources, at least one in Sanskrit and others in the Rajasthani vernacular, would later attest to this visit.[32] The Mughal writings of the period, though, largely gloss over this stay at Udaipur. Karan Singh, who was busy rebuilding his capital, is said to have lodged Khurram's family in a recently built pavilion on an island in Lake Pichola—a two-storied structure with a dome and canopied balconies.[33] It was small by the standards to which they were accustomed. But the lake glimmered all around, and the pavilion faced the labyrinthine Jagmandir Palace that Karan Singh had been constructing. Khurram, indebted to the man whose father had once kissed his feet, exchanged turbans with him in a gesture of friendship before they parted.[34]

Then Jahangir arrived in nearby Ajmer, and the imperial army headed by Mahabat Khan and Parwez moved in swift pursuit. After a few months' stay in Udaipur, Khurram's household accompanied him as he retreated to Mandu. Finding Mahabat Khan's forces close behind, they headed toward

Burhanpur. Khurram left the majority of his household staff—servants, eunuchs, and concubines—as well as his belongings, at the lofty Asirgarh Fort north of Burhanpur, and took with him only his three wives, children, and a few servants.[35]

At Burhanpur, Khurram discovered that his third wife's grandfather, the venerable Abd-ur-Rahim Khan of Khans, who had been in charge of the Deccan in his absence, had been corresponding with Mahabat Khan, the imperial general. Khurram put Abd-ur-Rahim and the khan's son Darab, who was also Khurram's general, under surveillance. Then, desperate, he begged the Khan of Khans to plead his case with Jahangir's men. Khurram even did the unthinkable and invited his father-in-law into the women's quarters, entry into which was reserved for only the closest of family members. There, his wives and children sobbed and pleaded for his aid—or so reports Jahangir, who was keeping a close watch on his rebel son's activities. Khurram's wife Arjumand played her part in trying to gain Abd-ur-Rahim, imploring him while her children, no doubt including Dara Shukoh, were by her side. The imperial army was drawing close, though, and Abd-ur-Rahim, wary of casting his lot with a rebel prince whose prospects were uncertain at best, defected to the imperial camp.

It was September 1623, and the monsoon was in full burst. Though Khurram had recently appealed to the Shah of Iran for support, his letter was ignored. Pursued from the north, Khurram could only go south, crossing the muddy, gushing Tapti River with his family and army. Many people along with their animals and cargo were swept away in the dangerous crossing, but Dara Shukoh and his family survived. Jahangir, exulting in his son's travails, notes that most of the imperial servants had by now deserted Khurram.[36]

Khurram knew that his only shot at regaining his footing was to leave Burhanpur, travel south through the neighboring kingdoms of Ahmadnagar, Bijapur, and Golconda, and then try to seize the empire's eastern provinces. But no assistance was forthcoming from either Malik Ambar, who wished to avoid another war with the Mughals, or the ruler of Bijapur, who wanted nothing to do with the rebel contingent. Qutb-ul-Mulk, ruler of Golconda, allowed Khurram to pass through the kingdom provided that he did not halt long. He even provided some money, which Khurram gratefully accepted.[37] Golconda, though farther away from Burhanpur, bordered the Mughal provinces of Orissa and Khandesh, the southern province of which Burhanpur was the capital.

By early November, Khurram arrived at Machilipatnam, a thriving Mughal entrepôt where British, French, and Dutch merchants came to trade, its hinterland lush with paddy fields and coconut-palm groves. Though he had lost many men and animals along the way, according to one English account, he still had four-and-a-half thousand horses, over ten thousand infantry, and five hundred elephants.[38] By imperial Mughal standards, this was a smallish army but it was large enough for a quick attack in a frontier province. Khurram's men and elephants went on a rampage to fill their bellies, destroying fields and trees and killing chickens in a prelude to their Orissa campaign. The governor of Orissa, Ahmad Beg, who had not expected Khurram to arrive so soon, was away fighting a local feudal chieftain named Giridhar. Unwilling, or perhaps afraid, to face Khurram's troops, Ahmad Beg sought refuge in the Burdwan region of Bengal. Within a month, Khurram took Cuttack, the province's capital.[39] Finally, it looked as though the rebel prince's fortunes were ascending.

Khurram's next stop was Bengal, the northeastern frontier of the empire. Here lay the fertile rainy delta where the Ganga joined the ocean; an area that had relatively recently been incorporated into the Mughal empire. Although large tracts of the region remained forested, over the course of the previous century, peasants had been settling the land, moving eastward. Religious men—Sufis—came with them, attracting their own followings. Gradually, with each successive generation, more and more of the population of Bengal came to identify as Muslim. But the river itself and the surrounding network of tributaries, waterways, and swamps, clogged the swift movement of cavalry. It was only under Jahangir, in 1610, that the Mughal state was able to infiltrate farther and capture the city of Dhaka, which was renamed Jahangirnagar in his honor.[40]

During Khurram's incursions in the eastern provinces, he started amassing allies from among the local nobility. One of those whom he pressed into his service was a *khanazad,* or "house-born" military commander of Isfahani origin, which meant that his father, too, had served the emperor—in this case, in the navy. Ala-ud-Din Isfahani, the commander in question, was also known as Mirza Nathan, an honorific meaning "lord of the nose ring," probably because his nose had been pierced in childhood as a talisman against illness.[41] A couple of years earlier, in 1621, Jahangir gave him the title Shitab Khan after he successfully put down a landowner's rebellion. Though he had never met Jahangir or been summoned to court, Shitab Khan had managed to get officially inducted as the emperor's *murid,* or disciple, which was a privilege, drawing on Sufi practice, of only a select few nobles.[42]

Once Khurram had made inroads into Bengal and seized Jahangirnagar, Shitab Khan joined the rebel prince with alacrity. By April 1624, Khurram's army, led by Abdullah Khan, had defeated and killed Ibrahim Khan, governor of Bengal and uncle of Ahmad Beg of Orissa. The prince sent a decree summoning the services of Shitab Khan and other nobles, which they received reverently, as though in the presence of the emperor. We know this because Shitab Khan penned a long autobiographical history of Bengal, a work that opens a window onto the life of a nobleman on the court's fringes, at the empire's eastern frontier. The last part of the chronicle treats Khurram's revolt. Because Shitab Khan goes out of his way to show his closeness to Khurram, we can catch here intimate sightings of the rebel prince's family life that we would not otherwise see in official histories.[43]

We learn, for example, that Arjumand Bano was involved in negotiating the surrender of Mirza Salih, the commander of the Burdwan garrison who initially held out against Khurram's siege. She was in touch with Mirza Salih's wife, who in turn convinced the nobleman to awake "from his sleep of negligence" and submit to Khurram. Children, too, were expected to play their part. Before finally choosing to take on the governor Ibrahim Khan, Khurram proposed that the soon-to-be six-year-old Aurangzeb stay with the governor in Bengal as a sort of figurehead. The plan, which never came to pass, was for Khurram to then go ahead with the rest of the family as he sought to conquer Bihar. Aurangzeb was likely chosen for Dara, as the eldest son, could not be spared, and Shuja in any case was still living apart from his parents with the emperor and Nur Jahan. But Ibrahim Khan made the ultimately fateful decision to resist and was eventually killed. And thus Aurangzeb remained with his family.[44]

Khurram's military forays during his rebellion entailed a slew of responsibilities. Apart from managing a stream of new supporters, rewarding loyal servants with gifts and positions, punishing deserters, and planning his next moves, he also had to arrange the travel and housing of the women and children with him. Arjumand's pregnancy was advancing, and her child was due any day. Shitab Khan's status as a house-born imperial servant often meant that he was charged with overseeing the women's well-being. One letter from Khurram ordered him to send from Bengal five boats to Patna, in the province of Bihar, for the ladies' use. Among many other tasks, Shitab Khan was instructed to arrange for Itimad Khan, a eunuch who came from Arjumand's father's household, to accompany the ladies to Rohtas via Patna, facilitate the safe passage of several elephants to the warring prince Khurram, and give one hundred gold coins to a prominent Sufi, Shaikh Abdullah of Ghazipur. In his account, Shitab Khan deftly handled all these logistics and was granted the opportunity to pay his respects to the ladies in person.[45]

By this point, Dara Shukoh and Aurangzeb were old enough to live among the menfolk, with guardians and tutors watching over them, so initially they were not sent to Rohtas with their mother. But then Khurram had second thoughts and entrusted them to the safety of the fort, where they entered at an astrologically auspicious hour.[46] Khurram got wind that the imperial forces led by Parwez and Mahabat Khan had crossed the Ganges with their armies. He retreated to Banaras, then crossed over to nearby Bahadurpur. Both sides prepared for battle, keeping a close watch on the other.

Shitab Khan notes that the imperial army had "eighty thousand brave horsemen, one thousand nine hundred elephants, and a hundred thousand experienced infantry." It was tiny in comparison with Khurram's forces, which numbered "one hundred and eighty thousand iron-clad horse-men, one hundred and ninety thousand brave infantry, two thousand four hundred war-elephants, seven hundred of which were in a state of heat, five hundred war-boats and fifteen hundred cannon." The sight of Khurram's army was so impressive, it blinded the eyes of the opposing side, he added.[47]

The khan exaggerated wildly. But perhaps the point of his description here lies not in its accuracy or lack thereof, but in the clear way it states the author's loyalties. Another later account estimates the size of the imperial army at a more reasonable forty thousand and Khurram's at a more plausible ten thousand. A host of allies had joined Jahangir's forces, including Raja Bir Singh Bundela. The battle moved to the banks of the Tons, a Ganges tributary. Abdullah Khan and other commanders, seeing that they were outnumbered, wanted to retreat. But Raja Bhim, who had helped secure Patna, insisted that they fight. The result was disastrous for the rebel forces, who were quickly surrounded just "as a ring encircles the fingers." Raja Bhim, for all his bravado, was killed, his body sliced by swords before being pulled off his horse.[48] Khurram's mount was slain and he too barely escaped with his life. Abdullah Khan gave him a horse to get off the battlefield, and they fled toward Patna.[49]

Meanwhile, in Rohtas, on the ninth of October 1624, while Khurram was in the thick of preparing for battle, Arjumand Bano gave birth to a son. He was her tenth child, the sixth so far to live. There was no question now of Jahangir giving him a name, so his parents called him Murad Bakhsh, "wish-fulfiller," after one of the divine attributes. A messenger conveyed the happy news to Khurram, who, according to Shitab Khan, held an "assembly of joy" for three days and nights, and asked Arjumand to issue a writ to Shitab Khan for any items she might need for the celebrations. The commander furnished the money and got the wife of the deceased Ibrahim Khan to make the purchases. If the widow was reluctant to assist relatives who were responsible for her husband's killing, he does not tell us, though Shitab Khan's memoir reveals that he himself took care to cultivate a good relationship with the noblewoman. Ibrahim Khan's wife bought, he reports, at Arjumand's request, huge quantities of expensive perfumes and rare aromatic substances. These included thirty seers (equivalent to almost sixty pounds) of "white ambergris of the sea," "two thousand pods musk of Khata and Khutan," "ten thousand bottles of the rose-water of Yazd," and fifty maunds (about four hundred pounds) of saffron.[50] One suspects that, just as with Shitab Khan's description of Khurram's army, these enormous numbers need not be taken literally. They are useful to Shitab Khan's story by making him sound important and indicating his regard for Khurram's family.

At the time, the acts of sprinkling, burning, and appreciating pleasant fragrances were prized ingredients of a social gathering. From Shitab Khan, we learn that even in the midst of war, Khurram's family strove to uphold social rituals. But Shitab Khan's anecdote also calls to mind another story about a Mughal birth. Roughly eighty years earlier, Khurram's grandfather, Akbar, was born to parents in exile. When the newborn's father Humayun heard the news of his son's birth, he cracked open a pod of musk in his tent. It was all he had in his abject state then. But the scent filled the air just as he hoped, no doubt, that his son's renown would one day spread. Humayun's water carrier, Jauhar, related this story years later when interviewed for his reminiscences of the previous emperor.[51]

After Khurram's defeat, the rebel prince, along with those commanders who remained with him, traveled for a night and a day without halting. Then, Shitab Khan writes, the prince rested under a tree, using his quiver as a pillow, while his companions too caught some sleep before setting out for more grueling hours of riding. The next morning, some of those in this starving group pilfered a goat and roasted its meat, but they were too embarrassed to offer this coarse repast to the prince. After the insistence of two religious shaikhs in the group, Khurram put aside his pride and ate a little. They were now close to Rohtas, and Khurram proceeded there alone, sending the others to Patna.

There, Khurram met Arjumand with their newborn son Murad Bakhsh and their other children. She soothed him, blaming his generals for the defeat. For two of them in particular, Abdullah Khan and Sher Khan, she had harsh words. "Both these men are shameless, they ought to die by taking poison," Shitab Khan reports her as saying.[52] Khurram had wanted to send them on individual expeditions and remain in Rohtas, but she dissuaded him from doing so. The family made plans to retreat eastward, via Patna, leaving behind baby Murad. Given his age and the perils of their situation, they decided against taking him with them. They put him in the care of nurses and appointed caretakers for the fort—Sayyid Muzaffar Khan of Barha, and Raza Bahadur of the infamous Khusrau incident, who had been

Khurram's trusted childhood slave.[53] Khurram, Arjumand, and the rest of their children left for the Deccan by way of Akbarnagar. But the imperial army led by Parwez and Mahabat Khan soon chased after them.[54]

Though Khurram and his family stayed in Akbarnagar for only twenty-four days, Shitab Khan describes this period in detail. He includes an anec-dote about the six-year-old Aurangzeb. On one occasion, Khurram distrib-uted bananas, of the choice "Martaban" variety, to his nobles. But the portion allotted to Shitab Khan was missing. After investigating, the ser-vants found that just two bananas remained, because little Aurangzeb had gobbled up the rest. Khurram was furious. Only Shitab Khan's pleas stopped him from punishing his son.[55]

Khurram had asked Darab Khan, who was in Jahangirnagar, to meet them in Akbarnagar, but the governor made excuses that the road was blocked and never turned up. The prince and his family headed south the same way they had come, but without the pomp that had accompanied his recent victories. With nowhere else to turn, Khurram approached the aging Malik Ambar. This time the Nizamshahi prime minister placated him, hoping to enlist Khurram's help against an alliance that Mahabat Khan had formed with the neighboring state of Bijapur. He sent his commander, the Ethiopian Yaqub Khan, to Burhanpur with ten thousand horsemen. Khurram arrived with his family and pitched camp at Lal Bagh, on the city's outskirts. They raised a siege, attacking the fort from two sides. The in-tense fighting lasted some months. At times it looked as though Khurram's men were about to make a breakthrough, but on each occasion they were thwarted. Then Parwez and Mahabat Khan arrived at the Narmada, and Khurram decided to quit. Exhausted and ill, he moved to Balaghat, at the empire's southern edge, and finally, in March 1626, wrote his father beg-ging for forgiveness.

Jahangir, pleased by this contrition, replied in his own hand. His son per-formed the appropriate obeisances before opening the letter. The emperor made two principal demands: Khurram was to ask his men to vacate the fortresses at Rohtas and Asir and to send Dara Shukoh and Aurangzeb to the imperial court in Lahore. If he complied, he would be pardoned and receive Balaghat province as his fief, recently wrested back from Malik Ambar.[56]

Not only was Khurram's status severely diminished from what it had been before his rebellion, but he and Arjumand now also had to relinquish their sons, with no certainty that they would see them again. There was no knowing how long Jahangir would remain alive or what would happen to the boys should he die. Nur Jahan may have insisted that Jahangir take the children hostage so that she would have some control over Khurram if a struggle for succession were to take place.[57] Khurram arranged for the infant Murad Bakhsh to be brought to them and for Rohtas and Asir to be handed over to Jahangir's men. He then moved to Nasik, in Malik Ambar's territory, with Arjumand, the rest of their children, and a small band of soldiers and retainers.

As Dara Shukoh and Aurangzeb prepared to leave their parents to join the emperor, suddenly the monarchy's foundations quaked—and almost crashed. It was mid-March 1626, just before the New Year celebrations. On his way to Kabul, Jahangir camped on a bank of the Bahat River, now known as the Jhelum, along with Nur Jahan and a handful of attendants. Mahabat Khan, accompanied by hundreds of Rajput soldiers, stormed into his tents. He forced the emperor to ride an elephant, accompanying him as though the two were going on a hunting expedition. Mahabat Khan had seized advantage of a glaring oversight in Jahangir's security: Nur Jahan's brother Asaf Khan had already crossed the river with the rest of his army, entourage, and baggage. Mahabat Khan got his men to block the bridge and cut the emperor off, effectively taking him prisoner.

The problem, actually, had been rumbling for a while. Mahabat Khan's rising station and military successes alarmed both Asaf Khan and Nur Jahan, because through him Parwez was becoming more powerful. Kami Shirazi, a panegyrist of Jahangir and Nur Jahan, wrote a narrative poem about this incident, in which he blames Mahabat Khan for luring Parwez into disobedience: "During that time, Mahabat Khan cast a spell / He threw out all the emperor's *farman*s from [Parwez's] heart."[58] Though Nur Jahan had backed Mahabat Khan's crushing defeat of Khurram, she was afraid that with the khan's support, Parwez would prevail over the younger, sheltered Shahryar. Asaf Khan's friction with Mahabat Khan was older; Thomas Roe had mentioned it ten years earlier.[59] But Asaf Khan, always careful to appear on the side of his sister and the emperor, remained circumspect about his concern for the fate of his daughter, Arjumand Bano, and son-in-law, Khurram. If Mahabat Khan could somehow be subdued, Khurram could hope to make a realistic bid for the throne.

Nur Jahan and her brother convinced Jahangir that Mahabat Khan was incompetent for having let Khurram escape into exile. An imperial decree ordered the nobleman to leave Parwez and take up the governorship of Bengal. But, at Asaf Khan's behest, another decree followed, stripping Mahabat Khan of the position and summoning him to court to return the elephants and wealth that he had acquired while beating back Khurram's armies from Bengal.[60] The latter decree intimated that the emperor suspected Mahabat Khan of financial impropriety. Mahabat Khan rushed to court, on the pretext of salvaging his reputation with the emperor. But in fact, he sought more than just to clear his name, for he brought with him several thousand (Kami's poetic account has ten thousand) Rajput soldiers from his fort in Ranthambore.[61] What is more, their wives and children accompanied them as well; apparently this would spur them on to greater acts of valor. The able general, banking on his tactical prowess and his good rapport with Jahangir, decided that a show of strength was the best way forward.

As Mahabat Khan drew near the emperor's camp on the Bahat River, the emperor summoned him to come alone, without his army. The khan instead sent his son-in-law, Khwaja Barkhurdar. Jahangir had him hauled off with his hands bound around his neck. The Khwaja's stated crime was that he had married Mahabat Khan's daughter without the emperor's permission. Until then Mahabat Khan's plan of action was perhaps not entirely clear, but he was now willing to risk what no nobleman had ever done before. He forced his way to Jahangir's tent and sweet-talked the emperor into mounting a horse and going over to his own camp. When describing this humiliating moment, Kami the panegyrist insists that Jahangir kept his cool. The poet writes, "Because, at the moment, it was a delicate time / The emperor revealed neither too much nor too little."[62]

Mahabat Khan took the emperor, securely in his custody, over to Shahryar's tent. The khan soon discovered to his dismay that Nur Jahan had somehow broken free of the cordon and escaped to the other side of the embankment. Kami relates that when Jahangir tried to reach Nur Jahan in a boat rowed by his attendant, Mahabat Khan had the boatman, Chajju, brutally killed. The emperor did not dare protest.[63]

Asaf Khan, together with his son and a couple of hundred soldiers, expediently locked himself up in the nearby fortress of Attock. Over the next days, Jahangir placated Mahabat Khan by playing along with his confinement. Meanwhile Nur Jahan, riding an elephant with her daughter Ladli, her granddaughter, and the infant's nurse, led the imperial army against Mahabat Khan's troops, with Asaf Khan's support. Nur Jahan almost drowned when her elephant was wounded while crossing the river, and an arrow struck her granddaughter. In Kami Shirazi's account, the empress's injured elephant represented her own valor: "Then, in rage, like a roaring lion / the Begam's elephant charged towards the battlefield."[64]

The imperial forces proved no match for Mahabat Khan's Rajput army. They were forced to surrender. Kami, the imperial couple's loyal poet, spins Nur Jahan's defeat to make it seem as though it was part of a deliberate strategy. Asaf Khan vacillated and then withdrew his forces, Kami suggests, partly because Jahangir had warned him not to fight and ultimately because Mahabat Khan's brother had been killed in the skirmish, and for this reason

Asaf Khan feared the nobleman would take his wrath out on the emperor.[65] But in any case, all the members of the imperial family present were now Mahabat Khan's captives: Nur Jahan, Jahangir, Shahryar, Ladli, their infant daughter, Asaf Khan, his son and daughter-in-law, and Dawar Bakhsh, Khusrau's son. It is likely that young Shuja was also with them, though the sources do not mention him.

Shortly thereafter, ten-year-old Dara and seven-year-old Aurangzeb journeyed to the court, leaving behind their father and mother, brothers and sisters, milk siblings, foster mothers, tutors, and other familiar people. They brought lavish gifts, including elephants, jewels, and chased weapons worth at least seven lakh rupees.[66] Khurram had to provide an entourage he could ill afford to spare, in order to protect the boys and the bounty they carried. Around May, the boys reached Agra, from where they traveled westward through the subcontinent's northern plains in the hottest months of the year.

There were new developments at Jahangir's court. Mahabat Khan had allowed the imperial party to continue onto Kabul and to carry out their activities as usual, except that they were constantly under his watch. There, his overconfident soldiers had a run-in with some elite members of the imperial guard, and the khan lost a good number of men. In the Deccan, Malik Ambar, Khurram's host, had died, at the age of eighty. By June, Khurram heard about Mahabat Khan's coup and headed north from Nasik to join the fray with a straggling band of soldiers, which was all he had left. Perhaps he thought he and Mahabat Khan would join forces against the emperor, or that he and his father would make amends by uniting against a common enemy, Mahabat Khan, and that by proving his loyalty he might draw his father away from Nur Jahan. On his way, his makeshift army dispersed, leaving him with only about five hundred men. Realizing that his earlier plan was not feasible, Khurram went to Thatta, in Sind, to fight against the imperial army, crossing the blistering Thar Desert. Arjumand, heavily pregnant, made the difficult journey with him. It is likely that the rest of their children, apart from the three eldest sons, also accompanied them.[67]

Word had recently arrived that Parwez was seriously unwell. When the imperial couple was in Kabul, official reports from the Deccan mentioned that the prince was ill with colic. Then, after the family hastened toward Hindustan, Khan Jahan Lodi, whom Jahangir treated as a foster son, wrote, saying that Parwez had become unconscious and the physicians had decided to cauterize him on the head and face. He drifted in and out of consciousness. The doctors diagnosed him with the malady caused by excessive drink, the same illness that felled Parwez's uncles Murad and Daniyal.[68]

In August, by the time Dara Shukoh and Aurangzeb arrived at their grandfather's court, Mahabat Khan's grip over the emperor and Nur Jahan had loosened. Kami's panegyric to Nur Jahan's stand against Mahabat Khan's insurrection depicts the empress riding on horseback and showing off her skill in archery and hunting. Kami has Jahangir, impressed, exclaim: "You and I are partners in kingship."[69] The imperial household was returning back from Kabul to Lahore. The boys met up with the camp along the way. Entering Jahangir's audience tent, the young princes thrice bowed low in the *kornish*, bringing their right hands to the ground and then to their foreheads, before performing the ceremony of kissing the ground, the *zamin bos*. This elaborate set of obeisances had, since Akbar's reign, been reserved for the emperor. The boys must have been duly coached to perform it correctly, as even the slightest breach of etiquette was looked upon sternly. The chronicler Mutamad Khan tells us that they then presented their tribute of three hundred thousand rupees in addition to the other gifts they brought in kind.[70]

The emperor and Nur Jahan were still under Mahabat Khan's surveillance when Dara and Aurangzeb arrived. Then, at the beginning of September, the princes witnessed Mahabat Khan's final undoing. The end of his coup was far less dramatic than its beginning. Jahangir lulled him into complacency by letting him believe he was a close confidant. Apparently, though, Nur Jahan and Shahnawaz Khan's daughter, who was also Ladli's daughter's nurse, were out to kill Mahabat Khan. Nur Jahan secretly arranged for military reinforcements from her eunuch Hoshyar Khan. At the Bahat River, the emperor ordered Mahabat Khan to go ahead of the imperial party. The khan complied, now more docile after his Kabul misadventure. Jahangir and his retinue swiftly outpaced him and crossed over to the other bank. Nur Jahan then sent Mahabat Khan a list of orders, including one directing him to go to Thatta and to fight against Khurram. The commander instead fled to the mountains of Mewar.[71]

It is during the period in Kabul, with Jahangir and Nur Jahan now emerging from Mahabat Khan's clutches, that Kami composed his panegyric for the empress. Kami's epic flows with devotion to Ali, whom the Shia particularly revere as the first Imam, and the Prophet's family. He presents Jahangir as a second Solomon and Alexander and a champion of Ali. Kami likens Nur Jahan, the poem's heroine, to Bilqis, Solomon's wife, and extols her piety in very Shia terms. Years later, the question of Nur Jahan's Shiism and its influence over the court would be associated with her ward Shuja.

The young princes Dara and Aurangzeb had an uneasy status as hostages in their grandfather's household. They did not know when they would see their parents again or even how long they would be allowed to live or re-main unmaimed. While they were under Jahangir and Nur Jahan's watch, imperial artillery fired upon their parents' tent in Thatta.[72] Khurram's siege failed and his army was cornered and trapped. The Shah of Iran had once again rebuffed the prince's plea for help or refuge. Khurram fell severely ill.[73] Amidst all this, in the third week of October, Mumtaz gave birth to a son whom they named Lutfullah, God's grace.[74]

Then a threatening missive arrived from Nur Jahan. She wrote that Ma-habat Khan was upset that the imperial retinue went off without him. She added, "Hopefully he is not in such a foul temper that anything would happen to your sons along the way." Of course, Mahabat Khan, now prac-tically disarmed, was not in a position to harm the boys. Nur Jahan, grasping the reins of power more tightly after emerging from the coup, had no com-punctions about using Dara Shukoh, Aurangzeb, and probably Shuja, too, as pawns. Khurram was forced to take his family and retreat; he traveled in a palanquin because he was too unwell to mount a horse. Lutfullah was only four days old when they departed. They returned to the Deccan where Malik Ambar's son found them a house.[75]

Parwez had died in the first week of October, his body ravaged by drink.[76] Khurram, however, did not know the fate of his fallen brother and one-time rival until he left for the Deccan, by which time word had swiftly reached the court. When she wrote her aforementioned letter to Khurram, Nur Jahan could see that the real battle for succession would now be be-tween Khurram and Shahryar, unless Khusrau's son Dawar Bakhsh sud-denly found himself some very strong supporters. Between the lines of her letter was also the wish to prevent Mahabat Khan from joining forces with Khurram. But eventually Mahabat Khan, who had once pursued Khurram as the emperor's general, decided to cast his lot with the rebel prince. No longer bound by loyalty to Parwez, and in rebellion against the emperor, Mahabat Khan traveled to Khurram's camp with gifts and a plea to make amends.[77]

By this point, Khurram's sons had already journeyed south to Lahore with Jahangir's party. The city, one of the largest and most populous in the world, spilled out beyond the Ravi River's banks. A decade earlier, the late English traveler Coryate had recorded that Lahore "contayneth at least six-teen miles in compasse and exceedeth Constantinople itself in greatness."[78] Hewn from dusty red sandstone, Lahore's expansive fort rose sharply from the Punjab's flat terrain, its massive ramparts extended over roughly fifty square acres. The Ravi flowed along its north side, adjoining gardens and pavilions from which the imperial household and select guests watched el-ephant fights and other spectacles put up for their entertainment.

The boys, confined in the fort, would have had scarce opportunity to sample the city's sights and pleasures. The sources provide very little insight into the private lives of the children during this time. We may picture their reunion with their younger brother Shuja, who had entirely grown up in the court, having lived with Nur Jahan throughout his father's rebellion. There were other princely grandchildren of Jahangir, older than Khurram's sons, whom Nur Jahan had rounded up and placed under close guard in the sprawling fort: Khusrau's sons; the sixteen-year-old Dawar Bakhsh and his younger brother Garshasp; as well as sons of Jahangir's younger brother named Tahmuras and Hoshang, who had been missing for years and were recently found and sent over by Mahabat Khan. All these male scions were possible threats to Shahryar's enthronement, which Nur Jahan openly championed. Shahryar kept a special eye on Dawar Bakhsh and supervised his confinement. As potential claimants to the throne, the emperor's grandsons were highly valuable in the governing economy of kingship. Others more experienced and capable could use them as fronts to wield their own power. These boys and young men were likely kept from mingling amongst themselves or developing any sort of camaraderie.

Nur Jahan may have also discouraged her brother Asaf Khan, the maternal grandfather to Dara Shukoh and his brothers, from spending much time with the boys. After Mahabat Khan's failed insurrection, Asaf Khan was disgraced and sidelined. He had been stripped of his rank and land allotment. Jahangir now rehabilitated him somewhat by restoring his rank to that of seven thousand cavalry.[79] Nevertheless, Asaf Khan would still have to tread carefully so that his loyalty to the imperial couple was not questioned.

Dara's time as a hostage in Lahore with his brothers, though long in the life of a child, was not interminable. It was interrupted by a trip north to the mountains. By March of the next year, the heat was beginning to affect Jahangir, whose constitution had taken a turn for the worse. The members of the imperial household, including the confined princes, wound their way toward the higher elevation of Kashmir. Yet, even in the shadow of the towering peaks, the emperor's chronic asthma bothered him and his appetite declined. Even worse, Shahryar, once a rival to Khurram, came down with an embarrassing illness. He was afflicted with what Mughal physicians referred to as "fox-mange," a term drawn from the ancient Greek medical tradition. The prince's hair, perceived as a symbol of manhood, fell out from his head, as well as his beard, eyebrows, and elsewhere. The doctors could not treat him successfully and it was rumored that he been stricken with syphilis. Regardless of the cause, the ailment was exceedingly humiliating. Shahryar decided to retire to the Lahore Fort with the hope of privacy, if not a cure. Jahangir gave him permission to take leave. Before departing, Shahryar entrusted the custody of Khusrau's son Dawar Bakhsh to Iradat Khan, courtier and brother to Asaf Khan and Nur Jahan.[80]

Meanwhile, Jahangir, who was still unwell, also set off on the journey back. Despite his ill health, he continued his habit of stopping to hunt along the way. In one incident, his attendants drove stags to the top of a precipitous cliff so that the emperor, in his weakened state, could easily shoot them. Jahangir fired at one but missed. The animal fled to a bush on the sharp edge of the mountain face. A servant chased after it, and crashed off the precipice to his death. The emperor was deeply troubled. After returning to camp that night, Jahangir's condition worsened. By the next morning, on the seventh of November 1627, the emperor was dead. At sixty years old, Jahangir had ruled India for over two decades.[81]

Khurram's boys saw Asaf Khan, their maternal grandfather, take charge instantly. At the time of the emperor's demise, Asaf Khan was with the royal entourage. Though he had just recently made amends with the court, the nobleman faced a unique, if perilous, opportunity. The once powerful khan, who had been keeping close tabs on Jahangir's health, quickly appraised the situation. Shahryar's move to Lahore gave Asaf Khan an opening. But there was no time to lose. With the aid of his brother Iradat Khan, Asaf Khan immediately had Jahangir's grandson, young Dawar Bakhsh, freed and proclaimed emperor. He persuaded the wary prince that his motives were genuine. Only days before, Dawar Bakhsh had been in Shahryar's custody. But Asaf Khan's loyalties at this point were by no means transparent.

The khan placed Nur Jahan, his own sister, under guard, ignoring her requests to meet him. He then entrusted his signet ring to one Banarsi, a Hindu manager in the elephant stables, with instructions to convey the news as swiftly as possible to his son-in-law Khurram. Banarsi started the long journey to the Deccan, traveling almost nonstop, day and night, on a series of post horses. His speed became legendary and some even claim that he ran the whole distance on foot. Asaf Khan also seized custody of his three grandsons, Dara Shukoh, Shuja, and Aurangzeb, as well as the other young princes, from Nur Jahan.[82] But, fearing their fate under Dawar Bakhsh, Asaf Khan soon then transferred his grandsons into the care of Sadiq Khan, who was both his nephew and son-in-law. The historian Qazwini later writes that Khurram's three sons, mounted on an elephant on their way back to Lahore, were like "three jewels in one treasure-casket" or "three stars in one constellation."[83]

Meanwhile, when Shahryar, who was back in the fort of Lahore, heard of his father's death, he raided the imperial treasury and bought the support of as many noblemen as he could muster. As Asaf Khan approached

Lahore, leading his troops with Dawar Bakhsh, the two armies faced off. The experienced officers and soldiers of the imperial guard on Asaf Khan's side were more capable than the army Shahryar had hastily put together. After many of the prince's soldiers scattered and fled, Shahryar and his wife scrambled for shelter in the women's quarters of the Lahore Fort's imperial apartment. Two of Jahangir's chief eunuchs located and imprisoned the couple. Shahryar was brought before Dawar Bakhsh. A searing punishment was yet to come. A day or two later, on Asaf Khan's orders, Shahryar was blinded. Qazwini puns with wordplay to describe this incident, as the term for blinding someone (*mil kashidan*) and desire or inclination (*mayl*) have exactly the same spelling in Persian: "The good-for-nothing's eyes were scratched out so that the desire for rulership would no longer remain." The loss of the prince's eyesight extinguished the possibility that he might become emperor.

Banarsi's epic journey lasted twenty days, during which time he was said to average seventy miles daily. The messenger found Khurram through Mahabat Khan, who had cast his lot with the estranged prince. Asaf Khan's signet ring allayed any doubts the prince might have had as to Banarsi's mission. After a perfunctory period of mourning, Khurram set off toward the north with his household and men, Mahabat Khan accompanying him. Along the way he sacked disloyal governors and issued royal *farman* injunctions, as if he were already the emperor. It was a while before he would even know of Shahryar's defeat, and Dawar Bakhsh's new position.[84]

In Lahore, Dawar Bakhsh, too, was stamping his seal on imperial decrees, as Sher Shah, "Lion King," a short-lived regnal name. One decree, addressed to Rai Suraj Singh, vassal ruler of Bikaner, announces Sher Shah's accession but devotes far more space to praising Nur Jahan, through whose support, Dawar Bakhsh writes, he inherited the throne. Dawar Bakhsh also advises the empire's servants to carry out their duties scrupulously. Another farman written to Raja Jai Singh of Amer conveys a similar message. While Dawar Bakhsh ruled from Lahore, Khurram independently sent an edict to Jai Singh informing him of Jahangir's death and his own intention to ascend the throne.[85] The Rajput vassal was more likely to have confidence in the seasoned, battle-worn rebel prince than in his callow nephew Dawar Bakhsh.

As Khurram marched through Gujarat on his way to Mewar, allies old and new paid homage. Quickly, he sent his trusted servant Raza Bahadur, infamous for his alleged role in the death of Khusrau, ahead with a decree for Asaf Khan: "In these times trouble roils the sky and sedition rises up in the earth." The decree continued by declaring that if Dawar Bakhsh, Khurram's "good-for-nothing" brother, Shahryar, and Daniyal's sons were all made "wanderers in the plains of nothingness," the empire's well-wishers "would be freed of their mind's anxiety and heart's unrest."[86] Merely blinding the princes would not completely eliminate them as threats, as Khurram knew from his experience with Khusrau. The princes had to be killed—not stealthily but with full public knowledge. Then, all the kingdom's nobles and chieftains would learn that Khurram was the unassailable emperor. Besides, this would also be the ultimate test for Asaf Khan, who throughout the rebellion had at least outwardly sided with the emperor and Nur Jahan. How could Khurram be sure that his father-in-law would not conspire with Nur Jahan to eliminate him once he arrived and then position himself as the power behind Dawar Bakhsh's throne? If Asaf Khan were to execute the lethal command to turn against Dawar Bakhsh, he would prove his eternal loyalty.

While Raza galloped to Lahore, Dawar Bakhsh continued to rule. Dara Shukoh and his brothers saw this sudden transformation of one of their cohort of hostage princes. They, too, would have had to pay their respects to him as well, participating in the performance that their grandfather directed. Asaf Khan needed to keep Dawar Bakhsh under tight control. The adolescent emperor, his life marked by the pain of his father's blinding, imprisonment, and murder, would have had no choice but to comply, even if he saw through Asaf Khan's scheme. Dawar Bakhsh also no doubt expected to contend with Khurram one way or the other, even if he did not know of his impending arrival, which his patron Asaf Khan had all but orchestrated.

The reign of Dara Shukoh's older cousin lasted only a little more than three months. On the nineteenth of January 1628, Asaf Khan arranged for the Friday sermon in Lahore to be given in the name of Khurram, now known as Shah Jahan. He also had Dawar Bakhsh thrown into prison.[87] A little more than three weeks later, on the second of February, Raza himself killed Shahryar, the last living brother of the new emperor, as well as Khurram's nephews, Dawar Bakhsh and Garshasp, and his cousins, Tahmuras and Hoshang, who had been imprisoned for good measure. The cold horror of the murders leaked through the euphemisms and justifications that writers and poets of the new order used to describe them. A few years later, the celebrated poet Qudsi, who had migrated from Mashhad in Iran, spoke approvingly of Shah Jahan's relief at the murders of his young relatives: "His mind's tablet was cleared of anxiety / For the thicket was purged of tiger cubs." The poet also compares these murdered princes to fingernails and toenails—extraneous features of the body that needed to be pared, just as potential threats to dynastic succession must be trimmed and discarded.[88]

A story in a much later source, most likely apocryphal, relates Dawar Bakhsh's calm courage in accepting what was in store for him. Apparently, in captivity, he was playing chess with his brother Garshasp when he heard the infamous Raza arrive. "It isn't contentment (*raza*) that has come but fate (*qaza*)," he remarked, punning on his assassin's name.[89] Raza was soon amply rewarded with a ceremonial staff and the rank of Mir Tuzuk, or master of ceremonies, at the court. Later he would be known by a special title—Khidmat-parast Khan, "the khan for whom service is worship." Asaf Khan was granted the title of Yamin-ud-Daula, "right hand of the state," for his crucial role in settling the question of Jahangir's succession.

Earlier Mughal emperors had also dealt severely with their brothers and rebelled against their fathers. But in terms of the sheer number of princes killed, Shah Jahan's route to the throne set a new standard for bloodiness. For Timur's descendants in India, the problem of succession had never found a single, easy solution. Humayun, son of the dynasty's founder, Babur, began the trend away from a concept of shared rulership to that of a solitary sovereign ruling over an indivisible kingdom. This new practice served well a young dynasty seeking to consolidate its power in the subcontinent. As time went on, claimants to the throne had to actively find a way to suppress other contenders. A prince with Khurram's persistence and valuable connections at court and beyond would have had a good chance of prevailing over the others. One could argue that the disarray and violence that succession struggles wrought on the empire were perhaps unavoidable evils that ultimately produced strong rulers. This approach to succession that allowed the ablest prince to rise to the top may indeed have been advantageous to the state.[90] But Mughal rulers often ended up undermining this system by seeking to anoint their own successors. Jahangir and Nur Jahan's support of Shahryar in the emperor's last years is a case in point; here, the matter is complicated by Nur Jahan's understandable reluctance to cede her own authority.

Dara Shukoh and his brothers were now finally reunited with their parents and siblings after a tumultuous year and a half of confinement and uncertainty. Their grandfather Asaf Khan took them from Lahore on the long journey to Agra, with a massive entourage befitting the emperor's children. Shah Jahan was already there. On the day of the killings in Lahore, he had alighted nearby, waiting for the astrologically determined auspicious time to enter the capital. The new emperor joyfully received his father-in-law, Asaf Khan, who presented to him his three eldest sons.

Only two years later, the artist Bichitr enshrined this scene in a lustrous illustration. It would eventually adorn the imperial copy of the *Padshahnama,* an official chronicle of Shah Jahan's reign. The inscriptions above

Shah Jahan at his accession meeting sons accompanied by Asaf Khan.

Shah Jahan's head announce him as the *sahib-qiran*, master of the astral conjunction, as potent as the prophet-king Solomon who commanded men, jinn, and animals. In the canopy above, a sun radiates directly over the emperor's head which itself shines with the luminous halo of kingship. Shah Jahan sits on the pinnacle of the world, directly above the pole of the globe guarded by two ulama. The image of the singular pole draws directly on the cosmic language of the *qutb*, or axis of the universe, popular amongst both kings and mystics. With the others standing some distance behind him, Dara Shukoh bows low before his father, while Shah Jahan clasps his shoulders in an embrace, as if to lift him up.[91] A new phase had begun for Dara Shukoh. Once the hostage son of a rebel prince, he had now become the favored heir of Hindustan's emperor.

3

YOUTH

1628–1634

W HEN SHAH JAHAN MOVED his court and household to Burhanpur
in March 1630, Dara Shukoh was about fifteen, the age when Muslim
jurists say a boy is mature and able to discriminate between right and wrong.
The imperial family settled into one of their former homes: an old, labyrinthine palace-citadel on the bank of the Tapti. It was built by the Faruqi sultans who ruled Khandesh for over two hundred years until Akbar annexed
the kingdom in 1601. Colorful glazed tiles clad the stone fortress, which
faced the city on one side, and on the other side, across the river, overlooked
expansive gardens and hunting grounds with pleasure houses.

Abd-ur-Rahim, the Khan of Khans, who earlier lived in Burhanpur as
governor and military chief, had left his imprint on the palace complex, setting up luxurious bathhouses painted in the Iranian style, gardens with
crisscrossing water channels fed by the Tapti River, and a library housing
hundreds of books populated by the many writers and poets he sponsored.[1]
Here, Dara, now old enough to have his own residence within the fort,
learned to manage a princely household.[2]

Until recently, Burhanpur hummed with trade, especially in textiles—
satin, wool, velvet, and calico, as well as in such metals as lead, tin, and
mercury. But toward the end of Jahangir's reign, the administration of the
territory had grown lax under Parwez, who reportedly never paid his troops
on time and generally let the city decline and trade suffer.[3] Shah Jahan's
arrival brought a new phase of stability and renewal to Khandesh, though

his main purpose in coming to his kingdom's southern frontier was to put down the second rebellion of his rule. The first, by the Bundela ruler of Orccha, Shah Jahan had easily quashed. This he managed with the help of Mahabat Khan and Khan Jahan Lodi, the Afghan noble whom Jahangir had adopted and also made his son-in-law. But in October of the previous year, Khan Jahan fled south from the court at Agra. After Jahangir's death, he had unwisely hedged his bets and held back from supporting Shah Jahan's bid for the throne.

Now, barricaded in the Asir Fort, Khan Jahan escalated his earlier recalcitrance into a full-scale revolt. The emperor swiftly left Agra for the Deccan and pursued him with the hope of also eventually making inroads into neighboring Ahmadnagar. Not that this rebellion was a great cause for alarm. In a Mughal emperor's life, the crushing of uprisings was par for the course, along with defending and expanding the kingdom's borders. The frequent movement of the peripatetic court that this required had some very practical benefits for the state. It kept the armies in good working order and the courtiers at the ready. It also relentlessly reminded the kingdom's subjects of the emperor's power and presence.

During the heady days after Shah Jahan seized the throne, Dara Shukoh, Shuja, and Aurangzeb enjoyed a reunion with their parents and siblings after a long separation. The boys joined their sisters, Jahanara, the eldest, Roshanara, who was a year older than Aurangzeb, and young Surayya Bano, as well as their brothers little Murad Bakhsh and baby Lutfullah, whom they had not yet met, as he had been born amid the stress of the battle at Thatta. Now, in Burhanpur, future joyous events beckoned. Dara and Shuja were of marriageable age, so brides had to be found and wedding arrangements made.

But soon after Shah Jahan's accession, the family began to suffer a string of losses. First, in April 1628, Surayya Bano died at age seven. Only days earlier Arjumand, now known as Mumtaz Mahal ("elect of the palace"), had given birth to an infant boy, Daulat Afza ("fortune increaser"). Less than a month later, death's shadow fell on the nineteen-month-old Lutfullah. Then shortly after reaching Burhanpur, in May 1629, the infant Daulat Afza passed away. Mumtaz Mahal, by now nearly forty, continued to bear children. The following year, in April 1630, she had a daughter who died immediately after she was born, even before she could be named.[4]

On the seventeenth of June 1631, the Burhanpur summer was at its burning peak when Mumtaz Mahal experienced the throes of labor for the fourteenth time. Jahanara was with her. At the mature age of seventeen, she had likely assisted with her mother's deliveries before. This time, something was wrong. Mughal doctors believed, following the ancient

Greek physician Galen, that the body was made up of four humors that had to be perfectly balanced for optimal health. In Mumtaz Mahal's case, these elements slid rapidly into disequilibrium.

The empress delivered a baby girl, but she bled heavily and her condition swiftly deteriorated. She probably suffered from what modern medicine would call a postpartum hemorrhage.[5] Still conscious, she asked Jahanara to send for Shah Jahan. Distraught, he came and sat by her pillow. There was no time for Dara Shukoh and his other siblings to come to her side, but she told the emperor that she entrusted their children and her mother into his care. Then she left this world.

Shah Jahan's chronicler, Abd-ul-Hamid Lahori, writes in the *Padshahnama* that, in her death, she dutifully heeded the Quranic injunction, "Return, to your lord, content and offering contentment."[6] She was in her fortieth year. The baby daughter survived and was named Gauharara, "Jewel-adorned." Qazwini, one of the earliest authors to chronicle Shah Jahan's reign, lauds her procreative accomplishments: "When she adorned the world with these children/like the moon, she waned after the fourteenth//When she brought forth the last single pearl/she then emptied her body like an oyster."[7]

Shah Jahan's historians focus on describing the emperor's grief, though the children must have been deeply afflicted as well. Lahori in the *Padshahnama* uses elaborate metaphors to contrast Shah Jahan's usual resplendence with his current state: "From the steam of sighs and the moisture of tears, the mirror of the sun gazer's mind, which, like the sun's looking glass had never seen the face of darkness, acquired turbidity's rust."[8] The emperor filled oceans with his tears and donned white clothes; all the children, courtiers, and servants, too, wore mourning attire. For a week, Shah Jahan did not appear at his balcony or carry out the affairs of state. Though before his wife's death he had no more than twenty white hairs, he soon acquired many more. For a while he was unable to control his weeping.[9]

Later writers recounted the scene at Mumtaz Mahal's deathbed with even more detail. An anonymous writer in Persian relates that her unborn child, called Dahrara according to one manuscript of his work, let out a loud cry while still in the womb. Upon hearing this, Mumtaz Mahal knew that her life was drawing to a close.[10] He also reports that the empress's last words to Shah Jahan were that eight children were enough of a legacy, and he says she extracted from him two promises: he would never father children with other women and he would build a magnificent, unique structure in her memory.[11] While no contemporary source attests to its veracity, this anecdote, and others like it, powerfully shape the memory of Shah Jahan and Mumtaz Mahal.

The emperor had lost not only his "longtime confidante," as Lahori refers to Mumtaz, and the mother of his children, but also an advisor and a true partner in the daily business of governance. A *hukm,* or edict stamped with her seal, remains until this day. Here she addresses the state's deputies in Erandol, a Marathi-speaking district of Khandesh. She endorses the new *deshmukh* (headman), named Kanoji, and advises him to take care of the populace's well-being so that they would feel grateful to the emperor.[12] This edict was likely only one among many that the empress sent out. Her trusted assistant, Sati Khanam, who had been Jahanara's governess, acquired an official position as her seal bearer. Sati Khanam drew up lists of deserving cases from the petitions that women in financial trouble sent her; Mumtaz Mahal then brought them to the emperor's attention. The empress also interceded in death-penalty cases and often procured Shah Jahan's pardon.[13]

The sixteen-year-old Dara saw his mother buried near the palace in the Zainabad Gardens, on the banks of the Tapti. Shah Jahan would visit the canopied grave every Friday, likely with Dara Shukoh and some of his brothers accompanying him. The poet Kalim describes the emperor's grief: "As soon as he cast his shadow on that grave / the moisture of his weeping would penetrate her shroud."[14]

But the emperor never intended Burhanpur to be his favorite wife's final resting place. He had his eye on a picturesque location in Agra, on the banks of the Jamuna River, southeast of the citadel. The land was an ancestral tract belonging to Raja Jai Singh, a fourth-generation vassal of the court, on which the raja's grandfather's house once stood. Shah Jahan exerted his royal prerogative to seize it from Jai Singh, eventually gifting him four grand houses from the imperial estate in return.[15] Raja Jai Singh dared not openly express his disgruntlement. Though he did his best to impede the construction, he was was compelled by his position to cooperate.[16]

In December 1631, Mumtaz Mahal's body was exhumed, and Shuja traveled with her bier to its new burial spot in Agra. Sati Khanam accompanied the young prince. Along the way, the procession flung coins to the crowds and distributed food. Once the body was interred in Agra, Shah Jahan had a small domed structure built over the grave as a kind of shield from the gaze of outsiders. Even in death, too, as befitted an elite royal or noblewomen, Mumtaz Mahal's seclusion had to be guarded.[17]

The grieving emperor, who had honed his interest in architecture during his princehood, plunged into the project of building a magnificent tomb. He summoned a bevy of architects, including the Iranian-born Makramat Khan, Jahangir's architect Abd-al-Karim, and Ustad Ahmad of Lahore. They drafted plans that Shah Jahan would regularly pore over, discuss, and alter. The cost, two decades later, ran up to fifty lakhs. Shah Jahan knew that this was not just a memorial to his beloved consort but also his own enduring legacy and future mausoleum. He planned to eventually relocate the Agra tradespersons nearby, so that the tomb, even during his lifetime, would attract a steady crowd of pilgrims and travelers.[18] It is now famous the world over as the Taj Mahal.[19]

IN THE SAME YEAR THAT DARA SHUKOH and his siblings mourned their mother, and the emperor his wife, a Sufi scholar in his mid-thirties, living in the north Indian town of Rudauli, finished writing a short treatise in Persian. He was known as Abd-ur-Rahman (d. 1638) and he belonged to an offshoot of the famous Chishti order named after Ala-ud-Din Sabir. The work he had just composed was no run-of-the-mill tract on Muslim piety or the Sufi path; instead it was based on an Indic book that he had discovered, written, he says, by Basisht.

Basisht, or Vasishtha in the Sanskrit version of his name, was one of the seven legendary sages of ancient India, but Abd-ur-Rahman Chishti calls him a prophet of the community of jinn. Muslim tradition holds that God created the jinn many years before creating Adam, the first human and the first prophet. Though the jinn are created from "smokeless" fire and humans from clay, they are very much like us, except for the fact that we cannot see them. The jinn whom Abd-ur-Rahman identifies here belong to the past; they were the people who lived in India before the coming of Islam.

Abd-ur-Rahman had read several books on the history of the Hindus, though they did not interest him because, unsurprisingly enough, they had no mention of Adam. But Basisht, he explains, was an exception, an author who actually wrote a book describing the greatness of Adam as well as the Prophet Muhammad. Basisht received much of his learning from Mahadev, another name for Shiva, the leader of the jinn, whom they called their father and considered a divinely appointed messenger. The jinn did have their own prophets; even authoritative Muslim texts, like the world history by Abu Jafar Tabari, attest to this, writes Abd-ur-Rahman.[20]

Some ignorant people, the Chishti scholar adds, think that Ramchandra, Krishna, and Arjun were children of Adam, but they are absolutely wrong. Rather, these three were born in the *treta jug,* the second of four cycles of time in Indic tradition, just like Mahadev, whom the Almighty brought into being not from a father and mother but from light and wind. Adam, on the other hand, was created at the end of the *dwapar jug,* the third era. The current era, *kal jug,* is due to last four hundred thirty thousand years, out of which 4,733 have already passed.

According to Abd-ur-Rahman, the Prophet Muhammad's migration to Mecca happened in the *kal jug* too, 1,040 years ago. He thus inserts the

Islamic calendar into a Hindu notion of time. There are no more jinn left in India, he says. Long ago, as the *Mahabharat* describes, there was a war between the angels and the jinn. All the jinn were wiped out and then the children of Adam came and settled in the clime of India.[21]

During the rest of this short work, Abd-ur-Rahman intertwines even more Hindu and Islamic narratives about the cosmos, in the form of a dialogue between Mahadev and his consort Parvati. In writing this book he does not see himself as deviating from the Prophetic example, which all believing Muslims are meant to follow. Indeed, he says, citing the Prophet's own words, it is a Sufi's spiritual duty to learn good things from every religious community.[22] Abd-ur-Rahman was not particularly concerned with studying Indic religious concepts on their own terms. If he were, he would not have turned deities into jinn and sages into angels. But in the process, a double transformation occurs, as the jinn and other Islamic figures also acquire new meanings.

Abd-ur-Rahman's particular cosmological project appears to be original and uniquely his own, though his engagement with Indic thought followed the example of many other Chishti Sufis before him. There are texts on yoga attributed to the order's founder, Muin-ud-Din Chishti (d. 1236), regardless of whether he actually wrote them.[23] Abd-ur-Rahman traced his spiritual lineage to Shaikh Ahmad Abd-ul-Haqq, who had died in Rudauli a couple of centuries earlier and who very likely learned yogic practices from Nath ascetics in Bengal.[24] Later, around 1480, the Chishti Abd-ul-Quddus Gangohi (d. 1537) composed the *Rushd-nama* (The Book of Correct Conduct), a multilingual work of Islamic mysticism. Drawing on materials in Persian, Arabic, and Hindavi, this work also incorporates discussions of yogic breathing practices. Here Gangohi assembles Hindavi verses alongside Persian couplets, interspersing these with Arabic quotations from the Quran and the Prophet's sayings.[25]

At least some Muslim scholars of Shah Jahan's era would have frowned on Abd-ur-Rahman Chishti's openness to using Indic texts in order to explore the histories of revered Islamic figures. The Naqshbandi followers and successors of Shaikh Ahmad Sirhindi, the Mujaddid, or Renewer, offer perhaps the sharpest contrast with Chishtis such as Abd-ur-Rahman. In multicultural India, many of them sought to follow the model of Muslim-majority Central Asia, where in the second half of the sixteenth century, Naqshbandi shaikhs such as Khwaja Hasan closely counseled the Kabul ruler Mirza Hakim.[26]

Sirhindi uses strong language to admonish Shaikh Farid Bukhari, a high-ranking noble and religious scholar under Akbar and Jahangir, over the presence of Hindus in the Mughal administration. If employed at all, he argues, they should be given insignificant jobs; indeed they should be avoided like dogs, taxed and disgraced. Such vitriolic bigotry, though, does not encapsulate the whole of Shaikh Ahmad Sirhindi's attitude toward Hindus. In other letters he writes of Hindus who were capable in his eyes of achieving a certain level of spiritual experience, and he addresses at least one letter to a Hindu. But in Sirhindi's ideal world, sharia-observant Muslims would have far more political power and freedom to observe practices like cow slaughter or eating when Hindus were fasting, without being hemmed in by the majority of the population.[27]

In the past, there was a point at which the lineages of Shaikh Ahmad Sirhindi and Abd-ur-Rahman Chishti had intersected. Sirhindi's father had in fact studied with Abd-ul-Quddus Gangohi. Moreover, Gangohi's attitude toward non-Muslims was complex; in a letter to the emperor Babur, he voices sentiments that sound similar to those of Sirhindi, if a shade less harsh. These prejudices did not prevent him, however, from taking pleasure in Hindi poetry and music.[28]

Though Sirhindi's imprisonment weakened his authority and his claims of being the Renewer attracted derision, his influence spread posthumously during Shah Jahan's rule. In 1623, the year before his death, Shaikh Ahmad Sirhindi appointed as his successor one of his sons, Muhammad Masum, whom he also identified as the Qayyum, the Sufi who acts as the world's central pole, through whom God reaches other human beings.[29]

Like his father, Muhammad Masum wrote copiously and persistently to religious scholars, Mughal officials, and members of the imperial family. His collected letters include one to Janan Begam, who was the daughter of Abd-ur-Rahim Khan of Khans and the fourth wife of Jahangir's brother Daniyal. Here, he refrains from discussing social and political issues, meditating instead on the Islamic mystical notion of love for the divine. This letter is replete with couplets from Persian love poetry such as this one, which evokes an image of the lover ineluctably drawn by the beloved's tresses: "I don't go to the neck's nape of my own free will/those two amber lassoes take me, pulling, pulling.[30]

But in a letter to the nobleman Shamsher Khan, who later became governor of Ghazni, Muhammad Masum champions his view of correct religious observance. He had heard about Shamsher Khan's kindness to Sufis, he says, from Maulana Muhammad Saif. Masum writes about the importance of subduing the carnal soul, the correct creed of the people of the Sunna, the five pillars, the desirability of Sufi practice, and the superiority of the Naqshbandis.[31]

While Naqshbandi leaders cultivated contacts among the Mughal governing elites, prominent Chishtis maintained their order's longstanding relationship with the state. Several years later, in an addendum to a collection of Sufi biographies, Abd-ur-Rahman Chishti writes of his association with Jahangir and Shah Jahan. He praises Jahangir highly and notes that he spent time with him when the emperor visited the Ajmer shrine; later, he met Shah Jahan as well. Abd-ur-Rahman criticizes Nur Jahan severely for her "misbehavior" and hints that she threatened the Sunni order—after all she was known to be Shia. We do not learn the full extent of Abd-ur-Rahman's association with courtly circles, although in this work as in others, he refers to one Shaikh Sufi whom he knew and who was very much in the ranks of both Sufi scholars and court nobility.

Shaikh Sufi had studied under the Chishti scholar Nizam-ud-Din of Amethi and later went on to read the major writings of Ibn Arabi with Wajih-ud-Din Gujarati of the Shattari order.[32] Subsequently he joined Jahangir's court, and tutored the prince Shah Jahan in works of history, theology, and mysticism.[33] Like other scholars at the time, the shaikh was expected to also demonstrate military prowess in the emperor's service and was attached to the imperial campaign in Telengana. Once Shah Jahan ascended the throne, he rewarded Shaikh Sufi with a mansab, a rank with the right to the revenues of a particular region.[34] But his official roles aside, Shaikh Sufi, too, was greatly interested in Indic thought. A number of Persian renditions of Indic works bear his name. These tend to be brief and didactic, lacking Abd-ur-Rahman's colorful equivalences between Indic and Islamic concepts and figures.

The contrast between the broad-based eclecticism of some Chishtis and the Naqshbandi promotion of a narrower, more tightly bounded view of religion might very well have widened as the two orders grew in prominence. At the heart of this divergence lay the notion, which Abd-ur-Rahman and Shaikh Sufi would have held, that all *wujud,* or existence, including God and God's creation, was ultimately one; this was an idea that Ibn Arabi's later followers distilled from the great shaikh's thought, and they felt that a Sufi might actually experience this unity with God. In contrast, Shaikh Ahmad and Muhammad Masum believed that the *wujudis,* as they called such thinkers, fundamentally misinterpreted Ibn Arabi. "Saying 'All is God' . . . [refers to] the various manifestations of God, not that it is the Essence of God in Reality," Shaikh Ahmad argues.[35] He wrote a letter to Shaikh Sufi on this very issue; however, the latter did not convert to the Naqshbandi leader's view.[36] But there is no straight line of causality or even correlation between the study of Ibn Arabi's thought and the openness of early modern Sufis in South Asia to Indic forms of knowledge. Many wujudi Sufis felt no need whatsoever to learn from Indic texts or practices.

It is hard to measure the precise influence that Shaikh Ahmad Sirhindi and Muhammad Masum had on the Mughal administration. Though their followers collected and carefully preserved their letters, we do not have records of the responses they might have received from Mughal officials. It would seem, though, that like Sirhindi, some of Shah Jahan's courtiers envisioned a more central role for the sharia, the normative basis for Islamic legal authority. While the Quranic revelation together with the Prophet's words and deeds are at the core of Islamic legal reasoning, the significance and scope of these two scriptural sources have been inextricably bound to the authoritative interpretations of jurists over the centuries.

Early in 1633, these defenders of a more exclusionary idea of governance achieved a small victory. The planning and building of Mumtaz Mahal's tomb in Agra had barely begun when Shah Jahan ordered the razing of all temples in the kingdom that were currently under construction. He focused especially on halting the building of temples in Banaras, the ancient city on the Ganga that Lahori's *Padshahnama* describes as "the great stronghold of infidelity." No fewer than seventy-six unfinished temples were destroyed. "In accordance with the edict of the infidelity-scorching, faith-nurturing emperor," writes Shah Jahan's court historian Qazwini, "they were returned to dust, and a strong foundation made for constructing the manifest religion."[37]

If it had been routine for Mughal rulers to trample on the religious expressions of the kingdom's Hindu majority, Hindus would have thought twice before building so many new temples in one city alone, even though it was an important pilgrimage site. For generations, the Mughal state had offered financial support to Hindu and Jain places of worship. What, then, brought about this destruction?

Qazwini explains that religious scholars had issued a fatwa, or legal opinion, regarding these unfinished temples. The document was intended to ensure the kingdom's protection from calamity. Shah Jahan then acted upon the ruling, though as ruler he was not compelled to do so, as a fatwa is not legally binding. Spies and investigators, part of the state's vast information machinery, were sent out to report which temples in Banaras would fit this category.

The basis for these jurists' ruling, though Qazwini does not mention it here, was a document concerning the religious rights of non-Muslims purportedly written in the time of the Caliph Umar, in the seventh century. Though it almost certainly dates from a later period, Umar's edict enjoyed a lasting canonicity in some Muslim legal circles. The text frames itself as a letter detailing a pact between the Christians of Damascus and the caliph, which included the condition that they would not establish any new places of worship but could keep the ones that existed before the Muslim conquest.[38]

Who were these ulama? Did the emperor placate a lobby of religious scholars who, like Ahmad Sirhindi, were more sharia-minded and felt that Hindus had been given too much of a free rein at the expense of Muslims? Or did Shah Jahan himself engineer the fatwa to justify a move aimed at Hindu rulers, just like Jahangir's desecration of the temple at Pushkar? The pragmatic emperor must have realized that he could reap both effects from this act, to mold his image as a sovereign guided by religion and assert his power in the empire's heartland.

But Shah Jahan continued to support those existing temples that already received state assistance. On the thirteenth of August 1633, a few months after the Banaras temples were demolished, an imperial farman confirmed a tax-free grant, originally bestowed by Akbar, to the temples of Gobind Rai. A line on the reverse of the edict states "it is not the rule (*hukm*) to make grants in the name of temples," suggesting that there might have been misgivings about supporting non-Muslim places of worship. Later that year, on the thirtieth of October, a decree was issued ordering compliance with an earlier imperial edict that had given a grant of land to custodians of the temple of Madan Mohan, which the *sevak* of the temple, a certain Sri Chand, had held previously.[39] Evidently the emperor had no intention of obliterating all the existing temples of the subcontinent or of denying his Hindu subjects access to worship.

WHILE THE CHASE FOR THE REBEL Khan Jahan dragged on and the kingdom's religious scholars debated theological positions, in Burhanpur, Dara Shukoh worked on cultivating his aesthetic sensibilities, as befitting a Mughal prince. Court records do not offer many details of his activities, but one splendid record endures: a *muraqqa* (album) that the prince compiled, even now nearly intact, containing miniature paintings arranged in pairs, interspersed with doubled leaves of calligraphic panels. Dara Shukoh also composed an introduction to his album, which today survives only separately, as a copy.[40] Here was an opportunity for the emperor's eldest son to raid the imperial collection of paintings and calligraphy produced by past masters, commission new images of his own, and display his own penmanship and literary finesse.

Dara's father, Shah Jahan, a consummate connoisseur, had also acquired considerable skill in calligraphy in his youth, and he too assembled an album while he was a prince.[41] We do not hear of Mughal princes or princesses learning how to paint; however, like Salim, as Jahangir was known before he became emperor, they could be closely involved in the details of an image's production.[42] But the art of beautiful writing was a crucial part of Mughal elite education. Indeed, calligraphy was considered to be superior to painting. Abu-l-Fazl, court chronicler of Akbar, Dara Shukoh's great-grandfather, calls the written letter "the source from which the light confined within it beams forth"; it is "a world-revealing cup" just like that of the legendary emperor Jamshed of ancient Iran, and it is "spiritual geometry" and the "portrait painter of wisdom."[43]

In fact, going by Dara Shukoh's preface, we could be forgiven for thinking that the album's sole purpose was to showcase the young prince's calligraphy. Here, the young prince exhibits his mastery of the ornate Persian language typically used in formal prose writing. He adorns the obligatory praise of God, the Prophet, and the first four caliphs of Islam with metaphors about writing. Here, he often plays on the double connotations of the word *khatt*, which means both writing or calligraphy and the downy fuzz on the upper lip of an adolescent boy. The reason for the latter being that, in Persian literature, particularly poetry, the ideal beloved is not a woman but a young lad.

Frequently the earthly beloved is a substitute for God—the true object of a lover's devotion—but here the divine is the supreme calligrapher, who brings forth "the adolescent beard's soft down." When it comes to introducing his own project, Dara Shukoh's tone is bold, even boastful:

> I have crowned the pen with writing's spear, and conquered the realm of calligraphy. The calligraphers of the seven climes have with one pen bowed their heads before the writing ... I've tied down the hands of this craft's masters, and with folded hands, I've accomplished the hand's work, and adorned this collection with my own flowing writing. To this bright meadow I've granted lushness from the exudations of my own pen.[44]

This kind of hubris is often part of the album-preface genre, in praise of the riches within the covers.[45] After next writing of the pleasing complementarity of the paintings and the calligraphy, the prince then showers tributes on his father. "The coronet-possessors wear a picture of his likeness on their heads, and the mirrors of the mind guard his image in their hearts." Here he refers to the practice, carried on from the time of Akbar, in which select imperial servants placed a small painted likeness of the emperor in their turbans to signal their relationship to the sovereign as disciples. He also alludes to the anxiety about visual representation that pervades some Muslim approaches to figural art as well as to his father's attempts to fashion himself into a more Islamic ruler than his forefathers: "Under [Shah Jahan] the work of the sharia has taken shape and through him the designs and paintings of Islam have acquired rectitude."

But Dara Shukoh has not finished talking about himself. For quite a while now, he says, with the aid of a pen, he has "made calligraphy's territory flourish." Through prose and poetry he exalts his own calligraphy: "Sight becomes drunk on the bounty of viewing it / for its script is intoxicating like the line on a goblet" and the "stars' eyes grow bright from its dark kohl."[46]

One might be surprised, then, to find not a single leaf of Dara Shukoh's calligraphy in the album's current form. This does not mean, however, that the prince's decorative writing was never part of the collection. There are actually fifteen folios missing from the album. One of these, facing a painting of a bustard, was in all likelihood an illustration of a bird, if it followed the pattern of all the other image pairings in the album. But some or all of the others may very well have contained the prince's calligraphy, later ex- cised or defaced like so many other surfaces that his pen had touched. We know that Dara practiced calligraphy in Burhanpur, because some surviving folios of Persian verses written in his skillful hand date to the period in 1630–1631 while he was there. Painted between the lines are decorative gold clouds, birds, and flowers, much like those adorning other calligraphic panels from that time in an album that Shah Jahan assembled.[47]

The pictorial contents of Jahangir's and Shah Jahan's albums were often complex mosaics of symbolic references that served above all to accentuate the emperor's power in relation to rival rulers, vassals, holy men, and court- iers. What, then, were appropriate subjects for a teenage prince, who was also constrained by the lack of an atelier that was his alone?[48] The first pri- ority of the court artists was, of course, to work for Shah Jahan.

But Mughal albums tended to juxtapose the old with the new. The young Dara Shukoh selected from a vast storehouse of images and examples of beautiful writing that Shah Jahan had inherited. He chose, for example, a couple of European engravings in black and white, one of St. Catherine of Siena and the other of the Virgin Mary and infant Jesus. These were set into a wider frame of calligraphed Chagatai Turkish and Persian verses, fin- ished with a thick, lustrous border adorned with gold flowers that was common to all the album's folios.

The prince also included at least thirteen calligraphy panels by the re- nowned calligrapher of Jahangir's era, Muhammad Husain Kashmiri, known as Zarrin-qalam, "Golden Pen," as well as several earlier Mughal and Persian pieces of writing. He obtained two earlier portraits of Hindu ascetics in the *nim qalam* technique, which involves a light wash applied over a pen-and-ink drawing, with results remarkably similar to lithographed engravings. These long-bearded yogis, with matted hair coiled in turbans atop their heads, sit cross-legged on craggy rocks. The one on the left fingers his prayer beads; his counterpart on the right lifts his hand in discourse. The city's domes and turrets in the distant background bring into focus the wilderness of their surroundings.

Dara also had court artists paint several new images especially for his album. The folios are profuse with pairs of blooming flowers, sometimes with butterflies, and several facing paintings of birds, alone or coupled. Though these themes were common in Mughal albums, some scholars describe the contents of Dara Shukoh's album as being particularly "feminine."[49] There is a note of dismissiveness in such remarks, the implication being that the paintings have lighter, less serious themes. This is uncalled for; such simple, single-subject images were common in the princely albums of Dara's father and grandfather as well.

But at first glance, there appears to be good reason to believe that the album was assembled for a woman. On the album's flyleaf is an inscription, signed by Dara Shukoh and dated almost a decade after this period in Burhanpur, to the year 1646–1647. It mentions the album's recipient—his wife. "This precious album was given to his most intimate companion and sharer of secrets, Nadira Bano Begam, by Muhammad Dara Shukoh, son of Shah Jahan, emperor and conqueror."[50]

Nonetheless, these so-called feminine themes aside, Dara Shukoh also collaborated with his artists to fashion and project a particularly princely persona in this album. Of the sixty-eight surviving paintings here, eighteen depict a young prince, at times seated with a teacher or facing a religious man on the opposite folio. Though in some he appears to be in his early teens and in others an older adolescent, the marked resemblance between them suggests they depict the same person. In light of the similarities with other paintings that we know to depict the prince, these portraits are likely of Dara Shukoh himself.[51]

Indeed, as the art historian Jeremiah Losty points out, there are compelling reasons to believe that this album was produced in the early 1630s and not later, when Dara gifted the album to his wife Nadira. For one, all the prince's portraits here show him in his youth—if it were compiled later, he likely would have included some contemporaneous portraits. Moreover, several paintings reveal the style of the artist Chitarman, who was known to have been active in Shah Jahan's atelier during the early years of his rule and who painted several signed portraits of Dara, both then and later. Then there is the evidence that the prince practiced calligraphy while in Burhanpur, matched with the celebration of calligraphy in his introduction.[52] Furthermore, the art produced for Dara Shukoh in the 1640s and later is conspicuously different in its complexity and motifs. Once we discard the notion that Dara specially designed the album for Nadira years into their married life, we can more clearly see it as a cherished first foray into understanding and appreciating the visual arts and the art of the pen.

Dara Shukoh's album, unlike many previous Mughal ones, also includes several images of royal women. Mughal women tended not to sit for portraits before male artists (and most, though not all, Mughal painters were men), who, as a result, had to conjure up their subjects' likenesses from verbal descriptions. Attempts to identify the woman represented in a portrait, or to distinguish an idealized figure from a portrait are on tenuous footing at best.

One such painting of a woman, resplendently bejeweled with a somewhat prominent nose, could be Mumtaz Mahal. She strongly resembles another likely depiction of the empress. Another, holding a betel cone, might very well be Jahanara, whose fondness for the stimulant was legendary. And a princess on the left side of a double spread, facing a young prince who is almost certainly Dara, may well be Nadira.[53] Though we cannot say for sure, these may indeed be portraits of the women closest to Dara Shukoh. It is not hard to imagine that the teenage prince found solace in composing the album after his mother's death, including among its artwork the likenesses of those dear to him. But though he had lost his mother, he would soon enter into a new phase of his life with his marriage.

IT WAS DARA'S MOTHER WHO SUGGESTED the union between her eldest son and the daughter of Jahangir's late brother Parwez.[54] Marriage between first cousins had become less common in the imperial family after Akbar had objected to the custom, but Nadira's impeccable pedigree made her an exemplary match. She was of doubly royal lineage, as her mother was the daughter of Sultan Murad, Akbar's second son from a concubine. True, Nadira's father had been Shah Jahan's rival for the throne, but Parwez, unlike Khusrau, had conveniently brought about his own death through excessive drinking. Mumtaz Mahal also identified a bride for Shuja, though, as befitted the spouse of a second son, the prestige of her station was perhaps just a notch lower than Nadira's. She was the daughter of Mirza Rustam Safavi, a direct descendant of the sixteenth-century Iranian emperor Shah Ismail. She also happened to be the cousin of Shah Jahan's first wife, whom we know only as Qandahari Begam. Both weddings were to have taken place earlier, but were postponed because of Mumtaz Mahal's death.

After twenty months had elapsed since the empress's death, it was considered appropriate to begin the marriage ceremonies. The imperial family had moved to Agra, a bustling city of about fifteen square miles, its bazaar teeming with so many people that it was hard to squeeze past them, according to Peter Mundy (d. 1667), an English traveler who was in the city during the wedding.[55] In luxurious contrast, the spacious mansions of the empire's most privileged aristocrats and royals curved around either side of the Jamuna River. These inviting abodes were set in large waterfront gardens. On the right bank, the palace complex rose up from the midst of the mansions and pleasure gardens, like the crowning jewel of a diadem. Dara Shukoh's own residence was the closest of all to the palace, nestled right beside its red sandstone walls.[56] Further upstream, along the same bank, the construction of Mumtaz Mahal's tomb was already under way.

In November 1632, Dara Shukoh's family made the formal procession, laden with gifts, including rare jewels, rich fabrics, and one lakh in cash, to ask for Nadira's hand. Afzal Khan, a high-ranking noble who had been close to Shah Jahan while the latter was still a prince, went with Mumtaz Mahal's mother, sister, and trusted aide Sati Khanam, as well as with Jahanara, whose participation was crucial. A trio of the empire's most important officials accompanied the entourage: Sadiq Khan, paymaster general; Mir Jumla, overseer of the imperial household; and Musawi Khan, head of the judiciary and charitable endowments. Shah Jahan's court chronicler Jalala Tabatabai lauds Jahanara's aplomb while performing all the rituals of the day, as she stood in for her mother and proved that she had full command of the complex etiquette the event demanded.[57]

The marriage festivities began in full swing three months later, in February 1633. Writing after the event, the emperor's historians made sure to record the details of the expenditure on the most expensive Mughal wedding ever staged, costing, in all, thirty-two lakh rupees.[58] Of this, ten lakhs came from Nadira Begam's family, who must have felt obligated to contribute as much as they possibly could.[59] The gifts alone were worth over sixteen lakhs, financed with the money that Mumtaz Mahal had set aside for her firstborn's wedding and from what Jahanara had contributed: rare jewels and bejeweled weapons costing seven and a half lakh rupees and materials for gifting to the emperor's courtiers, worth a lakh and a half. Elephant howdahs of pure gold, umbrellas embellished with pearl ropes that cost seventy-seven thousand rupees, and a handsome sum of ten thousand rupees was set aside solely for strewing and scattering among the public. A further six lakhs and forty thousand went toward an array of items that a prince and a princess might need for their household, such as gold implements, both enameled and plain, silver vessels and utensils, gold-embroidered napkins with gem-studded flowers stitched onto them, varicolored carpets, and velvet tents woven and embroidered with gold. Animals, too, were presented, including horses of all types—Arabian, Iraqi, Turkish—as well as Kacchi horses from western India.[60]

These lavish gifts, signs of the emperor's fabulous wealth and generosity, were meant to be exhibited. Before Dara Shukoh and his bride could take them home, Jahanara and Sati Khanam had them artfully displayed in the hall of public audience in Agra. This hall, with its forty pillars, was an opulent wooden structure that Shah Jahan built; painted green and gold, its pillars were like cypress trees, said his Iranian poet laureate Kalim.[61] First, the women of the palace were given an opportunity to see the presents in seclusion from the men, and then all the princes, nobles, and other courtiers attended the gift-viewing celebration.[62] Later, Shah Jahan made sure that this splendor was recorded for posterity; the imperial manuscript of Lahori's *Padshah-nama* illustrates in a double spread the staggering quantities of these presents, the rows of elephants and horses flanking a mass of men bearing trays.[63]

All the festivities thus far were primarily hosted and enjoyed by Dara Shukoh's own family rather than the bride's. One incident, though, hints that Nadira's mother, Jahan Bano Begam, pressed for a role in her daughter's wedding. On the occasions when Mughal court historians do refer to royal women, they very often address their chasteness; so we hear that Jahan Bano Begam, "face-veil chooser of veiled chastity," requested of Shah Jahan's courtiers that she also be allowed to host a function in her home to display her contribution to the dowry. She had acquired jewelry worth eight lakhs for her daughter and decoratively arranged the jewels for viewing together with other gifts. First the women had their gathering, and then the emperor himself graced her home with his presence.[64]

On the eleventh of February, the night before the actual wedding, the henna ceremony took place in the Agra Fort's glittering *ghusl khana*. This was literally a bathhouse but was far less private than we might now imagine such a place to be; it was where the emperor held audiences for an intimate few. A Dutch traveler described it as a square building made of gold-plated alabaster.[65] As was the custom, Nadira's family sent across trays heaped with henna.[66] That night, the imperial librarian Inayat Khan tells us, so many candles, lamps, torches, and lanterns were lit that the earth's quadrangle became the envy of heaven's court.[67] Peter Mundy concurs, estimating that one million lamps must have been kindled. Music filled the air for the first time since Mumtaz Mahal's death. A gigantic display of fireworks illuminated the riverbanks, covering an area of at least half a mile in length, writes Mundy. Rockets, squibs, and crackers, placed within the forms of elephants, giants, monsters, turrets, artificial trees, and more, created a most fearsome blast and made night seem like day. Meanwhile, following the Indian custom, the palace ladies, concealed behind a curtain, applied henna to Dara Shukoh's hands and feet as well as to the fingertips of the elegant "silver-bodied" guests, which they then bound with gold handkerchiefs.[68] The attendees received sashes woven of gold thread, and the harem servants laid out for them the ingredients of a tasteful social gathering: a spread of flowers, betel-leaf stimulants, perfumes, and an array of appetizers and fruits.[69]

Where were Nadira and her family during these festivities? The sources continue to keep the bridegroom and the emperor at the center of their narrative. Mughal chroniclers would have thought it unseemly to describe the fourteen-year-old bride's preparations or how she looked and bade her family farewell.

The next afternoon, Dara Shukoh's brothers, Shah Shuja, Aurangzeb, and Murad Bakhsh, along with their maternal grandfather Asaf Khan and a host of nobles, visited the bridegroom in his house. They then took him in a procession for an audience with his father in Agra's forty-pillared hall. Shah Jahan gave Dara Shukoh a number of gifts, including a special robe, a gem-studded dagger and sword, a string of pearl and ruby beads, horses, and an elephant. It was only after midnight that the actual marriage ceremony was performed, during which the court's chief justice, Qazi Muhammad Aslam, delivered a sermon. The qazi then announced the dower, a necessary condition of the Muslim marriage contract. Nadira was to receive five lakhs, just as Arjumand had done when she married Shah Jahan. With that, the wedding was solemnized. The cries of congratulations and the sound of celebratory drums rent the heavens.[70]

A week later, Shah Jahan paid a visit to his son's house, something an emperor only did on exceptional occasions. This was also an opportunity for the seventeen-year-old Dara Shukoh to show that he could shoulder the adult responsibility of hosting the emperor with due respect and ceremony. The prince had the entire path from the palace to his own house covered in the most sumptuous textiles. He then offered his father precious gifts worth one lakh rupee, including some Badakhshan rubies that cost forty thousand.[71]

Shah Shuja's marriage took place within days of Dara Shukoh's. The emperor wanted it solemnized before the upcoming month of Ramazan. It would have been unsuitable to have a royal wedding when everybody was fasting; also, it was uncommon to celebrate marriages during the period between Eid-ul-Fitr, which marks the end of Ramazan, and Eid-ul-Azha, which takes place after the month of pilgrimage to Mecca. The events and festivities were similar to those at Dara's wedding, except that the costs and grandeur were diminished a shade.[72]

If ever cracks had formed in the relationships between Shah Jahan's three eldest sons, we only manage to glimpse them a few months after Dara's wedding. It was the seventh of June, when the summer was well underway. Two elephants, each goaded into a mad rage, fought fiercely on the banks of the Jamuna, beneath the imperial balcony. One, with tusks, was called Sudhakar, and the other, tuskless, was named Surat Sundar. Dara, Shuja, and Aurangzeb joined their father to watch the spectacle. This kind of entertainment was reserved for emperors alone and took place several times a week in Shah Jahan's court.[73]

The sibling trio and their father were all on horseback so as to better follow the elephants, who moved ahead as they battled each other, their trunks knotted and writhing like serpents. On each of these enormous animals an elephant driver balanced precariously, holding tight.[74] Dara Shukoh was on the elephant on Sudhakar's right, while his brothers were on the left, with Aurangzeb closest to the beast. It was common for sparring elephants to separate momentarily and stare at each other before resuming the fight. At one such instance, Sudhakar, whom intoxication had made reckless, broke through the cordon of guards and viewers and charged at Aurangzeb. The young prince, not yet fifteen years old, calmly steadied his terrified horse and thrust his lance more than four fingers deep into the elephant's skull.[75]

The onlookers, in a state of panic, could do no more than utter prayers. But Sudhakar became even further enraged despite, or rather because of, his wound. He gouged Aurangzeb's fleeing horse with a tusk, throwing the prince onto the ground. Just then Shuja joined the attack, riding up to strike the elephant with his gleaming spear. Guards had ignited fireworks to distract Sudhakar. The air was thick with smoke and dust. A flaming wheel crashed into Shuja's horse, who then reared, throwing the prince off.

Both princes needed help desperately. Raja Jai Singh proved his loyalty by joining the fray, but his horse shied. Then fortuitously, Surat Sundar, the other elephant, saw that his rival's attention was elsewhere and took the opportunity to attack him. Sudhakar fled with Surat Sundar in pursuit, and the incident ended as suddenly as it had begun. Shah Jahan's historians like to say that Sudhakar gazed upon the imperial countenance and was thereby chastened enough to resume his fight.[76]

The written sources are silent about Dara Shukoh's role amidst all this. In an illustration in Lahori's *Padshah-nama,* made for Shah Jahan, Dara is at some distance behind Aurangzeb, the farthest away of all the brothers from the elephant.[77] He holds a spear poised straight upward, almost, but not quite, ready to defend himself. The painting collapses all the stages of the episode into one frame, so Aurangzeb strikes Sudhakar while Shuja aims his lance, and Jai Singh attacks from the elephant's rear. It does not depict the ignominy of the princes flung to the ground. The historical narratives and the visual representations effectively sideline Dara Shukoh from the main course of action.

Later writers would try to scour this incident for clues about the brothers' personalities, for what they perceive as the seeds of Aurangzeb's daring and Dara's cowardice. There is the surely apocryphal story that, after Shah Jahan rewarded Aurangzeb for his bravery, the emperor expressed relief that his son had not let himself suffer the disgrace of being killed by the elephant. Aurangzeb apparently replied, "If it had ended differently there would have been no dishonor in it. The shame lay in what my brothers did." However, this anecdote, recorded more than half a century later, is so rife with inaccuracies, relating, for instance, that the incident took place in Lahore, that the veracity of Aurangzeb's alleged remark becomes highly questionable.[78]

But does Dara Shukoh's lack of participation in this incident tell us anything about the brothers and their relationship? Was the eldest prince simply too far away to act? After all, if Dara had foolhardily plunged into the melée, it would have done little to help the situation. Though the prince would have displayed his courage, the risk may not have seemed justified. The structure of the anecdote would lead one to think that Dara, already favored by his father in so many ways, did not particularly need to prove himself. Aurangzeb, the third son, was entering adulthood in the shadow of his two elder brothers, who had just had extravagant weddings. His performance ensured him a place in the history books and in the sort of poem, by the celebrated Kalim, that would acquire wings and travel to gatherings where people would recite it.

After Aurangzeb struck the elephant's forehead, in Kalim's words, "Out of that crack which formed in his head from the spear/Left the intoxication which had been in his head."[79] Kalim emphasizes Aurangzeb's bravery and portrays the prince as choosing to spare Sudhakar, glossing over the fact that he did not actually succeed in subduing the elephant: "As it would not be agreeable to the brave/to capture one when there are two in the midst//Out of chivalry he withheld his hand from him/though he had seized him, he restrained himself//Through his innate sense of duty, he displayed courage/at an age when he was not yet accountable for religious duties."[80]

Even as Shah Jahan's sons were finding their feet, on the pages of the court histories, at least, they were settling into roles in a partially written script. A poet or chronicler could not know for sure which prince would eventually succeed to the throne.

Aurangzeb facing the elephant Sudhakar.

A couple of months after the elephant duel, the emperor appointed the seventeen-year-old Shuja governor of the Deccan. The aging Mahabat Khan, headquartered in Burhanpur, was waging a series of grueling campaigns against Ahmadnagar and Bijapur, and needed reinforcements. The tenuous bonds between these kingdoms and the Mughal state had frayed. Now with Malik Ambar dead for nine years, various parties had begun to scramble for power in the Deccan. Mahabat Khan wrote a missive to the emperor, urging him to send one of the princes at the soonest instance. Shah Jahan, instead of giving the eldest, Dara, a chance to hone his military skills, chose to send Shuja, his second son.

We might speculate, as at least one eighteenth-century British historian has, that Shuja, hankering to make his mark, pressed Mahabat Khan to write the emperor.[81] There is some merit in this conjecture. The khan's armies desperately needed a fresh infusion of support. Though Mahabat Khan had recently captured the Daulatabad Fort in Ahmadnagar, he could not seize the kingdom until Shahji Bhonsle, a Maratha chieftain, was removed from the equation. But Shuja had no military experience. He would be useful not for his prowess at fighting but for the renewed attention that the Deccan campaigns would attract. Both parties, Shuja and Mahabat Khan, would thus benefit.

In preparation for his departure, Shuja received an official rank before his elder brother did. He was given a mansab sufficient to support ten thousand men and five thousand horses, two magnificently ornamented horses, and a chariot.[82] A few months later, on the fifth of October 1633, also the emperor's birthday, Dara Shukoh received his first rank. His mansab supported twelve thousand men and six thousand horses.[83] Instead of leaving to head a military campaign, Dara remained at the court with his wife, who was now expecting their first child.

NADIRA HAD CONCEIVED A FEW MONTHS after her marriage. A daughter was born on the twenty-ninth of January 1634.[84] To commemorate his first grandchild, Shah Jahan made a special visit to his son's house, just as he had after Dara's wedding. The prince arranged a sumptuous reception for his father and the many important nobles in his retinue. Shortly afterward, the imperial household, including the new mother and her baby, set forth from Agra toward Lahore.

Before they arrived, the two-month-old infant died. The timing made the tragedy seem even bleaker. It was Eid-ul-Fitr, when they should have been celebrating the end of the Ramazan fast. Dara Shukoh was inconsolable and his grief took the form of a severe illness.[85] We do not hear anything, though, about the condition of Nadira, who had just lost her first baby and now had to contend with an ailing husband. The prince's fever soared and the court physicians could do little to cure him. Shah Jahan grew concerned and ordered that Dara Shukoh's tent be pitched beside his own, so that Jahanara, who had taken over Mumtaz's role in looking after the emperor, could better tend to her brother. The emperor also summoned from Lahore his trusted aide Wazir Khan, a physician of note who had often treated him and his sons. The khan managed to reverse the mistakes that the previous doctors had made, and Dara's health finally improved. A relieved Shah Jahan ordered a celebratory feast and gave generous alms to the poor. At least this is what Lahori tells us in the *Badshah-nama*.[86] For the imperial chronicler, the story ends here, on a cheerful note.

But what if Wazir Khan never actually cured the prince? Eight years later, in 1642, Dara Shukoh picks up the thread of this story in a book he wrote—his second—called the *Sakinat ul-auliya* (The Tranquility of Saints). It does not contradict the version of Shah Jahan's chroniclers but offers a completely different memory of what happened during the spring of 1634. An illness does feature in this, but it is not what Lahori recounts. And the death of his daughter for whom he grieved so deeply finds no mention whatsoever. Instead, Dara Shukoh describes an encounter and a miraculous healing, which, he believes, radically transformed the course of his life.

It was the seventh of April 1634. Dara Shukoh had been unwell for about four months now, and doctors had been of no help.[87] Perhaps the depression that Lahori mentioned never lifted, or Wazir Khan's ministrations provided only a temporary respite. But in either case, then, the chronology does not match; Dara's illness, which surfaced in January, must have preceded his daughter's death. Could the tragedy have simply worsened a condition the prince already had? We will never know for sure. For Dara Shukoh, writing in 1642, the particulars of his ailment are less important than the details of its cure and aftermath.

Lahori and Dara Shukoh agree on one point: that when the imperial party arrived in Lahore, the emperor made a visit to a Sufi ascetic who lived nearby.[88] He was known merely as Miyan Mir, a hybrid Hindi-Persian title meaning "respected chief," or by the more intimate Hindi appellation Miyan Jio, meaning "respected sir." Unlike many religious leaders close to the court, he did not boast of grand Arab, Persian, or Central Asian ancestry. In portraits of him made during Shah Jahan's reign, his dark, grayish brown skin stands out strongly, contrasting with the paler complexions of most other Muslim elites in Mughal paintings. As much as these depictions might reflect Miyan Mir's true appearance, they also hint at a conscious differentiation between Indian-born and immigrant Muslims. Miyan Mir's grandfather Qazi Qadan was one of the first mystics to compose Sufi poetry in Sindhi, the vernacular tongue of the region that stretches southward from the Punjab and comprises the Thar Desert as well as the Indus River's southern stretches and delta. Miyan Mir was not particularly eager to seek out imperial patronage. He was content to remain in Sindh where he lived for years before moving north to Lahore.

What Dara Shukoh mentions, and what Lahori's account omits, is that the emperor took Dara along, as well, to meet the saint, and that the main purpose of the emperor's visit was to find a remedy for his firstborn son's illness. Shah Jahan made a humble entrance into Miyan Mir's dwelling, writes the prince, by now a committed disciple of the Sufi teacher. The emperor took Dara Shukoh in by the hand and beseeched, "Revered Presence, Miyan Jio! This eldest son of mine has great affection for you. Physicians have been unable to treat him. Please look after him."[89]

Miyan Mir grasped the prince's hand and, with the other hand, picked up a clay pot that he regularly used for drinking. After filling it with water, he breathed a prayer over it and recited the fatiha. He then instructed Dara Shukoh to drink the water and said that the prince would be cured within a week. A week passed, and Dara Shukoh, who was completely healed of all afflictions, decided to send one of his aides to the holy man for treatment. The man was cured within four days, at the precise moment that Miyan Mir had also predicted.

Shortly after this encounter, Dara Shukoh joined his father on their annual trip to Kashmir, but upon their return at the end of the year, they visited the Sufi recluse again.[90] This time, the emperor and Miyan Mir conversed at some length. As far as the official court historians are concerned, these meetings were nothing but a harmonious communion of elevated souls. According to Lahori, the emperor often observed that "amongst the ascetics of India, there are two who have ascended to the level of perfection—Miyan Mir and Shaikh Muhammad Fazl Ullah, who made his abode in Burhanpur."[91]

But, as Dara Shukoh later reports, Miyan Mir did not let the emperor's esteem for him inhibit his own unsparing frankness. Dara recalls that when he visited the Sufi's dwelling again, along with his father, the emperor confessed that his heart had become cold to the world, meaning that his royal duties wearied him and that he was looking for some spiritual succor. Miyan Mir, unsympathetic, retorted, "You ought to do a righteous act that would gladden the heart of any Muslim. On that occasion, then offer a prayer asking for nothing but God." He then quoted a verse by the thirteenth-century mystic poet Jalaluddin Rumi to drive in his point: "You wish for God as well as the material world/This is mere fancy, impossible, insanity."[92]

Later during that meeting, the emperor gifted the saint a turban and a string of prayer beads, made from humble date seeds, not gemstones. According to Dara, Miyan Mir declined the turban but accepted the prayer beads, which he then gave to the young prince. The saint's bold independence contrasted with the manner in which many Sufis eagerly received imperial patronage. On the two trips to Lahore during which Shah Jahan met with Miyan Mir, he also visited another Qadiri, Shah Bilawal, each time giving the latter a generous financial gift, which the Sufi distributed among the members of his lodge.[93]

Why would the eldest prince diminish his father, the emperor, by relating this anecdote? Already, Shah Jahan had started to exercise tight control over the books and images that would portray him for posterity. Court historians, like Lahori, would certainly not dream of mentioning Miyan Mir's rebuff. Qazwini, who recorded an early, less sanitized history of Shah Jahan's first decade of rule, does explain that the Miyan Mir did not generally appreciate gifts, which is why the emperor's men only offered him a white turban and prayer beads. But he neither adds that the Sufi refused the turban nor discusses the further details of the conversation between the emperor and the recluse. Instead, he enthuses that their "felicitous meeting" was "the envy of all gatherings of sacred people and celebrations of spiritual folk."[94]

Eight years later, though, when Dara Shukoh wrote his *Sakinat ul-auliya,* he had become deeply immersed in Qadiri life. His description of the emperor's encounter with Miyan Mir follows a familiar pattern in Sufi literature: the indifferent ascetic, unmoved by wealth and power, nevertheless manages to impress a ruler accustomed to obsequiousness. There is always a paradox in these cases: Miyan Mir's charisma rested on his disinterest in the material world, yet he could not afford to completely reject connections with the imperial court, whose beneficence ensured the survival of his order. This account served the prince's own purposes: by revealing a Sufi's snub to an emperor, even his own father, he could thereby underscore his own spiritual precociousness. Perhaps Dara Shukoh's book was meant for private circulation among an intimate group of friends and not for Shah Jahan's eyes. Dara's description of his own interaction with Miyan Mir provides a vivid contrast.

"I considered his blessed house to be a sacred valley," Dara writes, of his second visit to Miyan Mir, "so I went inside barefoot. His Presence, Miyan Jio, was chewing and spitting out cloves during his conversation with the emperor. Some of those present found this annoying to their sensibilities."

The Sufi, displaying his disdain for temporal power, had no qualms about behaving in a way that would ordinarily never be permissible before an emperor.

What the prince did then must have astonished his onlookers. He gathered up these discarded, masticated cloves, and ate each one. As he swallowed them, he says, two simultaneous feelings arose in his heart: a sense of detachment from worldly matters and a knowledge of his intense belonging to Miyan Mir's community. Once the emperor and his entourage took leave of the holy man and set off, Dara Shukoh lingered and went to Miyan Mir alone. For a while, he recalls, he rubbed his head upon the saint's blessed feet. Miyan Mir, overjoyed, placed his hand on the prince's head. Thereupon, Dara felt such sublime happiness that, he says, his head transcended the very throne of God. Later, a certain Hajji Muhammad Bunyani would tell Dara Shukoh that when the prince's name came up in conversation, someone asked Miyan Mir, "Do you favor him?" The Sufi replied, "He is my soul and my eyesight."[95]

Dara Shukoh puts himself at the center of his account of the emperor's meetings with Miyan Mir. But there is yet another dimension to the story of Shah Jahan's visits to the Sufi recluse. This time we hear of it through an unofficial history written by a relatively ordinary man, at least, when compared to princes or the litterateurs of the imperial court. His name was Tawakkul Beg, and he was the son of a soldier from the Kulab highlands in Central Asia as well as a Qadiri devotee. In this work, which chronicles the life and times of Mulla Shah Badakhshi, Miyan Mir's deputy, he exposes a scandal emanating from Kashmir, where Mulla Shah lived with a community of followers, including Tawakkul Beg.

Mulla Shah was forty-seven when Shah Jahan ascended to the throne, and that same year, Tawakkul Beg tells us, the Sufi reached a singular level of spiritual realization, the full cognition of *tauhid,* or God's oneness. In honor of the occasion, Mulla Shah composed a special quatrain, which speaks of the two "shahs" each sitting on his own throne: "He, Shah Jahan and I, the two, emperor and beggar / One day sat upon two thrones of guidance // He sat upon his world-ruling throne / I on the throne of understanding God's essence."[96] The tone combines reverence with a hint of mockery. For a Sufi, it was clear which form of sovereignty was superior.

Word of Mulla Shah's spiritual attainments reached the ear of his pir, Miyan Mir, who heard that Mulla Shah could now witness the angelic realm with little effort, skipping the ascetic rigors and mortification that most Sufi adepts required. Students flocked to Mulla Shah in Kashmir. One of them, Mir Baqi from Turan, would lose control of himself when entering into a mystical state, uttering several statements that his fellow Qadiris found offensive.

Miyan Mir denounced him strongly and expelled him from the order. Although he cautioned Mulla Shah, too, to guard his tongue during heightened spiritual experiences, the Badakhshani Sufi uttered the following couplet that seemingly denigrated the Prophet: "I am hand in hand with God/Why should I care about Mustafa?"[97]

By the year 1634, the chatter about Mulla Shah's ecstatic utterances and verses had become loud enough to gain the attention of some elite ulama attached to the court. They accused him of unbelief and drafted an edict calling for Mulla Shah to be put to death. Three of the highest ranking among them stamped their seals on it before the others could follow suit: Mulla Fazil, Shah Jahan's household steward; Qazi Aslam, the chief jurisprudent of the empire under Shah Jahan who had officiated at Dara Shukoh's marriage; and the qazi's brother, Mirak Shaikh, who had been Dara Shukoh's tutor.[98]

Today we might think of the ulama and Sufis as two fiercely opposing camps, inhabiting separate worlds, but this was not the case in Mughal times. Though Tawakkul Beg does not say so, Qazi Aslam and Mirak Shaikh actually had strong Qadiri links. Qazi Aslam studied under the Qadiri Sufi Shaikh Bahlul of Lahore before entering court employment under Jahangir through his family connections.[99] Another famous disciple of Shaikh Bahlul was the ecstatic mystic Shah Husain. Stories abound of his love for a Brahmin boy, Madho. Though Mirak Shaikh studied under Mulla Abd-us-Salam, the magistrate of Lahore, before entering Shah Jahan's service, he also shared a teacher with Miyan Mir. Both were pupils of Maulana Nimatullah in Lahore, who in turn was a disciple of the Qadiri Sufi Sadullah, another of Shah Husain's teachers.[100] We might interpret the ulama's strong objection to Mulla Shah's verse as an attempt to bolster their own authority and quell Mulla Shah's growing popularity in Kashmir.

These religious scholars brought the edict to Shah Jahan, arguing that killing Mulla Shah would lead to rewards for the emperor in the next life. The emperor was reluctant to act without sending someone to Kashmir to verify matters. Just then, Dara Shukoh stepped in. He persuaded the emperor that, because Mulla Shah was a disciple of Miyan Mir, it would be inappropriate to act hastily. Shah Jahan praised Dara's insight and promised to put a hold on the decree.

It was an age before swift lines of communication, and more and more people heard news of the fatwa, but not the emperor's order to halt it. The news drifted from Lahore to Kashmir, and Mulla Shah eventually heard that an imperial decree had ordered his death. He rejoiced, saying that he would now witness the countenance of the divine. His disciples, fearful, pressed him to escape to Tibet, insisting, "the scholars have all belted the waist of enmity." Mulla Shah retorted that living and dying were the same to him, as he was not a mere imitator of authority.[101]

Apparently, according to Tawakkul Beg, Shah Jahan had brought up the matter at his first visit to Miyan Mir. Upon hearing about the death sentence prepared for his disciple, the Sufi put the tip of his finger to his mouth in astonishment. "Mulla Shah is a master of mystical experience," he explained. "When the spiritual state overtakes him, words just come out." As the emperor and son took leave of Miyan Mir, Shah Jahan turned to Dara Shukoh and commended him for opposing the ulama's edict.[102] Soon father and son, together with the rest of the imperial household, left for Kashmir.

4

DISCIPLESHIP

1634–1642

IN THE SUMMER OF 1634, Dara Shukoh's father waited until the heat had fully set in before he left Lahore for Kashmir. As usual, he took with him his family, the enormous staff of his household, and his army. There were four possible routes to the remote valley tucked within several ranges of high mountains. The imperial party had to choose their itinerary carefully to avoid dangerous landslides caused by the melting snow. By May, much of the snow would have already disappeared. They decided to approach the dense Pir Panjal mountain range from the Kashmir Valley's southeast, by way of Bhimbar, a town now in the part of Kashmir administered by Pakistan.[1]

At the beginning of June they arrived at the foot of the Pir Panjals. The mountain roads were exceedingly narrow. Dara Shukoh was one of the few permitted to ride along with some of the emperor's personal attendants, the hunt officials, and the imperial kitchen staff; the rest of Shah Jahan's massive entourage would walk. From Jahanara's own later accounts of the return journey from Kashmir, we gather that the imperial women sometimes traveled on elephants, seated in curtained howdahs. But in this case, when the trails were narrow, they would have used palanquins.

Mirza Amin Qazwini, the Iranian man of letters and court chronicler who later wrote his firsthand account of the trip, traveled with Asaf Khan. The lines of the emperor's men, as they trudged up and down the difficult terrain, must have stretched for miles. Before beginning the ascent, Shah

Jahan had arranged a *qamargha*, a special type of hunt that was the emperor's prerogative alone. Fifty thousand men made themselves into a
human barrier enclosing a large area, Qazwini tells us. Within it, the emperor shot some musk deer that were trapped inside.[2] One can only imagine
how many more men and women the imperial retinue must have included.

They would have had to cross about seventy miles of rocky, mountainous
terrain before reaching the Kashmir Valley, a long, slim oblong plateau
about six thousand feet high. There were some particularly treacherous
patches along the way. The poet Muhammad Jan Qudsi, who was also in
Shah Jahan's entourage, writes that some of the mountain passes were so
narrow, the sky above seemed like just a strand of hair. His narrative poem
describing this journey includes the following verses about the Pir Panjal
range: "The east breeze struts gracefully at its skirt/Because it cannot climb
to its top ... A bird cannot fly on the route/It must slice a path with its
wing's shears."[3] Though there must have been some truth to Qudsi's descriptions, he was also invoking stock images of the tortuous road to
Kashmir, tropes that earlier Persian poets had popularized.[4]

The city we know today as Srinagar was then usually referred to simply
as Kashmir. It spread out at the foot of the hilltop Koh-i Maran fortress,
alongside the Dal Lake, which shimmered silvery blue and green. Ever since
Shah Jahan's grandfather Akbar had annexed Kashmir in 1586, Mughal
and Iranian writers and poets never tired of comparing Kashmir to paradise. In Dara Shukoh's time, one never spoke of it as just "Kashmir"; it was
always "paradisical Kashmir" (*Kashmir-i jannat nazir*) or "matchless
Kashmir" (*Kashmir-i benazir*). Despite the difficulties of the journey, the emperor took time to appreciate the natural beauty along the way, inhaling
the fragrance of jasmine or stopping to sit and gaze at a giant, roaring waterfall. Qazwini describes the reason for the imperial visit to the spectacular mountainous region as "sightseeing in Kashmir's eternally vernal rose
garden."[5]

By idealizing Kashmir through language, or by constructing elaborate
gardens there, Mughal elites tamed and possessed its landscape. Kashmir
was not an unknown, wondrous territory in a strange realm; it was the emperor's own pleasure ground, the empire's jewel. Akbar laid out a garden
in his citadel on the Hari Parbat mountain. Jahangir, Nur Jahan, and Asaf
Khan built gardens that channeled bubbling springs into orderly tree-
flanked waterways. These streams divided the ornamental grounds vertically and cross-sectionally, with the water cascading down inclines carved
out of stone or shooting up in jets as fountains. When Shah Jahan was a
prince, he had designed one such garden around a mountain spring, known
as Shalimar, and now it was ready, with thousands of flowers in bloom and

trees laden with fruits and nuts about to ripen. He renamed it Farahbakhsh, "Granter of joy," to commemorate his arrival in Kashmir.[6]

The emperor cultivated this Mughal paradise and gifted shares of it to his family. Three gardens went to Jahanara, including one that had formerly belonged to Nur Jahan. Dara Shukoh, Jahanara, and Murad Bakhsh each received gardens built on islands in the midst of the Dal Lake. Shah Jahan also gave Dara a garden named Karna, which had been his as a prince. Aurangzeb was granted his first estate, a village near Achabal, in the valley's southeast, though his father does not seem to have bestowed on him a garden.[7]

Apart from partaking of the valley's scenic pleasures, Dara Shukoh was eager to meet Mulla Shah to further deepen the Qadiri connections he had recently made in Lahore. Dara treaded cautiously. He did not wish to upset the famously aloof Sufi, and he also wanted to show that he was a sincere supplicant and not a mere dilettante. Tawakkul Beg relates that the prince had made up his mind to perform the kornish obeisance before Mulla Shah. This show of respect was generally reserved for the emperor. Dara pitched camp near the Sufi teacher's home and waited to catch a glimpse of the master. But Mulla Shah was away in the wilderness on a spiritual retreat. When he finally returned home, he was told that Dara had been there for some days. His disciples coaxed him into allowing the prince to pay his respects. The Shah graciously agreed. As Dara's forehead touched the ground, he felt a desire arise in him to serve the pir as a disciple. But for now, the two seem to have had no further interaction during Dara's time in Kashmir.[8]

During this same year, a Hindu youth called Banwali, sometimes also known as Banwalidas, also made his way to Kashmir. We know of his journey through the *Dabistan-i mazahib* (The School of Religious Sects), a Persian work from the mid-seventeenth century. Authored by one Mubad Shah, a disciple of the Iranian "freethinker" Azar Kaiwan, the *Dabistan* sketches colorful accounts of various religious traditions in South Asia and the people associated with them.[9] It related that from a young age, Banwali had a penchant for dervish assemblies. He had heard of the Kashmir-based Qadiri mystic, Mulla Shah Badakhshi, and acquired an overpowering wish to see him. In accordance with the dictum, "A Sufi has no religion," says the *Dabistan*, Banwali "is well acquainted with the idol and the idol temple, neither is he a stranger to the mosque."[10]

Banwali was the son of one Hiraman Kayasth. The Kayasths were a caste of scribes who traced their origin to Chitragupt, son of the god Brahma. Associated with justice, Chitragupt constantly records the actions of every sentient being in his role as secretary to Yama, the god of death. By Shah

Jahan's time, many Kayasths had come to work in the administration as record keepers, letter writers, and accountants. Persian was the language in which they most easily wrote, and young Kayasth boys would study the classics of Persian prose and poetry with the hope of securing government employment.

Banwali might well have arrived in Kashmir with the emperor's entourage. At some point, he became associated with Dara Shukoh's retinue and may have acquired his devotion to Mulla Shah through contact with the prince. Tawakkul Beg discusses Banwali in his chronicle of the Kashmiri mystic: "A Hindu named Banwalidas was a seeker of God. He performed a lot of ascetic exercises, always practicing mystical wayfaring and breath control. One day, he was ennobled by the service of Mulla Shah. He revealed his search for the divine truth, spending day and night at the threshold." In this telling, the Sufi teacher was not one to accept disciples easily. "Become a Muslim," ordered Mulla Shah. Banwalidas replied, "I've gone past infidelity and Islam, and broken both the sacred thread and the rosary. No shackle remains on me." During this occasion, however, Banwalidas affirmed the *shahada*, the Islamic testimony of faith. As he grew more absorbed in his spiritual practice, he left Dara Shukoh's employment and moved to the wilderness, where he lived in solitude. For a while, we hear nothing more about him, though later it becomes apparent that he would keep up his ties with Dara Shukoh. Immersing himself in the practices of Sufi devotion, Banwalidas would one day become an accomplished poet and author.[11]

IN MID-DECEMBER 1634, after the Kashmir trip, the imperial family returned to Lahore, where they remained for the rest of the winter. Shuja was still away in the Deccan. The sixteen-year-old Aurangzeb had just received his first rank of ten thousand horsemen. This was an intimation that he, too, would soon be called to the line of duty away from the court. Dara Shukoh and his father once again met Miyan Mir, as we heard in the previous chapter. Upon impressing the aged Sufi with his devotion, Dara dived headlong into the company of the Lahore Qadiris. Though he was not yet formally inducted into the order, he became Miyan Mir's *de facto* disciple for a brief but intense period.

From Dara Shukoh's later recollections, we gather that he must have had several further meetings with Miyan Mir, enough for the Sufi to entrust the prince with special mystical knowledge. Dara would practice a Sufi technique of gazing upon his master, called *tawajjuh*, which literally means facing or confronting. During these sessions, Miyan Mir's divine grace, focused on his disciple, would enter the young prince. Though the prince does not use quite this simile, this process of charismatic transference may have felt like a shaft of light piercing through a windowpane. Dara engraved Miyan Mir's physiognomy on his heart. Years later, writing in the *Sakinat-ul-auliya,* he would recall his master's light-filled eyes; his wheat-like complexion; his strikingly high nose and wide forehead; his beard, which was the length of four fingers and completely white; and his frail body, weakened by years of ascetic rigors and exertions.[12]

Miyan Mir was too feeble to perform the movements of the namaz even from a seated position, so he offered his prayers lying down. "Most of this group [of Sufis] constantly suffer from afflictions," remarked Dara, but the truth was that Miyan Mir did not have much longer to live. On the eleventh of August 1635, he closed his eyes to the world for the last time.[13] The prince made sure to build a mausoleum for his pir near Lahore. A square structure, raised on a plinth amid a spacious courtyard, the tomb still attracts throngs of devotees today.

But Dara received most of Miyan Mir's instruction through visionary experiences after the Sufi teacher's death. Such visions, the prince referred to with the word *waqia,* literally meaning an incident, event, or occurrence, using a term drawn from the name of the Quran's fifty-sixth sura. As a technical term of Sufi practice, a *waqia* means a mystical vision witnessed either while awake or while dreaming. In one such vision, on a Monday night, Dara found Miyan Mir in repose, outside his house. When he approached him to pay his respects, Miyan Mir grasped the prince's hand and asked him to come close. In Dara's words, "He exposed my chest, and having pulled the clothing away from his own chest under the left nipple, rubbed it against my nipple on the same side, and declared 'Take that with which I have been entrusted.' And such a multitude of dazzling lights from his blessed chest entered mine that I cried, 'Enough!'" After this overwhelming event, Dara says, his heart became "pure, luminous, and imbued with the taste of mystical experience and ecstasy."[14]

A modern reader might see homoerotic tinges in this episode. But for a seventeenth-century Sufi, it would have represented a very literal heart-to-heart transmission of divine grace and mystical insight from a pir to his disciple. Sufis tend to view the heart as the locus of mystical knowledge and experience that the mind cannot comprehend. Dara's anecdote also evokes a well-known incident in the biography of the Prophet Muhammad. Before the Prophet set off on his night ascent into the heavens, the angel Gabriel, who had been the bearer of the divine revelations, opened his chest and took out his heart. Gabriel then cleansed it with water from the Zamzam spring in the Meccan sanctuary before returning it to its place.[15]

Several years after Miyan Mir's death, in December 1641, Dara Shukoh sat, facing west in the direction of the Kaaba. It was no ordinary day. By the Islamic calendar, it was the twenty-seventh of the sacred month of Ramazan: the *Lailat-ul-Qadr*, the Night of Destiny or Power, when more than a millennium earlier the first verses of the Quran were revealed to the Prophet.[16] A restlessness overcame the prince and he sprang up. Suddenly, a large building appeared before his eyes, which he soon recognized as Miyan Mir's tomb.

Miyan Mir emerged, saying that he had something to teach Dara, and proceeded to thrust his index fingers into each of the prince's ears. Dara Shukoh was immediately overpowered by a sound that he called *sultan-ul-azkar*—an expression which literally means the "emperor of divine remembrance," and here reflects a Sufi practice associated with higher states of divine gnosis. Miyan Mir embraced the prince, held his chest close to his, and then let him go. Upon this, relates Dara, "I then lost consciousness. He gave me a spiritual elixir, and intimated to me something which neither speech, writing, verbal expression, nor allusion could express. My object had been attained. Pleasure multiplied upon pleasure; victory upon victory was fulfilled, and the distinction between proximity and distance from God vanished."[17] The prince's euphoric account of his initiation by Miyan Mir into a powerful, secret meditation practice announces his arrival at an elevated spiritual plane. Just as the Prophet Muhammad was gifted the divine revelation, Dara, through Miyan Mir's mediation, becomes the recipient of an esoteric truth.

But in 1635, Dara Shukoh was still very much a novice on the Sufi path. It was some years before he would fully immerse himself in the Qadiri *tariqa* or order. For now, he had a new opportunity to savor the life of a householder. Before his pir's death, he had become a father. In March, as the imperial camp stopped at Sultanpur on the way to Agra, Nadira gave birth to a son. He was named Sulaiman Shukoh, meaning "one endowed with the glory of the prophet-king Solomon." Festivities ensued, and Dara gifted his father jeweled weapons and luxurious textiles.[18] This was Shah Jahan's second living grandchild. Shuja and his wife Bilqis already had a little daughter named Dilpazir Bano, born in 1633. For Dara and Nadira, after the loss of their first child, the birth of a male heir would have been an occasion of immense relief and comfort.

With his wife, Nadira, Dara shared the joys of family life, but his eldest sister Jahanara remained a cherished confidante. They had been close since early childhood, and as they matured, they cultivated a mutual interest in seeking nearness to the divine and finding an appropriate spiritual master. Since the age of twenty, as she tells us in a short autobiography that she later penned, she had been especially drawn toward the Chishti order. In Dara Shukoh's company, she could open her heart:

> For my brother, Sultan Muhammad Dara Shukoh Qadiri, victorious, powerful, gnostic of secrets, master of spiritual experience and divine presence, the eye's light and light's vision, possessor of inner meaning and glorious deeds, heir to the inner and outer kingdom, felicitous God-seeker, of high dignity and ex- alted rank—may God increase his shadow's glory and ease his deeds—I have and have had the utmost personal love, the highest notional affection, perfect religious and worldly accord, and a unity of form and meaning. We are both one spirit, blown into two forms. One soul come forth in two bodies. As my brother, the perfect gnostic, has acquired complete benefit from knowledge of spiritual mysteries, and ineffable fortune from divine truths, he has always con- veyed to me truth-pointing utterances, and described the spiritual states and stages of the great ones, the shaikhs and the friends of God—may their secrets be sanctified.[19]

In the summer of 1635, Jahanara, at twenty-one, was one of the wealthiest persons in the empire, and by far the most powerful woman. She was still single, and she must have sensed her father's reluctance to arrange a match for her. There was no man whose rank could equal hers, and moreover, if she had children, they might one day compete for the throne with young Sulaiman Shukoh and other future grandchildren of Shah Jahan. Unmar- ried, she could, and would, carve out an enduring role for herself at her father's court. But the project that consumed her during these years was her own spiritual fashioning.

FOR THE NEXT FEW YEARS, Dara Shukoh would be at his father's side, witnessing closely the tasks of imperial rulership, which included defending and expanding borders, and constructing extravagant edifices as symbols of power and majesty. Only a week after his grandson's birth, at an auspi- cious time arranged by prior notice, the emperor entered Agra. This date, the twenty-second of March 1635, was the eighth anniversary of his acces- sion and a rare conjunction of the two major festivals celebrated at the court: Nauroz, the Persian New Year, and Eid-ul-Fitr, which marked the end of a month of fasting. In a court where astrology and religious calen- dars ruled supreme, this was no doubt seen as an especially felicitous mo- ment. Dara Shukoh and his siblings accompanied the emperor to Agra.[20] The chroniclers do not reveal if Nadira accompanied the others; if she did go, she would not have had much of a chance to rest after Sulaiman Shu-koh's birth.

It was a fitting time for Shah Jahan to inaugurate an opulent new throne, which had taken seven years to build, at a cost of over ten million rupees. This replaced the simple black stone slab that Jahangir had proudly used.[21] Here, from a gold platform encrusted with innumerable jewels, twelve pillars rose gracefully to support a canopy, all of which were made of solid gold. The throne glistened with rubies, garnets, pearls, emeralds, and diamonds. Lustrous tapestries and fabrics cushioned and draped the seating area. Atop the canopy, two delicately fashioned peacocks faced each other, each holding a glowing ruby in its beak. Though these birds gave it its later appellation of the Peacock Throne, Shah Jahan's chroniclers referred to it simply as the Jeweled Throne (*takht-i murassa*).[22]

The emperor, who had a shrewd sense of how to craft his image for the present day as well as for posterity, would have realized how strikingly this new throne framed him as he sat for his daily audiences. It resembled the jharokha window at which Mughal emperors sat daily in a practice dating from Akbar's rule. However, this entire edifice served to encapsulate the emperor in a golden blaze. Poets like Kalim and Qudsi rhapsodized about the Jeweled Throne—indeed Qudsi's verses were carved on it—and it would often appear as a central compositional element in paintings of court scenes. In Qudsi's words, "Hail, auspicious throne of the emperor!/Completed by divine assistance//The day the firmament made it/It first melted the sun's gold."[23]

Shah Jahan had news writers regularly document major events taking place in the court and empire, but in 1636 he asked the Iranian man of letters, Mirza Amin Qazwini, to chronicle his reign from the time of his accession. We may recall that a few years earlier the emperor had seen and approved of a piece that Qazwini wrote on Aurangzeb's encounter with the elephant Sudhakar. Unlike his father, Jahangir, Shah Jahan was not much of a memoirist. The emperor had in mind a sweeping, panegyric history. Qazwini embarked on this lengthy project that would later take shape as the first version of the *Padshah-nama* (The Book of the Emperor). Other litterateurs had written earlier accounts of Shah Jahan's reign. For instance, Jalala Tabatabai, soon after arriving from Iran in 1634, had already chronicled the first years of Shah Jahan's rule. But now he had been displaced by Qazwini, who, however, drew on Tabatabai's chronicle among other sources for his new history.[24]

The three oldest princes, who were boys when the emperor first ascended the throne, had come of age. It was an appropriate time for the emperor to delegate more responsibilities to them, though he keenly supervised their every move. He had recently dispatched Shuja on what would eventually become an unsuccessful campaign in the Deccan, to capture the Parenda Fort now occupied by the Bijapur rulers. In September 1635, Shah Jahan sent the seventeen-year-old Aurangzeb on his first campaign to head an army sent to quell the rebel Jajhar Singh of Orchha, a densely forested state in the subcontinent's central region. Jajhar Singh's father, Bir Singh Bundela, had been a Mughal vassal. But the son, who since Shah Jahan's accession had exhibited rebellious tendencies, attacked and killed another raja. Now, along with his heir Bikramajit, Jajhar Singh openly resisted the emperor.[25]

Aurangzeb, still inexperienced, did not have a significant role in the expedition. He arrived after the imperial army had already driven Jajhar Singh and Bikramajit out of the Chauragadh fortress. The raja and his son were eventually murdered by Gond tribesmen in the jungle where they had fled. Court chroniclers recounted with gusto the cruelties that Jajhar Singh and his men inflicted on their womenfolk, killing or wounding them or forcing them to commit suicide lest they be captured by the enemy. As a price for their father's sedition, Jajhar Singh's male descendants were forced to renounce their faith and to convert, as were the surviving women in the household.

When Shah Jahan was on his way toward the city of Orchha with Aurangzeb, he ordered his army to destroy the grand Chaturbhuj temple built by Bir Singh Bundela, adjacent to the royal palace.[26] The destruction did not claim the entire edifice.[27] But through desecrating the temple, Shah Jahan stamped out the most important symbol of the Bundela ruler's sovereignty. It was turned into a mosque. The emperor's men also recovered the considerable wealth that Jajhar Singh had stashed away.

Mughal chroniclers interrupt their account of the Orchha campaign with interludes featuring descriptions of the area's natural beauty. In his numerous missives to his father, Aurangzeb described the delights of the Bundelkhand landscape—its rivers, lakes, and little pools; its gardens, meadows, mountain peaks, and plains; and the abundant wildlife available for hunting.[28] The emperor accompanied by his other children took a detour to enjoy these sights. It is telling that this scenic terrain is likened to Kashmir, even though the lush foliage and climate could not be more different. The imperial party spent four days at a magnificent waterfall near Dhum Ghat.[29] This episode of repose offers a vivid example of the ways in which, for Mughal royals, hunting and sightseeing, as well as the memorialization of these acts in prose or poetry, served to mark their possession of conquered territories.

When not at war, Shah Jahan often took care to ensure that non-Muslims could go about their daily business without obstruction. Only recently, in December 1634, had he issued a decree allowing the sounding of a gong in the Madan Mohan temple at Vrindavan for the sake of "divine worship."[30] Surviving records attest that he also protected the interests of Shantidas Sahu, an influential Jain purveyor of jewels to the court. In August 1635, he sent a decree to the officers of Ahmedabad, instructing them to ensure that nobody interfered with Shantidas's shops, gardens, or mansions. Like many other decrees of Shah Jahan, it carries Dara Shukoh's seal at the back, which certifies that a copy was sent to Afzal Khan, an Iranian nobleman who had been close to the emperor since Shah Jahan was a prince.[31] This exemplifies how Dara Shukoh was involved with the minutiae of governance, albeit from his imperial perch.

Soon after his first Deccan expedition, Aurangzeb started coming more and more into his own. Later that year, in July 1636, Shah Jahan appointed him governor of the Deccan. As his father had done years earlier, Aurangzeb would hone his administrative and military skills dealing with the empire's turbulent southern frontier. The next summer, in May 1637, Aurangzeb was granted leave to come to the court in Agra, as his marriage had been finally arranged. The bride, named Dilras Bano, was actually Shuja's wife's niece. Dilras Bano's father, Shahnawaz Khan, was the son of Mirza Rustam Safavi, whose daughter Shuja had wed. The festivities followed the pattern of Dara Shukoh's and Shuja's marriages, but they were significantly smaller in scale and grandeur. Following custom, the wedding began with the henna ceremony in the imperial bathhouse and ended with Aurangzeb receiving his father in his own residence. Since Jahanara had released considerable monies from her own funds for her two other brothers' weddings, Shah Jahan contributed ten lakhs for this occasion.[32]

A year and a half after his first marriage, Aurangzeb married again. He'd already had a child with Dilras Bano, a daughter born in February 1638 called Zeb-un-Nisa, the "ornament among women." But this time, Aurangzeb wed a Rajput princess, the daughter of the raja of Rajouri, a hill-state in present-day Jammu. His bride, later known as Nawab Bai, belonged to the Jarral clan of Rajputs, who were converts to Islam, but preserved their Rajput identity. There were pragmatic reasons for this union. After all, Shah Jahan, too, had sealed multiple marriage contracts to forge political alliances. There had been no Mughal emperor since Akbar, who had not married a Rajput princess, though Aurangzeb's siblings had not yet done so. Most of the time, these marriages took place just as a Rajput ruler was being inducted into Mughal imperial service. But in this case, although there was no ongoing campaign in Rajauri, it was to prove an expedient match. Rajauri was located in a strategic area, which Mughal emperors invariably passed through en route to Kashmir. The union with Nawab Bai soon produced a son, Muhammad Sultan, born at the end of 1639.[33]

Meanwhile, sorrow once again struck Dara Shukoh and Nadira. In July 1638, Nadira had given birth to another son, who was named Mihr Shukoh, the "sun's splendor." Three-year-old Sulaiman Shukoh now had a brother. A month later, the four of them set off with the emperor on an extended trip that would eventually take them to Kashmir. Not even two days into the journey, the baby died.[34] After the death of Dara's firstborn, the prince had plunged into a severe illness. This time we do not hear how Dara, let alone Nadira, dealt with the loss. But we do know that around this period, Dara immersed himself in the study of practical philosophy and mysticism.

The prince, now in his mid-twenties, had not yet returned to meet the Qadiri Sufis of Miyan Mir's lineage. But he had not forgotten them all this while. Though he did not now have a living teacher, he made sure that throughout his peregrinations and royal duties he continued to pursue his own religious studies. He had been perusing the biographies of Sufi mystics in Persian compendiums called *tazkiras*, which assemble narrative accounts of these saints and arrange them either chronologically or according to their orders and lineages. It occurred to Dara that he, too, might compile his own book of saints' lives. He may have shared this idea with his sister, Jahanara. Or perhaps it was her suggestion that he write a tazkira. Or maybe her own reading and writing planted the seed of scholarship in his mind, for she, too, was working on a book.

In preparation, both brother and sister immersed themselves in Sufi literature, reading widely from what had by then been established as a Sufi canon. Dara read from such classics as the esoteric Quran commentary by the Sufi Sulami of Nishapur; the *Kashf-ul-mahjub* (The Unveiling of the Concealed), a biographical manual on Sufism by Hujwiri, a great mystic from Ghazni, whose shrine in Lahore still attracts throngs of devotees; the tazkira of saints by the renowned Iranian poet and biographer Farid-ud-Din Attar; a range of works by Ghazali, the influential Iranian Sufi, theologian, and jurist; and the *Nafahat-ul-uns* (Breaths of Intimacy), a sprawling tazkira by Jami, who was an enormously prolific poet and scholar based in Herat. The prince was not an uncritical reader; in fact, he noted gaps and chronological inconsistencies in some of the saints' biographies that he read and vowed to improve on these in his own compilation.[35]

Jahanara mentions that her brother gave her a copy of the *Nafahat-ul-uns* at a time when she was faced with a temporary parting from him and in need of succor. She also indicates that she read the *Akhbar-ul-akhyar* by Abd-ul-Haqq, the illustrious Qadiri hadith scholar who had established his own educational complex in Delhi. Perhaps she obtained from the imperial library the very copy that the author had presented to her grandfather, Jahangir, when she was very young. Among other works, she read Abu-l-Fazl's *Akbar-nama,* which includes short notices on the empire's saints. She also closely followed her brother's ongoing writings and must have shared his library.[36]

Elite Mughal women were no strangers to education. There are court paintings of the period featuring girls or young women studying with a male teacher.[37] The princess would have received a solid education in Persian and Arabic from her governesses, who, in her adulthood, now assisted her in her administrative duties. They included the aforementioned Huri Khanam, her childhood nurse, and Sati-un-Nisa Begam.[38] Jahanara was thus fully equipped to embark on these intellectual and spiritual explorations.

Though Dara Shukoh does not tell us about the actual process of reading and writing, we can glean some clues from Jahanara's autobiography. The brother and sister composed their respective volumes during a time of intense movement and travel—from Agra, to the city of Shahjahanabad that was being planned north of Delhi, to Lahore, to Kabul, then back to Lahore. Jahanara started her readings of saints' lives in earnest on her way to Kabul from Lahore, but Dara had been on this path for a while. Their libraries would have accompanied them, and they must have picked up new books along the way and had scribes create new copies of especially rare or valuable works. Dara regularly provided his sister with books, she tells us. While they rested between journeys in their palatial tented complexes, they read, meditated, wrote, and discussed. Jahanara suggests that she might even have browsed through books on saints' lives while traveling in her palanquin: "I kept busy with divine remembrance, rosary-telling, and reading the lives of shaikhs and thus passed the stations on the way to Kabul," she writes.[39]

But time and again, the siblings' other responsibilities punctuated their spiritual and intellectual labors. Both Dara Shukoh and Jahanara had to serve and assist their father and prepare for the numerous ceremonial occasions that court life entailed. Dara Shukoh was not away in the field like Shuja and Aurangzeb were, but he came very close to setting forth on his first military expedition.

Qandahar, always a trouble spot in Mughal-Safavid relations, had suddenly flipped back into Mughal hands. In March 1638, Ali Mardan Khan, the Persian commander who had fallen out with the reigning emperor of

Iran, Shah Safi, gave Qandahar over to Shah Jahan and defected to the Mughals. Shah Jahan was jubilant but justifiably concerned that Shah Safi
would launch an attack to retrieve the garrison town. He sent Shuja to
Kabul with an army. The prince waited there, and when no attack seemed
forthcoming, was recalled back to court. Then, in early 1639, intelligence
reports intimated that Shah Safi was planning an invasion. This time, it was
Dara Shukoh's turn to be dispatched to Kabul. The emperor would join
him later. If need be, Dara would himself lead the army to Qandahar.

Jahanara, who remained with her father, was consoled by her brother's
regular letters. While he marched northwest, he met Sufis, including Shaikh
Daulat Gujrati and a reclusive young ascetic, Hajji Abdullah. As she followed in his path, she, too, met these same holy figures. When she reunited
with Dara in Kabul, they continued their conversations about books and
shaikhs. She sensed her heart growing cold to the world and its seemingly
useless activities. Then she began to feel increasingly unwell: "This was the
time of my youth but I saw the strength of my limbs decline day by day
and was often in pain. I knew that my outward strength was diminishing
hour by hour." Jahanara drew a modicum of comfort from a saying of the
Prophet that enjoined, "Die before dying." This she understood as an injunction to bind the heart more firmly to the divine essence than to finite
existence.[40]

To Jahanara's great relief, the Qandahar expedition was called off. A
famine in Kabul meant that there would not be enough food for the troops.
The imperial family turned back and headed for Lahore. Dara and his sister
continued to read, talk, and write, each putting together an impressive work
requiring considerable research.

In a remarkable coincidence, Dara Shukoh and Jahanara completed their
books on the same day. The siblings both mention the same date for the
composition of their works: the twenty-seventh of Ramazan, 1049, which
corresponds to the twenty-first of January 1640. By then they were in Lahore with their father and would all soon head to Kashmir after the Eid
festivities. The twenty-seventh of Ramazan, we recall, was the Night of
Power and Destiny, a date charged with religious significance. It would be
hard to find a more auspicious day to finish a book. This striking concur-
rence further suggests the close alignment between the siblings' spiritual
quests.

The scope of Jahanara's and Dara's works differed, however. The princess called hers *Munis-ul-arwah* (Confidant of Souls) after, she says, a book
by Muin-ud-Din Chishti with a similar title. This is a shorter work than
Dara's and it focuses on Chishti saints alone. Jahanara first gives a fairly
lengthy biography of Muin-ud-Din Chishti and then provides brief sketches

of five other saints from his order. She frequently quotes sayings and conversations attributed to these Sufi masters. At this point, unlike Dara, she did not have any affiliation with the Qadiris. Her piety was directed toward the Chishti order alone.

Dara Shukoh entitled his book *Safinat-ul-auliya* (The Ship of Saints). Literally, the word *safina* means a ship, but it came also to signify an anthology, often of poetry, for its all-encompassing size, and his title evokes both senses of the word. With over four hundred biographical notices of saints, it has a wider sweep than his sister's book. Like all such tazkiras, the choices that the prince made about whom to incorporate and how to label particular figures reveal that the *Safinat-ul-auliya* is not a merely neutral spread of information. Dara's classification includes four major Sufi orders: the Qadiris, Chishtis, Kubrawis, and Suhrawardis. Dara also has a larger miscellaneous category for those who cannot be categorized by a single order. Further, he lists only three Indian Qadiri saints, including Miyan Mir, in his section on Qadiris, placing other Indian initiates of the order in the miscellaneous section or ignoring them altogether. The prince also entirely leaves out the more somber Naqshbandis from his collection.[41]

At the end of his book, Dara appends biographies of women mystics, beginning with those from the Prophet's own family and ending with Bibi Jamal Khatun, Miyan Mir's sister. This was also relatively standard in tazkiras, but in light of Dara's affinity with his sister, this may have had a special resonance, showing that women, too, could attain this special spiritual state.

Dara Shukoh introduces himself in the *Safinat-ul-auliya* as "Muhammad Dara Shukoh, Hanafi, Qadiri." Hanafi, because he identified as a Sunni rather than a Shia Muslim, and most Sunnis in the subcontinent followed the legal school of the eighth-century jurist Abu Hanifa. Qadiri, because he had come to think of himself as a Sufi in the Qadiri lineage of Miyan Mir. Throughout the work, the prince refers to himself in the third person as "this *faqir*," literally meaning "a poor person," but also denoting a Sufi dervish. Though this kind of self-deprecation was common in Persian prose writing, it was by no means necessary for a prince and certainly reflects his personal choice. The prince writes explicitly in the introduction that he considers himself to be one of the group (*taifa*) of Sufis.[42]

It is very rare indeed to find a copy of one of Dara's books from his lifetime, and rarer still to find one actually written in his own handwriting. The Khuda Bakhsh Library in Patna has what looks like a very early manuscript of the *Safinat-ul-auliya,* with the prince's own annotations and emendations.[43] The British Library in London also holds an autograph copy of *Munis-ul-arwah*, in Jahanara's distinctive, large hand, each page bordered with stylized flowers rendered in gold.[44] Only a handful of manuscripts survive of the *Munis-ul-arwah,* but there are countless copies of the *Safinat-ul-auliya* in Persian collections all over the world. This indicates that Dara's book later circulated far more widely than his sister's. At the time of writing, though, the siblings' main audience seems to have been each other.

While Shah Jahan's eldest two children were absorbed in composing their books, the emperor himself had been engaged in shaping his own kind of literary project by proxy, through his historians. Around the year 1638, he dismissed Qazwini. The chronicler had just completed a mammoth account of the first ten years of Shah Jahan's reign. Rumors floated of the superior literary skills of another scholar, Abd-ul-Hamid Lahori, who had been leading a relatively anonymous life in Patna when he was summoned to Shah Jahan's court. Lahori recalls that the emperor was looking for someone who could emulate the *Akbar-nama,* which Abu-l-Fazl composed for Shah Jahan's grandfather Akbar. He also cites the *Akbar-nama*'s manner of "stringing together heart-pleasing expressions" and the "vividness and freshness" with which it was "embroidered." [45]

It appears, though, that the emperor was looking for more than a skilled wordsmith. Instead of having Lahori pick up from where Qazwini left off, he ordered the scholar to rewrite the first ten years. Moreover, Shah Jahan had recently changed the calendar system used by his court. Qazwini's history relied on the "divine era" solar calendar instituted by Akbar, a system that began at Nauroz, the spring equinox, and had 365 days in the year. This time, Shah Jahan had Lahori use the Islamic hijri calendar, which was lunar and had approximately ten fewer days in each year. The emperor had ordered work on its calculations some years earlier.

What motivated the emperor to make this change? Historians have tended to attribute the new calendar to Shah Jahan's growing religious conservatism.[46] The other changes he enjoined upon Lahori also bolster this view. For instance, Lahori expunges key details in Qazwini's account of the care with which the emperor oversaw the work of his court's visual artists. They still continued to produce magnificent paintings, though.[47] Was Shah Jahan trying to appease the ulama? But this would be too simplistic an explanation. It is hard to gauge precisely the extent of the religious scholars' influence and the nature of their inclinations. We cannot rule out that Shah Jahan, ever in close communication with his eldest son and daughter, was undergoing his own parallel form of pious self-fashioning, just as they were, in a process that also took the form of engaging with Sufi authorities.

On the eighth of February 1640, shortly after completing their books, Dara and Jahanara left Lahore for Kashmir. Their official role there was to accompany the emperor, but they also intended to visit Miyan Mir's successor, Mulla Shah, hoping that he might impart to them some further knowledge. Jahanara, for her part, had of late been troubled by thoughts about her mortality. A spiritual teacher, she thought, would help: "My blessed life, every breath of which is precious and dear, the passing of which cannot be recovered, was wasted in nothingness and fruitlessness. My age was twenty-seven. Perforce, when I turned my attention to the real matter, that is reaching God, I desired to grasp the holy hem of a perfect spiritual master . . ."[48] Her brother appears to have had similar aims.

This time, Dara Shukoh was more forthright in approaching the reclusive Sufi. But the prince left no record of these early encounters with Mulla Shah. Once again, Tawakkul Beg fills in some of these silences. He tells us it was Shah Jahan who met the Sufi first. He reports that the emperor set up camp in the garden of Zafar Khan, governor of Kashmir, whose wife, incidentally, was Mumtaz Mahal's niece. Once ensconced in a pavilion with a view of the Dal Lake, Shah Jahan sent a message to Mulla Shah, saying that he wished to hear the Sufi teacher's discourses on divine truths and gnosis. Mulla Shah retorted, "Day and night you're in the company of people who only understand the external world. You've moved far away from spiritual matters. If you were to hear about these, what effect would they have?" Shah Jahan was undeterred and pressed his case. Mulla Shah relented and came to visit the emperor. There, at Shah Jahan's request, the shaikh explained the subtle distinctions between three Sufi terms, using the analogy of himself and the emperor: Cognitive certainty (*ilm-ul-yaqin*) occurs when Mulla Shah knows that the emperor Shah Jahan exists. Seeing and recognizing the emperor is an example of visual certainty (*ain-ul-yaqin*). Absolute certainty (*haqq-ul-yaqin*) takes place when he is actually in the emperor's presence.[49]

Dara Shukoh and Jahanara did not participate in this conversation, though they might have seen the pir from afar. The prince had a desire to visit Mulla Shah, which intensified late one night while he was still awake praying. He set out impulsively, taking with him a close and trusted servant called Mujahid. The darkness provided a cover for them as they crept into the courtyard of Mulla Shah's house. They could discern the shadowy form of the Sufi pir as he sat in meditation under a chinar tree.[50]

The prince left Mujahid by the entrance and approached Mulla Shah. Tawakkul Beg relates that he stood silently near the pir. For a whole hour, Mulla Shah ignored him. Finally, the pir asked, "Who are you?" though of course he knew full well who his visitor was. The prince gave no reply. "Why don't you speak? Tell me your name!" Mulla Shah asked again.

"My name is Dara Shukoh," the prince responded feebly.

"What is your father's name?" the pir demanded.

Dara answered, "The emperor Shah Jahan."

"Why have you come?" asked Mulla Shah.

"I'm a seeker of God and have come to this threshold for spiritual guidance," replied the prince.

Mulla Shah did not suppress his annoyance any further. "What have I got to do with emperors and princes? I'm an ascetic with no desires. What sort of time is this to come give me a headache and make trouble? Get lost and don't come again!"

Dara Shukoh became despondent and tears flowed from his eyes all night. He took Mujahid and went back the next day, but Mulla Shah completely ignored him. The prince became even more upset and left crestfallen in tears. As they walked back, Mujahid, who was disturbed to see his master in such a state, asked, "What miracles and greatness do you see in this dervish to make you come every night and suffer so much? Dervishes are good-natured and manifestations of mercy. They aren't bad-natured and bad tempered like this one." He spoke this way about Mulla Shah so that the prince's heart would grow cold toward him, explains Tawakkul Beg. Dara Shukoh retorted that if the Sufi were truly a hypocrite, he would not have behaved as he did but would have welcomed him warmly.

That night, Mujahid suddenly fell ill. For some hours, he lay burning with fever. By the time morning came he was already dead. The prince was distraught. This was divine punishment, he felt. He blamed himself for not admonishing his servant more severely when he criticized Mulla Shah. Seeing Dara's pain, Qazi Afzal, a religious scholar of the court, interceded with the help of Mulla Muhammad Said, a disciple of Mulla Shah. "The prince's heart is very delicate," they explained. Mulla Shah softened and gave leave for the prince to come to his home.[51]

Dara Shukoh waited until night to visit the Sufi master. For the prince to go by daylight would attract unnecessary attention. At the door he performed a kornish, the deep obeisance generally made before the emperor, and hesitated. Mulla Shah beckoned him inside the room where he was seated. Dara noticed that the lamp was dying out and he fixed the wick with his own fingers in order to better appreciate the pir's luminous beauty. Impressed, from that moment, Mulla Shah took him on as a disciple. After some days had passed, he initiated the prince with a mystical vision. He first asked Dara to blindfold his eyes. Then he concentrated intensely upon the young prince, channeling his divine grace to him. That exhilarating infusion of the pir's charisma revealed to Dara Shukoh the world of angels, otherwise invisible to humankind.[52]

Dara confided in his sister about these mystical experiences, though we do not know if he shared the story of his initial rebuff as told by Tawakkul Beg. Jahanara had acquired a great devotion to Mulla Shah, however she had not met him. Presenting a gift to the reclusive Sufi would be inappropriate, so she cooked some green leafy vegetables herself, which she sent along with bread and a note. For a month, Jahanara received no reply, though she heard secondhand that Mulla Shah had muttered his usual line about not having any dealings with worldly people and royalty. She persisted, sending him more letters. Dara Shukoh, too, made sure to speak highly of her. Eventually, Mulla Shah began to reply to the princess. He would advise her, through their correspondence, about specific prayers and spiritual exercises to perform.[53]

Imperial women did not, as a rule, meet unrelated men face to face, so Jahanara continued her relationship with her teacher without ever stepping out of her seclusion. She had caught a glimpse of him, probably through a curtain or latticed window, while he conversed with Shah Jahan. For now, she was content with a portrait of Mulla Shah that Dara Shukoh gave her, painted by a master artist. She committed his features to memory so that, even with eyes closed, she could visualize him.

Over the coming years, Dara Shukoh, and presumably Jahanara as well, worked with artists to produce several portraits of Mulla Shah and Miyan Mir. In many of these portraits, Dara is featured along with them. There is one surviving image, now in Tehran's Gulistan Palace, that the prince might well have had made to commemorate his initiation as Mulla Shah's disciple. Here, Dara kneels before his master, holding an unrolled scroll. Behind him stands a young courtier. The Sufi pir raises his hand, index finger stretched, while making a point, an open book or scripture before him. Another disciple sits farther away. The trio are seated on a mat outside a modest hut. Steps lead up a mound to the dwelling, and at their foot Dara's groom sits by his waiting horse. Many of the compositional elements in this image resemble the painting of Jahangir's visit to Chidrup—the riderless horse, the hut standing in for the cave, the distant city. Here, though, Dara is not a haloed emperor indulging his inquisitiveness, but a humble disciple.

A handful of single portraits of Mulla Shah are still extant. Does the portrait that Dara gave to Jahanara survive among these? We cannot be certain, though there are some possible candidates. In one painting, Mulla Shah is standing, shown in profile.[54] His right hand holds a rosary, and with his left he holds a volume bound in crimson and gold—the Quran, perhaps, or his own collected poetry. His pose and the green background popular in Mughal portraiture evoke a common style of depicting Mughal royals and nobility. In another portrait, the seated shaikh, clad in bright yellow, leans lightly against a mauve bolster, his hands clasped around his knees.[55] A golden nimbus frames his face. His snowy beard betrays his age, as does the green ascetic's sash that he uses to support his posture.[56] The accoutrements

Portrait of Mulla Shah.

of his devotional work are strewn beside him: his armrest, rosary, books, pen case, and even a white kerchief, which in Mughal art is often associated with royalty. This image certainly reflects the special relationship between the shaikh and his imperial disciples. But in 1640, Mulla Shah would have been younger. In a third portrait, there is still some black in his beard. He sits here, too, gazing into the distance. A book and armrest are tossed nearby. The shaikh's features are rendered in exquisite detail, but the background is only partially sketched out. Was it such a painting that Dara Shukoh commissioned for his sister during their trip to Kashmir?

None of these surviving portraits give any concrete indication that they were in Jahanara's possession. The princess's autobiography does tell us, though, how these portraits might have been used. After studying her image of Mulla Shah "with the gaze of sincerity and eye of belief," she readied herself to perform a special spiritual exercise, for which her pir had coached her via her brother. On the appointed day, she rose early and bathed. All day long she abstained from food, breaking her fast in the evening with some quince that Mulla Shah had sent. Then she supped on a frugal meal cooked in the house of the Qadiri Sufi Mulla Muhammad Said. After praying until midnight in her private mosque, she retired to her room. There she sat facing the direction of Mecca and concentrated on the portrait of Mulla Shah. A doubt flickered in her mind. Was she being disloyal to the Chishti order by accepting the guidance of Mulla Shah, a Qadiri? Then, suddenly, a state came upon her of neither sleep nor wakefulness. Here she saw the Prophet Muhammad, surrounded by his companions and saints. Mulla Shah was among them. He reverentially placed his head on the Prophet's feet. "You have lighted the lamp of the Timurids," said Prophet Muhammad to him. This vision not only dispelled Jahanara's doubt, it confirmed to her that she and her brother, the only ones among Timur's descendants to join the Qadiri order, had a unique spiritual role to play.[57]

At the end of her six-month sojourn in Kashmir, Jahanara made a special request of Mulla Shah. They had been corresponding repeatedly, but before she left for Lahore she wanted to see him in person. He rode his horse up to an elevated area by her path, dismounted, and sat under a mulberry tree with a red blanket thrown over him. She paused her elephant and gazed at him for a while from her howdah before resuming her journey. He never saw her directly; that would have been a severe violation of propriety. Jahanara, however, was overcome. "My eyes were blinded and out of intense longing (*shauq*) the hair on my body trembled," she wrote. It is perhaps this incident that the princess commissioned to be memorialized in a painting. In a seventeenth-century portrait, her pir sits beneath a

مولوی روم

Portrait of Mulla Shah.

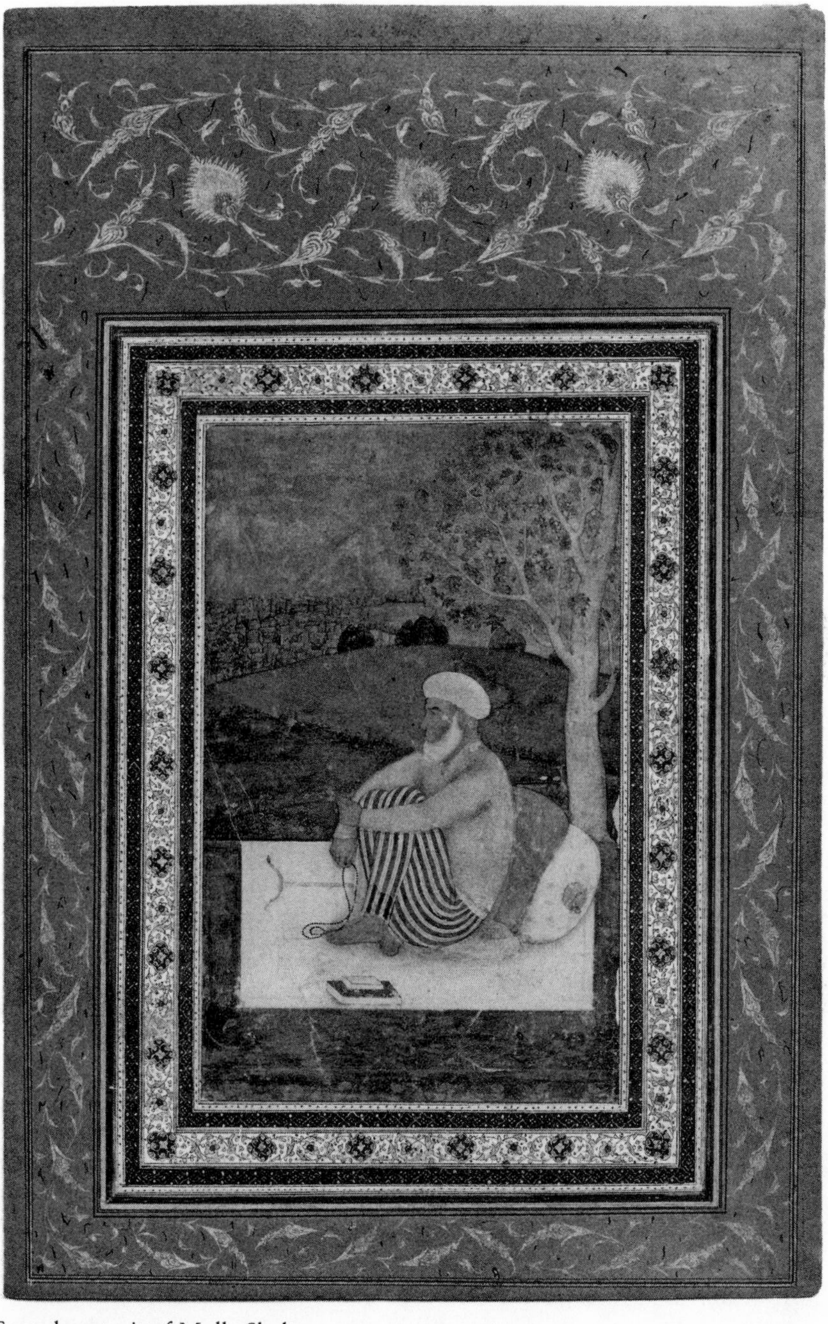

Seated portrait of Mulla Shah.

tree, his scarlet shawl having slipped off his shoulders onto the bolster behind him.[58]

DURING HIS REMAINING TIME IN KASHMIR, Dara Shukoh threw himself fully into learning from Mulla Shah as much as he could. One day, Mulla Shah asked the prince to choose if he wanted to learn Miyan Mir's spiritual exercises, or his own. He explained that Miyan Mir's method involved plenty of hardship and would necessitate abandoning the world. On the other hand, he had devised a vastly simplified practice, one that even Miyan Mir had endorsed. Dara requested that Mulla Shah impart to him these accelerated techniques of spiritual practice.[59]

In the prince's later recollections, he credits divine providence as well as Mulla Shah's ingenuity for his swift progress. It was God, Dara Shukoh believed, who "brought me to the intimacy of friendship with his own friend." Regarding his teacher, the prince recalled, "this dear one showed me such kindness, so that that which a person would achieve under him in a month, I achieved in a day, and that which a person would achieve in a year, became possible for me in a month."[60]

Mulla Shah had arrived full circle from his earlier hard-hearted rejection of the prince. A prolific poet, especially since Miyan Mir's death, he now composed poetry especially for his royal disciple. In one poem, he invokes a motif that Sufi poets often use, contrasting the ruling sovereign with the true ruler: "The world ruler of the body's globe isn't an emperor / The world ruler is he who rules the heart // What is comparable to the first and second Lords of the Conjunction? / Our Dara Shukoh has become the heart's Lord of the Conjunction."[61] Mulla Shah provocatively compares Dara with the prince's Central Asian ancestor Timur, known as "Lord of the Conjunction," as well as his father Shah Jahan. This Sufi, who outwardly had once prided himself on his independence from worldly concerns, now came to write much like a court poet would for his patron.

When the time came for Dara Shukoh to leave Kashmir, the prince paid one last visit to his pir. Mulla Shah arranged an occasion to ensure that the prince would remain involved with the Qadiri order. The Sufi teacher had invited several prominent people from the order to be present, and he introduced them to Dara one by one, praising their spiritual prowess and loyalty. Mulla Shah then gave a discourse on divine truth and gnosis. As the prince took his leave, the pir presented him with a letter that said, "Please guide my friends [namely, the disciples of the path], as your intellect is greater than that of the rest. I would be happy if you could guide them. If one of my faqirs crosses the limits of appropriate speech, please admonish and restrain him."[62] Even though Mulla Shah had known the prince for only a few months, he was effectively giving Dara Shukoh authority over the other members of the order. Once entrusted with this responsibility, the prince's ties to the Kashmir-based Qadiris would only deepen.

As Dara bade farewell to Mulla Shah, he requested two favors of his pir. One was that he recite the fatiha to ensure that Dara would eventually depart from the world in a state of true faith. The prince may have believed that he would soon be called up for a military assignment. Mulla Shah acquiesced after admonishing the prince that the end of life for a Sufi was perforce devoid of sorrow and separation from the divine. The second request was that his master point out his faults and shortcomings. At the same time, the prince wanted him to disregard anyone who, perhaps jealous that Mulla Shah favored Dara, might allege that the prince had sought the company of other spiritual teachers as well. Mulla Shah reassured him, saying, "I am completely satisfied with you. . . . From the day that you came before me, every step that you have taken has been on the path of propriety, and in agreement with my wishes; nobody else has set forth on the path who has adhered to my wishes with such solicitude."[63]

Through their correspondence, the sibling's relationship with Mulla Shah thrived after they left Kashmir. The prince includes eleven more of his mentor's letters in the *Sakinat-ul-auliya*. Mulla Shah starts each letter with the invocation, "May the good fortune of the divine vision be your lot." His tone is warm and intimate, addressing Dara as a friend or spiritual companion rather than a junior disciple. He refers to the prince as, "You who are initiated into the divine mysteries," mentioning in another letter, "I repose great confidence in your sagacity and farsightedness," addressing him again as "my sincere friend whose equanimity of mind and love for truth is established."[64] In yet another missive, he calls Dara "emperor of the external and internal realms."[65]

Dara Shukoh also quotes two letters that Mulla Shah wrote his sister, Jahanara. In one, the Sufi praises the prince, saying, "whatever [divine knowledge] you acquire from your brother, God has given him. He is a credit to all the great personages, past and present." Though there was a precedent for women mystics in this Qadiri lineage, here Mulla Shah implicitly encourages Jahanara to defer to her younger brother's spiritual authority.[66]

Shah Jahan and his family remained in Lahore for a while after the trip to Kashmir. Jahanara and Dara, fresh from the heady spiritual heights that they had recently achieved, continued their journeys of mystical perfection. Jahanara began to write a slender autobiographical book about her Sufi inclinations and her recent encounters with Mulla Shah. This, too, like her *Munis-ul-arwah,* she completed on the auspicious twenty-seventh day of Ramazan, the Night of Power and Destiny. She entitled it *Risala-i sahibiya* (Epistle of Companionship).[67]

We know that Dara Shukoh wrote mystical poetry, and though we do not have exact dates for his poems, it is likely that he composed many of these in the first flush of his devotion to the Qadiri order. His form of choice was the ghazal rather than the longer, narrative masnawi that Mulla Shah favored. Eventually he would write enough verse to compile a concise diwan of poetry. His poetic pen name, which he uses in the final couplet of each poem, is simply "Qadiri."

The ghazal, in the hands of several of its masters, such as the thirteenth-century Indian poet Amir Khusrau or the sixteenth-century Iranian poet Urfi, often blurs the boundaries between earthly and spiritual love. Dara's poems, in contrast, are univocally infused with devotion to God and to the saints of the Qadiri order. His couplets share a thematic unity whereas the ghazals of other poets often string together disparate verses like "pearls on a thread."

In one poem, Dara equates Lahore, the residence of the late Miyan Mir, to the holy Kaaba of Mecca. Here he vividly expresses his desire to go to Miyan Mir's mausoleum at Darapur, of the way a lover seeks to visit his beloved:

> My passionate desire for Punjab has no respite,
> For the imprint of the Friend is in Punjab.
> When I step into his city on foot,
> Out of respect I fashion my foot out of my head.
> * * *
> Until I circumambulate my own pir,
> My turbulent soul is like quicksilver.
> For this Qadiri, [the tomb at] Darapur has become his Kaaba,
> For in it there is much to be revealed.[68]

Dara takes up the Kaaba motif again in another ghazal praising Mulla Shah:

> As my Lord and master is the pir,
> My Kaaba is the blessed Kashmir.
> Whoever has seen the Shah has not sought the Kaaba,
> This is the effect of gazing at his countenance.
> O Kaaba-goer, grasp the Shah's hem!
> Since you are the Kaaba's hem-grasper.[69]

The prince not only equates Mulla Shah's residence of Kashmir with the Kaaba, but also likens it to the saint's countenance itself. Mulla Shah is a

Kaaba to rival the Meccan sanctuary, and is himself a destination for pilgrims. Dara's repeated mentions of his pir as the *shah* have the double effect of not only referencing the Sufi teacher's name, Mulla Shah, but also imbuing him with imperial attributes.

The prince and his pir had been corresponding for a while, when, early in 1642, a sudden and new responsibility caused Dara to seek Mulla Shah's blessings and guidance. The emperor's intelligence agents reported that the young Safavid ruler, Shah Safi, harbored designs on regaining the fortress city of Qandahar. Shah Safi had sent his commander Rustam Khan to wait nearby in Nishapur, a city in the Iranian kingdom's eastern province of Khurasan. Quick action was needed to preempt the Safavid Shah. Shuja was occupied in distant Bengal where he was governor, while Aurangzeb administered the Deccan. This left Dara Shukoh as the obvious choice to lead the campaign.[70]

The twenty-seven-year-old prince had not yet had a chance to fight on the battlefield, having been recalled early from his previous expedition to Qandahar. He was no doubt waiting to prove himself by carrying out such an important assignment. He turned to his pir for guidance. In response, Mulla Shah wrote part of a Quranic verse in the header of his letter to Dara: "You threw not, when you threw, but God threw."[71]

Dara Shukoh would have immediately grasped the context and intent of this excerpt from the divine revelation. The interpretive tradition associated with the Quran views this verse as originally addressed to the Prophet Muhammad during the battle of Badr against the Meccan infidels who persecuted the early followers of the Prophet. One popular classical commentary in Arabic explains: "O Muhammad, you did not strike the group of [infidels] when you threw stones, rather it was God who did so by making the stones reach them."[72] Dara Shukoh, as a true seeker of God, should not fear, his teacher tells him, because ultimately it is the divine who will act. But this is not all, for a wujudi-inflected interpretation of the verse goes a level further. Mulla Shah elaborates in another letter to Dara that the words "You threw not" signify our unity with the divine. Indeed, he says, there is not a single particle in all of existence that is independent of God.[73]

Shah Jahan made sure that his eldest son would be well prepared to take on the Iranians. He sent Dara Shukoh with an army of fifty thousand horsemen and forty high-ranking chiefs. Among these officers were the Rajputs Raja Jai Singh and Raja Jaswant Singh. The emperor also ordered Ali Mardan Khan, the former Safavid governor of the city now stationed in Kabul, to assist Dara as best as he could. He sent Murad Bakhsh to wait at the banks of the Indus in case his support was needed. Dara took leave of the emperor at Lahore in a ceremony during which his father gave him several gifts, including a valuable turban ornament, his own string of pearls and rubies, and several bejeweled weapons.[74]

As soon as Dara Shukoh crossed the Indus River, in May 1642, he received word that the Safavid emperor had died. In Lahori's words, Shah Safi, "drunk on the wine of ignorance and intoxicated by the dreams of youth . . . filled up the measure of his life in Kashan."[75] He was not yet thirty-two. This was divine intervention, Dara Shukoh felt, aided by Mulla Shah's intercession. He would write, recalling Mulla Shah's recent letter to him, "God, the glorious and exalted, that very month dealt the ruler of Iran such a blow that he could not rise up. The people killed him by giving him poison."[76] The prince's attribution of the cause of Shah Safi's death contradicts the official Safavid accounts. Indeed the Persian ruler's well-known affinity for both opium and wine may have contributed to his untimely demise.[77]

Dara Shukoh informed his father of Shah Safi's death, but Shah Jahan wanted the news doubly confirmed. He instructed Dara to dispatch the officers Khan-i Dauran and Said Khan with a contingent of thirty thousand to Qandahar. Meanwhile, Dara Shukoh was to wait at Ghazni. After the initial news was corroborated, Dara hastened to Lahore.[78]

The prince may have had mixed feelings about Shah Safi's untimely death. On the one hand, it was a welcome miracle, ridding the empire of a hostile neighbor. The Shah's successor, his son Abbas, was still a young child, and it would be some time before he would become a serious threat. But this time, again, Dara had been deprived of the chance to achieve glory on the battlefield. He was the only one of his brothers not to have fought in a military expedition.

Upon his arrival in Lahore on September 10, 1642, he was greeted by high-ranking nobles such as Islam Khan, who brought him to pay his respects to the emperor with an offering of a thousand gold coins. Shah Jahan, pleased at the elimination of his Iranian rival, rewarded Dara Shukoh by conferring on him the same title that his own father, Jahangir, had earlier given him, "Shahzada-yi Buland Iqbal" (Prince of Lofty Fortune).[79] The title stamped a seal on what the emperor had already made clear: Dara Shukoh was his favored heir. Henceforth, all those addressing the prince and writing about him were ordered to use it.

Once back at court, Dara Shukoh returned to his studies and his writing on spiritual perfection. He continued working on a new book that he had been composing, a sequel of sorts to his *Safinat ul-auliya*. This was a tribute to his Sufi masters, Miyan Mir and Mulla Shah, and to the Qadiri order, interspersed with his own spiritual autobiography. He had already started to pen accounts of his time with Miyan Mir, the aged Sufi's disciples, and his sister, Bibi Jamal Khatun. During and after his time in Kashmir, he may well have written about Mulla Shah and his companions. Now, sometime during the Hijri year 1052, between April 1642 and March 1643, he completed a collection that he entitled *Sakinat-ul-auliya* (The Tranquility of Saints).

This work is more than a mere collection of admiring anecdotes compiled by a faithful disciple about his teachers. We also cannot dismiss it as the journal of a naive young prince's spiritual experimentation either. There is a deliberately crafted set of arguments running throughout the *Sakinat-ul-auliya*. The collection is a multilayered religious manifesto. Its opening lines introduce the premise that Dara Shukoh has been uniquely and divinely endowed with the capacity to attain great spiritual heights. Here, Dara refers to his early wish to join a group of Sufis and relates God's promise to him of a gift that no emperor had ever received before:

> The faqir without a care, Muhammad Dara Shukoh, says: Because I had always desired of the omnipotent emperor and the master of unity that he should put me among his friends and lovers ... and that my heart be attached to a group of dervishes ... God the most high ... deigned to answer the petition of this helpless one. On a Thursday of my twenty-fifth year, I was asleep when a hidden voice called out and repeated four times, "That which had not been possible for any emperor on earth, God the most high has given to you." After awakening, I said to myself that such felicity must of course be gnosis. Indeed, God the most high would give this good fortune to me ... for his best gift is the gift of his love which has no equal and no price, and is hard-won and rare. This blessing is tied to his endless favor and mercy.

Emperors, implies Dara Shukoh, were generally dilettantes when it comes to spiritual matters. By comparing himself to past sovereigns, the prince is already coming to think of himself as a ruler. And only he, Dara Shukoh, blessed with divine grace, can resolve the opposition between dervish and ruler. He separates himself from Mughal nobility and the scholarly class by disavowing any connection with the *ahl-i zahir*, "literalists" or "exotericists," a label that Sufis use for people concerned with only the external elements of religious practice, who fail to cultivate its interior aspects. The prince writes that he was transformed by Mulla Shah's instruction, "Now, even though I appear to be of the exotericists, I am not one of them, and I know their ignorance and wretchedness. And even though I am removed from the dervishes, I am one of them."[80]

Dara Shukoh further establishes his religious credentials by quoting the Persian mystic Hujwiri, who said, "A man is not worldly by virtue of the abundance of possessions and is not a dervish by their scarcity." The prince explains Hujwiri's statement in the following way: "He who holds poverty to be superior, does not become worldly by virtue of his wealth, even if it is proprietary. He who rejects poverty is worldly, even if he is in distressed means. . . . He who is named by God 'faqir,' is poor though he may be wealthy. He is doomed who thinks he is not a prisoner, though his position may be a throne."[81]

While Dara uses Hujwiri's statement to establish that, for him, there is no contradiction in remaining a prince while pursuing his spiritual agenda, he does not believe that this applies to other royals as well. The underlying theme of the *Sakinat-ul-auliya* is that Dara alone, among all the other Mughal dynasts, possesses the characteristics of a true spiritual master and has been divinely chosen to play an important role through his ties with the Qadiri order.

Dara contrasts the warm welcome he received from the Qadiris with the experience of the late emperor Jahangir, who had also approached Miyan Mir. He does not hide his dislike of his grandfather. The months he spent in his childhood as a hostage of Nur Jahan and Jahangir must have been deeply etched in his memory. In this regard, his assessment of his grandfather in the *Sakina* is quite telling:

> The Emperor Jahangir did not believe in saints and dervishes, and would inflict torments on this group, and exhibit bad behavior. Despite this, he sent one from among his close circle to the service of *Hazrat* Miyan Jio, and invited him to his own residence, saying apologetically, "Had I heard of you when I was in Lahore, I would have gone to be at your service. But because I departed from the city at an opportune time, I cannot come again. You come to see me, please."[82]

Jahangir, as we remember, had imprisoned Shaikh Ahmad Sirhindi, the Naqshbandi Sufi, who wrote prolific missives that were sometimes critical of the Mughal state. Even Abd-ul-Haqq did not escape the emperor's ire.[83] Dara Shukoh must have been referring to these instances when he mentions his grandfather's repressive measures against Sufis.

Would Dara, a Qadiri, have sympathy for Sufis from rival lineages? Many modern writers treat Sirhindi as a bastion of Islamic orthodoxy, in contrast to the religious figures associated with Dara.[84] But such polarized divisions between mystical piety and orthodox authority did not operate in the same way during the seventeenth century: though a devout jurist, Sirhindi was importantly also an initiate of both the Naqshbandi and Qadiri orders. The *Safinat-ul-auliya* even mentions a meeting between Miyan Mir and Sirhindi. Dara represents the latter in a positive light, as someone capable of producing miracles.[85]

According to Dara, Miyan Mir agreed to visit Jahangir. The emperor became greatly affected. He even offered to abandon his empire and all his wealth if the Sufi pir so wished. Miyan Mir retorted, "The true Sufi is he for whom rocks and jewels are the same. Whenever you say 'In my view, a rock and a jewel are equal,' then you are also a Sufi." When the emperor pleaded with him, Miyan Mir relented, saying that Jahangir could appoint a substitute to supervise the kingdom and that he would train the emperor in spiritual matters. Pleased by these words, the emperor asked, "Do you wish for anything from me?" Miyan Mir responded, "Will you give me what I seek?" He replied, "Of course I'll give it to you." The Sufi said, "I ask for just this, that you give me leave to go." The emperor was then forced to allow him to depart.[86]

By demonstrating the reverence that Dara's own forebears had had for Miyan Mir, this anecdote elevates the Sufi as a great spiritual figure worthy of respect, and underscores his charisma and independence. Here, as in the earlier story where Miyan Mir rebukes Shah Jahan, the former comes across as a stronger spiritual force, one who was not afraid of emperors.

But Dara's anecdote is not a mere fabrication. Jahangir's meeting with the holy man was important enough for him to include in his memoirs. After hearing of the the Sufi's piety and freedom from need of the world, wrote Jahangir, his desire to meet him increased and he invited Miyan Mir to the court. His ill health notwithstanding, the Sufi complied and went to visit the emperor. Jahangir recalls their meeting as follows: "He is a truly noble person, a rarity in this age. I went out of my way to sit with him, and from him I heard many lofty words on mysticism. Although I wanted to offer him a token of my esteem, since I found him too high-minded for such a thing, I couldn't do it. I offered him a white antelope skin for a prayer mat. Immediately thereafter he bade me farewell and returned to Lahore."[87]

Though Jahangir's account of their meeting does not entirely contradict Dara's, it offers a different perspective on the encounter. The ailing Sufi cannot afford to ignore the ruler's invitation; when he visits him, the emperor is impressed by his erudition, reticence, and modesty.

But for Dara Shukoh, these anecdotes about his forebears meeting Miyan Mir served a function beyond eulogizing his teacher. They underscore that Dara, unlike his father and grandfather, has been able to successfully integrate himself into a community of the spiritual elect. He is a unique royal for whom there is no contradiction in also being a Sufi adept.

5

THE CHOSEN

1642–1652

M ORE THAN THREE YEARS would pass before Dara Shukoh and Jahanara returned to Kashmir. The siblings remained by their father's
side, as usual. For much of this period, they were based in Agra, where their
mother's splendid mausoleum was nearing completion.[1] In the autumn of
1643, Shah Jahan made another pilgrimage to the tomb of the revered Chishti saint, Khwaja Muin-ud-Din, at Ajmer. There, in a very public display
of devotion, he asked that food prepared for the devotees be cooked with
the meat of *nilgai* (antelope) that he himself had hunted.[2] Dara and Jahanara, who almost always also traveled with their father, would have
taken part in this trip. Jahanara, of course, was a long-term devotee of the
Chishtis. For Dara, too, there would have been merit in paying homage at
the shrine even though his recent writings elevated the Qadiris above all
other orders.

Meanwhile, the links between Mulla Shah's Qadiri order in Kashmir and
the court were unbroken, even strengthened. As we learn from Tawakkul
Beg, several imperial servants joined Mulla Shah's community of Sufis, some
actually withdrawing from imperial service. One Muhammad Shafi, the son
of Qazi Afzal, a religious scholar and jurist at the court, became Mulla
Shah's disciple after taking leave of Dara and Jahanara at Akbarabad.[3] A
servant of Dara's younger brother, Shuja, governor of Bengal, received permission to enter Mulla Shah's order.[4] (Tawakkul Beg may have had a hand
in this, as he had earlier served under Shuja.) The nobleman Mutaqid Khan,

son of the "house-born" courtier, Najabat Khan, also visited Kashmir to receive Mulla Shah's initiation.[5]

Mulla Shah even interceded with Dara on behalf of the religious scholar Mulla Juki Kabuli. The *Nuskha* describes Mulla Juki as an outstanding man of learning, with complete mastery of the rational sciences. Dara Shukoh became upset with him over an unspecified fault. Mulla Juki took leave of the emperor and went to Mulla Shah. The Sufi shaikh consoled him. He let Mulla Juki participate in his mystical gatherings and imparted to him the "mysteries of self-knowledge," which, Tawakkul Beg explains, was the same as "knowledge of the eternal."[6] After a year had passed, Mulla Shah wrote Dara, interceding on Mulla Juki's behalf. The prince replied warmly, expressing appreciation that Mulla Juki had attained the felicity of being with Mulla Shah. He inscribed the letter in his own hand, a gesture expressing high regard for his spiritual master. Dara Shukoh also wrote separately to Mulla Juki, declaring that, for his part, he had cleared away the "dust of resentment."[7] Though Mulla Juki would have been considered one of the ulama, it was perfectly normal at the time for him to associate with Sufis.

This movement of people back and forth, between the centers of power and Mulla Shah's order in Kashmir, reflects the pir's growing influence at court. Previous Mughal emperors, especially Akbar and Jahangir, co-opted the charismatic authority of sufis.[8] Much as a Sufi pir would, they initiated a special set of courtiers as their disciples. In this case, select members of the court became Mulla Shah's disciples, instead of Shah Jahan's. Moreover, it was common for leading Sufis to style themselves as alternative rulers—emperors of the spiritual realm. Mulla Shah also had a court, albeit without all the trappings of pomp and glory that earthly emperors possessed. In his case, now, the rival "court" of the Sufi merged into an extension of the imperial court.

Tawakkul Beg's account suggests that in addition to Dara and Jahanara, the emperor was a driving force in fostering close relations with Mulla Shah. For instance, one of Shah Jahan's own servants, Marhamat Khan, had previously been a disciple of Mulla Shah.[9] Similarly, during this time, Tawakkul Beg came from Kashmir, at Mulla Shah's behest, to work in Dara Shukoh's retinue.[10] Imperial servants, especially those who had inherited their positions from a family member, were considered part of the emperor's household and enjoyed a special status.[11] Here, with some leaving the court to join Mulla Shah's household, and others coming from Mulla Shah's service to that of the emperor, the retinue of the imperial family began to overlap with the Sufi's household. This fostered a unique kind of intimacy between the two. It would be hard to imagine anyone else with whom the emperor could be so familiar that their households shared this mutual permeability.

BY EARLY APRIL 1644, it was warm in Agra, though summer's most scorching heat loomed ahead. The emperor's family had not yet left for their next trip to the Himalayas. "During these days," says Lahori, "when the clouds sowed imperial favors, and the hopes of mortals sprung lush and green, all of a sudden, treacherous fortune and the crooked heavens brought forth despicable dispositions, and unlikeable characteristics. The world's happiness mingled with sorrow."[12]

Jahanara had suffered a terrible accident. The princess was walking to her bedchamber at night when her robes brushed against a burning lamp. Her clothes, made from the lightest muslin, were drenched with the oils of flower, especially the "Jahangiri" perfume that her great-aunt Nur Jahan had concocted. This made them fragrant as well as highly flammable. The flame licked her hem and then immediately swallowed her up. Four of Jahanara's nearby attendants rushed to help, but the fire engulfed them as well. The princess barely survived. Her torso and hands were horribly charred. A week later, two of her attendants died.[13]

Another version of this story eventually reached Mulla Shah. Tawakkul Beg reports that the garments of a dancing girl employed in Jahanara's quarters burst into flame during a performance. Her clothes, "in the manner of the Indian fairy-born," were doused with perfume oil. When the princess went to rescue her, their clothing touched. Jahanara immediately caught fire and fell unconscious. The emperor shed tears of blood on seeing her condition. He abandoned all affairs of the state to tend to his daughter.[14]

Jahanara's recovery was far from smooth. Shah Jahan gave away enormous sums of money in charitable donations, in the hope of a divine cure. Eminent physicians sought to heal her, including Hakim Daud, a Safavid court physician who had migrated from Iran.[15] After five months her wounds started to fester again. Eventually a servant in the imperial household named Arif prepared an ointment that gave her some relief.[16] At the end of July, Shah Jahan suggested that she move temporarily to Dara Shukoh's waterfront mansion for a change of scene. In an unusual step, the emperor, who could not bear separation from his daughter, himself stayed for a couple of weeks in his son's residence, which Dara had completed building only the previous year.[17]

Tawakkul Beg suggests that Mulla Shah had a hand in Jahanara's recovery. Marhamat Khan, Shah Jahan's servant with Qadiri ties, had written Mulla Shah informing him of the accident. The shaikh's reply arrived, and Marhamat Khan shared it with the emperor. "God has two attributes," Mulla Shah writes, "beauty (*jamal*) and majesty (*jalal*)." At times the Almighty displays one; at times the other. He prays that in Jahanara's case, this divine majesty would be transformed into divine beauty.[18]

Upon reading the letter, Shah Jahan took it up to Jahanara's apartments. She felt rejuvenated after merely listening to it read aloud. After this, says Tawakkul Beg, God granted her the strength to read and write.[19] Jahanara might have written to Mulla Shah, for she then received a personal letter from him. "May you have the fortune of the divine vision," he begins, asking that God grant her a speedy recovery. He speaks of the "heart's sickness," which he explains as "distance from the divine." He prayed that Jahanara's own physical affliction be transformed into *suhbat*, an intimate nearness to the divine. After receiving this letter, Jahanara regained complete health, according to the *Nuskha*. Marhamat Khan sent Mulla Shah a message from the emperor to the effect that the princess's health had turned around.[20]

But this story finds no mention in the official chronicles. Shah Jahan's historian, Lahori, makes not a single reference to Mulla Shah's contact with the imperial family during this time. Of course, as Mulla Shah's disciple, Tawakkul Beg had a vested interest in extolling his pir. His report of the princess's miraculous healing should be read with this in mind.

Nonetheless, if we take at face value the fact of letters being exchanged and the interpenetration of Mulla Shah's circle with the royal servants, fissures appear in the personas that Dara Shukoh and Shah Jahan created for themselves. Dara's writings thus far show him to be the ideal Qadiri disciple. Based on these, one would imagine that of the three—Shah Jahan, Dara, and Jahanara—it was Dara Shukoh who was most attached to the Kashmir Qadiris. Shah Jahan's glittering self-presentation in the paintings and histories he commissioned does little to show his devotion to Sufis or other holy men. But this Qadiri chronicle of Tawakkul Beg opens a door onto the Mughal sovereign's domestic sphere. Here we glimpse imperial servants who might otherwise have no mention in histories, the princess and emperor in her private quarters, and Mulla Shah acting very much as an advisor and guide to the emperor along with his two eldest children.

While Jahanara recovered bit by bit, Shah Jahan and Dara Shukoh faced another series of anxieties. Aurangzeb, who had been away serving in the Deccan, sped north to visit his sister upon hearing the news of her illness. He arrived with impressive alacrity in May, bringing with him his eldest son, Muhammad Sultan, who had not yet met his grandfather. But within a month, the emperor had stripped him of his official rank and governorship of the Deccan. This was an act almost equivalent to disowning him.

What had caused such a sudden change in Aurangzeb's relationship with his father? The official sources are deliberately vague. Lahori lays the blame on Aurangzeb and the bad company the prince fell in with: "Owing to the company of some rotten-minded ignoramuses and short-sighted fools, Prince Aurangzeb Bahadur decided to withdraw his hand from matters of state and retire from the world."[21] The prince had "determined, without any apparent cause, to resign from worldly occupations and lead a secluded life," Inayat Khan explains in his later abridged history.[22]

Aurangzeb's purported desire to become an ascetic recluse was of a completely different order from Dara Shukoh's own journey on his spiritual path. His threat to withdraw from the world and evade his own princely duties hinted at a deeply held resentment, one strong enough to make him stand up to his father. Shah Jahan construed it as open disobedience. We can only infer the layers to this story that the bland euphemisms of chroniclers conceal. Whatever role Dara Shukoh played in all of this remains unmentioned in Shah Jahan's official histories. Regardless, the extended spell in Agra during long months of disgrace would have weighed heavily on Aurangzeb. Bereft of his position and much of his household in Burhanpur, Aurangzeb surely seethed at Dara's comfortable status in the court.

Jahanara took on the role of Aurangzeb's confidante and consoler. From her own sickbed, she sought to assuage her father's anger at his third son. Eventually, in February 1645, a mellowed Shah Jahan reinstated Aurangzeb's rank and assigned him the jagir of Gujarat, where he would serve as governor.[23]

By the following year, 1645, Jahanara had recovered enough for a journey to Kashmir to be deemed safe. She would accompany her father, Dara Shukoh, and Murad Bakhsh, together with their mammoth entourage. Dara Shukoh's immediate family was joined by an infant son, three-and-a-half-month-old Sipihr Shukoh.[24] The imperial family decided first to visit Ajmer, to honor a vow that the emperor had made while Jahanara was ill, that he would go on pilgrimage there when she recovered. But they were quickly forced to put the Ajmer trip on hold when the strain of the journey caused Jahanara's wounds to fester again. This time, in Mathura, a mute mendicant named Hamun prepared a healing poultice, which helped her greatly. After a rest in Delhi, they proceeded slowly to Kashmir, arriving at the end of April.[25]

By this point, Aurangzeb had parted from the imperial family to take up the governorship of Gujarat. He approached his new role zealously. One of his most memorable acts, soon after he took charge, was to desecrate a temple built by the Jain merchant Shantidas and his brother in Saraspur, outside Ahmedabad. The temple was dedicated to Parshvanath, the twenty-third *tirthankara*, one of the ancient teachers, or "makers of fords," of the Jains who taught how to transcend the cycle of birth and death. A German adventurer, Johann Albrecht von Mandelslo (d. 1644), visited it a few years earlier in 1638, describing it in great detail. Two elephants hewn from black marble guarded the temple's entrance; on one of them sat a statue of the patron Shantidas himself. Inside, rows of alcoves framed a courtyard, each with a statue in black or white marble, which von Mandelslo mistook for sculptures of naked women seated cross-legged, but which were far more likely to have been representations of tirthankaras.[26]

The French traveler Jean de Thévenot (d. 1667), writing over two decades later, recounted that Aurangzeb, "who has always professed an affected devotion," had a cow killed in the temple. This was in order to defile it so that no worship of the "Gentiles" could take place. The prince then had the noses of all the statues lopped off, and converted the temple to a mosque.[27] The structure, though, was still intact for Thévenot to see—replete with figures of men, animals, and naked women "seated in the oriental manner." Judging from this account, most of the damage seems to have been confined to defacing the statues.

Aurangzeb's action was evidently taken independently of his father. It served to assert his authority in a new territory. The prince mirrored, on a small scale, his father's attack on Benares temples early in his reign. But Shah Jahan and Dara Shukoh had earlier gone out of their way to protect Shantidas's business interests.[28] By desecrating Shantidas's temple, Aurangzeb also struck a blow at his father and eldest brother.

Meanwhile, once in Kashmir, Shah Jahan and his two eldest children once again enjoyed the company of Mulla Shah. Dara Shukoh's writings do not record this trip in detail, though Tawakkul Beg, who was in the prince's entourage, filters into his chronicle events that he considers significant. Soon after arriving in Kashmir, Tawakkul Beg relates, the emperor sent his chief steward Sadullah Khan to invite Mulla Shah to court. The Sufi acquiesced. The night that Mulla Shah was expected, Shah Jahan had already retired to his private quarters, instructing one Hayat Khan to alert him to the Sufi's arrival. Mulla Shah greeted Shah Jahan with a "Salam alaikum," to which the emperor replied, "Salam." Out of respect, the Sufi sat a short distance from the emperor, who then pulled him near by the arm so that they could have "warmer companionship."[29]

There is no mention that Mulla Shah performed obeisance to the ruler. Moreover, none but a religious recluse or the closest of family members could even sit by an emperor. Shah Jahan then commented on their similarity, "You are a servant of God, and I am a servant of God. We do not depend on anyone external." Mulla Shah did not wholeheartedly agree. He pointed out that the emperor only occasionally occupied himself in God's remembrance. In contrast, Mulla Shah's main task was to lead people to God. But the emperor silenced him, declaring, "Yes, that is true . . . but you and I have no need of any other than God the Most High, and that is why it is appropriate for us to commune." Shah Jahan then offered the Sufi a bolster pillow that had belonged to his great-grandfather Humayun, saying that it was a fitting gift for one who was indifferent to money. Mulla Shah accepted it and took his leave. Shah Jahan returned to the inner apartments and told Jahanara about the meeting.[30]

The anecdote highlights the Sufi's independence—he comes when he pleases and does not hesitate to voice his opinion. It also displays Shah Jahan's desire for Mulla Shah's company. There is something self-serving in it, as with many of Tawakkul Beg's anecdotes about his spiritual master. But here Tawakkul Beg's account is more than a mere formulaic component of a Sufi hagiography as it does not show Mulla Shah simply triumphing over the emperor.

In Kashmir, Jahanara continued to cultivate her bonds with the Qadiri order in a manner that befit her rank and gender. Mulla Shah's disciple, Muhammad Halim, was getting married, and she sent lavish gifts—money to the house of the bride, a headdress made with strings of pearls for the groom, and a present for the bride's mother so that she would not feel left out. All of Mulla Shah's disciples participating in the wedding received perfumes as well as tobacco leaves.[31] Tobacco was a luxury reserved for the aristocracy; European merchants had introduced it in India only a generation or two earlier.[32] These gestures, reminiscent of the ways Jahanara funded and organized the weddings of her brothers, signal that she forged kin-like relationships with her Qadiri brethren.

We hear little about Dara Shukoh's own encounters with Mulla Shah on this visit, though the prince visited his spiritual master frequently. Tawakkul Beg writes that he had received the opportunity to serve both Mulla Shah and the prince during these months. Tawakkul Beg also carried messages between Mulla Shah and the imperial siblings Dara and Jahanara.[33]

But the prince would soon write about an episode that took place four months into his stay in Kashmir. Here, on the eighth of Rajab (one of the four months designated in the Quran with special sacred status) Dara Shukoh experienced another mystical vision.[34] Unlike his first visionary experience with Miyan Mir, Dara now saw the Prophet Muhammad. An unbroken chain of spiritual descent immediately became apparent to him. From the Prophet Muhammad, most beloved of God, the "line of leadership" went straight to Abd-ul-Qadir Jilani, founder of the Qadiri order, eventually reaching Mulla Shah—and through Mulla Shah to Dara Shukoh himself. In the vision, the prince was then appointed to write a treatise showing the path to the divine. He writes that as he opened the Quran at random, to take an augury (*fal*), as was his custom before starting a book, the title of his new book entered his mind: *Risala-i Haqqnuma* (The Truth-Directing Treatise).[35]

The precocious prince of the *Sakinat-ul-auliya* had become a teacher in his own right. He had long believed that he had been uniquely gifted with spiritual powers, but now he had been commissioned to instruct others as well. Would he still require his pir, Mulla Shah? Who were the intended readers of his book? He had yet to begin the project, though, for soon after his vision he set off for Lahore from Kashmir.

Dara Shukoh's divine vision appeared against the backdrop of some recent political developments. For one, he had recently come into a new position—his first governorship. In June of that year, 1645, Shah Jahan appointed him his deputy in the province of Allahabad, with the additional charge of two important forts—Chunar and Rohtas. Ordinarily, the emperor would have dismissed the prince from the court, and sent him on his new task, as he had done with his other sons. But this time, Shah Jahan maintained his policy of keeping Dara close by his side. Instead, they sent Baqi Beg, a trusted member of Dara Shukoh's household, to oversee the actual governance of the province. Baqi Beg was the tutor and guardian of Dara's eldest son, Sulaiman Shukoh, who was now ten years old. According to Mughal custom, Baqi Beg was bound by ties of loyalty to his charge and Dara Shukoh's family.[36]

But before he completed his book, following his appointment as governor of Allahabad, Dara Shukoh spread the wings of his intellectual and religious explorations even wider. Though he did not actually go to Allahabad, he initiated a correspondence with a famous Chishti Sufi who lived there—Shaikh Muhibbullah Mubariz (d. 1648). At the time, Muhibbullah was one of the empire's preeminent and most prolific commentators on Ibn Arabi's writings.[37] He also happened to be a close associate of Abd-ur-Rahman Chishti, who, in a decade or so, would include Muhibbullah in a collection of biographies entitled the *Mirat-ul-asrar* (Mirror of Secrets).[38]

Dara wrote to pay his respects to Muhibbullah, and referred to himself as a faqir and as a "lover (*muhibb*) of the faqirs," in a word play on the shaikh's name that emphasizes Dara's devotion. The prince expresses great happiness about Muhibbullah's presence in Allahabad and offers the services of his representative Baqi Beg, should the shaikh require anything for the sake of the "believers" there. Then Dara lists questions, sixteen in all, for Muhibbullah to answer. They cover sundry topics: What is the beginning and end of the task on this mystical path? Did prophets of an earlier age know of God's unity and of divine gnosis? When might one perform the ritual prayer without being distracted by stray thoughts? Does the mystical seeker become annihilated or does he become that which he seeks? What is the distinction between love and pain?[39]

In reaching out to Muhibbullah, Dara was not disavowing his Qadiri teachers. It was not uncommon for Sufis to seek more than one teacher, even to take initiation in multiple orders. Recall that earlier, in a conversation with Mulla Shah, the prince had expressed anxiety that some jealous people would accuse him of seeking other teachers.[40] But through this letter, Dara, flush from his latest experience of revelation, is making himself known to other accomplished mystics. His questions stem from curiosity, but also from a desire to show Muhibbullah how spiritually advanced he had become, because he was not particularly interested in the shaikh's answers.

In his reply, Muhibbullah praises the prince to the heavens, humbly referring to himself as an "insignificant speck." He expresses great joy at Dara Shukoh's connection with Allahabad and he addresses the prince's questions in great detail, dwelling, in his answers, on the themes of God's unity and that of the individual with the divine, as well as the proper conduct for a faqir. All the while Muhibbullah quotes profusely from two important works of the Andalusian mystic Ibn Arabi: the *Fusus-ul-hikam* (Bezels of Wisdom) and the *Futuhat-ul-Makkiya* (Meccan Revelations). He takes care to cite the exact chapters in these works whenever he refers to a point in them. Muhibbullah also sprinkles his replies abundantly with quotations from several other Sufi authorities and Persian poets—such early mystics as Abu Bakr Wasiti (d. circa 928) and Abd-ur-Rahman Sulami (d. 1021). Also featured are the influential martyr Ain-i Quzat al-Hamadani (d. 1131) and the commentator of Ibn Arabi, Sadr-ud-Din al-Qunawi (d. 1274), along with the famed poets Rumi (d. 1273) and Hafiz (d. 1390).[41]

In his lengthy response, Muhibbullah seeks to meticulously address the prince's queries touching on various fine points of spiritual perfection and divine gnosis. Although Dara expresses tepid appreciation for some of Muhibbullah's answers, he is hardly impressed by the shaikh's erudition:

> Regarding the replies in which [Muhibbullah] everywhere referred to the sayings of the ancients and considered them to be true, according to this faqir the ecstasy that does not accord with the words of God and the Prophet is much better than that which is written in books. For [this faqir] has spent much time studying books about the saints. But because so many discrepancies became apparent, he completely abandoned the study of books, and engaged in the study of the heart, which is a limitless ocean from which fresh pearls emerge: Do not refer me to any book/For I know my own inner truth to be a book.[42]

Whatever he retrieved from his heart's ocean, Dara adds, he planned to put into written form. He would then send this to the shaikh for amplification. This suggests that he had already begun thinking further about the *Haqqnuma* but might not have completed it at the time of his correspondence with Muhibbullah.

Muhibbullah's reply to the prince sugarcoats rebuke with blandishment. After the usual praise of God, he expresses thanks that a few words of his letter were acceptable to the prince's sensibilities. Quoting the verse rejecting book-learning at the end of Dara Shukoh's letter, the pir tells the prince that he has erred. He cites Quranic verses invoking the idea of the revelation as contained on a celestial "preserved tablet" and others about God's omnipotent power. Muhibbullah then refers to Dara's comment about preferring the ecstasy that did not accord with the Quran and the Prophet's sayings. "This would be a good determination," the shaikh says kindly, instead of dismissing Dara's declaration outright. But, Muhibbullah asserts, "The truth is that people's words and chatter about the knowledge of spiritual mysteries and divine unity have no credibility." Indeed, the shaikh continues, it is forbidden for a perfect gnostic (*arif-i kamil*) to describe these matters to just anyone. All perfect gnostics have their own special connections with God. Continuing in this vein, Muhibbullah gently attempts to nudge Dara Shukoh away from his provocative remark toward a deeper understanding of spiritual states in Islamic mystical thought.[43]

This marks the end of their preserved correspondence. When he wrote Muhibbullah, Dara Shukoh was already well set on the path he illuminates in his *Haqqnuma*. As his epistle shows, at this point in the prince's spiritual evolution, he privileged the experiential religious quest over book knowledge. He remained open to new techniques and ways of soaring to further spiritual heights. The prince's impatience with formalized religious learning may indicate Dara's growing interest in exploring Indic thought. But the painstaking study of Ibn Arabi's philosophy was now increasingly less appealing to him

Dara Shukoh's rather grandiose self-assurance in his spiritual path echoes his father's large gestures of power on the world stage. Now that Shah Jahan no longer had to fear for Jahanara's life, the emperor turned his attention to fulfilling some political ambitions that he had long nurtured. Mughal rulers had, since Humayun, aspired to recapture the Central Asian territories associated with their fourteenth-century ancestor, Timur. But they were too preoccupied with invasions, rebellions, and the endless efforts to subdue the subcontinent's southern kingdoms to actually do so. Now the time seemed ripe. Nazar Muhammad, ruler of Balkh, faced a rebellion led by his own son, Abd-ul-Aziz, who had proclaimed himself ruler in Bukhara.

Shah Jahan, who had been preparing for this campaign for over a year, first stationed Ali Mardan Khan in Kabul to assess the situation. Nazar Muhammad was eager for the Mughals to help him recover his kingdom, though Shah Jahan's motives, of course, were hardly altruistic.

Shah Jahan and his courtiers were well aware that the economic benefits of capturing the Uzbek lands, with revenues equal to only a small portion of Indian territories, would not have offset the huge cost of the campaign.[44] There may, however, have been strategic reasons to annex, or at least weaken, Balkh and Badakhshan, whose recent rulers had raided Mughal territories.[45] And the symbolic value was high. Shah Jahan identified more closely with Timur than either his father or grandfather. Timur's famed astrological epithet, "Sahib Qiran," the Lord of the Auspicious Conjunction, affirmed imperial rule through the divine destiny of the stars. Shah Jahan used this as part of his own title; he appeared on coins, in paintings, and in the imperial chronicles of the day as the second Sahib Qiran.[46] Timur conquered vast swaths of territory comprising today's Iran, Iraq, and parts of the Levant and north India. Shah Jahan's Central Asian campaign would now be enacted on a world stage with the Safavids and Ottomans as a suitably awed audience.

Such grand moves also accompanied an increased emphasis on Timur in Shah Jahan's court. Recently, in 1637, a new book had reached the emperor—a rather obviously spurious autobiography of Timur. Supposedly translated from the Chaghatai Turkish, the collection celebrated the exploits of the progenitor of the Mughal dynasty. From Qazwini's telling, it was clear that the emperor realized the translation was actually a recent composition. Shah Jahan nonetheless greatly appreciated the work and had a copy sent to Aurangzeb for his edification.[47]

In the spring of 1646, Shah Jahan dispatched Murad Bakhsh to Balkh via Kabul at the head of sixty thousand soldiers. He accompanied Murad to Kabul in order to more closely oversee military operations. En route, Dara Shukoh, as usual accompanying his father, halted his own journey northwest of Lahore, in the town of Sheikhupura, which was apparently named after the young Jahangir whose father would affectionately refer to him as Sheikhu Baba. Here Jahangir had built a striking tower, over a hundred feet tall, which in Dara Shukoh's time may have been adorned all over with deer antlers embedded in its stonework.[48] Dara would remain here, rejoining the emperor's party in Kabul after only four months. According to Lahori's *Padshah-nama*, Nadira was seriously ill and needed time to recover. It would be eleven months before she fully regained her health.[49]

Sometime in 1056 AH (1646/7), Dara gifted his wife Nadira the richly illustrated album of paintings and calligraphy that he had earlier assembled as a young prince. The loving inscription he pens for her does not mention the month. Yet we can imagine that he might have made this gesture on a particularly momentous occasion, such as her recovery from illness, or that she leafed through it during her convalescence.[50]

During the same year, Dara Shukoh finished the *Haqqnuma,* which he had first conceived of in Kashmir. He may have penned the treatise in Sheikhupura during his months of relative respite from travel and state duties. Unlike Dara's previous writings, this was not a book about the lives of Sufis or their comparative excellences. Neither was it an encyclopedic compilation based on the major writings of the Sufi canon. Rather, the *Haqqnuma* served as a guide to the techniques of cultivating the heart so that it "blooms" in divine union.[51]

Dara Shukoh is critical of the famous Sufi writings and manuals that had become standard fare for those wishing to advance their spiritual journey. These books are very difficult for people to understand, declares the prince; he lists such foundational works as Ibn Arabi's *Futuhat* and *Fusus,* the *Sawanih-ul-ushshaq* (Intuitions of Lovers) of Ahmad Ghazali (d. 1126), the *Lamaat* (Celestial Flashes) of Fakhr-ud-Din Iraqi (d. 1289), as well as the *Lawaih* (Rays of Light) and the *Lawami* (Heavenly Beams) of Abd-ur-Rahman Jami (d. 1492). The *Haqqnuma* distills the truth of these writings into an easier to imbibe "pure font of divine unity."[52] Dara Shukoh adds a quatrain to further illustrate his point: "If for you the inner essence of the law is abstruse/And to really criticize Sufi texts you're far too obtuse//Know the One and no other in this world and the next/This is the truth taught in the *Futuhat* and the *Fusus.*[53]

The prince's verses condense Ibn Arabi's complex meditations into an utterly simple dictum: "Know the One." They simultaneously elevate and diminish the importance of the *Futuhat* and the *Fusus* to centuries of Islamic thought. In the passages that follow, Dara Shukoh quickly proceeds to once again privilege the experiential over the study of books. The *Haqqnuma*'s sources of authority are not books; rather, they are the spiritual practices in which Miyan Mir and Mulla Shah trained their disciples. The prince attributes their origin, however, to Prophet Muhammad. As though anticipating objections, Dara Shukoh is quick to add that nothing in his treatise contravenes the words and deeds of the Prophet himself.[54]

The *Haqqnuma* traces the mystical path through four successive realms: it starts from the human realm (*nasut*) and proceeds through the realm of sovereignty (*malakut*) and the realm of divinity (*lahut*), to the final destination of the realm of omnipotence (*jabarut*). This idea of four states of existence is a common one in Sufi writing.[55] But here, for the first time in

Dara Shukoh's works, we see small hints that he might have expanded his spiritual investigations beyond more mainstream Islamic sources.

It is often hard to distinguish, though, the Indic ideas and practices that Miyan Mir's Sufi order might already have appropriated from those which Dara Shukoh might himself have recently come across. For instance, Dara's discussion of the first realm lists three types of hearts that the spiritual seeker possesses: the "fir-tree heart," located behind the left breast; the "mind's source," inside the brain; and the "lotus heart" in the center of the buttocks.[56] The descriptions of these hearts echo the concept of *chakra*s, literally "wheels," or "centers" of energy in the yoga tradition, which are located in similar areas of the body. Although Dara does not explicitly compare these hearts to *chakra*s, other Sufis in India have been known to develop this concept, identifying the *chakra*s with the Sufi notion of subtle centers. In a work called *Yoga Qalandar,* Dara's contemporary, the Bengali Sufi Sayyid Murtaza (d. 1662), maps onto the *chakra*s four realms: the human realm and those of sovereignty, divinity, and omnipotence.[57] The *Haqqnuma* indirectly participates in these dialogues with the yoga tradition.

But another instance in the *Haqqnuma* suggests that Dara Shukoh might have also begun to add to what his teachers imparted to him, using concepts drawn from Indic thought. He describes the second realm, in which he cautions the seeker not to stay for long, no matter how appealing this station is. Here the traveler on the mystical path must buff away the rust from his heart so that it can reflect the Divine Beloved's beauty. This is accomplished by softly repeating Allah's name in the heart, without moving the lips—a practice that Miyan Mir disclosed to select disciples. Dara then reveals the mystical secret of the name: "My friend, this name is extraordinarily great. It contains infidelity and Islam. It gathers into unity all the divine names. Apart from this name, nothing exists. The inner meaning of this greatest name is this: It possesses three qualities: creation, sustaining, and annihilation."[58]

Sufi writings commonly invoke the *coincidentia oppositorum* of infidelity and faith, while still emphasizing a devotion framed by Islamic paradigms. Dara Shukoh goes further. Not only does he suggest that Allah's name encompasses what is not Islam, that is, kufr, or infidelity, he also identifies as divine characteristics that could only be the key attributes of the Indic *trimurti*—a triad of divine manifestations in the forms of Brahma, the creator; Vishnu, the preserver; and Shiva, the destroyer. Here, Dara Shukoh treats them as attributes of a single divinity instead of as separate deities.

The prince does not disclose how he started engaging with Indic ideas. In fact, he does not even acknowledge them as Indic. While discussing the realm of sovereignty, Dara describes a breathing exercise that closely resembles a technique of *hatha* yoga. Sitting in the manner of the Prophet, the seeker seals his ears and eyes with his fingers, placing his middle fingers on both nostrils. Alternately blocking and releasing one nostril after the other, he utters the first half of the Islamic witness to faith, "There is no God," while inhaling. He then gently exhales out the second half, "but God." Cultivating this technique, Dara recounts, together with focusing on the heart, leads to a heightened state of divine remembrance, the *sultan-ul-azkar*, which he had obtained through a vision of Miyan Mir five years earlier.[59]

Dara Shukoh likens this practice to the Prophet Muhammad's own account of the moment before receiving a revelation. He reports the Prophet saying, "A sound comes to me sometimes like the boiling of a large vessel, sometimes like the buzzing of a honeybee, sometimes in imaged form as an angel in the shape of a man who speaks to me, and sometimes I hear a sound like a string of tinkling bells."[60]

Though the *Haqqnuma* establishes impeccable Islamic credentials for the *sultan-ul-azkar,* similar practices of breath control and the subsequent auditory experiences have an important place in hatha yoga traditions.[61] The account in the *Shivasamhita* (c. 1300–1500), an influential work of hatha yoga, is particularly close to Dara's description: "When the *yogi* restrains the wind by tightly closing his ears with his thumbs, his eyes with his index fingers, his nostrils with his middle fingers, and his mouth with his ring fingers, and intently carries out this practice, then he immediately sees himself in the form of light. . . . And moreover, through its practice, *nada* (sound) gradually arises. The first sound is like a line of drunken bees or a lute. After practicing thus there is a sound which is like the ringing of a bell and destroys the darkness of *samsara* (transmigratory existence). Then there is a sound like thunder."[62]

But the *Haqqnuma* makes no mention of an overlap between the *sultan-ul-azkar* and Indic practices. It does not tell us whether Dara's description of this practice arises from his association with the Qadiri order or reflects the seeds of his interest in yoga, broadly defined. We do know, though, that Sufis in the Indian subcontinent have a long history of engaging with and appropriating yogic techniques of breath control. For some Sufis, the techniques of hatha yoga became part of the available repertory of esoteric knowledge passed down through a chain of spiritual masters, whose lineage was traced back to the Prophet himself. There are several examples of texts describing Indic bodily techniques of liberation and then furnishing them with Islamic antecedents.[63] Dara Shukoh, consciously or not, enters into conversation with this body of practices and writing.

Though we may not have a precise record of Dara Shukoh's interactions with Hindu religious figures during this period, we know that Shah Jahan's court continued the earlier Mughal tradition of hosting Sanskrit scholars and employing Hindus. Chandarbhan Brahman, a skilled writer in Persian, had been in Shah Jahan's employ since 1639.[64] He would eventually join Dara Shukoh's household staff. In 1643, Malajit, Shah Jahan's chief Brahmin astrologer, composed a lexicon of astronomical terms in Sanskrit and Persian to present to the emperor. Shah Jahan himself had awarded Malajit the august title *Vedangaraya*, "Lord of Vedic Sciences," an honorific that surpassed the title *Jyotisharaja*, "Lord of Astral Knowledge," which had been conferred upon earlier chief Brahmin astrologers in the Mughal court.[65]

Later, in 1651, at the court in Lahore, Shah Jahan awarded fifteen hundred rupees to the renowned Sanskrit intellectual from Benares, Kavindracharya Saraswati.[66] There are indications that Kavindracharya interacted with the emperor and other members of the imperial family. Kavindracharya composed a series of poems in Brajbhasha, a form of literary Hindi, which he called *Kavindra-kalpalata* (Wish-Fulfilling Vine of Kavindra). About half of these extol Shah Jahan, while others praise Dara Shukoh, Jahanara, and Murad. The emperor, says Kavindracharya, knows not only the Quran and the Puranas; he knows the secret of the Vedas too.[67] Dara Shukoh, in the poet's estimation, was "Indra-like, moon-like, Macchindra-like in yoga."[68] Here, Kavindracharya lauds Dara for his knowledge of Indic traditions, comparing him to the Hindu deity Indra as well as to Matsyendranath, the perfected master (*siddha*) revered amongst yogis. Kavindracharya even mentions Dara's wife Nadira, likening Dara and Nadira to the legendary and revered lovers of the Ramayana, Rama and Sita: "Dara and Nadira are made thus, just like Sita and Ram / Image of renown, great wisdom, abode of supreme bliss."[69]

The *Kavindra-kalpalata* also includes a series of philosophical meditations on *tattvajnana*, the knowledge of reality or truth. Here, Kavindracharya elaborates the positions of various Indic schools of philosophy regarding the world and the nature of its cause. Kavindra himself firmly avows a non-dualistic position. For the poet, the world itself is *brahman,* the ultimate reality, a claim which he exhorts his listeners to repeat: "Say again and again, the world itself is *brahman.*"[70] This concept of the unity of existence would have resonated with Dara's Sufi proclivities. But, Shah Jahan, too, would have been its intended audience. As Kavindracharya's primary patron, the emperor played an important role in hosting the Sanskrit pandit.

Persian writers at the court also attest to Dara Shukoh's public persona as a philosopher-prince. Shah Jahan's chronicler, Qazwini, repeatedly distinguishes Dara with such honorifics as "prince of wisdom," "nurturer of the arts," and "seeker of knowledge."[71] This is also the image cultivated in a massive Persian medical encyclopedia completed in 1646/7 by Hakim Nur-ud-Din Shirazi, a physician in Shah Jahan's court. Its title, *Ilajat-i Dara-shukohi* (Remedies of Dara Shukoh), derives from Dara's name.[72] Its opening dedication celebrates Dara as a philosopher-prince—an Alexander, a Solomon, a second Plato. Shirazi identifies Dara Shukoh as the rightful "heir apparent" and a champion of universal knowledge.[73]

Echoes of the intellectual and spiritual legacy of Dara Shukoh's great-grandfather Akbar resound throughout Shirazi's collection. Opening verses praising the prince gush, "We've drunk at the font of universal peace (*sulh-i kull*)."[74] The phrase identifies Dara and the Mughal court as a source of universal or total peace. *Sulh-i kull* was a key concept in Akbar's political theology.[75] Moreover, the eclectic purview of Shirazi's encyclopedia evokes Abu-l-Fazl's *Ain-i Akbari* (Institutes of Akbar), a work that similarly presents the emperor as tending to the collective health of society and the state.[76]

These allusions to Akbar were not accidental. The Indian-born Shirazi hailed from an illustrious family of doctors and bureaucrats who had long served at the Mughal court. Nur-ud-Din Shirazi's father was a physician, while his maternal uncles were the famed historian Abu-l-Fazl and the poet Faizi. All three brothers worked in Akbar's service. Shirazi celebrated the literary heritage of his uncles, who had both developed notable interest in Indic philosophy and learning, by editing and publishing volumes of their letters. But, like his father, Shirazi dedicated his life to tending the soul by curing the body.[77]

The philosophical system that Shirazi advanced in Dara Shukoh's name was remarkably ambitious. Shirazi's encyclopedia spans an ethical universe centering on the perfection of the human body and the mind, though the bulk of the work focuses on cures to physical ailments. Yet, both the opening and conclusion engage explicitly the fields of philosophy and mysticism, with extended commentaries on sundry topics such as anatomy, music, mathematics, numerology, physics, geography, astronomy, and language. The collection culminates with a treatment of occult knowledge and power. Shirazi's detailed instructions for preparing drugs and various medicaments transition almost seamlessly into recipes for magical spells and charms, many of which the author confirms he tested himself. One of the most important sources that Shirazi cites for his knowledge of the occult is the *Zakhira-i Iskandarani* (Treasury of Alexander). This collection of spells and talismans, originally written in Arabic, was particularly well known within the Mughal court during Dara's time. Even more noteworthy for Dara Shukoh's interests during this period, Shirazi integrates into the concluding chapters a detailed account of yogic practices of breath control and meditative practices developed by the sages of India as a form of obtaining occult power and knowledge.[78]

BOTH SHAH JAHAN AND DARA SHUKOH managed affairs of state even as they sought wisdom through their intellectual and cultural activities. The military adventure in Central Asia did not live up to Shah Jahan's expectations. The beginning was very promising. Murad Bakhsh easily seized Balkh, though the ousted ruler Nazar Muhammad managed to flee to his son, their rift forgotten. When Shah Jahan, waiting in Kabul, heard the news of Balkh's capture, he announced eight days of celebration.[79] The northern part of the kingdom, including Samarqand and Bukhara, was next, he hoped. But soon afterward, Murad Bakhsh sent a letter asking for permission to come home. Governing an alien land was proving to be much harder than the conquest itself. The morale of his men was low, and with a famine in the region they had no idea how they would secure enough provisions to survive the Central Asian winter. Taking Samarqand and Bukhara did not appear at all feasible.[80]

Dara Shukoh remained in the Punjab during much of the Balkh expedition. While his father anxiously steered the campaign from afar, Dara helped oversee the governance of Hindustan. It soon became clear that nothing could induce Murad to remain in Balkh. The emperor rushed the experienced Sadullah Khan to take over the operation. Murad returned in disgrace, and was stripped of his rank. Shah Jahan forbade him from coming to court and had him remain in Peshawar for several months. The following year, in February 1647, the emperor sent Aurangzeb to reinvigorate the stalled campaign, albeit with a much smaller army. Shah Jahan moved to Lahore and appointed Shuja to administer Kabul. According to Tawakkul Beg, Shah Jahan also corresponded with Mulla Shah about the campaign, asking him to pray for victory in Central Asia.[81] In March that year, he added the Punjab to the portfolio of provinces under Dara Shukoh's governorship. This time, because the prince was actually stationed in Lahore, he was able to acquire some hands-on administrative experience.

By October 1647, it was clear that Aurangzeb had not made any headway in Central Asia. Shah Jahan instructed him to retreat, relinquishing Balkh to Nazar Muhammad. The emperor was forced to drop his cherished goal. In total, the expedition had cost forty million rupees and an untold number of lives.[82]

While Dara Shukoh's brothers were entangled in this costly and disastrous mission, the eldest prince expended at least some of his energy on architectural patronage. Building was a passion that he shared with his father, for whom it formed a crucial aspect of his image as a powerful sovereign. While still in Sheikhupura in 1646, Dara sent Tawakkul Beg back to Kashmir to oversee projects that he had been planning there. The *Nuskha* offers a rare contemporary account of how a site now popularly known as Pari Mahal, the "Fairy Palace," came into being.

Today all that remains of the Pari Mahal are the ruins of six pavilioned terraces, set halfway up a mountain overlooking Srinagar's Dal Lake from the southeast. Apart from the stairs and terraced walls, some built structures survive: a *baradari* (pavilion), a couple of water tanks, and an arcade on the lowest terrace covered in a lattice of small holes that suggests it once housed pigeons. The expansive views of the sky merging into the translucent lake, the clouds both above and reflected below are magical. To the Pari Mahal's east, at the foot of the mountain range, lies a garden designed around an effervescent spring known today as Chashm-i Shahi, the "Shah's Spring."

Little is known, though, about the Pari Mahal's origins or how the site might have been used. In the nineteenth century, a British doctor based in Kashmir heard a legend that it was the abode of an evil magician who kidnapped princesses. One such king's daughter eventually managed to track him down and have him captured.[83] Others believe that Pari was a misspelling of Pir Mahal, named for Dara's Sufi pir, Mulla Shah, which eventually replaced the original name.[84] Several layers of historical memory, including oral tradition, enwrap the site. But the details of Dara's own involvement with this terraced pleasure palace lie largely buried and forgotten.

Tawakkul Beg provides some tantalizing insights into the Pari Mahal's creation. There is a mountain, he recounts, overlooking the Dal Lake, named *Koh-i Pak,* the "Pure Mountain." Two springs flowed from it. One the Kashmiris called "Salma," and the other, on the mountain's spine, they called "Qatalna." When the prince learned about these springs and realized that at least one of the sites was suitable for building, he sent Tawakkul Beg from Sheikhupura to locate the origins of the Salma Spring and enclose it within a marble tank in such a way that it would bubble from its midst. Jahanara built some grand structures by this spring, which she renamed Chashma-i Shahi, after Mulla Shah. Mulla Shah, however, felt that it would be more appropriately named Chashma-i Sahibiya, referring to the Prophet's companions, as its original name referenced Salman the Persian, closely associated with the Prophet. But Jahanara's name for the spring endured through time. Tawakkul Beg's description corresponds to the site now known as Chashma-i Shahi. Today, though, the word Shah in the place name is generally thought to refer to the emperor.[85]

Meanwhile, according to Tawakkul Beg, Mulla Shah had been exploring the mountain with his servant Hasan Raina. The Sufi shaikh discovered another spring farther up the mountain, though this one did not flow as freely. He remarked to Hasan that it would be nice if a portion of the mountain were cut away, so that the spring could gush forth. Then the governor of Kashmir requested from Mulla Shah permission to build in that location. Courtiers in Jahanara's employ constructed other buildings. It was Dara Shukoh, though, who built an "extraordinary heart-enchanting, pleasure-granting place," with magnificent views of the Dal Lake and all of Kashmir. According to Neve's nineteenth-century description, the Pari Mahal's buildings showed evidence of having been colored chocolate-red, green, and yellow, so we can imagine that decoratively painted plaster covered the stone.[86] The spring, now tamed, cascaded down the terraces, filling pools. "This spring should be named *Chashma-i shahi*," declared Mulla Shah. He would delight in visiting the *Chashma-i sahibiya* with some select disciples, then after a night spent there, proceed uphill to the *Chashma-i shahi*, visiting the Qatalna Spring on the way. The return journey would follow the same pattern. While the place names have not been identified, Tawakkul Beg's account fits well with the Pari Mahal's location.[87]

The imperial embrace of Mulla Shah continued during and after the Balkh debacle. While stationed in Lahore, Dara Shukoh entreated Mulla Shah to come down from Kashmir to winter there. The weather in Lahore was far more temperate, he argued. So the shaikh set forth. As he approached Lahore, Tawakkul Beg, along with Mir Abu Talib, Jahanara's deputy in the city, went to greet him reverentially in Shahdara, on the banks of the Ravi River. Jahanara arranged for Mulla Shah's stay in a mansion that had belonged to the late Firoz Khan, the eunuch superintendent of the female quarters in Shah Jahan's household. The building seemed to have reverted to her possession. Tawakkul Beg and Abu Talib served Mulla Shah day and night. Qazi Afzal, the religious scholar who a few years ago had interceded with the reluctant Mulla Shah to accept Dara Shukoh as a disciple, now assisted the prince in governing the city, and visited Mulla Shah daily.[88]

Tawakkul Beg's account makes it plain that Mulla Shah was a guest of the entire imperial family. During his stay in Lahore, Jahanara sent food for him and his companions through her deputy, Abu Talib. In April 1647, Shuja was passing by on his way to his new post in Kabul. The prince sent a messenger to pay respects to Mulla Shah, apologizing for not coming in person. As Mulla Shah was housed within the precincts of the Lahore Fort, he could not enter without the emperor's permission. Shuja gifted the Sufi two thousand rupees, which Mulla Shah promptly refused. Shah Jahan, too, sent a handwritten letter welcoming Mulla Shah to Lahore.[89]

When the Sufi returned to Kashmir, he felt comfortable enough with the imperial family to make his own needs known. Mulla Shah desired a *khanqah*, or Sufi lodge, where his disciples could stay, near his home perched on the skirt of the Koh-i Maran hill overlooking the city. He also wanted a congregational mosque attached to the khanqah, because it was incumbent upon Muslim men to offer the Friday midday prayer in a congregation rather than in solitude. A mosque of his own would enable Mulla Shah to pray all the five daily prayers in a congregation. Mulla Shah instructed Jahanara's deputy in Kashmir to gather stones for construction. The official repurposed a heap of stones originally belonging to an idol-temple (*but-khana*). "Tell your mistress to make a khanqah for God," Mulla Shah directed. Tawakkul Beg reports that the imperial family released sixty thousand rupees for constructing the mosque-khanqah complex. His figure concurs with the official account.[90] It would take at least a couple of years for the building work to be completed.[91]

The following year, in 1648, Mulla Shah decided to winter in Lahore again. "Kashmir is paradisical only in the summer," his disciples told him. Tawakkul Beg received the group near Lahore. He was accompanied by Muhammad Hakim, the son of Qazi Aslam, who years before had participated in issuing the fatwa against Mulla Shah. Now the same qazi made arrangements for Mulla Shah's accommodation in the mansion of Shaikh Abd-ul-Karim.[92]

Mulla Shah did not meet his imperial hosts empty-handed. That year, he prepared a handsome manuscript of his poetry, containing ten masnawis, long narrative poems, interspersed with occasional prose passages. Its folios brim with Persian calligraphy penned in an excellent hand and glisten with gold leaf. Mulla Shah corrected the manuscript, annotating it here and there with notes written in the margins, and at regular intervals, he certified that he had inspected the text.[93] Several of his masnawis meditate on religious topics—the *diwana*s, or those crazed with spiritual ecstasy, or the *basmala,* "In God's name" with which the Quran begins. But two *masnawi*s directly speak to Mulla Shah's imperial connections, though he infused these also with a spiritual dimension. One is about Kashmir and its delights—starting with his home and proceeding on to sights such as the hammam, the chinar trees, the main congregational mosque, the water of Dal Lake, the imperial gardens, including the Nishat, Faiz-Bakhsh, and Farah-Bakhsh gardens, and a lone cypress tree. In this poem, Mulla Shah also journeys onto the gardens and residences of Jahanara, Shah Jahan, and Dara Shukoh. The other *masnawi*, the *Risala-i Shahiya* (The Imperial Epistle), begins with an address dedicated to Shah Jahan and his two eldest children: "O Shah Jahan, and you, Dara! / And O Dara and you, Jahanara! // To you, the eternal rulership of the world/May you possess the world, forever//Dara, to you, in entirety, is world-rulership/To you all the ornaments of the world."[94]

Mulla Shah puns with the names of these three members of the imperial family, wishing for their continued power and authority. Dara, the heir, receives special mention. The poem exploits to full effect the literal meanings of their names: Shah Jahan, "emperor of the world," Jahanara, "ornament of the world," and a form of the Persian infinitive *dashtan* ("to have" or "to possess"), which sounds similar to "Dara." The rest of the *masnawi* continues to laud Mulla Shah's imperial patrons. We can glimpse this poem's reception at the court through a painting in an album produced for Shah Jahan; it has an elaborate, illustrated border, and is attributed to the artist Bichitr, On the top right-hand corner of the border sits a poet with an open book on which is inscribed the first verse from this poem.[95]

The Sufi struck a fine balance between his lavish poetry of praise and his own independence. While he was in Lahore, Shah Jahan sent a message citing his great desire to see him. The emperor also mentioned the agreeable air in the Faiz-Bakhsh and Farah-Bakhsh imperial gardens. Mulla Shah was reluctant. It was raining, and the gardens were far away. If the emperor really wanted to meet there, he could make it in a week's time. Shah Jahan persisted, "Your desire to meet is evident, delay is not suitable." The emperor suggested Shah Burj—a secluded quadrangle in the northwest corner of the Lahore Fort with a sparkling mirrored hall—as an alternative. There he interrupted his private audience to enjoy Mulla Shah's company.[96]

On another occasion, the emperor sent Sadullah Khan to fetch Mulla Shah. It was time for the evening prayer, but the Sufi sensed that the emperor needed his company. Shah Jahan left the meeting that he was holding in his bathhouse and met Mulla Shah privately. A new crisis had erupted. In late 1648, the young Safavid emperor Shah Abbas, emboldened by the Mughal debacle in Balkh, managed to recapture Qandahar in a surprise winter attack.[97]

Daulat Khan, the Mughal governor stationed there, quickly capitulated. For over a decade, the Mughals had managed to retain their grasp on this strategic city. But ever since Shah Safi's sudden death, the threat of another Safavid invasion loomed. Shah Jahan dispatched Aurangzeb, now governor of Multan, to recapture Qandahar. He was the obvious choice for this mission after Murad's poor showing in Central Asia.

Aurangzeb and the Mughal forces embarked on the difficult journey. The prince sent regular dispatches to his father, who liked to be apprised of every detail. But he also found time to write his sister, Jahanara, addressing her as the *sahiba* (mistress) of the age, or merely *sahib* (master). All the way from Kohat to Ali Masjid (both today in northwest Pakistan), recent rains had made the mountains verdant. She was on her way to Kabul with the emperor and would be taking the same route. "If the weather remains in this state, perhaps Sahib too will be much cheered by this landscape."[98]

The rest of Aurangzeb's journey was less pleasant. Near Ghazni, he found that provisions were scarce, but Shah Jahan urged him to soldier on. Marching through bad weather, delayed by snow, the Mughal forces finally laid siege to the walled city at the end of May. Within three months, the hastily assembled army was forced to withdraw, bruised by its lack of heavy artillery, its rations depleted. Plans would have to be made for another attempt, this time with due preparation.

At the beginning of 1651, Aurangzeb went all the way from Multan to Delhi at his father's summons. While traveling, he kept a brisk correspondence with his oldest sister. Or rather, she was a more regular correspondent, and he often apologized for his neglect or delay in writing her.[99] En route, Aurangzeb stopped in Lahore, where Dara still served as governor. There, he tells her, he reveled in the poppies, yellow jasmine, and irises of the imperial family's gardens. But he also suffered an annoying experience. Dara Shukoh's *gumashta,* or agent, emerged from the city to welcome his master, when Aurangzeb had dismounted in the environs of Lahore. When he saw Aurangzeb, the gumashta got on his horse and rode off. There was no ceremonial obeisance, or acknowledgment of the prince's presence. This must have been a deliberate ploy by Dara to insult him, Aurangzeb thought: "The reason for this depraved action wasn't clear. He probably committed these unbecoming gestures on his own master's direction."[100]

Jahanara, ever the peacemaker, facilitated Aurangzeb's meeting with Dara. The younger prince seems to have been mollified. "Thanks to God the Most High, due to the sublime one's [i.e., Jahanara's] favor, I had a good conversation. I was most pleased by our meeting. Because no music is performed on the tenth of Muharram, we did not have a musical gathering (*suhbat-i rag*)." This little snippet from the prince's letter shows us that Aurangzeb was quite accustomed to musical performances and that it might well have been Dara's decision not to listen to music on *Ashura,* a day of fasting for Sunnis and mourning for the Shia. Aurangzeb also thanks his sister for arranging a meeting with their younger brother, Murad.[101]

During his journey, Jahanara plied Aurangzeb with gifts and letters, including fruit preserves from the imperial provisions. As he neared Delhi, she sent a document drawn up by her astrologer. It contained the calculation of the auspicious time at which to meet the emperor. This one example reflects the integral role of astrology in Mughal court functioning. Aurangzeb was much appreciative of his sister's gesture. The prince also speaks of visiting the tomb of his great-great-grandfather, Humayun.[102] He no doubt experienced other visual delights as well. After his losses in Central Asia and Qandahar, Shah Jahan had attacked an older project with fresh enthusiasm—turning Delhi into a magnificent new capital—with Jahanara's and Dara Shukoh's participation as well.

That year, 1651, Shah Jahan and his eldest two children summered in Kashmir to escape the heat of the plains. The emperor visited Mulla Shah's newly completed mosque complex. Jahanara's attendants gave the shaikh a valuable diamond, which he apparently accepted. The shaikh composed a poem commemorating its completion, beginning, "Of stone did Begam Sahib make a building/The noble child of the faith-protecting emperor of the worlds."[103] It ends with a chronogram that he coined, "The date of my khanqah is 'Khanqah-i Shah,'" corresponding to the year of the edifice's foundation.[104]

While in Kashmir, Dara Shukoh, with the emperor's permission, organized the marriage of his sixteen-year-old son, Sulaiman Shukoh, to the granddaughter of Khwaja Abd-ul-Aziz Naqshbandi. The Khwaja had been Jahangir's general in Qandahar during Shah Abbas's capture of the city in 1623. His name reflects a link with the originally Central Asian Naqshbandi order. Dara Shukoh must have thought it expedient to forge networks with Naqshbandis as well as with the Central Asian nobility at this time. Of late, the Turanis, as they were called, were forming an increasing proportion of the rank-holders in the Mughal state, though their numbers did not supersede the Iranians.[105]

After the Kashmir visit, Shah Jahan, Jahanara, and Dara stayed in Shahjahanabad for a spell. Aurangzeb visited the court, leaving for Multan after paying his respects to the emperor. Shah Jahan had already started to plan his next stab at retrieving Qandahar. When he was in Kashmir, he had recalled Shuja from Bengal for this task.[106] But eventually, in February 1652, Aurangzeb set off to lead the campaign alone.[107] Dara Shukoh, fearing an alliance between his two younger brothers, may have dissuaded his father from sending both to Qandahar.

The emperor peppered his son with frequent letters, keeping close tabs on Aurangzeb's every act and movement. Aurangzeb's replies provide an invaluable insight into the relationship between father and son, as they reflect the tight control that Shah Jahan kept over the princes at all times. We know from Aurangzeb's replies that the letters Shah Jahan sent before the prince launched his second offensive on Qandahar were often accompanied by lavish gifts—pearl rosaries along with pearl and cornelian armlets, a ring studded with lucky stones, fragrant perfumes and precious incense powders of musk and ambergris, a diamond turban ornament, a fine Arab steed and a female elephant. Along the way, even when knee-deep in military preparations, Aurangzeb went out of his way to supply his father with the fruits that Babur's descendants in India craved, particularly musk melons and pomegranates.[108]

By January 1652, Shah Jahan, too, was on his way to Lahore, along with his entourage. His plan was to proceed to Multan in Sind, while Dara Shukoh would go on to Kabul with Ali Mardan Khan, the Safavid governor who had surrendered Qandahar to the Mughals in 1638. In his next letter, he proposed a new strategy, a two-pronged attack on the Safavids, with a separate army led by Dara.[109] Was Dara Shukoh himself behind this idea? The eldest prince may have hankered to prove himself in battle, especially since his previous expedition to Qandahar ended abruptly, though fortuitously, with Shah Safi's death. Joining his more experienced brother would enable him to bask in the credit should the siege be victorious.

Aurangzeb, as we might expect, did not leap at the prospect of a role subordinate to his older brother. He dared not openly cross his father, but referred to the issue in a veiled way: "May the desire of the happy heart [of your Majesty] be splendidly displayed in the choicest manner upon the platform of manifestation!"[110] Shah Jahan sensed his son's reluctance and chose not to pursue the suggestion any further.

In other matters, though, Shah Jahan applied firmer, more direct pressure. Both Shah Jahan's instructions and Aurangzeb's plans changed again and again during the lead-up to war. The emperor supervised from a comfortable distance. Aurangzeb was on the ground. With the help of local contacts among landowners, he investigated which route to Qandahar would be the safest, would offer provisions along the way, and not unduly tax his men. He first inclined toward the most direct route, along which he hoped to dig wells and set up armed posts. But by the third week of February, when his army was camped outside Multan waiting for the auspicious hour at which to depart, his heart was set on another, more roundabout route. He would head north from Multan via Bhera, a town on the banks of the Jhelum River, instead of directly west toward Qandahar.

Then a letter from Shah Jahan arrived, exhorting Aurangzeb to take the more direct route, via Deh-i Shaikh. The emperor made clear that his son was expected at Qandahar on the fifteenth of the Persian month Urdibihisht, corresponding to the fourth of May. Aurangzeb politely outlined his reservations about this route, explaining that it had a long stretch completely devoid of water and that provisions would be scarce along the way.[111] Nevertheless, the prince acquiesced to his father's command, knowing that by doing so, some of the responsibility for the troops would transfer to Shah Jahan himself. Soon afterward, Aurangzeb blamed the route for a delay. Eventually he would reach in good time, and the imperial astrologers would postpone the auspicious date for arrival at Qandahar to the twenty-third of Urdibihisht.

Early in Aurangzeb's journey, Shah Jahan urged Shuja to join the campaign and directed Aurangzeb to do whatever he could to ensure a smooth relationship with his older brother. This time, Aurangzeb was more effusive in his praise for the emperor's suggestion, though he still seemed reluctant to share the glory with a brother. Eventually, as he approached Qandahar, he heard from his father that Shuja was ill, but insisting on carrying on. At least his arrival would be considerably delayed. Aurangzeb, probably relieved that he would reach Qandahar first, sent loving wishes for Shuja's recovery. Fortunately for him, Shuja never came.

At Qandahar, Shah Jahan posted his prime minister, Sadullah Khan, to guide and assist Aurangzeb and act as a conduit for his own orders: "We have given suitable instructions in all matters to the Khan, the head minister of all viziers, to inform the *murid*, who should act accordingly."[112] But both Aurangzeb and Sadullah Khan soon found themselves at a loss. A couple of weeks after arriving, Aurangzeb had to halt the siege because they had already run out of guns. He wrote to Shah Jahan for permission to acquire more artillery.

By the first week of June, the Mughal army had been in Qandahar for almost a month without making significant progress. They fired ten cannonballs at the fort every day, causing minor damage that the Safavids easily repaired overnight. It was painfully clear that their artillery was inadequate. Eventually, Sadullah Khan hatched a plan with Aurangzeb to try to breach the garrison wall. They would line up all the guns in one area, with the khan leading an army in the entrenchment. Raja Rajrup and Raja Madan Singh would support him with their men. But, they would have to find a way to tow all the artillery to one place without Safavid interference. And they needed the emperor's approval before proceeding.

Meanwhile, in Aurangzeb's account to his father, Rajrup had boasted that he would enter the garrison with his men in the dead of night. Sadullah Khan let him execute his plan, but Rajrup botched the task. Afterward, a Safavid sortie in Sadullah Khan's trench took many lives. The Mughal soldiers' bows, arrows, and swords were of no use against the heavy gunfire blasting from the fort.

Amid these setbacks, a letter from Shah Jahan arrived on the sixth of July, forbidding Aurangzeb to consolidate the guns in one area: "An attack from two sides is indeed possible and must be made. Attacking from only one side, however, is entirely inappropriate."[113] Why not just breach the wall using the two massive guns from Surat that they had, along with a handful of others? It must have been difficult for Aurangzeb to swallow his frustration. Did the emperor not understand that even their largest guns were no match for the fortress walls?

In the end, Aurangzeb never managed to execute his plan. First, the emperor learned about the Mughal army's recent losses, and had a change of heart. Now he felt it best that Aurangzeb make his own decision about the artillery. But then soon afterward, on the twelfth of July, Shah Jahan ordered Sadullah Khan to lift the siege.[114] Five days later, by the time the emperor changed his mind again to order that the siege continue, the army had already dispersed.

The recriminations started even before Aurangzeb reached Kabul: "It astounds us, that after such preparations the fort was not taken." Aurangzeb was still on his way when he received word about his new appointment. Shah Jahan ordered him to tell his sons in Multan (and presumably his wives and daughters too) to meet him in Lahore. After Aurangzeb paid his respects at court, he was to proceed directly to the Deccan, where he would serve in the position he had last held in 1644. This was essentially a demotion. To make matters clearer, Aurangzeb's annual salary was to be cut by seventeen lakh rupees.

That was not all. There would be another campaign against Qandahar the following year. This time, Dara Shukoh would lead it. Moreover, Sulaiman Shukoh, now a young man of seventeen, had been made governor of Kabul. Aurangzeb probably wondered if Dara was behind Shah Jahan's lack of support for his Qandahar campaign. That Shah Jahan wanted to wrest Qandahar back from the Safavids, there is no doubt. It did not matter which of his sons accomplished the victory. But in Aurangzeb's failure lay a new opportunity for Dara.[115]

Aurangzeb did his best to protest within the tight confines of propriety that governed his relationship with the emperor. First he claimed that he had, at the outset, wished to serve in Qandahar under "Dada Bhai," the Hindavi term of respect he used in his letters to refer to his elder brother. Might he not attempt Qandahar again? The emperor dismissed him with a Persian proverb recited by the wise: "Something already tested, need not be tested again."[116]

6

MISSION

1652–1654

AURANGZEB HAD BARELY BEEN on the road for a week after leaving Kabul, when a monsoon flood forced him to halt his journey at Naushera. The Indus raged. The river was so swollen, it destroyed the bridge that he and his entourage would have used to cross to the other bank. There was no point trying to construct even a temporary bridge before the waters abated. The few boats available were not enough to carry all his men across.

But the prince was not in a terrible hurry. He had to convince his father that this was a serious emergency and that he was not just dawdling—a hard task, but by this point he was accustomed to the emperor's rebukes. More importantly, he saw an opportunity: his brother Shuja, bound for Bengal, was also held up on the same side of the river. While writing his father, Aurangzeb mentions Shuja's presence in the briefest, most casual way possible. Did the two manage to meet?[1] The emperor, so keenly supervising his sons' movements, made sure that they rarely saw each other, unless, of course, two princes were required to cooperate for a military campaign. When they carried out their duties separately in far-flung regions of the empire, the princes posed less of a threat to his authority.

In a letter to Jahanara, though, Aurangzeb suggests that he and Shuja missed crossing paths by a hair. "If the prince of mortals had stayed on this side of the river two or three days longer, and pulled in his reins [to stop], a meeting with him would have quickly come to hand." He hoped to meet Shuja in Lahore. Perhaps Jahanara could help. "God-Most-High willing, whenever his delight-increasing company, of which I have long been desirous, is obtained, it would be the manifestation of Sahib's [Jahanara's] grace and kindness . . ."[2] Aurangzeb stopped in Shahjahanabad for a few days on his way to Agra. While his father was away on the road, he received imperial permission to enter the private quarters of the palace-fort so that he could meet his sisters. Certainly, he would have seen Roshanara and Gauharara, but Aurangzeb spent the most time with Jahanara, whom he hosted at his own mansion in the city and visited again to take leave before proceeding to Agra.[3]

A later account reports that Aurangzeb and Shuja finally did manage to meet in December, at Agra. Aurangzeb was headed back to the Deccan after stopping there, and Shuja was going to travel farther east to Bengal. Jahanara herself may have arranged their meeting, per Aurangzeb's request, though the outcome of their encounter would not have pleased her. Aurangzeb's pent-up bitterness against his father and Dara, his eldest brother, seemed to have touched a chord in Shuja. The two brothers secretly committed to a pact. They would further solidify their sibling relationship through the marriages of their children. In any case, for Mughal royals, fraternal bonds were, by themselves, too weak to count for much. One of Shuja's daughters would marry Aurangzeb's eldest son, Muhammad Sultan. A daughter of Aurangzeb would wed Shuja's eldest son, Zain-ud-Din. The marriages could not take place immediately. Muhammad Sultan was not yet thirteen. For now, though, the betrothals sufficed. The brothers would not breathe a word about this to their father, for it was Shah Jahan's prerogative to approve, or reject, the matches of all in his extended household.[4]

The marriage alliance did not reflect a plot to overthrow the throne. But it signaled a deeper agreement. After all, the question of succession could at any time burst on the horizon. Shah Jahan was almost sixty-one. He had already lived longer than his father, Jahangir. Aurangzeb saw a good opportunity to enlist his brothers' support in advance. Once in the Deccan, he would also arrange to have a separate meeting with his younger brother, Murad.[5]

DARA SHUKOH STAYED BEHIND IN LAHORE after his father passed through the city in August, en route to Shahjahanabad from Kabul. There was plenty of work to do, and the prince had the wherewithal to carry it out. Dara was assigned new territories that placed enormous revenues at his disposal. Under his jurisdiction were now Kabul, Lahore, and Multan. Sulaiman Shukoh, now nearly eighteen, remained in Kabul to oversee affairs there. The prince's trusted aide, Tawakkul Beg, was dispatched to Ghazni with the duties of court reporter and overseer of revenue collection. Shah Jahan's chroniclers tell us that these new governorships were given to Dara Shukoh in accordance with the prince's own requests.[6] This suggests that Shah Jahan allowed Dara a fair amount of independence while planning the Qandahar siege.

The prince believed that he had divine favor on his side. Earlier, in Kabul, he had invited two Sufis to a gathering in his quarters. They sat in a meditative trance, with sleeved hands shrouding their faces. After about an hour had passed, one lifted his head and reported that he was witnessing there before them the situation of Iran as it unfolded. "The ruler of Iran has passed away, having bid farewell to the kingdom and to fortune." The other Sufi echoed him, saying that he could see the ruler's funeral. Indeed, Dara Shukoh, too, announced that he had recently beheld a mystical vision that Shah Abbas would die before he spent even seven days in Qandahar.

But Dara was determined to leave nothing to fate. Inayat Khan reports, "During the period of three months and some days that he remained in Lahore, he used such profuse exertions that he accomplished what otherwise could not have been done in one year."[7] The prince summoned some Europeans in Mughal employ to build a model fort. For assistance, they consulted books that they brought with them, which were illustrated with diagrams of every possible type of fortress as well as potential lines of attack. Then Dara had European and Indian gunners, in turn, stage a mock siege. They hurled cannonballs at the fort from battle stations at the foot of its wall. The prince was more impressed with the European battery.[8]

Such an extravagant spectacle needed an audience. Dara invited choice guests to view the military exercise. A chronogram marking the date, "The first victory of Dara Shukoh," rose above the congratulatory murmurs to be recorded in a contemporary chronicle.[9] Its author, Muhammad Badi, also known as Rashid Khan, was an official in the service of Mahabat Khan (a son of Shah Jahan's old ally, who had inherited his father's title). Rashid Khan accompanied his master to Qandahar. Much later, in 1678, Rashid Khan published his military diaries of the expedition and the preparation leading up to it, which gives detailed insight into the Qandahar campaign.[10]

Dara Shukoh guided his troops toward Qandahar in February 1653.[11] The army was magnificently supplied with men, animals, wealth, and guns—the cavalry numbered seventy thousand, there were ten thousand foot soldiers and sixty elephants from the imperial stable in addition to the 170 that the prince and his accompanying nobles already had. Dara carried with him a whole crore of rupees for his expenses. Boats transported several heavy cannons separately via the Ravi River. The army stopped for provisions in Multan along the way, where in the third week of March, Dara Shukoh celebrated *Nauroz*, the Iranian new year, according to court custom. There, Mahabat Khan contributed thirty lakh rupees toward the campaign, while another sixty lakhs arrived from Lahore.[12] The prince was anxious not to tarry too long in Multan and ordered that a bridge of boats be built.

Though Dara Shukoh radiated enthusiasm for his first true taste of battle, several of the nobles with him were more jaded. Rajrup and Jai Singh, among others, were two-time veterans of the Mughal-Safavid wars. They had barely returned from a grueling campaign and journey, only to receive orders that they should turn around and march back. If they held any reservations about the expedition's feasibility, they dared not voice them publicly.

A small part of what must have been a longer correspondence between Raja Jai Singh and Dara's wife, Nadira Bano, still survives. It is a decree, written in her hand, advising the raja to discharge the duties assigned to him and not to worry about attending to her. The date corresponds to the second week of April 1653, when Jai Singh would have been marching toward Qandahar.[13]

This little fragment, lifted from its context, raises more questions than it answers. Why would Jai Singh and Nadira correspond, and why would she feel it necessary to remind him to focus on the task at hand? Was he deliberately stalling, looking for a way to escape the military action? Jahanara had also written to Jai Singh the previous year, informing him that he had to go fight at Qandahar.[14] These examples show that the imperial women played a role in corralling Shah Jahan's nobles toward the Mughal state's war efforts. In Jai Singh's case, it appears that Jahanara and Nadira were specially roped in to motivate the reluctant Rajput warrior.

AS HE LEFT FOR QANDAHAR, Dara had no way of knowing that he would never come to reside in Lahore again. He would visit, of course, but not stay there for any significant length of time. For the prince, Lahore was not merely a city. It was sacred land. As Dara's poetry attests, its earth mingled with the dust of interred saints, chief among them his beloved spiritual guide, Miyan Mir.[15] Over the years, after becoming governor, Dara had worked to leave his architectural imprint on the city's landscape. It was already splendid enough. The citadel, walled in red sandstone, rose south of the Ravi River, elevated by its hilly ground. Outside the city's eastern Delhi

Gate, Shah Jahan's physician Wazir Khan had built a jewel-like mosque embellished all over with vivid, Iranian-style tiles. Its minarets gazed over a city complex nearby that Dara had been constructing over the years. Farther east, upstream of the Ravi, Dara laid out a garden alongside other gardens, including Shah Jahan's Faiz Bakhsh, lining the main road to Shahjahanabad. He also changed the royal route to Shahjahanabad so that it went southward, past the tomb complex that he had built for Miyan Mir.[16]

The military preparations leading up to the siege of Qandahar consumed Dara. But he made time for another project that he had recently started. In 1652, sometime after he turned thirty-eight, the prince began to compile a book of ecstatic sayings by notable Sufis, both past and present. He would call it *Hasanat-ul-arifin* (Fine Words of the Gnostics). There is a special term for this kind of utterance in Persian and Arabic—*shath*, which connotes bold, even shocking, speech that only a mystic in a state of ecstasy might get away with. The poet Farid-ud-Din Attar (d. 1221) included in his memorial on Sufi saints an influential telling of a story about the master Mansur Hallaj (d. 922), who was executed by the ruling Abbasid regime in Baghdad. Hallaj famously equated himself with God, declaring *"ana-al-haqq"* (I am the Divine Truth). Attar vividly describes Hallaj's brutal execution, after which even his ashes continued to cry out his *shath*.[17] Hallaj's crime, the Persian poet Hafiz explains, lay not in the idea he expressed but in his divulgence of a secret so momentous it ought to be revealed only on the gallows.[18] Such revolutionary utterances, by Hallaj and others, came to be themselves (paradoxically, perhaps) institutionalized. Four centuries before Dara Shukoh, the Iranian mystic Ruzbihan Baqli (d. 1209) collected several of these aphorisms, which he then annotated with commentaries, first in Arabic and then an expanded version in Persian. In his own collection, the prince freely borrowed from Baqli, simplifying the renowned Sufi's ornate prose, and supplementing the entries with other material such as Jami's magisterial *Nafahat-ul-uns* (Breaths of Intimacy) as well as with expressions relating his own personal experience.[19]

However canonical these ecstatic utterances had become, though, Dara Shukoh used his project to draw a line between mystics immersed in divine unity and advocates of a more sober religiosity. The prince had grown weary of the usual Sufi literature, he confesses, in the *Hasanat*'s introduction. Nothing but "pure unity" (*tauhid-i sirf*) would suffice for him.[20] Dara began to gush lofty verities and spiritual mysteries in his states of ecstasy. Then, he says, some "base-natured people of low aspiration, and dry, insipid ascetics" set about slandering him, accusing him of blasphemy, and rejecting him, all because of their short-sightedness. For this reason, Dara Shukoh relates, he decided to collect the exalted sayings of the great mystics that he had read and heard to serve as definitive proof against those "Christ-faced imposters, those Moses-resembling Pharoahs, those Abu Jahls of the Muhammadan flock."[21]

Should we conclude that Dara Shukoh's religious inclinations invited the ulama's wrath? Certainly here, as in his earlier writings, there is a rhetorical function to framing his own work as a riposte to opponents. This is a way for the prince to build himself up and use the weight of leading Sufi authorities on his side. Moreover, it was common in Persian mystical texts to preemptively criticize one's adversaries.

It is also quite possible that the prince's detractors were not just imaginary concoctions. Dara paints them colorfully, but their identities remain blurred. We do not know what public roles they may have inhabited. They might have been Sufis, or individual scholars also affiliated with a Sufi order, or even rival factions within the court who sought a pretext to defame. Regardless, the stark social division between Sufis and ulama is a very modern notion in South Asia. And the idea of an Islam bereft of mystical piety or devotion was not even conceivable.[22]

But in neighboring Safavid Iran, a clerical elite was gradually gaining ground over the eroding power of Sufi shaikhs, in their own attempt to claim the mantle of divine knowledge and authority.[23] It is possible that Dara heard murmurs of opposition to his newfound proclivities, though it is hard to imagine an open campaign against the prince, given that he had the full backing of the state apparatus for his spiritual explorations. One of the most frequently cited poems from Dara's *diwan*, reflects his disdain for custodians of religious orthopraxy, known in popular parlance as *mullas*:

> Paradise is where no mullas are found,
> Where there is no bickering and clamor from the mullas
> May the world be free of the mulla's noise
> May no one care about their fatwas . . .
> In the city where a mulla has his home
> There isn't a wise man to be found
> Don't gaze, O Qadiri, upon the mulla's face!
> Don't go where there is no madness for love![24]

In the world of the ghazal, the literal-minded mulla or the puritanical ascetic (*zahid*) did not have a very high standing. So, for this particular poetic genre, Dara Shukoh's statements are not particularly shocking. Moreover, in his own daily life, Dara Shukoh constantly engaged with Islamic religious scholars. Mulla Fazil, who had once signed a fatwa against Mulla Shah, now accompanied the prince to Qandahar. Qazi Aslam, the jurist with Qadiri connections, had long been part of Dara's intimate group. Further, many of the nobility were trained in the Islamic sciences, just as many of them also held Sufi affiliations.

But then, who precisely was a mulla or, to use a term without such derogatory connotations, an *alim*? Surely village judges or provincial bureaucrats were not worthy of Dara Shukoh's ire. In the mid-1630s, the scholar Muhammad Sadiq of Kashmir compiled a biographical anthology of learned men from the time of Timur to Shah Jahan. For each era, he further divided his compilation of lives into: (1) *sayyids*, namely descendants of the Prophet, along with leading Sufi authorities; (2) ulama, who generally focused on jurisprudence, together with physicians and accomplished scholars of theology and speculative philosophy, referred to as *fuzala*; and finally (3) poets. There are subtle hierarchies here, to be sure, but also a remarkably capacious understanding of who an *alim* or learned scholar might be. And within these classifications lie tangles of further complexity. Qazi Safa, a jurist, is listed as a poet. Shah Jahan's minister and confidant, the courtier Afzal Khan, has pride of place among the ulama.[25] Mulla Abd-us-Salam, who wrote on Islamic law, was also classified as an *alim*, though he possessed a "dervish-like disposition."[26] As for Muhammad Sadiq, the compiler of this collection of biographies, he was associated with Shaikh Ahmad Sirhindi, as well as with the famed hadith scholar, jurist and Qadiri Sufi Abd-ul-Haqq of Delhi, both of whom occupied many of these categories as well.

Shah Jahan's reign thus did not have anything resembling a homogeneous group of conservative clerics. Dara's censure of literal-minded conservatives certainly functions as a rhetorical device designed to lend authority to his own enterprise. But as with the fatwa that once threatened Mulla Shah over his own ecstatic utterances, there were clearly factions who also sought to police the boundaries of probity. Were the critics whom the prince ridicules, then, closer to home—the more soberly-inclined scholars and Sufis of the empire's highest echelons? The ranks of Shah Jahan's nobility had been expanding for some time. Men with some formal religious training thickly populated this elite group who held imperial assignments. The prince might have been justly wary of some sections of the noble classes. In response, rather than quelling his spiritual explorations, he sought to strengthen his position by collecting the testaments of canonical authorities.

Moreover, Mulla Shah, too, was suspicious of those religious authorities who, he felt, did not fully appreciate the higher stages of esoteric knowledge. As the Sufi master rose in stature at the court, prominent religious figures flocked to see him. Among them were the scholar Mulla Abd-ul-Hakim Siyalkoti and the Naqshbandi Sufi Khwaja Khurd Dihlawi, neither of whom managed to achieve a deep spiritual intimacy with Mulla Shah. In Tawakkul Beg's words, they merely "thirsted after literal knowledge," the kind found in books of theology and philosophy, rather than the inner wisdom that Mulla Shah imparted to a select few.[27]

Dara felt comfortable sharing his own ecstatic declarations with another Sufi to whom he had become very close—the Qadiri Shah Dilruba, whose honorific means "heart robber."[28] Six of the prince's letters to Dilruba survive, unfortunately without the shaikh's replies. Dara Shukoh's correspondence with Dilruba effervesces with passionate devotion to God and love for the shaikh. Though they are not dated, the ideas they convey are in line with the prince's remarks to Muhibbullah. These letters, which express mystical secrets, were probably not meant for the general eye. There is no mention of them in Dara's books, though he would include a section on Shah Dilruba in his *Hasanat-ul-arifin*.[29]

Dara's first letter expresses thanks for a letter and a poem the Sufi had sent. He laments that they have not met—it is not clear if they had not met for a while or if they had never met in person. "Wherever I am, whether Agra or Lahore, my heart is fettered to you."[30] His missives to the shaikh are letters of deep affection, replete with longing. One of his letters ends with this couplet: "Why have you become estranged from me?/You and I are but old friends."[31]

Both Dilruba and Dara share a mutual reverence for their Qadiri teachers. In one letter Dara Shukoh rains countless supplications on "Miyan sahib."[32] In another, he mentions "Miyan Jio" in the context of the Sufi's relationship with his addressee.[33] But Dara and Dilruba themselves also seem to share the closeness of master and favorite disciple. Dara holds his addressee in high regard, referring to his joy upon receiving a "letter of forgiveness" from the sheikh absolving the prince of any personal faults. In his correspondence, Dara reiterates the point he had earlier made to Muhibbullah, but phrases it differently. He declares, "Praise God, praise God, that from the blessing of love of this noble, revered, great community (*taifa*), insincere (*majazi*) Islam has fled the heart of this faqir, and true infidelity (*kufr-i haqiqi*) has shown its face."[34]

Is Dara really saying that he has renounced Islam to become an infidel, a kafir? Some modern readers, focusing on the second part of his utterance, believe so.[35] But one key to understanding the statement lies in its first part, where Dara gives credit to a "noble community," which can only be identified as the Qadiri order (he uses the same term, *taifa*, to refer to it in his *Sakinat-ul-auliya*). Dara Shukoh's commitment to the Sufi order into which he was initiated has not wavered. Instead, through his mystical practice, under the tutelage of his pir, new worlds opened up to him.

Dara now knows more palpably that God and the universe are one. Rather than preparing to leave Islam—the insincere, superficial, or external Islam that he contrasts with the real—the prince clings tight to a dominant strand of Islamic devotional thought that might be thought of, if imperfectly, as "mystical infidelity."[36] Dara draws on the juxtaposition of true infidelity (*kufr-i haqiqi*) and insincere Islam (*islam-i majazi*). This pairing was famously advanced by the renowned mystical poet Mahmud Shabistari (d. 1340) and championed earlier by the famed Sufi martyr Ain-i Quzat al-Hamadani.[37] The vocabulary of infidelity had been well-ingrained in Persian poetry for centuries. For a mystic, claims of embracing infidelity were often a means of conveying the extent of one's passionate love and longing for the divine. Underlying such utterances is the recognition that God transcends all duality, including the duality of faith and infidelity. Unlike God, faith and infidelity are created and therefore transient. Thus the seeming rejection of faith is actually a way to get closer to God's unity.

The prince's critique of "insincere Islam" also had a longer history at the Mughal court. Dara's great-grandfather Akbar instituted a special mode of imperial discipleship called the *din-i ilahi,* which in modern times has often been misunderstood as a newly invented religion.[38] One of Akbar's courtiers, Abd-ul-Qadir Badayuni (d. 1605), secretly poured out his critique of the goings-on at court in a chronicle revealed only after his death. Here, he reports that new initiates in Akbar's circle of devotees took vows promising to renounce the "religion of insincere (*majazi*) and derivative (*taqlidi*) Islam which they have seen and heard from their fathers," and to embrace the "divine religion" (*din-i ilahi*).[39] In the structure of imperial discipleship, the emperor became the supreme religious authority of esoteric knowledge. While Akbar's din-i ilahi did not continue beyond his reign, the practice of imperial discipleship very much shaped the hierarchical relationships governing the court. Dara's denunciation of "insincere Islam" echoes Akbar, without acknowledging his influence.

At this point in his religious trajectory, it was not enough for the prince to verbally embrace infidelity as a mark of his adherence to the ultimate truth of divine unity. He stretched out to explore new spiritual territories, though he always stayed rooted in the vocabulary of Islamic monotheism. From the *Hasanat-ul-arifin,* which Dara Shukoh finished in 1654, we gather that the prince had begun to delve even deeper into Indic thought. Other sources indicate that he read as widely as he could; his studies included the *Ramayana,* the stories of Krishna, and likely Abu-l-Fazl's writings on Indic religions.[40] He would have had access to the Akbar-era Persian translations adorning the imperial library and to people at court, like the pandit Kavindracharya Saraswati, to guide his explorations of Hindu learning. Shah

Jahan gladly aided Dara Shukoh's new studies. In fact, between January 1652 and March 1653, Kavindra received no less than six handsome awards from the emperor, ranging from a thousand to fifteen hundred rupees.[41]

Dara Shukoh was not the only one balancing military and administrative work with ambitious literary endeavors. While the prince was leading his men to war, his deputy in Ghazni, Tawakkul Beg, also used his time in the Afghan city to engage in literary activity, though his primary duties—writing news reports and administering revenues—no doubt kept him busy enough. Shamsher Khan, Shah Jahan's governor in the province, had charged him with an additional task. The governor desired to read a history of the past kings of Iran. He had in mind the famous *Shah-nama* of Firdausi, the renowned poet who claimed to have labored for thirty years on his epic poem peopled with ancient Iranian rulers and demons. But the governor was put off by the effort required to plow through the *Shah-nama*'s ornate and lengthy verse in order to access the moral of each story.[42]

So, Tawakkul Beg condensed Firdausi's epic into easily digestible prose, and also summarized its main lessons at regular intervals. He named the abridgment *Tarikh-i dilgusha-yi Shamsher Khani* (The Heart-Pleasing Shamsher Khani History), after his patron. Tawakkul Beg completed the work in 1063 AH (1652/3), in the same year when the Qandahar campaign was unfolding. Though Firdausi's poem did not, of course, treat contemporary Iran, it is hard not to see parallels between the war in Qandahar and Shamsher Khan's interest in Iranian history.

Tawakkul Beg could not predict how popular his prose version of the *Shah-nama* would be in years to come. There are hardly any manuscripts left of the *Nuskha*, his personal account of Mulla Shah and the imperial family. But over 150 copies of his *Shah-nama* still exist, and this figure does not account for those in private or uncatalogued collections or the many that must have decayed or disappeared over the years.[43]

BY THE END OF APRIL, Dara Shukoh's men had taken up positions by the city's gates. Qandahar was set in a fertile oasis watered by the Arghandab River and its tributaries. The garrison city lay on a steep, rocky ridge rising sharply up from the plain. At the uppermost levels of the ridge, several peaks soared above the fort. Lakah, the highest, was used to store precious water reserves for the citadel's use. Massive ramparts enclosed the city, constructed from a mixture of clay, stones, and straw so solid that a British colonial officer in the nineteenth century reported that a bullet could only pierce its outer surface.[44] Halfway down the northeast side of the ridge lay a memorial to the conquests of Dara Shukoh's ancestor, Babur—a vaulted chamber hollowed out of the mountainside, with inscriptions on its walls praising Babur and his son Humayun. It acquired its name, Chihil Zina, from the forty steep steps leading up to it. Below the fort, the city with its large trading market straggled up an elevated plateau. A moat with a complex system for controlling the flow of water around the citadel added a further layer of impenetrability.[45]

The Mughal army hoped to breach the ramparts by blasting their way through the walls with an onslaught of cannon fire. They also had their eyes set on Chihil Zina. If this could be captured, its height would give them a strategic advantage for attacking the fortress.

The broad contours of how the Mughals fared at Qandahar are easy enough to discern, but the finer points vary depending on the different accounts. Shah Jahan's court historians dutifully reshaped and abridged whatever Dara must have sent to court by way of letters and the reports of his news writers. In contrast, Rashid Khan's far more detailed account, which circulated after the events, is colored by the author's primary loyalty to his patron, Mahabat Khan. The discrepancy between these versions hints at tensions between the prince and the khan during the campaign. The few modern historians who discuss Rashid Khan's *Lataif-ul-akhbar* (The Choice Reports) consider it a complete indictment of Dara Shukoh's military abilities.[46]

Yet the often bitter and partisan character of the work, with its focus on incriminations, makes it a difficult source for assessing the situation on the ground. Rashid Khan records the excruciating infighting between various nobles often in an effort to paint himself in a favorable light. The work narrates each day's events and conversations from the author's perspective. It is so detailed that its original form must have been Rashid Khan's own journal, which he made public only later. In this way it shares a similar form with Tawakkul Beg's own personal observations recorded in the *Nuskha* of his time in the service of Mulla Shah and the imperial family.

The beginning of the campaign was the easy part. Astrologers fixed the auspicious time for the siege on May 15, 1653.[47] The commander Rustam Khan went on ahead with an Uzbek contingent for reconnaissance. Dara Shukoh camped nearby for about a week before the appointed time. His men plundered nearby farms for provisions. Local chieftains made visits to pay their respects. On the thirteenth of May, he came to the outskirts of Qandahar and deputed his men to different gates of the fortress. Then came the digging of trenches and other elaborate preparations for the siege. The challenge was to accomplish this while the Safavids fired from the great height of their citadel. Meanwhile, Rustam Khan worked to capture the nearby fortress of Bust, which was easier to take, so that its loss would lob a psychological blow to the Safavids.[48]

But by far the Mughals' most pressing difficulty was their deficient artillery. This had been Aurangzeb's single greatest problem at Qandahar as well. First of all, they had to wait endlessly—four months—for the arrival of the two heaviest guns, named *Fath-i Mubarak* (Blessed Victory) and *Kishwar Kushai* (Clime Destroyer). Without these, there was no realistic hope that the Mughals could breach the citadel walls. In the meantime, they had to figure out how to make cannon shot locally. Thirty thousand cast iron cannonballs had been left behind in Lahore, as they were deemed too heavy to bring. The stonecutters accompanying the army were forced to use trial and error methods to figure out how to make cannonballs that did not immediately crumble when fired.[49] This also cost valuable time and led to missed opportunities. The Safavids easily spotted their enemy's vulnerabilities and exploited them with relish.

In the course of jotting down his diary, Rashid Khan mentions that various sorcerers frequented the Mughal army camp. As with astrology, the occult arts were cultivated as an accepted body of practice and knowledge throughout the period, both in Hindustan and among the neighboring Muslim dynasties. The author of the *Lataif* does not make too much of these episodes—he casually weaves them into a larger mass of detail on the day's happenings. One Indian sorcerer, named Indarkar, traveled with the army from Lahore, and managed, through well-placed contacts, to secure an audience with the prince. In Qandahar, he brazenly approached the besieged fort and asked to be let in so that he could smoke a tobacco chillum from the top. The Safavids played host to him there for some days. However, when Indarkar asked for permission to return, they tortured and killed him.[50]

A yogi and his disciples also lived off Dara Shukoh's largesse, without apparently doing much to earn their keep. But it was Jafar (fl. 1671), Dara's head of artillery, who fell for the claims of a certain Hajji, a sorcerer and illusionist. The Hajji wandered into the camp, claiming he had the power to command jinn.[51] He performed various rites for Jafar involving dancers and sacrifice of a dog, but the demons he controlled failed to quell the fort's cannons and guns. The Safavids heard about this Hajji's necromancy and retaliated with a magic rite of their own, stuffing a dog's carcass with boiled rice and flinging it into Jafar's trench. This, explains Rashid Khan, was a means of canceling out the Hajji's incantation with their own spell.[52] At the embattlements, as Mughal soldiers fell under torrents of artillery, high-ranking officials commanding artillery as well as footmen in the infantry wove spells, recited auspicious suras from the Quran, and invoked the sublime names of God. They sought to harness the influence of celestial powers so as to subjugate demons into their service, just as they sought to subjugate the citadel.[53]

It would be a mistake to view such appeals to divine and occult power as merely limited to the fringes of society. Mughal elites were intimately familiar with the occult arts and continually cultivated them. Take, for instance, the warrior, scholar, and man of erudition and taste, Muhammad Baqir (d. 1637). He came from the aristocratic family known as Najm-i Sani, the "Second Star." At least two members from the Najm-i Sani clan of Iranian émigrés fought alongside Dara Shukoh at the walls of Qandahar, including Muhammad Baqir's son, Fakhr Khan.

Muhammad Baqir migrated from Savafid Iran as a child, with his father. He entered Akbar's service in his youth and continued his illustrious career in the courts of Jahangir and Shah Jahan. A renowned archer and battle-tested commander, he was also a talented calligrapher and poet. With his skills on the page and the field of battle, Muhammad Baqir rose from commander of the garrison in Multan to governor of Orissa, then Gujarat, and finally Allahabad. He cemented his alliance to the royal family by marrying Nur Jahan's niece.[54] Muhammad Baqir is well known for a treatise on moral philosophy and the discipline of the soul, which he dedicated to Jahangir.[55] Much less remembered is his mastery of physics and observational astronomy, which had direct bearing on the military arts.[56] He also pursued an abiding interest in occult learning.

Numerous manuscripts survive in Muhammad Baqir's name dedicated to observing the movement of the stars, crafting sundry talismans, fashioning pin dolls, and casting spells, all promising the power to summon demons and jinn. Here are charms for lovers, enemies, emperors, and battles against invading armies, illuminated with fine talismanic figures.[57] Muhammad Baqir's occult writings draw inspiration from the Hermetic quest for universal knowledge and take as models for the hidden arts Aristotle, the paragon of sages, and his famed disciple, the world-conquering hero Alexander.[58] For many Muslim intellectuals of the day, steeped in Avicennian neoplatonism on the emanating power of the soul, both magic and miracles formed part of a larger body of legitimate knowledge on the nature of existence. In the Mughal court, much of this material also overlaps directly with earlier spellbooks by the likes of the great Ashari theologian and philosopher Fakhr-ud-Din Razi (d. 1210) and Siraj-ud-Din Sakkaki (d. 1229), a highly influential statesman at the Mongol court whose name has long been associated with the occult science. Muhammad Baqir, master of the sword and pen, produced a Persian rendition of Razi's book of astral magic, *al-Sirr-ul-maktum* (The Hidden Secret), and a translation into Persian of an Arabic collection of spells, *Zakhira-i Iskandarani* (The Alexandrian Treasury). The powerful Iranian aristocrat went on to compose and dedicate to Shah Jahan a Persian encyclopedia of theology and jurisprudence, which also touched on the occult arts, all filtered through a devout Shii perspective.[59]

All of this goes to say that Dara Shukoh was by no means unique in his willingness to entertain sorcerers during the Qandahar campaign. The imperial library was itself replete with manuscripts on occult learning, many of which were drawn from earlier Arabic and Persian manuals.[60] In addition to a lasting engagement with Indic astrology, the learned of the Mughal court browsed *Indrajala* works on illusionism and incantations produced in various vernaculars of India.[61] The elites sanctioned their embrace of magic through the precedent of the Prophet Solomon who commanded armies of jinn, mastered the speech of animals, and possessed knowledge of the unseen. The seal of Solomon, known as the quintessential master builder, features throughout Mughal architecture and serves as a lodestar for both Jahangir and Shah Jahan.[62] It was also common for Mughal warriors to wear under their armor talismanic clothing woven with Quranic verses, sacred sayings, and occult designs, as they outwardly decorated their shields, swords, helmets, banners, and guns with tightly woven calligraphy meant to protect them on the battlefield. In this, they shared much in common with their Timurid predecessors and their Ottoman and Safavid contemporaries.[63]

Waiting for reinforcements, dependent on an unstable supply chain, and in search of any means to breach the walls at Qandahar, Dara was forced to improvise. And so, apart from enchanters, he also called upon the practical knowledge of engineers from the Deccan to design mechanical cranes (*jarr-i-saqil*) that could launch missiles from above down onto the battlements.[64]

Given the inherently weak position of the Mughal army at Qandahar, it is not surprising that personalities clashed and tempers frayed. It did not help that, according to Rashid Khan's digest of the events, the prince's head of artillery, Jafar, made up for his inexperience with overenthusiasm, regularly promising more than he could deliver. Dara Shukoh, firmly set on reversing the previous Mughal losses at Qandahar, was inclined to listen to Jafar over the more measured judgments of others. At the beginning, too, it seemed that Mahabat Khan also had confidence in Jafar. "If there were ten people like him, we would take the fort in two or three days," the khan told Dara Shukoh. "O Lord of the World," Jafar would say, "why are they sitting heedlessly today when a hundred and fifty *gaz* of the city wall have fallen into the ditch and the Sher Hajji wall is more delicate than paper?"[65] But to inflict sufficient damage on the Sher Hajji wall was easier said than done.

Beneath the veneer of a united front, tensions brewed. Sectarian and ethnic strife mingled with personal animosities. Jafar and Mirza Abdullah, a paymaster (*mir bakhshi*) whom Dara put into the service of the infantry, bickered frequently. Jafar carped that Mirza Abdullah's sympathies, and those of his men toward the enemy could not be fully trusted: "He is Irani and I am Turani, there can never be friendship between the two of us. Between these factions of ours are essential disagreement, religious enmity, and external and eternal contradictions that have always endured and will continue to do so."[66] Mirza Abdullah was from the same family as the commander and occultist Muhammad Baqir Najm-i Sani.[67] Many Iranian émigrés rose to prominence in India making careers for themselves through the patronage of local potentates, and several served directly in Dara's retinue.[68] Yet, the incident with Jafar suggests that their status as outsiders came into focus during this war against Iran.

If Jafar optimistically boasted of imminent victory, Raja Jai Singh made up for him in his reluctance to fight. The prince had more than an inkling of this, for early in the campaign, he addressed the raja harshly. Jai Singh was "honored with the felicity of the kornish obeisance," reports Rashid Khan, and then Dara Shukoh gave him a tongue-lashing. "This is the third time you've come to the fort. If this time too, you do nothing and go back, what are you going to tell the servants of the venerable Shadow of God [Shah Jahan]? And how will you show your face before the women of Hindustan? Truly, women are better than men who repeatedly return unsuccessful. . . ." This dig at the raja's manhood must have rankled. "Even though there is no path open to the fort yet," retorted Jai Singh, "order us to attack, so that our manliness or unmanliness can become apparent." But, for all Jai Singh's bravado, he still defied the prince's commands whenever he could.[69]

By the end, morale was so low that even Jafar's motivation vanished. It was already the third week of August. Dara Shukoh and his commanders had planned a last-ditch attack in the hope of finally invading the fortress. They managed to breach the wall. But the hordes of Mughal soldiers who rushed to enter were shot down by Safavid gunners. In this crucial moment, according to Rashid Khan, rumor spread that Jafar sat down to enjoy a meal of bread with onion and watermelon. Another of Dara's commanders, Izzat Khan, indulged in some personal grooming, sprinkling himself with rose water.[70] The Safavids, who had furnished the citadel with reinforcements, were able to easily withstand the onslaught. All the Mughal efforts were ultimately for naught, as the siege reached its bloody end and the Mughal forces, overstretched and undersupplied, were forced to retreat.

In Iran, court poets exulted. The famous Saib (d. 1676) of Tabriz had spent seven years of his life in India. He had served Zafar Khan, governor of Kabul, when Shah Jahan came to the throne. Now, he wrote a panegyric for Shah Abbas, celebrating Dara Shukoh's retreat. Though the Mughal rulers were also Muslim, albeit mainly Sunni, Saib speaks of the tussle over Qandahar as a religious war:

> Shah Abbas the second, the Sahib Qiran's manifestation
> Became victorious in the greater *jihad* against the commanders
> Once again, from beneath the Indian crows' feathers and wings
> Appeared the egg of Islam like the sun
> . . .
> Like the Shah's standard, the faces of the fort-commanders whitened
> The Indians all at once grew yellow-faced and ashamed
> Even though no color is deeper than black
> In their flight, yellow-face overcame those black people.[71]

Not only is the Mughal-Safavid war termed a *jihad,* it is the "greater jihad," more commonly understood as a spiritual struggle against the baser self.[72] And here, Shah Abbas is the true Sahib Qiran, possessor of the felicitous astral conjunction and master of the world. The image of the Indians as crows fleeing to expose the shining sun anticipates Saib's description of them as "black." The pairing of black and Hindu with white and Turk in Persian poetry has many complex connotations, and darkness is not necessarily always a negative quality.[73] Here, though, it is. Only the yellow of liverless cowardice is worse.

AFTER THE DEMORALIZING FAILURE ON THE AFGHAN MARCH-LANDS, Dara Shukoh stayed at least two weeks in Lahore before reaching the outskirts of Shahjahanabad on January 4, 1654. When he had arrived in Lahore a little over a year earlier, the emperor treated him like a victor. But now the prince moved swiftly to other pressing concerns. He needed to finish the new book that he had started. We know from Dara's own account that he began the *Hasanat-ul-arifin* in 1652, before the Qandahar expedition, but different versions of the text give varying dates of completion. One manuscript used in the modern edition of the collection has the date as Muharram 7, 1065 AH (November 17, 1654).[74] It is certainly possible that Dara started the project, halted it during the war, and then finished it almost a year later. But especially since the *Hasanat* is a brief work— only thirty-odd pages in an earlier nineteenth-century lithographed edition—an earlier date is also quite plausible. The manuscript used for the lithograph has Rabi-ul-Awwal 1, 1064 AH (January 20, 1654) as the *Hasanat*'s date of completion.[75] This timeframe still gives Dara roughly two and a half weeks after arriving in Delhi to finish the *Hasanat*, add and insert final entries and updates.

But before he signed off on the compilation, Dara Shukoh accomplished another important task. He met a new religious teacher. This time, he was a Hindu named Baba Lal who lived in Dhyanpur, roughly a hundred miles northeast of Lahore. Some texts call Baba Lal a *gosain*, and others call him a *bairagi*, both terms that denote Hindu ascetics. We do not know when exactly Baba Lal visited the prince, but they seem to have had several meetings. Evidence from the manuscript tradition suggests that they met after the Qandahar expedition.[76] The shrine of Baba Lal in Dhyanpur also holds this view. Its modern custodians claim that the prince met the ascetic there, though they incorrectly say that Dara also avoided facing his father, out of humiliation after the defeat.[77] Even if the prince and Baba Lal had not met before Qandahar, there would have been ample opportunity for talks during Dara's fortnight in Lahore. It is most likely, as some Persian sources suggest, that rather than go to Dhyanpur, the prince requested Baba Lal to visit Lahore.[78] But these were not just casual meetings or sessions of private tutoring in Indic thought. Just like the earlier encounters between Akbar and then Jahangir with the ascetic Chidrup, these conversations became an event, for posterity if not for the public, shaped over time by several hands.

A particularly evocative imperial painting of an encounter between a young Dara Shukoh and a Hindu ascetic lends insight into how such encounters were portrayed and imagined. The art connoisseur Stuart Cary Welch has attributed this painting to the master artist Govardhan, who worked in the ateliers of three Mughal emperors: Akbar, Jahangir, and Shah Jahan.[79] The scene takes place in front of a pillared, carved pavilion, located in a verdant blossoming garden on a terraced platform. At first glance, the setting seems very much like the Pari Mahal in Kashmir. But the Shalimar Garden in Lahore too has terraces and similar pavilions

Mughal prince converses with Hindu ascetic and other holy men.

made of marble. The miniature could just as well depict another Mughal garden in Lahore, even Dara's own.

On a platform before the pavilion, seven men are seated in a circle. Their faces are detailed so sensitively that they seem to be the likenesses of actual individuals. The eye is drawn to the saffron-robed ascetic in the center right. A wooden platform elevates the serene sage slightly above the others. He gently holds a wooden armrest of the type Hindu sadhus use. His eyes are distant, gazing outward; in Mughal figural art this often implies a detachment from the material world.[80] The prince, shown in profile, kneels respectfully beside the ascetic. The two form a dyad on the same horizontal axis, though not directly facing each other. The prince's gilded sash and turban lend him a glow, though without the nimbus that portraits of his father include. Two religious scholars, identifiably Muslim from their garb and beards, refer to books. A musician plays the *santur*, while a supplicant in the patched robe of a Sufi mendicant bows down before the ascetic.

The miniature appeals to a type of naturalism in its treatment of flora and physiognomy common to the tastes of the time. It would be misleading, though, to view the painting as a window onto a concrete event, such as Dara's encounters with Baba Lal. For one, Baba Lal, as portrayed here, bears a striking resemblance to figures in two of Govardhan's other paintings—a *tanpura* player in one and a Muslim ascetic in another.[81] Moreover, the miniature recalls previous iconic Mughal paintings: Jahangir meeting Chidrup, as well as Narsingh's famous depiction of Akbar leading a discussion among scholars from diverse religious traditions.[82]

There is also a discrepancy between the portrait of Dara here and what his appearance must have been at the time as a thirty-eight-year-old, when he is known from the literary record to have held his famous dialogues with Baba Lal. For years now, Dara Shukoh had sported a beard, just like his father Shah Jahan. In the painting, the prince's youth and beardlessness lend him an aura of wholesome purity. The painting thus may belong to an earlier set of dialogues with Hindu ascetics.

Dara Shukoh's encounter, or meetings, with Baba Lal later became such an enduring literary and visual motif that it is hard, if not impossible, to tease out what transpired during their encounter. Manuscripts and then lithographs of their dialogues offer extremely different versions. These divergences far exceed the minor discrepancies common to hand-copied texts. There is nothing resembling a stable text. One version is concise and so highly stylized, written in often-rhyming, alliterative prose, that it seems more like a crafted literary piece than a dialogue that might have actually taken place:

> I asked: What is the faqir's repast in hunger?
> He replied: His own flesh.
> I asked: What is a morsel in the throat?
> He replied: The food of patience.
> I asked: What is the faqir's existence?
> He replied: Always in prostration.[83]

Though this excerpt lyrically renders one conception of a faqir's ideal qualities, there is little here that might resemble an actual encounter between Dara Shukoh and Baba Lal. In contrast to this absence of specificity, though, this particular text details seven precise locations in which the two met in Lahore.[84] This serves as a way to carve the cultural memory of the prince deep into Lahore's geography and architecture, whether or not he actually met Baba Lal at these different settings.

Some manuscripts present longer, more involved dialogues, though even these do not all seem to belong to one identifiable family of manuscripts. Further, these longer versions of the dialogues are not quite transcripts of actual conversations, rather, they have undergone clear literary reshaping. Yet some of the manuscripts offer information about the mechanics of the encounters. A certain Rao Jadav Das is said to have acted as a secretary during the meetings. He recorded their dialogues in the Hindi that the prince and the ascetic must have used as a spoken medium.[85] This raw material was then distilled into Persian prose, sprinkled with a few verses for embellishment. Some manuscripts attribute this transformation to Chandarbhan Brahman, the imperial scribe and litterateur, whose hometown was Lahore.[86] This is by no means impossible. Rashid Khan, author of the *Lataif-ul-akhbar*, notably mentions that Chandarbhan accompanied Dara Shukoh to Qandahar as his manager of household supplies (*diwan-i buyutat*).[87]

The longer versions of the dialogues refer to Dara as *Aziz*, which means both "illustrious" and "beloved". They call the ascetic *Kamil*, the "perfected one." This honorific evokes the ideal in Islamic mysticism of the perfect human (*insan-i kamil*), who has obtained the heights of divine knowledge. The prince comes across as an earnest seeker, and Baba Lal as a patient teacher. According to the memory of these encounters endorsed at the Dhyanpur shrine today, Baba Lal dazzled Dara Shukoh, Shah Jahan, and Aurangzeb alike, and they all became his followers. But in these Persian dialogues, there is no attempt to establish the superiority of either Baba Lal or Dara Shukoh, though their relationship is one of master and disciple. The prince asks thoughtful questions that reveal a serious interest in Indic religious thought and texts: What is the difference between the *nad* (creative utterance) and the Vedas? What do *dhyana* (meditation) and *samadhi* (complete absorption) really mean? Why did Sita remain untouched even after being held in the demon Ravana's house? Why wouldn't a demon magically assume Rama's form?

Dara Shukoh grapples with some concepts and practices that, to him, would have seemed incompatible with monotheism and Islamic views on representing the divine: "What exactly is idol worship in the land of India, and who enjoined it?"

"This was instituted to strengthen the heart," replied Baba Lal. "Just like unmarried girls who play with dolls and then stop doing this when they run a household . . . those who are unaware of the interior, [engage with] exterior forms, and when they become aware of the interior, [they] abandon the exterior."[88]

The dialogues also reflect the prince's emerging interest in Advaita, or nondualist Vedantic philosophy, an inclination that Baba Lal appears to have also shared. Dara Shukoh enquired about the distinction between *atma* (individual self) and *paramatma* (supreme self). "There is no difference," Baba Lal answered. The prince also asked several questions about the stages of waking, dreaming, and deep sleep, with which Advaitic philosophical traditions are deeply preoccupied. These states serve to explain the different levels of reality and illusion.[89]

An important problem for the prince is how to negotiate liberation while remaining wedded to the material world: "When it is clear that [a ruler] is a yogi, how can it be established that his rule isn't free from the business of external ornamentation?" Baba Lal's reply suggests that the ruler can accommodate both roles: "The yogi exists in the ruler, for this reason . . . whenever he seeks the company of God's people, at that time the world does not interfere."[90]

For a few days, Baba Lal responded to the prince's shower of queries. Then he suddenly fell silent. The prince was ready with fresh questions. Baba Lal explained that the prince's constant referral to books was getting tiresome. If they could pause a moment, then perhaps they could derive some repose, and also pleasure, from their discussion. Recall Dara Shukoh's undermining of book knowledge in his letters to Muhibbullah and the *Haqqnuma*. When it came to books on Indic religions, he apparently had a different attitude.

At another point in their conversation, Dara asked, "What ought a faqir do altogether?" Baba Lal remained quiet. The prince tried again. The ascetic still would not speak. Did this silence mean that "the seeker was an initiate of the glance's states?," asked Dara. Baba Lal replied that he had answered. When asked what his response was, he replied, "Silent."[91] The dialogue resumes again after this exchange.

It would take a while for Dara Shukoh to fully absorb and build on his lessons with Baba Lal. His immediate task was to complete the *Hasanat-ul-arifin*. Dara Shukoh begins this collection of ecstatic utterances with a divinely revealed shath from the Quran: "He is the First and the Last, and the Outward and the Inward."[92] This means, the prince explains, that God says, "existence is contained in me, and all is I." He also quotes a famous saying of the Prophet Muhammad, "I am Ahmad, without the letter *m*." Ahmad, like Muhammad, is related to the Arabic word *hamd*, or "praise," and is another name for the Prophet. Removing the "m" in Ahmad makes it *Ahad,* which means "the One." These examples set the tone for the *Hasanat.* This work is inflected with themes that Ibn Arabi and his followers developed on the nature of existence (*wujud*) and the ultimate unity of creation and the divine. The collection includes aphorisms from the Prophet's companions, early Sufis from Baghdad, later mystics from the Persian-speaking world, and Dara's own contemporaries.[93]

Though Mulla Shah and Miyan Mir merit their own entries, Dara devotes by far the longest section to another teacher of his, Shaikh Bari, who had died a short while earlier in 1651/2. He was a solitary mystic, Dara says, using the term *mufrad*, which connotes a Sufi who did not need supervision from the *qutb*, the guiding spiritual authority of the age. The prince relates some of his numerous memorable encounters with Shaikh Bari.[94]

Dara also commemorated Muhammad Sharif, "one of the profligates and free spirits of our times" who proclaimed that the Muhammadan ultimate truth or reality (*haqiqat-i muhammadiya*) had now manifested in him: "A thousand years ago there was the Prophet Muhammad / A thousand years later there is Muhammad Sharif."[95]

The entries in the *Hasanat* focus both on the saints of past generations as well as on Dara's contemporaries and stories from his own teachers. Take, for instance, Sandal, a mystic about whom the late Miyan Mir had spoken admiringly and who, according to Miyan Mir, had danced among the catamites of Lahore for forty years. Once, Miyan Mir recounted, a group of ulama were asked to petition the divine for rain. Their efforts went unanswered. Eventually Sandal was brought in and his exhortations resulted in rain. The lesson of this story is, for Dara Shukoh, "that in every community and in every garb, there are visible and hidden friends of the Divine Truth. On account of their blessings the heavens and earth stand, and emperors rule. On account of their blessings, the ulama prevail over the heretics."[96] Note that in this context, Dara uses the term "ulama" approvingly but subordinates them to God's friends, the Sufis, without whom they cannot perform their role.

The idea that God's favored friends exist in every community opens the door not only for social rebels and eccentrics but also for non-Muslims, two of whom make their way into the *Hasanat-ul-arifin*. One of them is, of course, Baba Lal, described here as the "shaven-headed." Baba Lal was "one of the most perfect gnostics," says the prince, "his knowledge of spiritual mysteries and constancy" unrivaled among the Hindus (*hunud*). It was Baba Lal who told Dara that every religious community had a gnostic, spiritually perfected person, through whose blessings God saved that community.[97]

The other is Kabir, the fifteenth-century poet-saint, whose hard-hitting Hindavi verses traveled the subcontinent. Like Dara's verses chastising literal-minded religious authorities, Kabir's poetry frequently inveighs against both mullas and pandits who fail to grasp the true nature of spiritual devotion and gnosis. Dara Shukoh would have heard more about the saint from Baba Lal, who counted Kabir as one of his own spiritual teachers. The prince narrates various anecdotes about Kabir, including the famous story regarding Kabir's imminent death and the ensuing struggle between Hindus and Muslims who each vied to perform his last rites. The Hindus wished to cremate him; the Muslims wished to bury him. In the end, Kabir, still powerful even in death, shut himself in his cell; when the door was opened his body had vanished and flowers were found in its stead. In this account, Dara could have used the term *hunud* (the Arabic plural of *hindi*) for Hindus here. Instead he casually refers to them as *kafir*s.[98] Dara does not use this term in an entirely pejorative sense; it had become a normalized way of designating a social category. But kafir does imply that these Hindus were not true followers of Kabir's monotheism. So while the term could hold a positive meaning in the inverted vocabulary of "mystical infidelity," here it serves the more prosaic purpose of rejecting Indian polytheists as infidels. Indeed, the prince would not dream of calling Kabir or Baba Lal kafirs, for he regarded them not as infidels but as genuine monotheists.

Kabir died roughly a century and a half earlier. Yet Baba Lal disclosed to Dara some of what he claimed to have learned directly from Kabir himself concerning the role of the spiritual guide (*murshid*):

There are four kinds of murshid: the first [are] like gold, which cannot create another like itself. Second, like an elixir that turns into gold whatever comes in contact with it . . . Third, like a sandalwood tree, which turns a favorable host tree into sandalwood, yet holds no sway over [a tree] that is not a favorable host. The fourth murshid is like a lamp, for he is known as a perfect murshid, for, from one lamp, a hundred thousand lamps are illuminated. With regard to this I [Dara] have said:

The gnostic bejewels your heart and soul,
   He plucks out a thorn and puts a rose in its place.
The perfect one draws out all from the form,
   One candle illuminates a thousand candles.[99]

Dara fuses a quatrain of his own composition with his report of Kabir's words.[100] These Persian lines of verse in no way resemble the Hindavi poetry commonly associated with Kabir. The Persianizing of Baba Lal and Kabir in the *Hasanat-ul-arifin* allows them and their sayings to seamlessly integrate into the company of the Sufi luminaries whom Dara Shukoh held in high esteem.

Other Muslim authorities in Dara's age also regarded Kabir as a monotheist. In the *Akhbar-ul-akhyar*, the renowned Abd-ul-Haqq of Delhi relates an anecdote involving Kabir that he heard from his uncle. Apparently, when Abd-ul-Haqq's father was a young child, he asked his own father, "Was this famous Kabir, whose utterances people recite, a Muslim or a kafir?" Abd-ul-Haqq's grandfather replied that Kabir was a monotheist (*muwahhid*). The child then asked, "Does this mean that a muwahhid is neither a kafir nor a Muslim?" to which the old man retorted, "To understand this matter is difficult. [Later] you will understand."[101]

WHILE DARA SHUKOH WAS STILL caught up in the exhilaration of war preparations, Aurangzeb trudged toward his punishment post in the Deccan. His wife, Dilras Bano, mother of three girls, was expecting a fourth child. On January 2, 1653, he met his brother Murad Bakhsh at the village of Doraha.[102] The emperor wanted Aurangzeb to proceed to Daulatabad, the Mughal capital of the Deccan, as swiftly as possible, though he recognized that there was administrative work to be handled in Burhanpur first. Shah Jahan also reminded Aurangzeb to supply him with mangoes and grapes when the season started—this being one of the prince's responsibilities, as we know from Aurangzeb's Qandahar campaign.[103] The Burhanpur palace had fallen into disrepair, so Aurangzeb lingered outside the city while it was renovated before entering on February 9.[104]

There, later writers say, the thirty-five-year-old prince fell passionately in love with a woman named Hira Bai, though the details of their accounts vary. The often-salacious collection of stories entitled *Ahkam-i Aurangzeb* (Aurangzeb's Edicts) attributed to one of Aurangzeb's servants, Hamid-ud-Din (fl. 1660), relates that Aurangzeb met her while visiting his maternal aunt, Saliha Bano, who was married to Burhanpur's governor, Saif

Khan. But the author of the *Ahkam-i Aurangzeb* appears to have the facts wrong: Saif Khan had long been removed from his governorship; moreover, his wife was Malika, not Saliha, and she had died over a decade earlier.[105] The author of the later biographical collection *Maasir-ul-umara* (Memorials of the Nobles), Nawab Shahnawaz Khan (d. 1758), relates that Aurangzeb took the ladies of his household for a stroll in the garden complex across the Tapti River from the Burhanpur citadel, where his mother had been once briefly interred. Female members of the Burhanpur harem also accompanied them. One of them, Hira Bai, who had earlier been in Aurangzeb's aunt's retinue, cheekily leapt up to pluck a mango from a tree, records Shahnawaz, though if this took place in February, the mangoes would have been terribly unripe. In *Ahkam*'s version, she merely held a branch and sang melodiously.

Whatever the case, the story goes that the prince immediately lost his heart, and along with it his senses. The *Ahkam* has it that he collapsed to the ground. His anxious aunt tended to him, but he could be assuaged only once he managed to acquire Hira Bai by giving his uncle two of his own concubines in exchange. According to the *Maasir,* for the next few months, Aurangzeb's besottedness for Hira Bai, a talented singer, took over his life. She once put a goblet of wine in his hand and mercilessly pressed him to drink it. The prince reluctantly brought the cup to his lips. Then she grabbed it and scoffed it down herself, saying, "My intention was only to test your love."[106]

There is something very formulaic about the anecdote—the sudden onset of Aurangzeb's passionate love and his desire taking the form of a malady borrow from the motifs of Persian narrative poetry. And the inconsistencies in the stories necessitate that these accounts be treated carefully. But the prince's correspondence with his father does hint that something inappropriate had taken place. On the fourteenth of May, Aurangzeb received a letter of reprimand from Shah Jahan. He hastily penned a reply, assuring his father that he was "guilty of no act which might be contrary to the will of God or of God's shadow on earth." Aware of the rumors circulating about him, Aurangzeb explains, he had preemptively sent a clarificatory letter to his agent at court. "I recognize that conduct of this kind is despised by all men; how could I sink to such a depth?"[107]

Aurangzeb's crime was not that he had an affair outside of his marriages; imperial and noble men would unquestioningly assume rights over the bodies of their wives and concubines. It was rather that he had lost control of himself. As Akbar's poet Faizi warned, in his poem on the Indian lovers Nal and Daman, a king could love, but his love must be tempered by sobriety.[108] The wine in the anecdote here not only reflects a real or imagined incident but serves as a metaphor for the prince's unquenchable emotions—in Persian poetry, wine and lovers are inseparably associated.

Aurangzeb's romance with Hira Bai ended as suddenly as it began, with her untimely death. If the *Maasir* is to be believed, she was buried in the city of Aurangabad, close to Daulatabad. Formerly known as Fatehnagar, Aurangzeb named this city after himself during his governorship of the Deccan and made it into his capital. Hira Bai must have accompanied Aurangzeb to Daulatabad when he made the monthlong journey there during November 1653.

The Venetian adventurer Niccolo Manucci (d. circa 1720), who traveled through India during the period, reports that after Hira Bai died, Aurangzeb "vowed never to take up wine or to listen to music," and would later claim that God had been very gracious to him by putting an end to that dancing girl's life, for through her the prince had "committed so many sins that he ran the risk of never reigning by being occupied in such vices."[109] Always one for a salacious story, Manucci exaggerates, though Aurangzeb later did, somewhat like his father, cultivate an austere persona, and it is possible that this incident influenced him to do so.[110]

There was no letup in Shah Jahan's admonitions. That summer, the ruler awaited a consignment of Deccani mangoes from a choice tree, the *padshah pasand* (Emperor's Favorite), and even commanded that Aurangzeb send men to stand watch over the tree after it flowered, waiting for it to bear fruit.[111] Aurangzeb replied to his father's command with the news that the crop that year had been bad. When fewer and poorer-quality mangoes arrived than Shah Jahan had desired, he railed, insinuating that Aurangzeb must have consumed them. Did Aurangzeb's childhood theft of bananas still linger at the back of his mind? The prince defended himself politely, "How could I permit mangoes, fit for Your Majesty's table, to be eaten here?"[112] Shah Jahan also complained to Jahanara, who wrote her brother. Perhaps, Aurangzeb explained, the mangoes were picked too soon, or the *dak chauki* (courier service) was running late, or the fruit fell out of the basket on the way. He then laid out in detail how he was going to ensure that the next shipment was better.[113]

7

CONFLUENCE

1654–1656

A DECADE AND A HALF after its plans were first laid out, Shahjahanabad was a thriving urban complex. The city was dominated by the imposing red sandstone palace-fortress where Shah Jahan, his household, and his army lived. Today, what remains of Shah Jahan's fort flanks the traffic-clogged Ring Road, one of Delhi's main arteries. In Dara Shukoh's time, though, the river Jamuna flowed picturesquely by the citadel's eastern ramparts. But the city in 1654 was still a site of ceaseless construction. The emperor had recently commissioned a massive wall to be put up around Shahjahanabad, which on completion would eventually measure twelve feet in thickness and almost four miles in length.[1] Sadullah Khan was supervising the ongoing building of a resplendent congregational mosque on a ridge in the walled city's center. Fazil Khan, now back from Qandahar, would also assist. Five thousand workers had already been toiling on it for four years; it would only reach completion in 1656.[2]

The founding of a new city gave the imperial women opportunities to shape their own architectural legacies. By 1650, several projects that they sponsored were completed. Jahanara was already a well-established patron in Agra, Kashmir, and Ajmer, and here too she created some of the city's most distinctive landmarks. West of the fort, she constructed a wide avenue running almost the full breadth of the city. It was lined on either side with arcaded markets and a canal coursed through it, the Nahr-i Bihisht (Stream of Paradise). Just north of the avenue, Jahanara laid out a vast garden, in-

tended primarily for women and children of the imperial household. However she also included a caravanserai for traveling merchants, and a public
bathhouse.[3]

Other women of the emperor's family too participated in molding Shahjahanabad and its environs. Dara Shukoh's other sister, Roshanara, built a
garden northwest of the city, as well as a grand tomb for her eventual in-
terment. Akbarabadi Mahal, one of Shah Jahan's nursemaids (*parastar*),
erected a mosque, a caravanserai, a bathhouse, and a grand market known
as Faiz Bazaar, running from the southern end of the fort to the city wall.
It was said to have had 888 shops, and its very own Stream of Paradise.
She also built a garden outside the city.[4] Sirhindi Begam, another esteemed
woman of the household, constructed a mosque and a garden tomb, near
Roshanara's. Fatehpuri Begam, a wife of the emperor, built a mosque and
a caravansarai.[5] These examples reflect the clout and wealth that elite Mughal women possessed. But they also show how Shah Jahan's capital city
was in many ways an extension of his household.

High-ranking nobles and their households commanded a good part of
Shahjahanabad's real estate. According to the French physician and natural
philosopher François Bernier, who arrived in India in late 1658, the city, as
a whole, had a population of close to four hundred thousand, almost the
same as Paris.[6] Shahjahanabad spilled out of the walls over to its suburbs,
as its elite inhabitants required labor sourced from outlying areas to maintain their lifestyles. South of the new imperial center lay what Chandarbhan
Brahman, Dara Shukoh's household superintendent and a noted Persian litterateur, called Delhi's "old city."[7] The landscape here was dotted with Sufi
shrines that over the years constituted an integral part of the city's identity,
such as the tombs of the thirteenth-century Chishti Sufis Nizamuddin Au-
liya and Qutbuddin Bakhtiyar Kaki. These flourished as vestiges of an authority rivaling that of the emperor—the charisma of these saintly inter-
cessors with the divine.

The prince's own waterfront mansion lay just northwest of the fort, in a
choice area reserved for the most elite nobles, such as the former Safavid
governor Ali Mardan Khan. Soon after his arrival, in mid-March 1654,
Dara made elaborate preparations to receive his father there with appropriate pomp and ceremony.[8] His mansion originally comprised two buildings, next to each other. Only a fragment of one building still stands, now
known as the Dara Shukoh Library.

Since the seventeenth century, the structure has had many incarnations.
It was the residence of Juliana, a Portuguese woman who eventually wielded
great influence at the court of the eighteenth-century emperor Bahadur Shah.[9]
Later, in the nineteenth century, it became the home of David Ochterlony

(d. 1825), the first British resident in Delhi in the court of Shah Alam II.[10] Ochterlony completely remodeled the facade to make it resemble a neo-classical mansion. Today it houses the Archaeological Survey of India.

Only a few remnants survive of the building's original form; these include a series of small red sandstone arched chambers at the rear that might have been stables, and other arches and columns in the interior. But we can imagine that Dara Shukoh's mansion would have been an even grander version of the stately Shahjahanabad homes. They were set in the midst of gardens, Bernier recounts, which were laid out with waterworks and fountains. Open courtyards allowed air to freely circulate, while subterranean chambers provided a cool respite from the summer heat. Little niches perforating the inside walls held lamps and decorative artifacts. The ceilings of the mansions glittered with intricate floral designs embellished with gold leaf.[11]

The new city of Dara Shukoh, Shah Jahan, and Jahanara was lacking in one aspect. It was bereft of their spiritual guide's physical presence. The emperor wrote Mulla Shah asking why he would not now come to Shahjahanabad instead of Lahore. "When you see this grand place, with its agreeable climate, you will forget Lahore," Shah Jahan declared to the shaikh. But the aging Mulla Shah was now too weak to make the grueling journey from Kashmir.[12]

ENSCONCED IN HIS PALATIAL QUARTERS IN SHAHJAHANABAD, Dara Shukoh had some respite from the frenetic life of the past year, when he went to Qandahar and back. By his father's side, he was closely involved in the inner workings of kingship. One of Dara's tasks was to mend and strengthen his own networks, some of which had suffered during the rancorous Qandahar campaign. With Shah Jahan's blessings, no doubt, he sought to build an alliance with Jai Singh, whom he had alienated in Qandahar. Late in 1653, probably after returning from Qandahar, he sent a princely decree to Jai Singh, assuring the raja that the emperor often spoke highly of him and considered him amongst his best generals.[13] At the beginning of February 1654, he sent another decree acknowledging a letter from Jai Singh and praising his loyalty to the court.[14] And on April 14 that year, he celebrated his son Sulaiman Shukoh's marriage with the daughter of the late Rai Amar Singh, a Rajput nobleman and Jai Singh's nephew.[15] This alliance had been in the works for some time, but now was a fitting occasion to seal it.

Shah Jahan too needed Jai Singh's help to deal with trouble brewing in the Rajput state of Mewar. Rana Raj Singh, grandson of Shah Jahan's loyal vassal, Karan Singh, had started to restore the fortifications of Chittor in violation of an agreement with the Mughal sovereign. In October 1654, Shah Jahan and Dara Shukoh set forth on a pilgrimage to the Chishti shrine at nearby Ajmer. The proximity of the imperial presence would deter Raj Singh, they hoped. They pitched camp at nearby Khalilpur. Dara Shukoh mediated between Raj Singh and the emperor, at the Rajput ruler's entreaty. The prince sent Chandarbhan, the superintendent of his household, along with a high-ranking imperial servant, Shaikh Abd-ul-Karim, with an ultimatum to Raj Singh. It was probably a deliberate choice to send Chandarbhan, a Brahmin, as the envoy to a Hindu ruler. Chandarbhan wrote a detailed report for the emperor, describing his successful coercion of the rana. Raj Singh was now obliged to send his six-year-old son to the imperial presence, and dispatch a contingent to serve in the Deccan. After conveying this threat, Shah Jahan and Dara Shukoh paid their respects at the Chishti shrine.[16]

Soon afterward, Shah Jahan commissioned a lustrous illustration of his visit to Ajmer for the official chronicle of his reign, the *Padshah-nama*. Like most Mughal paintings of forts or cities, it has a flattened, aerial perspective. At its center is the walled city, all sandstone and marble, with the shrine nestled within. Rolling hills stretch beyond it. In the foreground, the emperor, seated on a brown horse, is resplendent in golden attire with a glowing nimbus behind his head. Facing him, a green-robed Sufi, the legendary Khizr, offers him a globe. Dara Shukoh is close behind, mounted on a gray horse. The emperor and his heir bask in the embrace of both spiritual and political power.[17]

Aurangzeb's agent at court had informed him of the imperial plans in Mewar, and the third-born prince referred to this episode while writing his father from the Deccan. Ever since he heard of these preparations, Aurangzeb wrote, his "anxious desire to serve" left him restless night and day, so he petitioned the court, "exalted as the firmament," to summon him to join the expedition. Aurangzeb had not seen his father since his own ignominious campaign to Qandahar in 1652. He expressed his wish to be received at court. "I had already submitted to Your Majesty my desire to gain the honor of entering the luminous presence, and [I have heard that] it has fallen from the tongue, speaking words of grace: We shall summon him to wait upon us."[18] But the summons did not come.

The prince then concentrated his efforts on another goal. He had been eyeing the southern kingdom of Golconda, famed for its diamonds, fertile

Shah Jahan and Dara Shukoh meet Khizr en route to the Chishti shrine at Ajmer.

fields and delicately hued chintz fabric. Aurangzeb saw an opportunity to deepen the influence of the Mughal state there. He had established clandestine ties with the Qutbshahi sultan's powerful minister, the Iranian-born Mir Jumla, a former diamond merchant who had his own army. Soon Aurangzeb pressed Shah Jahan to lure Mir Jumla to Mughal imperial service. The minister, though, cleverly ensured that both the sultans of Golconda and Bijapur also competed for his loyalty. Mir Jumla was "twisting and turning . . . while disclosing his true intentions to nobody," wrote Aurangzeb to his father.[19] The prince awaited more opportune circumstances that would allow him to invade Golconda. With his father now approaching sixty-five, the prospect of succession could not have been far from Aurangzeb's mind. The more military victories he racked up, the better he would be placed to make a bid for the throne.

Even as Shah Jahan sidelined Aurangzeb in the display of Mughal might at Mewar, the prince shrewdly nurtured his relationships with prominent Rajput rulers. That year, 1654, he twice sent Jai Singh a gift of five matchlock muskets.[20] He also arranged an additional land assignment for Jai Singh, and added some of the raja's soldiers to his own Deccan campaigns.

Aurangzeb benefited from not representing the imperial position in the Rana Raj Singh affair. He used this opportunity to forge his own independent ties with the rana. In November of that year, the prince sent a Hindu envoy, named Indar Bhatt, to Raj Singh. The servant, whom Aurangzeb called a "palace of reliability," brought along for the rana a diamond ring and a special robe (*khilat*). The exchange of envoys and gifts between Aurangzeb and Raj Singh would continue into the near future.[21]

BACK IN SHAHJAHANABAD, DARA SHUKOH used this spell of relative stability to focus on an important aspect of Mughal kingship—the continued refinement of his inner self and his intellect. These months in 1654 afforded him the time to surround himself with interlocutors of his choice, to summon the presence of whomsoever he wished to see, in short, to behave like a sitting emperor. The prince's mansion in Delhi now functioned like a secondary court, a salon for dialogue and learning. His meetings with Baba Lal fresh in his mind, Dara Shukoh applied himself to a study of religious thought beyond Islam, in a far deeper manner than he had pursued before.

We know that Dara had been especially interested in Indic systems of learning for a while. He did not have to go far to find teachers, for Shah Jahan's court had continued the Mughal tradition, since the time of Akbar, of hosting and interacting with Sanskrit scholars. For some time now, Shah Jahan had been regularly rewarding Kavindracharya Saraswati for his musical compositions as well as for his writings.[22] Kavindra is one of the few pandits whom we can plausibly identify as one of Dara Shukoh's interlocutors and instructors. After Dara's return to Shahjahanabad, in February 1654, Kavindra again received his usual gift of one thousand rupees.[23] This would be his tenth such honor in a period of three years.[24] Few scholars at Shah Jahan's court were so generously and so frequently rewarded. But Kavindra would have to wait almost two years until his next gift at court, in the third week of January 1656.[25] We might surmise from this that Dara Shukoh had decided to branch out more in his choice of guides to Indic thought, or that he took a more independent approach to his explorations.

Kavindra seems to have introduced Dara to another Benares-based pandit known as Brahmendra Saraswati, who was a noted author on Advaita Vedanta. A letter, written in Sanskrit, has come down to us, addressed to Brahmendra (or rather, to Narasimha Goswami, his other appellation) and purportedly written by Dara Shukoh.[26] The prince must have had a pandit help him compose this, because it is laden with lavish, ornate expressions that would have taken years of Sanskrit learning to produce. According to this letter, the addressee was a recipient of Kavindra's praise. The author signs off as "Mohamad Dara Shukoh, who has ascended the seventh plane made possible through the driving away of the great delusions by the knowledge of reality in which the abundance of supreme bliss is revealed."[27]

There is also some evidence that the celebrated Sanskrit poet Jagannatha was associated with both Shah Jahan and Dara Shukoh. Jagannatha was a Brahmin whose roots lay in the southern region of Telangana. According to one Telugu account, he made his way to Delhi only to find it in chaos, during the turbulent period before Shah Jahan's accession to the throne. Undeterred, he changed course and headed for Udaipur, to the court of Jagat Singh, the ruler of Mewar. There Jagannatha wrote a paean in praise of his new patron, called *Jagadabharana* (Ornament of the world), with a play on the Udaipur ruler's name "Jagat," which means world or universe. The pandit also wrote a praise poem for Shah Jahan's father-in-law, Asaf Khan. The colophon of this work mentions that Shah Jahan bestowed on the poet the title of Panditaraja, literally "king of the pandits," an honor somewhat like the title of poet laureate.[28]

Jagannatha was not averse to reusing his earlier compositions for new patrons. In a reworked version of the *Jagadabharana*, he inserted the name of Dara Shukoh in place of the Rajput ruler. Some years later, when forced to leave Delhi, he sought refuge at the court of the Koch Bihar ruler, Prananarayana, and once again modified his *Jagadabharana* accordingly.[29] But these praise poems were but drops in the ocean of the panditaraja's *oeuvre*, as he focused his energies on producing a monumental work on Sanskrit literary aesthetics, or *rasa*, entitled *Rasagangadhara* (The Ganga-bearer [Shiva] of Rasa), in addition to several poems.[30]

In later accounts of his life, we find a tragic story about Jagannatha's illicit love. His grand-nephew related an early version, dated to 1673, fairly soon after the poet's demise. This account notes tersely that Jagannatha married a Shah's daughter, meaning a Muslim, and immediately found liberation in the Ganga, that is, through death by drowning.[31] There are also verses attributed to the panditaraja about his Muslim beloved, for instance: "That Muslim girl has a body soft as butter/and if I could get her to lie by my side//The hard floor would be good enough for me/and all the comforts of paradise redundant."[32]

An unattributed story links Jagannatha and his doomed romance more directly with Dara Shukoh. The panditaraja was regaling a salon with his poetry at the prince's house. A Muslim noblewoman listened in the women's quarters behind a screen. At the end of the evening, the prince, pleased, asked Jagannatha what reward he would like. Jagannatha replied that all he wanted was to marry the aforementioned lady. Upon enquiries, the noblewoman revealed that she too reciprocated these feelings. Dara Shukoh made arrangements for the two to go to Benares at the dead of night. Their union was too scandalous for the Brahmins of Benares to condone. All temple doors were closed to Jagannatha. The two made their way to Durga-khoh on the Ganga's banks where they lived out the rest of their days.[33]

This is all hearsay; we have no proof that this incident actually took place. True or not, these stories suggest that, in this period, the divide between the Sanskrit universe and that of the Mughals was more porous than it had ever been. But they also reveal a brewing unease about such interactions, which was expressed as gossip and rumor. Today, this anxiety manifests as complete denial, with scholars arguing that Jagannatha's romance was a fabrication concocted by his rivals.[34]

Dara Shukoh may also have had a more targeted political reason for pursuing his studies of Indic thought. After all, a potential revolt had recently been averted in Mewar. The Hindu rulers formed an important part of Shah Jahan's nobility. Their support, together with the troops they commanded, was crucial for any serious military action. Even Bernier comments that Shah Jahan had granted a pension of two thousand rupees to a certain pandit of Benares, likely Kavindracharya, partly as a reward for his great learning and partly so as to "please the Rajas."[35]

The workings of Mughal alliances and networks were highly complex. It is far too simplistic to assume that Dara's study of Hindu sacred texts, or Shah Jahan's rewards to a Brahmin scholar might in themselves guarantee the Hindu rulers' undying loyalty. After all, Dara's prior interest in Indic religion did not prevent his acrimonious spat with Jai Singh at Qandahar. Nevertheless, as for previous Mughal rulers, Dara Shukoh's universalism was an important ingredient in his idea of a perfect ruler, one who was also the perfect philosopher. So there were political implications to Dara's wide-reaching philosophical investigations.

Furthermore, Dara Shukoh's activities paralleled those of Jaswant Singh, the ruler of the Rajput state of Marwar. Despite being his father's third son, Jaswant Singh had inherited the throne in 1638. Now, in January 1654, Shah Jahan granted him the title Maharaja.[36] It was his niece whom Sulaiman Shukoh married that spring. The Rajput ruler was a prolific author, whose numerous works include the Advaita-inflected *Anandvilas, Aparokshasiddhant, Anubhavprakash, Siddhantasar* and *Siddhantabodh,* all in Brajbhasha, a literary form of Hindavi. He also commissioned translations of Sanskrit texts into Brajbhasha, such as the *Gita Mahatmya,* the *Bhagavad Gita,* and the *Prabodhachandrodaya,* a Sanskrit allegorical play.[37] Many of these works are hard to date precisely, so we cannot trace any direct links between the cultural activities at the Marwar and Mughal courts. But the broad themes here, of non-dualism, coexisting with a tinge of devotion to Krishna, avatar of Vishnu, mirror Dara Shukoh's own intellectual excursions in the 1650s. So did the sponsorship of translations. These similarities suggest that particular Indic texts and branches of knowledge were becoming associated with kings and emperors, forming a kind of spiritual and intellectual practice of rulership.

It is hardly a coincidence, then, that the period of Dara Shukoh's deepest involvement with what he viewed as ancient Indic thought coincided with his growing overtures to Rajput rulers. This is not to say that he was guided by a crude political expediency, believing that his studies would make him more popular amongst these prominent Hindus. Rather, he was engaged in a process of self-fashioning that, consciously or unconsciously, was also informed by the political context of his times. At this point, in Shahjahanabad, the prince was molding himself into the kind of ruler who mastered a grammar of universal kingship in which elite Rajputs like Jaswant Singh also partook.

We must note, though, that Dara's explorations did not just stop at Indic learning and texts. Bernier reports that the prince sought out a Flemish Jesuit, Father Henri Busée, also known as Henricus Busaeus, for dialogue about religious matters. Here too, Bernier suggests that the prince's true aim was to ingratiate himself with the European artillerymen serving the Mughal army.[38] Bernier seems to have had a narrow, somewhat cynical view of Dara's own spiritual proclivities, as well as of the long history, since Akbar, of the Mughal court's hospitality to Jesuit visitors.

In his later writings, the prince does speak of having studied the Jewish and Christian scriptures, particularly the Torah and the Gospel. Apart from Father Busée, he had another interlocutor in these matters—Muhammad Said Sarmad Kashani, a Jewish convert to Islam, who had been a merchant in Baghdad before traveling across the Persian-speaking world to India.

Similarly, we learn, that the *Dabistan*'s anonymous author made the acquaintance of Sarmad at Hyderabad, in the southern state of Golconda some time earlier, in 1647. Sarmad, who was descended from learned rabbis, perused the rabbinical creed and the Torah, but then became a Muslim. He studied with renowned philosophers of the day in Iran, such as Mulla Sadra and Mir Findiriski, who himself had visited India and written a commentary on an Indic non-dualistic religious text. Then Sarmad journeyed eastward to Sindh on business, but stayed for love. In Thatta he met a Hindu boy named Abhay Chand, and was immediately besotted. According to the *Dabistan*, just like a *sanyasi* (a world-renouncing Hindu ascetic), Sarmad shed his clothes, and remained naked as the day his mother bore him. He waited patiently at his beloved's door. When Abhay Chand's father finally realized the purity of Sarmad's love, he let him in. Abhay Chand reciprocated Sarmad's ardor and the two became inseparable. Sarmad used to say that the Bani Israel did not consider it necessary to clothe the private parts, and that indeed the prophet Isaiah too roamed naked in his final years.[39]

The two made their way across India, where it seems that Sarmad ultimately received patronage from Shaikh Muhammad Khan, a noble attached to the Qutbshahi ruler of Golconda. Sarmad wrote poetry in the khan's praise. Then in 1649 the khan died en route to pilgrimage in Mecca, just as Sarmad had foretold. At some point thereafter, Sarmad and Abhay Chand then went to Shahjahanabad, where they must have gained admission to Dara Shukoh's circle of associates.

Very little evidence survives, though, of Dara Shukoh's personal relationship with Sarmad. Bernier mentions that Sarmad was a famous faqir who flaunted his nudity in the streets of Shahjahanabad.[40] But he does not speak of any connection between the ascetic and the prince. It would not be surprising, however, if Sarmad's Persian poetry found a resonance with Dara Shukoh, drawn as he was to shocking, seemingly blasphemous mystical utterances like this couplet equating the sacred Kaaba with a polytheist's idol: "In the Kaaba and the idol-temple, the stone is he, the wood is he/In one place, the black stone, in another, the Hindu idol."[41]

This is the kind of ecstatic speech that Dara would have recorded in his *Hasanat-ul-arifin* had he known Sarmad while working on it. Sarmad's absence from this collection suggests that their acquaintance began at some point after early 1654. Such imagery, of course, was not unusual in Persian mystical poetry. Just like Mulla Shah, whose ecstatic poetry had landed him in trouble at the beginning of Shah Jahan's reign, Sarmad also composed quatrains praising the prophet Muhammad.

The correspondence between the prince and the ascetic continued to circulate after their time. A copy of one exchange ended up in a *bayaz*, an album of miscellaneous poetry and pieces of writing, belonging to a nineteenth-century collection. The letter attributed to Dara Shukoh begins:

> My pir and spiritual teacher. Every day I have the intent to serve you, but it is unattained. If I am I, why would my desire be in vain? And if I am not I, what fault is it of mine? . . . When the chosen Prophet would go to battle against the unbelievers, and the army of Islam suffered losses, the literalist ulama would say, "This is a lesson in fortitude." But what need does the Final One have of lessons?

In this account, Sarmad replied to the prince with the following couplet: "Whatever I've read, I've forgotten / Except the Friend's words, which I keep repeating."[42]

Abhay Chand, under Sarmad's instructions had translated sections of the Torah into Persian. The *Dabistan* preserves an excerpt from Abhay Chand's rendition of the *Book of Genesis*.[43] Dara Shukoh may well have accessed this text through the version prepared by the two.

But Dara Shukoh's enthusiasm for learning about Hindu religious thought would eventually eclipse his curiosity about the scriptures of Jews and Christians. He continued his studies, likely drawing on Kavindracharya Saraswati, as well as other unnamed pandits, for assistance. They would have introduced him to texts associated with the growing canon of non-dualistic Vedanta—works that espoused a unity of *atman*, the individual self, and *brahman*, the ultimate reality of the universe. Such ideas would understandably appeal to Dara, given his spiritual inclinations. It was also the case that at the time in many parts of North India, including Benares, the philosophical school of Advaita Vedanta held sway amongst the Brahmin scholarly classes.[44] In any case, the prince's initial intellectual forays during this period in Shahjahanabad were broad and eclectic, and he did not limit himself to Advaita Vedanta.

In late 1654, Dara Shukoh may have also crossed paths with a fellow seeker of Indic learning. Father Heinrich Roth (d. 1668), who was associated with the same mission as Father Busée, had recently made his way to the Jesuit college in Agra after alighting in Goa in 1652. Following his Mewar excursion, before the imperial party returned to Shahjahanabad,

Dara Shukoh stopped by Agra with his father.[45] From the outset, Roth had devoted himself to studying Indian languages—Persian, of course, and Hindi, as well as even Sanskrit. He was aware that the Mughals ruled over a large non-Muslim majority, and thought that studying Indic philosophy and religious traditions, which he saw through a Brahminical lens, would help him secure conversions.[46] Just like Dara Shukoh, Roth too sought the assistance of pandits in his studies. Not only would their Sanskrit circles have overlapped, it is also highly likely that they were reading some of the same things.

In addition to a Sanskrit grammar that Roth composed, two Sanskrit manuscripts hand-copied by the Jesuit have survived the years. One, by Venidatta, is the *Panca-tattva-prakasa* (Light on the Five Elements), which was originally composed in 1644. It is a beginner's text, a primer on concepts key to the Vaisheshika school of Indian philosophy, a branch of thought that had been undergoing a renaissance of sorts in Sanskrit intellectual circles.[47] Vaisheshika philosophers examined the stuff of existence, which they classified into several categories, including the elements and atoms, which they believed to be the tiniest indivisible units. The other manuscript that Roth copied is Sadananda's *Vedantasara* (Quintessence of Vedanta), a late fifteenth-century work that discusses some important ideas in Advaita Vedanta.[48] These include: ignorance about the true nature of the self, the metaphysical basis of being, and the attainment of liberation through understanding the identity of the self with brahman, the ultimate reality. The *Vedantasara* is part of a genre that compressed and synthesized the complexity of Advaitic philosophical ideas and debates into concise digests.[49] Roth's detailed marginal notes in Latin show how closely he read these texts.

The prince's intellectual pursuits, intensive and wide-ranging though they were, did not diminish his more public role as ruler. Early in 1655, Shah Jahan formalized Dara's status as preferred son and future heir. The occasion was the emperor's sixty-fifth lunar birthday, an auspicious time for the bestowing of largesse. Before a public audience of assembled nobles, he presented his eldest son with the most extraordinarily lavish gifts, the details of which his chroniclers duly recorded. They included a satin robe with a golden yoke tastefully sequined with valuable diamonds, while the collar, sleeves, and hem were decorated with pearls. This ceremonial garment was worth two and a half lakh rupees. In addition to other priceless jewels, the prince received the sum of thirty lakh rupees. But this was not all. Henceforth, Dara Shukoh would be known as "Shah Buland Iqbal," meaning "Emperor of Exalted Fortune," just as Jahangir had once granted Prince Khurram the title of "Shah Jahan." Dara was also conferred the privilege of sitting on a golden chair next to the emperor's throne.[50] According to Bernier, this made it seem that "there were almost two kings [ruling] together," though Shah Jahan was merely repeating the favor that his own father Jahangir had granted him when he was a prince.[51]

IN 1655, THE YEAR THAT DARA SHUKOH turned forty-two, he finished writing yet another book.[52] This was his most ambitious work yet, not in length—it was merely a short treatise—but in scope. The work was a direct result of his immersion in Indic learning, but also built on the steps that he had already taken with his *Risala-i Haqqnuma* and *Hasanat-ul-arifin*. The *Haqqnuma* assimilated yogic practices for liberation into an Islamic spiritual genealogy. The *Hasanat* made reference to the prince's wide-ranging dialogues with Baba Lal in its collection of ecstatic sayings by Sufis. Dara Shukoh titled his new book *Majma-ul-bahrain,* meaning the "meeting place of the two seas." Many modern readers assume that these seas stand for the two faiths of Islam and Hinduism, though what this phrase connoted in Dara's own context was infinitely more subtle and complex.[53]

"Majma" is an Arabic noun of place meaning confluence, and its root, *j-m-ʿ*, is associated with collecting, bringing together, and ordering. This quite aptly reflects the work that the book does to compile and arrange terms and ideas from Sanskrit, refracted through Hindavi and Persian. But Dara Shukoh's title would have had another immediate resonance for his readers familiar with the symbolic language of Islamic mysticism. It calls to mind the Quranic verse (18:60) in which the phrase *majma-ul-bahrain* occurs: "And when Moses said unto his servant: I will not rest until I reach the place where the two seas meet (*majma-ul-bahrain*), even if I journey for ages." This section of the Quran is famous in Sufi circles; it narrates the story of the meeting between the prophet Moses and an unnamed teacher, identified by many of the Quran's commentators as Khizr, a mysterious saint who gained the power of immortality. In this scene, Moses catches a fish only to see it slip away. He then sets out to find it at the meeting of the two waters. Sufi commentaries often interpret this passage as a reference to the waters of immortality, as here the fish appears to miraculously come back to life. During his explorations, Moses comes across a guide, usually identified with the ever-living Khizr, who in three instances acts in strange ways that flout social norms: He sinks a ship, kills a young boy, and repairs a wall in a village where the inhabitants had denied them hospitality.[54] Afterward, Khizr explains to Moses the inner significance of his actions, instructing him in the inscrutability of God's justice. For Sufi exegetes, this episode came to represent the distinction between esoteric and exoteric knowledge, suggesting that the legalistic approach of Moses depicted here could never adequately comprehend God's mysteries.[55]

It is precisely this arena of knowledge with which Dara Shukoh is concerned—the esoteric, inner learning of both Hindus and Muslims. The prince refers to two religious traditions, but these are not the crystallized, rigidly-bounded Islam and Hinduism that we know in modern times. His project does not seek to synthesize two separate streams of Islam and Hindu religion. Instead, he aims to uncover and document a common font of truth shared by Muslim and non-Muslim, Indian "monotheists."

This distinction proves essential to understanding the broader significance of Dara's work. The beginning lines of the *Majma-ul-bahrain* compare unbelief (*kufr*) and its antithesis, Islam, to two locks of hair that frame, rather than obscure, the divine countenance:

> The fullest praise to that unique One, who has made manifest the two tresses of unbelief and Islam, which are adversaries to one another, upon his beautiful countenance, without likeness, without an equal, and has not made either of them a veil for his handsome face.
>
> > Unbelief and Islam race down his path,
> > Crying, "He is one, he has no partner."[56]

Dara Shukoh borrows this verse from the twelfth-century mystical poet Sanai's *Hadiqat-ul-haqaiq* (Garden of Verities). In most versions, the verse contrasts unbelief (*kufr*) with religion (*din*) and not *islam*, the form that Dara uses, though this variant was widely known in the Mughal context.[57] Here unbelief also signifies the Indic knowledge that the *Majma-ul-bahrain* presents and is contrasted with Islam in religious terms. By this the prince implies that religious traditions outside Islam also offer a path to the divine.

Dara's comments on the "divine countenance" implicitly reference a saying attributed to Ali, the Prophet's son-in-law, which is popular in Sufi texts. Ali reportedly said, "Were the veil to be removed, I would not increase in certitude," meaning that he already had a clear vision of the divine.[58] In the brief introduction to the *Majma*, Dara also cites conversations and relationships with "monotheists" of India as the source of his knowledge:

> The faqir without a care, Muhammad Dara Shukoh, relates that he, after discerning the truth of all truths, ascertaining the mysteries of the subtleties of the Sufi school of truth, and attaining this magnificent divine gift, has approached

this purpose, [namely] to comprehend the nature of the school of thought of the monotheists of India (*muwahhidan-i hind*) and the attainers of truth (*muhaqqiqan*) among this ancient people. With some among them, who have attained perfection, who have reached the extremities of ascetic practice, comprehension and understanding, and the utmost levels of mystical experience, God-seeking and gravity, he [i.e., Dara Shukoh] has had repeated encounters and carried out dialogues.[59]

We recall that in some of his recent writings and in his correspondence with Shaikh Muhibbullah, Dara expressed his dissatisfaction with book learning, especially books that he thought to be overly abstruse and complex. Here, he credits his personal meetings with Hindu teachers instead of authoritative texts as the basis for his study.

The prince then identifies the basis for his comparative endeavor, "Apart from linguistic differences in discerning and knowing, I saw no divergence. From this perspective I brought together the words of both parties and collected some terms that are essential and valuable for the seeker of truth to know [and] arranged [them in] a treatise. Because it was a meeting place (*majma*) of the truths and mystical knowledge of two truth-knowing communities, it was named *The Meeting Place of the Two Seas*, in accordance with the saying of the eminent ones: 'Mysticism is justice (*insaf*) and mysticism is the abandonment of gratuitous ceremony (*takalluf*).'"[60]

There is an underlying mystical truth, the prince suggests, that Sufis and Indic ascetics of a monotheistic persuasion share beneath their linguistic differences. Through his choice of title, as well as his references to "justice" and the dislike of *takalluf*, gratuitous ceremony or insincerity, Dara Shukoh declares a preference for esoteric interpretations over external forms of religion alone. He then identifies his intended audience: "Thus, he who possesses justice and is from among the people of comprehension, discerns what profundity has been reached in the ascertainment of these stages. Surely the people of understanding, who possess comprehension, will obtain abundant fortune from this treatise, and no portion of its rewards will remain for the dimwits of the two parties. I have written this investigation in accordance with my own mystical unveiling (*kashf*) and experience (*zauq*), for the people of my household, and I have no dealings with the common folk of either community."[61]

Dara Shukoh's book was for an elite group of intimates, close enough to be counted as members of his household. It was certainly not meant for commoners, be they Muslim or not, but then how many works produced at the court were? Moreover, it was fairly standard for mystically-inclined authors writing in Persian to claim that only special readers, the "people of the heart," (*ahl-i dil*) could fathom their works. A prince's writings demanded attention, though. With whom would he share his latest discoveries? Half a decade had elapsed since Dara had last set foot in Kashmir, so physical distance, at least, stood between him and his teacher Mulla Shah. Certainly, he had an eclectic circle of companions in Shahjahanabad, some of whom—Father Busée, Sarmad, Kavindracharya, perhaps his sister Jahanara—we might identify. But Dara also took another step that reveals more about the readers he wanted to reach.

The same year, 1655, in which he composed the *Majma,* he likely also had it translated into Sanskrit, with the title *Samudrasangama* (Ocean's confluence).[62] The Sanskrit translation is a fairly faithful rendition, closely following the Persian text, though in many places it replaces Islamic terms with Sanskrit counterparts. So monotheist becomes *vaidika,* or a Vedic scholar; a hadith of the Prophet is rendered as a *bhagavadavakyam,* or saying of God; Allah is *parabrahmana,* or the supreme brahman; a Sufi is an *ekatmavadin* or someone who propounds one soul, a term denoting the absolute monists of Vedanta; and Muhammad is *mahasiddha,* meaning a great spiritual master or yogi.[63] The Sanskrit text also adds some details missing in the Persian; for instance, it mentions Baba Lal by name as one of the prince's main interlocutors.[64]

Who was the intended audience of the *Samudrasangama,* the Sanskrit counterpart to the *Majma-ul-bahrain*? These were not the vast numbers of Persian-literate Hindus working in the Mughal administration. The use of Sanskrit spoke directly to Brahmin intellectuals, some of whom held their Muslim rulers at a suspicious arm's length. Jain scholars too would be able to read it, but they may have not constituted a primary audience. We can assume that many of Dara's pandit contacts were, like Kavindracharya, residents of Benares, a city under the prince's own jurisdiction, as he still held the governorship of Allahabad. Regardless of its audience, the translation gave Dara's Persian project of comparison its mirror equivalent, in sweeping universal terms.

There were also clear political implications to Dara Shukoh's acts of writing and translating. The prince's studies had revealed to him a truth that he wished to promulgate amongst like-minded people, drawing monistic or monotheistic scholars into his fold. The *Majma*'s composition revealed not only the prince's spiritual journey, but also the type of rulership he was performing. As Shah Jahan's act of temple destruction early in his reign reveals, Benares was no isolated provincial outpost. Actions taken there would have an impact on imperial relations with Hindu chieftains and rulers elsewhere. Several prominent Brahmins in Benares had roots in South and Central India and were still linked to networks there.[65]

Most copies of the *Majma-ul-bahrain* present the following topics as areas for comparison and detailed commentary:

1. The Five Elements
2. The Senses
3. Meditation
4. Divine Attributes
5. Spirit
6. Winds
7. The Four Worlds
8. Sound
9. Light
10. Mystical Vision
11. The Names
12. Prophethood and Sainthood
13. Brahma's Cosmic Egg
14. Directions
15. Sky
16. Earth
17. Divisions of the Earth
18. The Intermediate State
19. Resurrection
20. Liberation
21. Night and Day
22. Perpetual Cycles of Time

To a modern reader, the *Majma*'s ordering might appear rather strange. In fact, Jatindra Bimal Chaudhuri, modern editor and translator of the *Samudrasangama*, finds the nature of this arrangement "haphazard." Chaudhuri offers his own alternative model of how the chapters ought to be more sensibly organized—under the rubrics of "matter," "soul," and "God," respectively, proceeding from lowest to highest in the hierarchy of the three realities.[66]

On closer inspection, Dara's categories are not as eccentric as they might seem. We can see that the *Majma* draws greatly on themes from his conversations with Baba Lal, even though the textual versions of these dialogues appear far removed from the actual discussions. But the prince did not receive information passively; rather, he absorbed, reshaped, and rearranged what he learned. For instance, when he met Baba Lal, he asked about the five elements in Indic thought, which he contrasts with the four that "Persian books" acknowledged. By the time he writes the *Majma-ul-bahrain*, Dara has found a fifth element in the Islamic view of the world—the "Great Throne" (*arsh-i akbar*) of God—to match the other five.[67]

The *Majma* is also often based on book knowledge, though the information that Dara presents cannot be traced to just one or two sources. The work's categories, taken as a whole, do not reflect any of the prevailing genres of Sanskrit knowledge traditions. And though some of the categories find resonance in certain aspects of Sufi literature, the selection appears to be the end result of a sophisticated individual process of inquiry and reasoning.

Some sections of the *Majma* engage deeply with specific religious texts. Yet, the only scripture it explicitly cites is the Quran. The chapters on the four worlds and on sound can be read as extended commentaries on the *Mandukya Upanishad*. The section on light offers an interpretation of the famous light verse in the Quran, bringing out its allegorical meanings. Dara's discussion of prophethood addresses a major problem in Islamic theology: Does God transcend all attributes of creation, or are some of his attributes similar to those possessed by his creatures? Following Ibn Arabi, Dara supports a combination of these two positions, integrating the perspectives of God's incomparability (*tanzih*) with his similarity (*tashbih*). This section invokes Ibn Arabi's discussion of the prophet Noah in his *Fusus* and related works. The *Majma*'s longest chapter, on liberation (*mukti*), offers a creative prose translation of verses from the *Bhagvata Purana,* a pre-tenth-century text detailing the story of Krishna, an avatar of Vishnu. This section from the *Bhagvata* describes the mapping of the universe onto the body of *purusha,* primordial man.[68]

The *Majma-ul-bahrain*'s enterprise is a comparative one. It compares and draws relationships between the Indic and Islamic concepts discussed within its pages. Yet the work does not assume a neutral vantage point from which it weighs equally these two systems of thought. Rather, the project takes as its primary object of study the domain of Indic knowledge, which it seeks both to describe using its own vocabulary, as well as translate into Islamic, largely Sufi, categories.

The novelty of Dara's project in the *Majma* lies in the connections that he draws between Indic and Islamic material discussed, rather than in the kinds of Indic knowledge that he introduces to his Persian readers. Several of the topics presented here on creation and cosmography had already been addressed by Mughal authors in some fashion, for instance, in the *Ain-i Akbari.* They also feature in the roughly contemporaneous *Dabistan-i mazahib.* These other works, however, aim to describe, enumerate, and categorize, outlining a range of Indic beliefs that are organized according to their school of thought. Though the *Majma-ul-bahrain* too regulates and organizes the knowledge it seeks to encapsulate, it also outlines its own monistic theology through the set of equivalences that it forges.

The umbrella category of *muwahhidan-i hind,* monotheists of India, allows the *Majma* a certain eclecticism in the concepts explored. Thus included within the purview of the collection are aspects of Nath yogic and some theistic strains of Vaishnava thought, as well as non-dualistic Vedanta. This eclectic collection is peppered with gleanings from the *Yoga Vasishtha* (about which we will read more in the next chapter), references to yogic meditation practices, and snippets of puranic cosmographies. Do these various strands point to the varying backgrounds and specializations of Dara Shukoh's interlocutors? Individually, they point to diverse, if overlapping, systems of thought, but taken together they indicate the bodies of knowledge that, in mid-seventeenth-century Persianate culture, had come to be seen as representative of Indic learning. The *Majma-ul-bahrain* also captures a broader trend in the development of Indic thought: here we witness the gradual integration of disparate Nath and Vaishnava forms of knowledge into Vedanta, though this process had begun centuries earlier.

Yet perhaps the most striking feature of the *Majma-ul-bahrain* is the prominent role it gives to the Quran. Wherever possible, Dara quotes and elucidates Quranic verses as proof texts to demonstrate the validity of the Indic concepts he describes. The Quran is a primary locus of authority in the *Majma-ul-bahrain,* guiding its representations of Indic ideas and narratives. One way of interpreting Dara's work is to view it as a type of scriptural commentary, albeit a nontraditional one, which builds upon methods developed in Sufi Quranic exegesis.

The *Majma,* like Dara's earlier *Risala-i Haqq-numa,* is also a manual for spiritual liberation, though not explicitly so. As we have seen above, the prince summons the vocabulary of Islamic gnosis—*kashf* (unveiling) and *zauq,* which literally means a kind of mystical tasting or experience—to explain his relationship to the new knowledge that he has acquired. The *Majma* takes the form of a lexical compendium of analogies and equivalences between Sanskrit and Persian terms. Dara Shukoh believes that these reflected the same core ideas. Liberation, he implies, lies in understanding this essential sameness.

There are obvious parallels between Dara Shukoh's project in the *Majma-ul-bahrain* and his great-grandfather Akbar's embrace of Indic learning, though the prince avoids referring to Akbar here. Dara would also probably never acknowledge that his pursuits resonated with the kind of rulership a Deccan king enacted only a generation earlier. Ibrahim Adil Shah II of Bijapur, who died in 1627, was an enthusiast of Indic music, dance, literature, and philosophy. Mughal royals tended to look down on these sultans of smaller kingdoms, derisively referring to them as "Deccan timeservers."[69] But the cultural productions of Ibrahim Adil Shah's vibrant court rivaled those of the Mughals. One of the sultan's own projects included a collection of songs that he composed, called the *Kitab-i Nauras* (Book of Nine Essences), arranged according to several different musical modes, or ragas. A couplet at the beginning praises the goddess Saraswati, and the first song eulogizes the prophet Muhammad.[70]

Coincidently, Shah Jahan too commissioned and curated a collection of Indian songs, also, like the *Nauras,* in the dhrupad style. The famous sixteenth-century musician Nayak Bakhshu, who worked at the courts of Gwalior and Gujarat, had composed several such songs in Brajbhasha. Shah Jahan ordered that Nayak Bakhshu's prolific compositions be collected over a period of two years. Then, the emperor had these winnowed down to the thousand best ones. He also had the original patrons' names changed out for his own. Much like Ibrahim Adil Shah, the Mughal ruler too saw musical connoisseurship as an important quality for a ruler.[71]

An eminent Persian litterateur at Ibrahim Adil Shah's court, Nur-ud-din Muhammad Zuhuri, wrote three exquisitely ornate prose pieces, which formed a supplementary preface to the *Nauras*. They read, in the context of Shah Jahan's court, as though they were composed for the emperor that Dara Shukoh wanted to become. In one of these, called *Gulzar-i Ibrahim* (Ibrahim's Rose Garden), Zuhuri portrays the sultan as specially endowed with the insight to perceive divine unity where others see only the veils of multiplicity shrouding the divine countenance. His vision, then, guides his subjects. "The sacred thread (*zunnar*) has no such [weak] joint with the rosary, that its snapping laughs at the priest's (*kashish*) wrangling. Between unbelief (*kufr*) and Islam there is no such secret that for [soothing] the latter's headache, healing sandalwood is not taken from the Brahmin's forehead."[72] Zuhuri's intricate wording suggests that the Brahmin's sacred thread shares a bond with the devout Muslim's prayer beads so solid that no petty caviling about religious niceties can break it. Islam needs its antithesis, unbelief, just as a headache needs balm.

The ruler who accepts both Islam and unbelief can truly witness the divine revelation, just like Ali, the Prophet's nephew and son-in-law and the first male to embrace Muhammad's mission. Indeed, Zuhuri quotes the same line attributed to Ali to which Dara later implicitly alludes in the introduction to the *Majma*. The parallels between Zuhuri's earlier description of his Sultan's attributes and Dara Shukoh's own vision of rulership were not merely a coincidence. Shah Jahan himself owned a collection of Zuhuri's writings that included the *Gulzar-i Ibrahim*.[73] Like Akbar, Ibrahim Adilshah exemplified how to successfully make one's political theology central to one's rule. Now, a generation later in the new city of Shahjahanabad, Dara Shukoh attempted to do the same.

8

THE GREATEST SECRET

1656–1657

AT SOME POINT DURING his intense study of Indic thought, Dara
Shukoh had a dream. We do not know the date or precise year, but we
know that it happened during or before 1066 AH (1655/6). It was not a
common sort of dream, because it was significant enough to be recorded.
The prince had witnessed special visions before, ones that involved his spiritual guide Miyan Mir. Here, too, Dara's dream evoked a longer history of
Muslim rulers who had visionary dreams and Muslim authors whose
dreams legitimized their literary projects.[1]

Dreams of the Prophet Muhammad abound, like the vision that famously
cured the blind poet Busiri of his blindness and led him to compose his celebrated Arabic ode on the mantle of the Prophet, the *Qasidat-ul-burda*,
still recited today in countless commemorations of the Prophet's birth.
Learned men, too, could legitimize rulers through their appearances in
dreams, like Aristotle, who materialized before the Abbasid caliph Mamun,
as a rationale for the translation movement in Iraq.[2] But Dara saw neither
the Prophet nor an ancient Greek philosopher. He saw the Hindu sage Vasishtha along with the legendary prince Rama, believed to be the Hindu
deity Vishnu descended on earth.

This dream was prompted by something the prince had recently read—a
slim work of only a few handwritten pages. Its author was Dara's contemporary Shaikh Sufi, who, as we remember, was a mystic and erstwhile
Mughal official whom the Sufi writer Abd-ur-Rahman Chishti knew well

and held in high regard. Shaikh Sufi claims that his book was a Persian translation of the Sanskrit *Yogavasishtha,* a work in the form of a dialogue between the legendary Rama, of *Ramayana* fame, and his teacher, Vasishtha. This dialogue is meant to have taken place while Rama was a young prince.[3] The Persian text, as usual, follows the North Indian vernacular pronunciation of these names, which has Rama as "Ramchandra," or "Ram" and Vasishtha as "Basisht."

The *Jog Basisht* (*Yogavasishtha*) that Dara Shukoh had in mind was not so much one text but a whole textual tradition. There are many versions and abridgments of this work: from the tenth-century monistic *Mokshopaya,* to the *Yogavasishtha Maharamayana* layered with Advaita Vedanta and Rama devotion, to the *Laghu Yogavasishtha,* a medieval abridgment of the latter by the Kashmiri scholar Abhinanda.[4] The version that Shaikh Sufi's text is based on, the *Yogavasishthasara,* is even briefer than the other works. In the longer texts, Basisht relates an interlocking series of stories to Ram, but this version omits the stories.[5] Apart from the *Mokshopaya,* these texts share the basic narrative frame: the prince Ram had become weary of this world and wanted to withdraw from it, but Basisht gradually guided him toward spiritual liberation of a type that he could attain while still remaining a ruler. Dara Shukoh did not particularly care for the shaikh's translation, but the figures of Ram and Basisht stayed with him long enough to penetrate his sleep.

Upon seeing Basisht, the prince said, he immediately prostrated himself before the sage. Basisht spoke. "O Ramchandra! This is a disciple who is absolutely sincere, please embrace him."

"With the utmost affection, Ram took me into his arms," Dara relates. "Thereafter, Basisht gave Ramchandra sweets to feed me with. I ate the sweets."[6]

Through words and actions, in the salutations and the giving of food, Basisht and Ram anointed Dara Shukoh as one of them, in much the same way that in his earlier visions, Miyan Mir imparted to him esoteric secrets heart-to-heart. But the prince saw Basisht and Ram as also ordaining him to perform an important task. The dream propelled Dara to carry out a translation project of his own. He would commission a translator to produce in Persian a new rendition of the *Jog Basisht,* one that was better than the version that Shaikh Sufi had made.

The prince leaves unmentioned the fact that previous Mughal rulers had also sponsored their own Persian renditions of the work. When his grandfather Jahangir was a prince, in 1597, he had the court litterateur Nizam Panipati collaborate with a couple of Sanskrit pandits to translate Abhinanda's abridged *Yogavasishtha* into Persian.[7] In 1602, Jahangir's father, the emperor Akbar, had commissioned his own translation of the abridged *Yogavasishtha,* carried out by one Farmuli, who self-deprecatingly identifies himself as the lowliest disciple of the poet-saint Kabir. Gorgeously illustrated with forty-one miniatures, the manuscript survives today. It bears Shah Jahan's imperial seal and inscription dating from 1627/8, the year he came to the throne.[8] The prince must surely have had access to this prized holding of the imperial library. Why then would he need a new translation?

By translating the *Laghu Yogavasishtha* anew, Dara Shukoh claimed the text for himself. Its argument that a prince could achieve full self-realization as an ascetic while acting as an exemplary ruler spoke directly to his own situation. It also continued a link to previous imperial engagements with the text by Jahangir and Akbar, the prince's grandfather and great-grandfather. Dara's dream of anointment fits into a broader imperial ideology that presented the emperor as a spiritual and temporal master of the world in decidedly Indic terms. Translation in the Mughal context had often been a way of asserting imperial authority. To translate a text that had been in India far longer than one's celebrated ancestors was to sprout deeper roots in the subcontinent's soil. It was also a way to mold this earth in new ways.

The translator, who relates Dara Shukoh's dream in his introduction, does not mention his own name. Some manuscripts identify him as an otherwise unknown Habibullah, though this could just be a case of mistaking a scribe for the author.[9] If so, he would be an uncommon, though not unique, example of a Muslim man of letters who also possessed a high level of expertise in Sanskrit and religious thought.

But stronger evidence lies in the Hindavi couplets drizzled throughout the Persian text. They provide the poet's pen name "Wali," the same that was adopted by Banwalidas, Dara's former secretary and fellow Qadiri disciple. Banwalidas, as a Hindu scribe turned Sufi adept, had the multilingual ability that would enable him to carry out this project, though one suspects that he used the help of a pandit or two to access the *Yogavasishtha* rather than work directly from the Sanskrit. As a Kayasth, he did not have the same access to Sanskrit learning that a Brahmin might; his other writings also suggest as much.[10] Banwalidas was doubly linked to Dara through his Qadiri discipleship to Mulla Shah and his imperial service, and he might have played an influential role in introducing the prince to the kinds of Hindu texts and ideas that already accorded with Sufi concepts of mystical gnosis.

It is also eminently likely that both Banwalidas and Habibullah were part of a larger team of translators who shaped the abridged *Yogavasishtha* into its new Persian form. The translations for Akbar and Jahangir had tended to follow this pattern. We can imagine that the prince was also an involved collaborator. By now, Dara Shukoh must have become familiar with many of the *Laghu Yogavasishtha*'s philosophical terms, which his *Jog Basisht* often preserves alongside their Persian equivalents.

Dara Shukoh's decision to commission this translation was very much part of an imperial project. But it also spoke to cultural currents outside the court in Shahjahanabad and even on its fringes. The prince tapped into an ongoing dialogue between Indic and Persian philosophical and literary realms. His own patronage also energized this conversation. At the same time that Dara worked on the *Majma-ul-bahrain* and oversaw the *Jog Basisht* translation, other writers in the subcontinent were undertaking their own acts of boundary crossing, whether through imaginative translations, by drawing on unconventional themes, or by trying on a different language and genre.

One such author was Mir Askari, a poet and writer in the Deccan, born in India of Iranian extraction. He had joined Aurangzeb's service and gained his trust. But he also was a prolific poet and disciple of the Sufi Burhan-ud-Din Razi Ilahi, in whose honor he adopted the pen name "Razi." In 1655, he rendered into Persian narrative verse the Avadhi Sufi romance *Madhumalati* (The Night-Flowering Jasmine), by Shaikh Manjhan (fl. 1545). Like Manjhan, Razi belonged to the Shattari order.[11] Razi's version of the Hindavi poem changed the names of the lover protagonists Manohar and Madhumalati to *mihr* (sun) and *mah* (moon). He entitled it *Mihr o Mah*: "Let me write a book on Manohar's love/Let me address him by the name '*Mihr*'//Let me sing a song of Madhumalati's beauty/Let me show a heart in her moon's veil."[12] For readers of Persian literature in India, Razi's narrative poem also calls to mind a mystical *masnawi* with the same title that the sixteenth-century Sufi poet Jamali Dihlawi composed, though Jamali's poem is set outside India and involves adventures from Badakhshan to Tripoli.[13]

The following year, 1656, the Sanskrit poet Nilakantha Shukla composed a narrative poem that he called *Chimani Charita* (Life of Chimani), whose heroine was the daughter-in-law of Allahwardi Khan, one of the generals who accompanied Dara to Qandahar.[14] Chimani, whose name literally means sparrow, falls in love with her handsome Brahmin tutor Dayadeva, though she is married to Allahwardi Khan's son Jafar. Soon, aided by an older woman, Anisa (who is meant to be her chaperone), Chimani and Dayadeva start having trysts. Chimani asks him if he really is a Hindu (she uses this very term). Dayadeva replies, showing her his sacred thread, that he was a Brahmin (*vipra*), and it was not suitable for her to go down that path of love. Chimani remonstrates with him. But eventually a romance brews between them.[15] The poem is reminiscent of Jagannatha Pandit's story in using the provocative motif of the love between a Muslim woman and a Hindu man. Its theme might well have been inspired by the Mughal connections with pandits in Benares that Dara Shukoh cultivated.

Soon after, in 1657, a North Indian poet named Surdas composed a narrative poem in Avadhi on the love story of the royal couple Nala and Damayanti. Though Surdas was a Hindu, the genre he adopted, the Sufi romance, was one used earlier by Muslim Sufis like Shaikh Manjhan. Surdas wrote in the eastern vernacular (*purab bhasha*), he says, so that people could comprehend it: "There the vernacular is everyone's intimate family (*mahram*)/He who reads it, can understand its meaning/That is the reason this love story/Is brought forth in the eastern vernacular."[16] Surdas dedicated this poem to Shah Jahan. We do not know whether the emperor ever received or read it, but it is significant that this Hindavi poet saw the emperor and his own literary creation as part of the same interconnected world.

DARA SHUKOH'S SPONSORSHIP OF THE *JOG BASISHT* translation marked a directional shift in his explorations of Indic thought. He had already dipped into a variety of texts on a range of subjects to compose the *Majma*. Now, his inquiry became more focused. He sought those ancient Indic books that most aptly conveyed the idea of divine unity he wanted to plumb. With the *Jog Basisht* translation in 1656, the prince now directed his energies to supervising translations of Indic texts.

The following year, in 1657, Kavindracharya, too, finished a translation of the *Yogavasishthasara* in Hindavi, the very text that Shaikh Sufi had rendered into Persian.[17] Presumably this was prepared for Dara Shukoh's benefit. Kavindra titled his version *Jnanasara* (Epitome of Knowledge). Though some scholars have speculated that this formed the basis for the *Yogavasishtha* translation that the prince commissioned, it is a wholly different work.[18] Mughal readers, though, do not seem to have distinguished between the various abridgments of the *Yogavasishtha*. When the prince developed an interest in the *Jog Basisht,* he might well have commissioned multiple people—for instance, Banwalidas and Kavindracharya—to work on producing accessible versions for his perusal.

We do not know what the prince thought of Kavindracharya's efforts, but he certainly would have been sympathetic to the text's general theme. The translation advances that there is no duality between the individual self (*atman*) and the supreme being (*brahman*), and that true liberation in this world is achieved through this realization. Kavindracharya's skill as a poet in Hindavi shines in this rendition of the *Yogavasishthasara*'s Sanskrit couplets into euphonious Hindavi verse. Whatever its reception at the court, the *Jnanasara* was part of a trend inching across the North Indian literary landscape, of writing Vedantic works beyond Sanskrit, in Hindavi and Persian.

Another slim Advaitic text, the *Ashtavakra Gita,* also appears to have caught Dara Shukoh's attention. Like the *Yogavasishtha*, it too is framed as a dialogue between a king and a spiritual teacher—in this case King Janak and the sage Ashtavakra. Manuscript copies of this are scarce, but at least one identifies the translator as a certain "Jadun Das Dara Shukohi." The last part of the translator's name signals that he was the prince's servant.[19] It is possible that "Jadun Das" is a misspelling of Jadav Das, the secretary who had transcribed the initial conversations between Dara Shukoh and Baba Lal in Lahore.

Other translations attributed to Dara Shukoh's sponsorship include a Persian rendition of the *Bhagavad Gita*.[20] Unlike all the other works that he composed or commissioned, this one has no preface or introductory remarks referring to the prince, so we cannot be certain that it was indeed connected with him. It is not unheard of for later copies of manuscripts to misattribute their authorship. For instance, works by Dara Shukoh have been credited to Abu-l-Faiz Faizi (d. 1595), the emperor Akbar's poet laureate, while other writings likely composed in a later era circulated under Dara Shukoh's name. Another Persian translation of the Gita is also attributed to Faizi.[21] At the same time, it is quite conceivable that Dara wished to read the Gita in a Persian translation specially produced for him. Though, in the mid-seventeenth century, the Gita did not have the status that it later enjoyed in colonial India as the representative sacred text of the Hindus, it did attract the interest of Abd-ur-Rahman Chishti, who composed his own eloquent Persian rendition of it.[22] Similarly, Dara Shukoh's reputation as a sponsor of Indic learning in Persian may well have contributed to the wide attribution of numerous writings to the prince.

At his court in Shahjahanabad, Dara Shukoh also extended his regard for Indian holy men to his patronage of art. During this period in the mid-1650s, artists in the Mughal workshops labored to create a complex miniature painting, which was also much larger than usual.[23] Given the theme, it must have been made for Dara Shukoh's eyes. The painting features the Ajmer hills in the background, but unlike the *Padshah-nama*'s illustration, it does not reference the recent imperial excursion to the city. In the upper third of the page, a long line of Sufi saints assembles on the plinth of a building, against a backdrop of European-looking marble colonnades.

Gathering of Holy Men.

Two European observers at the left look on in wonder. Some of the saints are clearly recognizable—the Chishti Qutb-ud-Din Bakhtiyar Kaki, Muin-ud-Din Chishti, founder of the Chishti order in the subcontinent, and Dara Shukoh's own spiritual teacher Mulla Shah. Before them, other Sufis dance and swoon in ecstasy, aided by young disciples who beat drums, strum music, and catch them as they fall. But the painting's most distinctive feature is at the very bottom of the composition: a frieze of twelve Indian saints seated in quiet repose. They represent a broad cross-section of monistic thought and popular theistic expression, from yogis on the right to *sant*s, holy exemplars of truth, on the left. Labels identify all of them. On the left sit the Vaishnava poet saints Ravidas, Pipa, Sena, and Namdev, all considered to be followers of Ramanand, as is Kabir, seated here next to his son Kamal. An Aughar Shaiva ascetic sits on the edge of this group, while on the other side are Matsyendranath and Gorakhnath, spiritual masters of the Nath yogis, Jadrup, recognizable from the paintings of his conversations with Jahangir and Akbar, and Baba Lal, while the last figure is likely Baba Lal's teacher, Chetan Swami. In later times, artists working in the Mughal style would often model portraits of these holy men after their representations here.

Whether intentionally or not, this painting captures the subjects of Dara's spiritual exploration in its various stages: The famous Sufi authorities whom he wrote about in his first two books, the *Sakinat-ul-auliya* and the *Safinat-ul-auliya*. The ecstatic mystics whose sayings Dara recorded in the *Hasanat-ul-arifin*. And finally the Hindu ascetics, including Baba Lal—the "monotheists," whose ideas the *Majma-ul-bahrain* gathers into a bricolage of mystical verities. At a visual level, though, the sants and yogis seated below the arched face of the plinth, are part of, yet somewhat marginal to, the main composition.

HAD DARA SHUKOH FOR ALL PRACTICAL purposes lost interest in rulership? In many retrospective perspectives on the prince, his rich cultural and spiritual pursuits in the mid-1650s seem to overpower all his other activities. On the face of it, his recent ventures stand in stark contrast with those of his brothers. While Dara focused intently on his learning and patronage, Aurangzeb in the Deccan was plotting to expand the empire by invading Golconda, seat of the Qutbshahi rulers. Shuja had been managing his own court and territories in Bengal for a decade and a half, out of his father's shadow. Murad Bakhsh, who in Malwa had earlier shown an aptitude for administration, was settling into his new role as governor of Gujarat.

But on closer examination, the gulf between Dara and his brothers was not as wide as it might seem. Shuja and Murad, especially, were active connoisseurs of literature and the arts. Shuja's patronage extended to the Hindavi poet, Varan Kavi. It also embraced the Persian poet Abd-ul-Baqi Sahbai, who took "Sai," the "striver," as his poetic nom de plume. From Sahbai's pen came a Persian rendition of the famed epic poem, *Padmavat,* which chronicles the desire of the Delhi Sultan Ala-ud-Din Khalji (d. 1316) for Padmavati, the Queen of Chittor. The romance was originally composed by Malik Muhammad Jayasi (fl. 1540) as a Sufi allegory written in Avadhi, a Hindavi vernacular of the northeastern plains.[24] Another prominent scholar in Shuja's orbit was the Indian-born Iranian Muhammad Sadiq Isfahani (d. 1651). Sadiq authored many works including a multivolume encyclopedia, which he dedicated to Shuja. Amongst other topics, the collection contains a section on Indian religions, biographies of prominent poets and scholars of Bengal, and a detailed geography and an atlas that closely follows the climatic model laid out by Ptolemy.[25] Moreover, Shuja was close to certain Sufi shaikhs. We have already heard of his relationship, through the exchange of letters and the movement of household servants, with Mulla Shah. Shuja also had his own special relationship with the Qadiri Sufi Sayyid Nimatullah of Bengal.[26]

Murad too fostered a vibrant literary culture in his court. He also forged connections with Brahmin scholars and musicians, evinced by the poem that Kavindracharya Saraswati wrote for him in his *Kavindrakalpalata* dedicated to the imperial family. Kavindra extols Murad's generosity: "Ask for a blanket; he'll grant you a splendid coverlet / Ask for a horse, he'll give you an elephant, he'll laughingly give you a diamond." The poet lauds Murad's other stellar qualities, including his knowledge of *dharama marama* (religious secrets).[27] In 1652, Shah Jahan's former chronicler Tabatabai translated into Persian for Murad Bakhsh an Arabic text, which itself was a translation of a Pahlavi work distilling the wise counsel of Anushirwan, the storied ruler of ancient Iran, legendary for his justice and sagacity. It consists of Anushirwan's answers to questions about governance that his courtiers put to him.[28] The poet Said Quraishi showered Murad and Shuja with praise-poems.[29] Muzaffar Husain Islahi, the prince's *mir-i adl* (chief of judiciary), became a distinguished poet.[30] The renowned Mulla Tughra of Mashhad was Murad's secretary; he infused his Persian poetry with Indic words and wrote an ode to the Rajput ruler Jaswant Singh.[31] Like Dara Shukoh and Shuja with their spiritual guides, Murad also cultivated a personal bond with the Sufi pir Jafar Shah of Gujarat.[32]

The courts of Dara Shukoh's brothers mirrored the eldest prince's activities of pursuing knowledge—just on a smaller scale. The emperor's court was Dara's own. He was so closely aligned with Shah Jahan that the usual limitations constraining princes did not apply. It is no surprise that Dara modeled himself instead on previous emperors both mythical and historical, fashioning himself as the quintessential philosopher-ruler. He was like Alexander, discoursing with his philosophers, or Akbar presiding over debates in his *Ibadat-khana*. Dara himself, though, did not explicitly draw on these examples of past kings. This would have undermined his declaration, recorded almost fifteen years earlier in his *Sakinat-ul-auliya*—that God had transported him to a spiritual plane much loftier than those of other rulers before him. The Benares pandits continued their association with the Mughal court, as Dara Shukoh needed their help navigating the Sanskrit texts that had seized his attention. His project of spiritual self-fashioning was an ongoing one.

Moreover, as the philosopher-prince soared to new heights of mystical knowledge, he closely monitored the affairs of state. Dara Shukoh kept an alert watch on Aurangzeb's activities. At the end of 1655, it appeared that Aurangzeb's plans to invade the wealthy kingdom of Golconda might bear fruit. Dara was concerned that a victory over Golconda would dangerously boost his younger brother's standing. With Jahanara's support, he sought to intervene.

The ruler of Golconda, Abdullah Qutb Shah, had recently imprisoned Mir Jumla's son along with the son's family. It now looked as though Mir Jumla would finally be swayed to join a Mughal campaign against Golconda. It would be much easier to defeat the weak Qutb Shahi ruler if Mir Jumla were not on his side. Aurangzeb sent his sixteen-year-old son, Muhammad Sultan, to take Hyderabad, Golconda's capital. Aurangzeb's correspondence with the emperor gently hints that he is aware of Dara Shukoh's opposition. It would be a quick victory for the imperial forces, yielding lucrative results, Aurangzeb says, provided there is no "interference from any quarter."[33]

The Mughal forces besieged Golconda, and sacked the city, but could not touch the ruler, who was barricaded in the impregnable fort. Abdullah Qutb Shah frantically wrote Shah Jahan, Dara Shukoh, and Jahanara, asking for a reconciliation. Dara exchanged several letters with the Golconda ruler. One of Dara's replies, written in March 1656, assures the Deccan sultan that Shah Jahan had not been in favor of the siege, and that the matter would be resolved soon.[34]

Meanwhile, Aurangzeb sent his father glowing descriptions of Golconda's beauty and natural resources, as he marched to Hyderabad: "How could I describe the goodness of this land, its abundance of water, and cultivation, the quality of its pleasure-increasing air, the sheer number of sown fields visible during the course of my journey?" The prince also rails against the religious heresies of the Shia ruler Abdullah Qutb Shah, who, "out of an abundance of ignorance and idiocy, has made abandoning the *sunnat* of [the Prophet], and flaunting heretical innovation, into his own custom." Aurangzeb accuses the ruler of causing his subjects to abandon the correct Sunni path, and encouraging them to revile the Prophet's companions, "which is pure unbelief (*kufr*) and heresy."[35] For Aurangzeb, the benefits of invading Golconda were self-evident. But at the end of March, Shah Jahan pressured him to lift the siege. Dara Shukoh had achieved a small victory.

Dara remained enmeshed within the material world in other ways as well. He participated in the imperial authority his father crafted through grand architectural gestures, for instance, as well as through the consumption and production of luxury goods. Both Aurangzeb and Dara Shukoh feature in a new chapter of the imperial relationship with Shantidas, the Jain purveyor of jewels for the emperor. This time, the brothers took turns to convey their father's irritation to the merchant, whom they suspected of withholding choice jewels. In late 1655, Dara Shukoh wrote Shantidas, rebuking him for sending quality wares to others (is this a veiled reference to Aurangzeb?), but not to him. He also included a threat. If Shantidas did not immediately dispatch a certain massive diamond weighing forty-four *surkh* (equivalent to thirty-eight and a half carats), the prince would complain to the emperor. In the middle of 1656, Aurangzeb took Shantidas to task for sending inlaid ware of inferior quality. Along with this scolding, he sent a robe as a gift.[36] Aurangzeb's past desecration of Shantidas's temple clearly did not prevent the prince from maintaining a relationship with the influential merchant. It was important for him to keep the channels of communication open, as Shantidas could be a potential source of funds, should the need arise.

IT WAS THE BEGINNING OF 1657. Dara Shukoh was once again fired with enthusiasm for a new translation project. This time, he would himself be closely involved in the process. He had discovered a text he believed to express truths about God's unity like no other—the key to unlocking divine mysteries that would otherwise remain hidden. Or rather, it was a collection of works, which the prince treated as one sacred book—the Upanishads, Sanskrit sacred texts which form part of the larger corpus associated with the four Vedas. Scholars tend to date the earliest Upanishads, the *Brihadaranyaka* and the *Chhandogya*, to the sixth or seventh century BCE, while some of the other Upanishads that Dara Shukoh translated can be dated to as late as the fourteenth century.[37] No previous Mughal royal had ever translated the Upanishads. The emperor Akbar had once asked the irascible litterateur Badayuni to translate the *Atharva Veda* into Persian, but the text does not seem to have survived.[38]

To carry out his ambitious project, Dara Shukoh summoned to Shahjahanabad a group of Sanskrit scholars from Benares. For six months he worked with them at his mansion near the Yamuna River's Nigambodh *ghat*, perhaps in the second building now known as his library.[39]

If we add just a dash of imagination to the details in Dara's own account, we might picture the following scene: The Benares pandits assemble on the floor of a hall. Piled amongst them are various long oblong bundles of Sanskrit manuscripts, written on palm leaves. Approximately fifty Upanishads are eventually selected for translation, perhaps fifty-two, mirroring the number of letters in the Nagari alphabet. The prince inaugurates the proceedings by performing an augury with the Quran. He opens up the holy book at random and finds this verse: "Alif. Lam. Mim. Sad. (It is) a Scripture that is revealed unto you, so let there be no misgiving in your heart from it, that you may warn by it, a Reminder unto believers."[40] Commentators on the Quran believe that these words, prefaced by the mysterious letters that begin some of the Quran's suras, were addressed to the prophet Muhammad instructing him not to have any fear or doubt about the divine revelation.

It is a felicitous time to start. A pandit reads out a Sanskrit passage, and another gives its meaning in Hindavi. They communicated in Hindavi, we gather, for the Sanskrit words mentioned in Dara's translation are given in their vernacular forms. Frequently the pandits refer to commentaries if they are available, like those on the twelve major Upanishads attributed to the famous eighth-century philosopher Shankara. From time to time, Dara Shukoh interjects with a question. A secretary helps the prince record the proceedings under his watchful scrutiny, as had happened during Dara's dialogues with Baba Lal. In the course of these exchanges, the Sanskrit verses eventually transform into rough Persian prose, which is refined over time. The prince and the pandits work through the chilly winter and the searing summer until the beginning of the monsoon.

After six months the voluminous collection is complete. It is the middle of the summer and the Islamic month of Ramazan is nearing its end. Just as with his first two books, Dara finished this work as the holy month of fasting drew to a close. One manuscript records the date of completion as the twenty-ninth of Ramazan, which, along with other odd-numbered days at the end of the month, is associated with the Lailat-ul-Qadr, the night when the Quran was first revealed to the Prophet.[41]

Dara writes a preface that collapses his entire life's work into a quest for the source of true monotheism. He recounts that even after reading and composing numerous books on Sufism, subtle concerns lingered in his mind. These could only be resolved through recourse to the divine word, though the Quran—God's revelation to the Prophet Muhammad—abounded in allegory, and those who understood its mysteries were so few! But had not God revealed more than one Book, each a commentary of the other, one explicating in detail where the other is ambiguous?

The scriptures of the people of the Book, though—the Torah, Gospel, and Psalms—did not satisfy the prince. They too were diffusive and allegorical, made even more obscure by the translations that selfish people had made of their works. (Was Dara Shukoh making a dig at Father Busée or Sarmad here?) He realized that he need look no further than his homeland, India, for a deeper understanding of divine unity. In his view, Indian scholars "do not reject unity, nor do they find fault with the unity-affirmers, rather, it is the foundation of their belief." Dara contrasts them with the "ignoramuses of today, who have established themselves as religious scholars and have fallen upon criticizing, tormenting, and naming as infidels the God-knowers and unity-affirmers." [42] The prince then discovers the Upanishads, "in which are contained all the secrets of the mystical path and meditative exercises of pure divine unity." He describes his project thus:

> As this self-examining truth seeker had in view the original unity of the essence, not the Arabic, nor Syriac, Hebrew, and Sanskrit languages, he desired to translate these *Upnikhats,* which are the treasury of divine unity, those who know it even in that community being few, into the Persian language, without additions or deletions or selfish motives, with the utmost accuracy, word for word, in order to understand what secret lies in it that this community conceals it and keeps it hidden so from the people of Islam. [43]

Dara Shukoh repeats the idea of the secret, which also references a Sanskrit meaning for the word "Upanishad," in the title of his translation. He calls it the *Sirr-i akbar,* which means, "The Greatest Secret." [44] There is a double edge to this enigma though, because for Dara this secret also reveals the hidden message of the Quran. The full import of the prince's project becomes clearer. Referring to himself in the customary third person, Dara explains:

> Each problem, and each lofty word that he had wanted, and of which he was the seeker, and had sought and not found, he obtained from that quintessence of the ancient book, which is, without doubt the first heavenly scripture, the font of truth-realization, ocean of divine unity, in agreement with the glorious Quran, and, not only that but its exegesis. It becomes clearly manifest that the

following verse is literally applicable to this ancient book: "It is a noble Qur-an, In a hidden Book (*kitab maknun*), which none save the purified touch, a revelation from the Lord of the Worlds." That is, the noble Quran is in a book, which is hidden. No one can apprehend it save that heart which has been purified. It has descended from the Sustainer of the worlds.

Dara makes the bold move of identifying the Upanishads with the "hidden book" mentioned in the Quran. His interpretation sweeps aside traditional explications of the verse, which either identify the hidden book with the Preserved Tablet, that is, the archetype of God's words inscribed upon a heavenly tablet, which has not been sent down to earth, or more generally with a celestial book.[45] He further elaborates:

> It becomes clear and evident that this verse is not applicable to the Psalms, or the Torah, or the Gospel, and from the word for revelation (*tanzil*, literally sending down), it is manifest that [this book] does not apply to the Preserved Tablet. As the *Upnikhat*, which is a concealed secret (*sirr*), is the origin of this book, and the verses of the glorious Quran are found in it literally; thus the "hidden Book" [mentioned in the Quran] is this ancient book, through which the unknown has become known and the incomprehensible comprehensible to this faqir.[46]

The prince finally has custody of the book, a collection of texts that have never before been translated. Dara Shukoh has moved beyond learning from sages and ascetics. He now has access to the very source of monotheism, the key to understanding all the celestial books. He who reads the *Sirr-i akbar,* Dara concludes, "having considered it the translation of the word of God, and having abandoned bigotry, becomes imperishable, fearless, without a care, and eternally liberated."[47]

Among all the sacred celestial texts, Dara explains, the oldest were a collection of four Vedas, which were revealed to the pure one (*safi*) of God, Adam, the first human and progenitor of all humanity. Early Islamic tradition had long associated Adam's first terrestrial home with India.[48] In Dara's telling, Sanskrit thus represents the original, primal language of humanity, an idea that had important afterlives in the development of modern comparative philology. According to Dara, the Upanishads represented a distillation of the Vedas and contained the ancient secrets of mystical knowledge and pure, original monotheism.[49]

Lodged between the *Sirr-i akbar*'s preface and the translated Upanishads is a glossary of about 114 Sanskrit terms, with their meanings in Persian. This list begins with one of its most striking equivalences, the syllable Om, which is interpreted as Allah. An explanatory note adds that it is the same as *pranava*, another word for Om, and means the "ender of secrets." The Hindu deity Brahma is the same as the archangel Jibril, who transmitted the revelation to the Prophet Muhammad, Vishnu is the angel Mikail, and Mahesh the angel Israfil. Brahmaloka, the abode of the deity Brahma, is the "farthest lote tree" (*sidrat-ul-muntaha*), which is Jibril's abode, referenced in the Quran. These equivalences function like a secret language that one has to master to understand the book—a symbolic code with which initiates could unlock the esoteric meanings of the text. The actual translations, though, tend to preserve both the Indic and the Persian terms side by side, instead of completely effacing one into the other.

Sometimes, manuscripts of the *Sirr-i akbar* take an alternate title with a similar meaning: *Sirr-ul-asrar*, "Secret of all Secrets." They share this other title with certain writings on mysticism as well as on a related tradition of esoteric knowledge.[50] The *Sirr-ul-asrar* is a title, for instance, of a manual on the Sufi way by the founder of the Qadiri order, Abd-ul-Qadir Jilani (d. 1166). It also is the Arabic name for a famed treatise of occult lore and political philosophy, known in Latin as the *Secretum secretorum*, and long attributed to Aristotle. Both titles were well known in India.

This occult collection purports to be an exchange of letters between Aristotle and Alexander. This work traveled from Arabic to Persian, Latin, and a host of European vernaculars. The Arabic text claims to have been translated from the original Greek on the orders of the Abbasid caliph al-Mamun. The work is filled with counsel for princes, esoteric knowledge, spells, and a fascination with India drawn from the Alexander romance.[51] Dara Shukoh would have also likely been familiar with the Mughal book of spells titled *Zakhira-i Iskandar* (The Treasury of Alexander) translated into Persian by the governor Muhammad Baqir Najm-i Sani. Like the *Sirr-ul-asrar*, this book of charms and talismans claims a royal pedigree. It was apparently discovered by the Abbasid caliph al-Mutasim, when he conquered the Byzantine city of Amorium in 838. Recall that Muhammad Baqir, who served as a high-ranking governor for both Jahangir and Shahjahan, also produced a Persian abridgment of Razi's *al-Sirr-ul-maktum* (The Hidden Secret), a book of astral magic, filled with talismans and charms, that came to be well known in the Mughal court.[52] These writings pay attention to the power of the soul or psyche (*nafs*) as a means of effecting occult or miraculous phenomenon. They also address how to harness the hidden forces of jinn and angels. At the Mughal court, the word *sirr*, or secret, in a title, thus had a long association with esoteric knowledge in the service of imperial power.

The prominence of the secret, the imperial translation bureau, the authority of primordial, celestial books, even the fascination with India, are all legible in a language of esoteric learning familiar to many in Dara

Shukoh's world. But the secret also had palpable Indic connotations as well. The very meaning of the word "upanishad" in Sanskrit, after all, is "secret" as Dara is quick to tell us in his introduction, as in a hidden or esoteric doctrine. One major theme in Dara's collection of Upanishads is cosmography and with it the attending interest in deities, demons, and heavenly structures. The Sanskrit word "upanishad" denotes the secret or esoteric connections uniting existence.[53] By opening up and harnessing these celestial writings for the first time in Persian, Dara, as the heir apparent, the consummate philosopher-prince, lays claim to an ancient knowledge of how to master the world.

Dara's *Sirr-i akbar* includes eleven of the principal Upanishads associated with the early corpus of the four Vedas. He also incorporates several later Upanishads, including ten Yoga Upanishads that assimilate hatha yogic practices into Vedanta. He avoids those Upanishads that have a pronounced sectarian tilt—those describing the worship of deities, and the different kinds of sectarian markings for devotees, for instance. Most probably, the *Sirr-i akbar* is the end result of a process of winnowing and selection of texts best reflecting the monotheistic message that Dara saw in the Upanishads. It is unlikely that it reproduced in Persian a preexisting anthology of Upanishads.[54] The *Sirr-i akbar* brings together an array of disparate, yet interconnected texts, and binds them into a sacred scripture.

The *Sirr-i akbar* adroitly tackles a problem that often vexed translators of Hindu texts into Persian—the conundrum of multiple gods. These deities appear so frequently in several Upanishads selected here that it would be very difficult to ignore or delete them. The main strategy that the *Sirr-i akbar* uses is to sidestep their divinity and enfold them within an Islamic framework. So a god (*deva*) becomes either an angel (*firishta*) or a spiritual guardian (*muwakkal*), a term often used to refer to the jinn. Sometimes, the *Sirr-i akbar* identifies individual deities as specific angels, as we have seen in the *Majma-ul-bahrain* and its own glossary, but as mentioned earlier, it never uses these equivalences as substitutes for their actual names.

For instance, the opening verse of the *Mundaka Upanishad* mentions that Brahma, who "arose as the first among gods" and is the world's creator and guardian, instructed his firstborn son Atharvan in the knowledge of Brahman, the foundation of all knowledge.[55] These two concepts—of Brahma, the creator and foremost god, and Brahman, the ultimate reality about which Brahma taught, do not quite equate to God and the knowledge of God, respectively. This would pose a problem for a Sufi who believed in the unity of all being. If Brahma is the same as the one God of the Quran and Islam, then how could he be distinct from Brahman, the ultimate reality? Besides, a Muslim translator would also be uneasy with the idea of Brahma having a son, because the Quran, pushing back against the Christian trinity, explicitly states that God does not beget progeny.

The *Sirr-i akbar*'s version closely captures the sense of the Sanskrit verse, but alters its texture: "Before all the spiritual guardians (*muwakkalan*), first Brahma, that is the spiritual guardian of creation, became manifest. Thus Brahma, who is the earth's cause and world's possessor, that Brahma, spoke to his eldest son, whose name was Atharba, of Brahmabidya, that is the knowledge of God's unity, which is the greatest of all the branches of knowledge, and which contains all the sciences."[56] By making Brahma a special category of being, separate from the one God, the *Sirr-i akbar* reshapes the text in a monotheistic mold. But, by assigning Brahma the divine power of creation, the *Sirr-i akbar* still keeps fairly close to the Sanskrit text, without offering a completely different retelling.

The *Sirr-i akbar*'s translation style is digressive and laden with explanations. It frequently reads more like a commentary than a word-for-word translation of the Sanskrit material into Persian. Once, the text explicitly invokes the non-dualist philosopher Shankara, though it often draws upon his commentaries without mentioning his name.[57] In many cases, Dara Shukoh uses Shankara's commentaries to layer the Upanishads with non-dualist or esoteric interpretations, making these ancient Sanskrit texts accord more with the prince's Sufi inclinations.

One such passage occurs in the *Brihadaranyaka Upanishad,* forming part of a series of creation narratives. It recounts that Prajapati, the primordial "lord of creatures," had two kinds of progeny: gods and demons, respectively: "Now, Prajapati's offspring were of two kinds: gods and demons. Indeed, the gods were the younger of his offspring, while the demons were the older; and they were competing for these worlds. So the gods said to themselves: 'Come, let us overcome the demons during a sacrifice by means of the High Chant.'"[58]

The *Sirr-i akbar* as usual substitutes angels for gods, and jinn for demons. But, inspired by Shankara's commentary, it understands the two categories of Prajapati's descendants as imbued with a deeper meaning. "Prajapat, what is meant by Prajapat here is this very person, his progeny are of two groups: angels and jinn. The external and internal senses, which are conjoined with possessing knowledge and acts in accordance with the Book of God, those are the angels. The senses, which are in agreement with one's own sensual pleasures and the desires, which contravene the Book, are the jinn. *Devta*, meaning angel, in the lexicon is a person who is good in comparison with the rest, and *asur* in the lexicon is he who is [immersed] in his own desires and sensual pleasures. . . ."[59] Following Shankara, the *Sirr-i akbar* makes a striking interpretive move. It maps these categories of gods/angels and demons/jinn onto the individual self. The implicit suggestion is that the individual self is identical to Prajapati.

But Dara Shukoh also frequently relies on other unnamed glosses to merely explain things that would have been alien or puzzling to many Persian readers of the day. For instance, the *Prashna Upanishad* discusses how the primordial lord Prajapati was food, which gave rise to semen, from which were produced creatures. It then relates: "So, those who undertake the vow of Prajapati produce a couple/To them belong the world of Brahman. . . ."[60]

The *Sirr-i akbar* does not so much translate these lines as discuss the finer points of the regulation of sexual relations for the householder: "A person, who, on this very night has intercourse with a woman/wife, and does not have intercourse during the day, does not waste his semen. From the intercourse that has occurred at night, from that semen a son or a daughter is born. A person who has intercourse with a wife at night will reach the world of the moon, which is a good world. A person who, from the fourth day, which is the period of purification after menstruation, until the sixteenth day, which are the days of attachment of the semen to the womb, approaches a woman one time in a month, this action falls within *brahmacharj*, the Sanskrit *brahmacharya*, that is, within devotion and ascetic practice, when he does not do this act for the sake of pleasure but rather does this, by the command of God (*khuda*) for the aim of fathering progeny." These detailed rules draw on injunctions elucidated in Hindu legal texts regarding the appointed times for intercourse, which in turn are based on Indic medical notions regarding a woman's fertile period every month.[61] In passages like this one, the *Sirr-i akbar* displays a taxonomic mode of inquiry, through gathering and listing Indic concepts and practices. The details it provides would have been the outcome of Dara Shukoh's discussion with his pandit collaborators.

At times the *Sirr-i akbar* blends its very own interpretive comments into the translation. For instance, it remarks on the horse sacrifice (*ashvamedha yagna*) discussed at the beginning of the *Brihadaranyaka Upanishad*. In ancient India, this sacrifice came to be associated with rites of sovereignty. The *Brihadaranyaka* allegorizes this sacrifice by identifying the sacrificial horse with the universe. The *Sirr-i akbar* adds this explanation: "*Ashmed* is a famous sacrifice (*jag*), not in the way that the literalists [view it] that a horse having been brought, must be sacrificed. Rather, *ashmed* connotes this meditative practice (*mashghuli*): that one considers oneself to be just as this horse that is going to be sacrificed. . . ."[62] Like a Sufi commentary on the Quran, the *Sirr-i akbar* distinguishes between an interpretation that only looks at the text's external, literal meaning, and one that reveals its inner,

hidden essence. By reshaping the horse sacrifice as an interior spiritual practice, this passage also reflects how Dara Shukoh sees these sacred Indic
texts as offering a path to liberation.

Dara Shukoh's Upanishad project cemented Kavindracharya's role as a
leader amongst his Brahmin peers, and a mediator of Indic knowledge for
non-Hindus. A few years later, the French traveler François Bernier sat down
with a group of six pandits in Benares in his own quest to understand Indian philosophy and religion. A prominent pandit arranged this meeting.
Though Bernier does not name him, this was almost certainly Kavindra,
whom Bernier describes as the "chief" of the pandits. These Brahmin
scholars discussed religious matters with Bernier, explaining that when they
worship images in a temple, their prayers are actually offered to the divine
and not to the idols, the images serving merely to focus their devotions to
God "who is the absolute master and the only almighty."[63] Bernier does
not doubt their sincerity, though he also suspected that the explanation was
part of an effort to make the veneration of idols more palatable to Christian doctrine. One might conceive that such an approach helped Dara
Shukoh derive a strong monotheistic message from texts about multiple
deities.

In the course of his own study of Indic texts, which he conducted in Persian, as he did not know Sanskrit, Bernier worked with one of the most
renowned pandits of India. Again, this may have been Kavindra, for Bernier notes that his Indian companion and teacher for some three years had
earlier been in Dara Shukoh's employ. Indeed, Bernier's presentation of the
Vedas and the antiquity of Sanskrit have notable parallels with Dara Shukoh's earlier explanations in the *Sirr-i akbar*, drawn from his own engagements with pandits.[64]

As for Kavindra, he became enormously popular amongst his fellow
Brahmin scholars, who composed two anthologies of verses praising
him—one largely in Sanskrit, and the other in Hindavi.[65] According to their
accounts, he had successfully convinced the emperor to abolish a tax on
Hindu pilgrims visiting the holy cities of Benares and Allahabad. In these
eulogies, he becomes a hero, journeying to the court to give an eloquent
discourse, stunning the diverse audience of nobles. There were present
Iraqis, Khurasanis, Abyssinians, Badakhshanis, Multanis, Balkhis, and
others, says the poet Hirarama. No promises of wealth could tempt the
Brahmin to temper his stand; he insisted that the tax be repealed.[66] Hirarama elides the fact that Kavindra had long been the recipient of imperial
largesse.

Shah Jahan's Persian chronicles remain silent on this incident. They also
do not mention any tax imposed on Hindu pilgrims. Whatever the actual

details of this event, we can assume that something must have taken place for Kavindra to be lauded thus by his peers. Nonetheless, the question of its timing remains unresolved. As Kavindra only seems to have enjoyed imperial attention after 1650, it is likely that he extracted this favor from Shah Jahan in the 1650s and not earlier. The *Kavindrachandrodaya* notes that the pandit managed to win the tax relief on the day of a Hindu festival dedicated to the sun deity, Surya, which occurs in January.[67] The last recorded monetary gift that Kavindra received at the court was in January 1657, before the *Sirr-i akbar* was completed. The occasion was the emperor's solar weighing, when scholars, poets, and others would customarily receive imperial largesse.[68] Though it is tempting to imagine that lifting the tax may have constituted a preemptive reward of sorts for Kavindra's work on the Upanishads, the story seems to have been more complicated. Evidence from Kavindra's own poetic composition, the *Kavindrakalpalata*, suggests that the tax may have been lifted earlier.[69]

Nevertheless, after the *Sirr-i akbar*'s completion, there would have been little opportunity for bestowing imperial favors. Shah Jahan soon fell seriously ill, and Dara Shukoh was consumed with his care.

9

SUCCESSION

1657–1659

SHAH JAHAN WAS TOO ILL to leave his bedchamber in the Red Fort—an inlaid and gilded marble structure where carved lattices filtered light and air and hanging blinds sealed the open archways. While the emperor ailed, Dara Shukoh guarded him fiercely. Shah Jahan's condition worsened day by day, relates the chronicler Muhammad Salih Kamboh, who lived through this period. The emperor was afflicted with strangury, or urination that was both excruciating and incomplete. Along with this, he suffered dehydration, swelling below the navel, and fever. In modern medical terminology, he would likely have had an acute bacterial prostate infection. Such illnesses could be especially serious in an age before antibiotics.[1] Medical doctors including the renowned Hakim Daud, known by the title Muqarrab Khan, as well as other unnamed "Christian physicians," strove to cure the emperor. Dara Shukoh tended to his father constantly, staying with him in his private apartments.[2]

Rumors surged out of Shahjahanabad to the rest of the empire. Many people thought that the emperor was dead and that Dara was keeping the news a secret. In truth, there was not much he could have done to avert the gossip. An emperor's illness was a calamity, toppling the equilibrium of humors that was thought to maintain the kingdom's health as well as his own. Shuja's retainer, Mir Muhammad Masum (fl. 1660), who felt the repercussions in distant Bengal, emphasized the importance of the emperor's well-being with a verse: "As long as the incomparable Shah's elements are healthy/The constitution of the age achieves balance."[3]

Masum was right about the empire's stability being threatened. Shah Jahan's ailment unleashed a series of events that would pit Dara Shukoh against his brothers. In an attempt to quell hearsay and speculation, Dara blocked most courtiers from all access to the emperor or his news, also detaining his brothers' agents at court. Masum claims Dara ordered for Mir Abu-l-Hasan, Shuja's representative, to be shackled and pilloried, and even threatened to rend the man's limbs. Such acts, according to Masum, planted in the kingdom's soil the seed of *fasad,* a word connoting corruption, sedition, and chaos, a threat to the state and to order.[4]

The events that took place soon afterward convulsed Hindustan. Eventually, more authors would write about the struggle for succession between Shah Jahan's sons than probably any other event in the dynasty's history before the 1857 rebellion against British colonial rule. But with the breakdown of power at the center, we have few substantial official accounts favoring Shah Jahan's or Dara Shukoh's perspectives.[5] And the prince, experiencing the biggest crisis of his life, would hardly find the opportunity to pursue his own writing. It is conceivable that many sources did not survive the ravages of time. Only a few of Dara's letters and decrees from this period remain.

Writing at the beginning of the nineteenth century, the court administrator Muhammad Faiz Bakhsh (fl. 1818) quotes in the course of his history from an unnamed report, which he claims was written by Dara Shukoh's private secretary.[6] But by all measures this source does not appear to survive independently. We are left with a shifting kaleidoscope of reports and anecdotes that take us further from Dara Shukoh and the perspective of his inner circle. Among the cacophony of voices, three chronicles stand out, each written by a partisan of a different prince. The *Waqiat-i Alamgiri,* composed after the events by a votary of Aurangzeb, is attributed to the poet Mir Askari Razi (d. 1696/7), who later received the title of Aqil Khan. Murad Bakhsh's tutor, Bihishti, an Iranian litterateur, composed the *Ashob-i Hindustan,* a versified synopsis of the turmoil in the late 1650s. Shah Shuja's retainer, Muhammad Masum, wrote a history of the succession wars, into which he sometimes inserts his own personal narratives as an eyewitness. Masum's history is known simply as the *Tarikh-i Shah Shujai.* Taken together, these three accounts offer valuable early insight into the momentous aftermath of Shah Jahan's illness.

Within a week, on September 24, 1657, the emperor had recovered enough to appear at the viewing balcony near his bedchamber, where Mughal emperors since the time of Akbar had customarily showed themselves to their subjects. His courtiers offered kornish obeisances. This was the occasion of an important proclamation. Dara Shukoh would have his rank increased to 50,000, with 40,000 cavalry. His annual income would also rise. With these gifts came an understanding that the heir would now be responsible for the affairs of state. By the end of October, the emperor's health had improved enough for him to travel to Agra for a change of air. This would now be their new base of operations. Care was taken to weed out potential traitors. Muazzam Khan, already summoned from the Deccan, was removed from the post of prime minister. The Shahjahanabad Fort was left in the care of Khalilullah Khan. The other nobles recalled from the Deccan, Mir Jumla, Mahabat Khan, and Rao Sattarsal, would now report to the court in Agra.[7]

All the while, writes Masum, the times were as agitated as the tortuous "ringlets of moon-faced beauties."[8] As Dara's brothers' informants were prevented from sending reports, news of the emperor's recovery may not have reached the other princes. Or, they did not trust what their agents conveyed. Shuja, believing the emperor to be dead, enthroned himself as emperor. He included in his grandiose title the epithet "Third Lord of the Auspicious Conjunction," after Shah Jahan and Timur. He also added the phrase "Second Alexander," after the Macedonian world conqueror, Alexander, the quintessential philosopher-king in Persian literature and a model for Mughal rule. Then, he loaded his army onto boats and headed upstream toward Shahjahanabad. On the tenth of December, Dara Shukoh prevailed upon Shah Jahan to send the twenty-two-year-old Sulaiman Shukoh to counter Shuja with an army of twenty thousand cavalry. The experienced Mirza Raja Jai Singh, who had now become Sulaiman Shukoh's relative by marriage, accompanied the young prince.[9]

The currents of the Ganges moved the imperial forces swiftly eastward. But uncertainty beset Mirza Raja Jai Singh, who preferred to tread cautiously. He was seemingly reluctant to anger the emperor, whom he thought might favor striking a deal with Shuja. It seems that his relationship with Sulaiman soured during their journey. Dara Shukoh and Nadira took quick action to appease the raja. Dara assured him that Sulaiman's reports would now be routed directly through Jai Singh. A communication from Nadira encourages the raja to spare no efforts toward victory and informs him that the emperor had granted him a generous monetary gift.[10] Soon afterward, Dara Shukoh urges Jai Singh to bring back Shuja's head.[11]

The imperial army pitched camp at Bahadurpur, near Benares. Shuja's army was nearby, in a secluded spot with easy access to the river for transport and supplies. Dara Shukoh wrote Jai Singh urging him to attack.[12] On February 24, 1658, the imperial forces stormed Shuja's camp.

Sulaiman Shukoh realized that the men under Shuja's command had been negligent in their surveillance, writes Masum. Apparently, over the past twenty-five years in Bengal, Shuja's soldiers had grown accustomed to sleeping in until the day's second watch, or noon. The morning of the attack, they were comfortably supine atop their charpoys, shielded by mosquito nets. When the invaders streamed into their camp, they drowsily rubbed their eyes awake. There was no time even to put on their armor or fasten their weapons. Shuja was nowhere on the scene. In Masum's words, "the Sultan of the horizons, too, by the dictates of fate, was at that time in a state of repose." When eventually he did emerge, having clambered onto an elephant, it was too late.[13]

It was an easy victory for the imperial army, but Shuja managed to escape. He and some of his men fled by boat to Patna and, from there, to the fort of Mungir, where he hoped to withstand a siege. Sulaiman Shukoh went in hot pursuit of Shuja. Raja Jai Singh, on the other hand, took his time in arriving.[14]

About a month later, the imperial court obtained news of the successful campaign at Bahadurpur. It provided some comfort. The Mirza Raja and Sulaiman Shukoh received increases in their ranks. Dara Shukoh took care to congratulate Jai Singh after the Bahadurpur victory, even though it was largely Sulaiman Shukoh's operation. It was the biggest military success the subcontinent had seen in over a century, the prince said.[15] He fondly addressed the raja as "Dada bhai" to reflect their recent kinship ties after Sulaiman's marriage.[16] But Dara Shukoh and Shah Jahan already had to deal with other new crises raging in Gujarat and the Deccan. There was still no resolution to Shuja's rebellion.

UPON HEARING OF SHAH JAHAN'S ILLNESS, Murad Bakhsh sprung into action. He put to death his diwan, Ali Naqi, whom he suspected of harboring sympathies for Dara Shukoh. Next, with the help of the eunuch Shahbaz Khan, he besieged and plundered the fort at the port city of Surat, extracting six lakh rupees. He also disobeyed the imperial order (via Dara Shukoh) to transfer to Berar, which was actually under Aurangzeb's governance. After this groundwork, he proclaimed himself emperor on the fifteenth of December 1657. Murad even had a poet to sing his praises— Bihishti of Shiraz, who was the prince's former tutor.[17] Bihishti extols the grand celebrations during Murad's enthronement, which, according to him, lasted for twenty days: "In that gathering, from one end to another/The air turned into jewel-scattering clouds/Gold, gems and silver, in the capital/Rained down like blossoms from a tree//Inasmuch as gold and silver were scattered/Hands refrained from collecting it."[18] Such rich detail was a feature of the epic poetry genre and not necessarily meant to reflect reality.

But since October, Murad, Aurangzeb, and Shuja had started corresponding with each other. What began as polite salutations discussing their father's illness became full-fledged conspiracies, complete with veiled language and arrangements to bypass imperial spies. If Murad's imperial aspirations troubled Aurangzeb, he hid it well. But Aurangzeb did take the lead in formulating a plan of action. In a letter to Murad, he mentions that a secret code would be sent subsequently. All further correspondence must be conducted using the code, Aurangzeb instructs.[19]

At the same time, reports Aqil Khan, Aurangzeb plied Shah Jahan with a stream of letters and gifts of grapes, no doubt attempting to dispel suspicion. Dara Shukoh, for his part, tried to preempt a third claimant to the throne. In Aqil Khan's account, Dara naively sent Aurangzeb's agent Isa Beg back to the Deccan, to convince the younger prince of the emperor's good health. This move backfired. Instead, Isa Beg persuaded Aurangzeb that Shah Jahan was too feeble to rule effectively and that Dara Shukoh had appropriated the reins of power.[20]

Aurangzeb could not afford to fight battles on multiple fronts. His strategy was to appease both Murad Bakhsh and Shuja, ignoring their recent betrayals of his previous agreements with them. As communications with Shuja would have to pass through imperial territory, Aurangzeb and Murad, it appears, exchanged more letters with each other than with Shuja. At this point, the correspondence between Murad and Aurangzeb seems mainly concerned with logistics and plans. Murad is eager to attack Agra immediately. Aurangzeb stresses the wisdom of biding their time, even suggesting that they invite the Iranian ruler Shah Abbas to attack from the west so that the imperial forces could be even further dispersed.[21]

These exchanges are occasionally tinged with religious undertones, at least in the forms in which they exist today. The letters of the imperial siblings have come down to us in various collections compiled much after they were written, and it could be that they bear the imprint of these later times. In early 1658, Aurangzeb was ready to march toward Agra. Appended to a letter to Murad that he wrote before going to war is an agreement (*ahadnama*), if an offer with an implied stick accompanying it could be called one. Apparently, it also included Aurangzeb's signature and hand impression, to underscore its seriousness and authenticity.[22]

The kernel of this agreement was this: Aurangzeb would ascend the throne, but he would share the empire with Murad. The terms of this arrangement are left conveniently vague. If Murad offered his full cooperation, and made Aurangzeb's "friends his friends" and his brother's "enemies his enemies," then he would receive all the empire's western territories, including the Punjab, Afghanistan, Kashmir, and Sindh.[23] Aqil Khan also discusses the details of the agreement but leaves out any suggestion of sectarian or religious motivations from his history. He does, however, repeatedly refer to Murad and Dara as "foolish" and "idiots without reason," quick to be duped by Aurangzeb's stratagems, but he gives no hint of religious animus.[24]

There is more to this document, though. The letter resounds with the bombast of religious war. Aurangzeb begins by announcing the main goal of his campaign, which is, "with the endeavors of the victorious standard's religious warriors, and the force of the victory-culminating forearms of the jihad-wagers, to pluck out the thorn of apostasy and heresy from the ever-blooming rose garden of the lands of Islam." He also wishes that the "leader of the apostates, together with his followers and partisans, would become nothing and non-existent." Later, he refers again to Dara as a "godforsaken apostate." From being a jealous, unjust brother, Dara Shukoh has now become an apostate from Islam. The charge of apostasy meant that not only would Dara be an illegitimate claimant to the throne but that his killing, too, would be justified.[25]

It is tempting to overstate this religious angle to the war of succession. Many modern writers perceive Aurangzeb's rhetoric through twentieth-century lenses—as the overflowing of a frothing discontent with Dara Shukoh's religious innovations.[26] But surely Aurangzeb, too, realized that the Mughal state's authority was only strengthened by its ability to absorb and include some of the subcontinent's diversity, a legacy that his great-grandfather Akbar had left for his successors. Moreover, in contrast to the prince's letter to Murad, the account of Shuja's courtier Masum makes no mention of heresy at this stage of the succession struggle; neither do the reports of the event by Bihishti, in Murad's entourage, or by Aqil Khan Razi, Aurangzeb's close servant.

At the same time, we cannot wish away the language of religious war. In his preparation for battle, Aurangzeb overtly references a model of the righteous conqueror, which Shah Jahan also drew upon during his rule. Babur, the dynasty's founder, was one example. But Shah Jahan appropriated and refashioned the image of a far older ancestor—Timur.

Years later, as an old man, Aurangzeb would recall the contributions of both Akbar and Timur in a letter to Bidar Bakht, his grandson. Ironically, Bidar Bakht was also Dara Shukoh's grandson, born to Aurangzeb's son and Dara's daughter Jani Begam . Aurangzeb refers to Mughal India as a "piece of bread," generously gifted to him and his forebears by Timur and Akbar.[27]

For now, though, the times demanded a warrior who waged a morally justifiable battle. The Mughals were no strangers to the rhetoric of *takfir,* the act of accusing other Muslims of unbelief. Such was the Safavid characterization of the Mughals after the last Qandahar war. Recall that Aurangzeb had also reviled Shia rulers in the Deccan as infidels.[28] Denouncing Dara as an apostate or infidel fit into a larger pattern. But it did not necessarily reflect the prevailing consensus on the prince's views and activities. Moreover, Aurangzeb, preoccupied as he was with the logistics of war, had neither the need nor the leisure to craft a full-fledged denunciation of Dara Shukoh's religious proclivities.

Did he, though, invoke his brother's "heresies" to galvanize support? Before joining up with Murad, Aurangzeb spent the month of March in Burhanpur preparing for battle. According to one history of Shah Jahan's reign, Aurangzeb went with the scholar Shaikh Nizam to visit the Sufi Burhan-ud-Din Raz-i Ilahi, who also happened to be Aqil Khan's spiritual teacher. Burhan-ud-Din, who was affiliated with the Shattari order, reportedly had a huge following. The Sufi had just come out of his house to perform his prayers. He was initially reluctant to sit down with Aurangzeb and Shaikh Nizam. Then, Aurangzeb managed to voice his complaints: "Dara Shukoh, crossing over from the religion of Islam, has stepped into the wasteland of error. Imitating the apostates who have abandoned divine injunctions, he has defamed Sufism, declared infidelity and Islam to be twin brothers—in this vein, he composed the *Majma-ul-bahrain*—rendered his great father helpless to rule, belted his waist in preparation for his false desire and to kill Muslims."[29]

The author of this anecdote is one Sadiq Khan, who purportedly served Shah Jahan when the latter was a prince, during the Mewar expedition of 1614. But other accounts mention that Sadiq Khan was still alive in 1686. The history attributed to him is most likely the product of the late seventeenth century rather than of an earlier time.[30] So it is by no means certain that Aurangzeb cited Dara Shukoh's writings to rally influential figures to his side.

Whatever Aurangzeb thought of Dara Shukoh's writings, in a letter to Rana Raj Singh, he went out of his way to extol religious harmony as the goal of great emperors. He pressed his own handprint onto the letter to show his sincerity and esteem for the rana. Rulers, Aurangzeb wrote, being shadows of God, ought to ensure that people of "different schools of thought and of variegated religious hues, are cradled in security and tranquility and pass their days in repose." Aurangzeb's flowery rhetoric signals his intent to get the Hindu rana's support. But in his letter, the prince also commits to a philosophy of rulership in which he explicitly aligns himself with the tolerance of his Mughal forebears. Those bigoted kings who torment their subjects, declares Aurangzeb, actually ruin what God has created. Should Aurangzeb succeed in his enterprise—that is, if "the goal's form, per the unanimous desire of the faithful, takes shape"—the prince's illustrious ancestors would "illuminate the four corners of the inhabited world."[31]

Aurangzeb had recently extracted considerable indemnities from the Adil Shahi rulers of Bijapur and was in a good position to launch a military campaign for the throne.[32] Jaswant Singh of Marwar went to the province of Malwa with an army of Rajputs to intercept the opposition. For additional support, Shah Jahan and Dara had also sent the general, Qasim Khan, with another army. The actual battle was brief. On the twenty-fifth of April 1658, at Dharmat, southwest of the ancient city of Ujjain, Aurangzeb and Murad's combined forces made easy work of the imperial armies. Jaswant Singh and Qasim Khan fled north.[33]

Masum was not an eyewitness observer to the battle at Dharmat, but he records these verses, which, according to him, involuntarily came to his lips when he heard accounts of the war:

> The row of Rajputs, chain mail clad
> > With lance-heads, cleavers of air
> Began the attack like crazed lions
> > On the Mughals, Indian sword in hand
> Faces ablaze with the flame of enmity
> > Their chests stitched with the points of spears
> By no means did they know the route to flight
> > For they knew no fear of battle . . .
> They displayed such fighting in that battlefield
> > That Arjun and Bhim were put to shame . . .
> The Musalman and Hindu mingled
> > Truth and falsehood united with each other.[34]

The battle at Dharmat was certainly not a fight between opposing armies of Hindus and Muslims. Masum's description, though, differs from the modern narratives that view Mughal history primarily through the lens of Hindu-Muslim conflict. Notice how, here in these verses, Masum romanticizes the valiant Rajput warrior. His gesture evokes how the sacred-thread-wearing, idol-worshipping Brahmin became a trope in Persian poetry, often presented with positive connotations.

After his victory at Dharmat, Murad wrote a jubilant letter to his Sufi pir, Sayyid Jafar Shah of Gujarat. It relates that Murad met up with his illustrious brother and that together they fought an army of fifty or sixty thousand, which the enemy had brought, in the "heights of arrogance." Such a battle "had not occurred in Hindustan for the last hundred years," he writes. Murad reveals that both he and his brother Aurangzeb planned to stay in Ujjain for three days and then proceed to Agra. He beseeches his pir to pray for more victory. Evidently, Dara Shukoh was not the only Mughal prince to confide in and rely on his Sufi teacher.[35]

Jahanara made a last-ditch effort for peace, sending Shah Jahan's envoy, Muhammad Faruq, to deliver her letter to Aurangzeb. To fight, she insists, was not merely a crime against one's family; it went against religious values. Indeed, the two were inseparably linked. Dara's alleged heresies do not figure at all in this correspondence.

The princess made sure to first dispel any doubts about the emperor's health. She upbraided Aurangzeb for taking up arms against his own father, "whose satisfaction is the satisfaction and pleasure of God . . . and the Messenger."[36] There was no justification for fighting against Dara Shukoh either, she argued, for according to both sharia and custom, the elder brother should be regarded as a father. She also urged Aurangzeb to avoid spilling the blood of the Prophet's followers during the blessed month of Ramazan. If he would only just halt and write down his grievances, the emperor would do his best to redress them.[37]

Aurangzeb ignored these sisterly appeals. Aqil Khan's chronicle includes a reply to Shahjahan that Aurangzeb sent himself. The prince is concerned that his father has lost control over the reins of governance. Here, he lists a litany of Dara Shukoh's wrongs, from his thirst for power to his attempts to sabotage Aurangzeb's potential success in annexing Bijapur. Aurangzeb blames Dara Shukoh for sending Jaswant Singh to Malwa. He does not spare his ally, Murad, either. He complains that Dara had transferred Berar from his assignment to Murad's, even though the younger prince, "having stepped over the line, became the perpetrator of a number of insolent and rude acts and the source of great shortcomings."[38] Notably, this long harangue against Dara Shukoh did not address the eldest prince's religious proclivities. After the easy victory at Dharmat, Aurangzeb was emboldened to push further in his bid for the throne.

Back in Bengal, Sulaiman Shukoh and Jai Singh, unaware of the other happenings in the kingdom, awaited instructions from the court. Jai Singh, for his part, probably wanted to see which way the winds were blowing in the rest of the empire. A letter from Dara arrived, writes Masum. The kingdom is aflame, it reported. More details would be provided in an imperial decree. Until then, Dara instructed that a peace treaty be negotiated with Shuja as swiftly as possible. Then, Sulaiman Shukoh and the raja must make haste back to Agra.[39]

Shuja sent his minister Mirza Jan Beg to Jai Singh's camp. For some days, the raja entertained him most graciously, serving up special delicacies to eat and drink, the likes of which "few people of Islam had seen," writes Masum. The negotiations occasioned a perhaps uncommon instance of Hindu and Muslim nobility dining together, which, like intermarriage, could in many contexts serve as a social taboo.[40] When Mirza Jan Beg returned to Shuja's capital, Rajmahal, where Masum was based, he recounted the details of their feasts. Masum's mouth watered. Jan Beg was kind enough to share with Masum some fruits that the raja had gifted him.[41]

Yet, with all his wining and dining, Jai Singh was deliberately stalling on his return to Shah Jahan's court. For months, he had failed to capture Shuja, although both Dara Shukoh and the emperor had repeatedly instructed him to do so.[42] Then, he kept Shah Jahan and Dara in the dark about his whereabouts and plans. The emperor had to order him to send an update.[43] Now, after Dharmat, Dara sent him anxious missives, calling Jai Singh the emperor's "greatest hope."[44] When he did not hasten, as requested, the prince and his father became desperate. They raised his rank again and sent him several edicts to come to Agra.[45] Dara Shukoh now had to face the advancing troops of Aurangzeb and Murad Bakhsh with a severely depleted army.

Murad and Aurangzeb, with their combined forces, marched northward toward Ujjain. Dara went south to try to prevent Aurangzeb from crossing the Chambal River. But Aurangzeb bypassed him and forded the river. Dara then returned to Samugarh, east of Agra, and there waited for the coalition armies of Aurangzeb and Murad to attack.

It was the sixth of Ramazan, which fell that year on the seventh of the scorching month of June. That year, the summer was particularly oppressive, notes Masum, who heard a firsthand report of the war from his brother Muhammad Said, employed as paymaster for Sipihr Shukoh's troops.[46] Even at night, there was little relief; the moonbeams were like "rays of fire."[47] On the day, the imperial soldiers sat ready on their mounts. The sun beat down on their armor. Their horses wilted. Yet there was still no movement from the enemy. The army waited until evening. They had very little opportunity to rest.[48]

The Venetian fortune-seeker Niccoló Manucci was among the few *firangis* who claimed to have participated in the events. Many years after the dust had settled, while living in Madras as a wealthy merchant and go-between,

Manucci penned an account of his time in India, which he sent to Paris for publication in 1700. Throughout his memoirs, Manucci frequently borrowed, without much in the way of acknowledgment, from earlier European writings. One of his main rivals was the immensely popular history of the civil war penned by the French physician François Bernier, which after its first appearance in Paris in 1670 became an immediate sensation across printing houses in Europe. But unlike Bernier, who only tended briefly to Dara as a physician at the very close of the drama, Manucci asserted even greater authority; at the age of twenty, he joined the service of Dara's army as an artilleryman just in time to witness the events as they unfolded.[49]

At midnight, recalls Manucci, three shots were fired from the opposing side, signaling their readiness for battle. An hour later, Dara emerged to renew battle preparations. Manucci slipped away on his horse shortly afterward and explored the area. He noticed other riders—soldiers trickling across to join Aurangzeb's camp.[50] After sunrise the next morning, the coalition army advanced, fresh from their planned rest the previous day. Murad, assisted by Shaikh Mir, led the right wing. The prince rode an elephant, his seven-year-old son Izad Bakhsh seated with him in the howdah. On the left was Aurangzeb's son, Muhammad Sultan, under the guidance of Aurangzeb's trusted foster brother, whom he had recently given the title of Bahadur Khan. Aurangzeb, mounted on an elephant, took his position in the center behind the artillery. Zulfiqar Khan led the vanguard. Aqil Khan estimates that they had forty thousand cavalry in all.[51]

Facing them, the weary imperial troops stood in formation, with Dara Shukoh at the center, also on an elephant. Sipihr Shukoh led the right wing and Khalilullah Khan led the left. The Rajput warriors, Rao Satarsal of Bundi and Raja Rup Singh Rathore of Kishangarh, helmed the vanguard along with Dara Shukoh's protégé, Daud Khan. The troops numbered about sixty thousand.[52]

A crucial battle in the subcontinent's history was about to begin. Each side had a victory under its belt—in Bahadurpur and at Dharmat respectively. The side that would prevail at Samugarh had a good shot at securing the throne. But did this struggle for succession also reveal some deeper religious and sectarian rifts in the empire's elite nobility? Some modern historians paint the following picture: The empire's sharia-minded Sunni Muslims allied with Aurangzeb and Murad. They fought against a diverse army that included large numbers of Shias and Hindus on Dara Shukoh's side. For instance, the modern historian Iftikhar Ghauri declares, "it was generally a war of the Sunni ideology on the forces of heterodoxy and infidelity led by Dara Shukoh."[53]

But this was hardly the case; in fact, Dara did not have a significantly larger number of Hindu nobility fighting with him at Samugarh. Athar Ali's painstaking research enumerating the seventeenth-century Mughal nobility disproves Ghauri's assertion with solid empirical data. He shows that at the outset of the succession war, an almost equal number of Hindu nobles supported Dara Shukoh and Aurangzeb—twenty-four versus twenty-one. And throughout his rebellion, Aurangzeb kept Iranian generals with their Shii sympathies on his payrolls.[54]

The pattern of support for Murad and Aurangzeb reflects their position as rebel princes, albeit powerful ones, challenging the reigning emperor. As Dara was based at the court as the emperor's favored son and heir, he was understandably joined by a much larger proportion of the nobility's highest echelons. For instance, of the uppermost tier of the nobility's ranks—those allotted a cavalry of five thousand and above—five out of nine supported Dara Shukoh. Dara did have more Hindus from this category. They included the Rajputs Jaswant Singh and Rai Singh Sisodia as well as the Maratha officer, Maluji Bhonsle. In this rank were also some Shia nobles, such as Rustam Khan, Jafar Khan, and Khalilullah Khan. The strong Shia and Hindu presence in Dara Shukoh's camp merely reflects the diverse composition of the elite nobility in Shah Jahan's India.[55]

But just before Aurangzeb arrived at Samugarh, he had enjoyed the help of a high-ranking Hindu noble, Champat Rai Bundela. To Dara's consternation, the Bundela royal enabled Aurangzeb to cross the Chambal River. Champat Rai, who had been resentful of Shah Jahan's attempts to assert control over the Bundela Kingdom, seized this chance to get back at the Mughal state.[56] The younger prince had also astutely cultivated ties with other disgruntled Hindu rulers. With Aurangzeb, at Samugarh, was the Malwa Rajput Indradyumna Dhandhera, whom the prince had recently freed from prison. His camp also boasted of at least ten Maratha nobles, with their respective troops; these included Jadu Rao and Damaji Deccani.[57] Then there is the question of tacit support, even among those not present at Samugarh. Mirza Raja Jai Singh, for instance, was no longer actively working for Dara Shukoh; neither had Raj Singh come to the eldest prince's rescue. In fact, early in April, Aurangzeb had overtly wooed Raj Singh. He wrote him, boasting of the crushing defeat he inflicted on Jaswant Singh at Dharmat, and pressured him to send his son along with an army. For that, the prince offered a material reward in the form of land assignments.[58] Indeed, as we shall see, loyalties evolved fluidly throughout the protracted struggle for succession. But the strong presence of Hindu support for Aurangzeb demonstrates that the allegiances of the nobility were not split along religious lines.

There are indications that Aurangzeb also enlisted some Muslim religious elites to join him in battle. It was not uncommon for religious scholars associated with the court to also engage in military action. Aurangzeb's tutor Mulla Abd-ul-Qawi reportedly fought at Samugarh. There he attended to the prince's stirrups, says a later biographical compilation of noblemen's biographies, using a Persian expression to suggest his close association with Aurangzeb. Just before the battle, Aurangzeb promised him the rank of fifteen hundred cavalry.[59] Shaikh Abd-ul-Aziz, a family member of Aurangzeb's Sufi teacher Shaikh Abd-ul-Latif Burhanpuri, fought against Jaswant Singh at Dharmat. He sustained numerous wounds, for which he was rewarded with a horse and a rank among the nobility.[60] Qazi Nizam Karhardawi, who had once served Dara's stirrups in Qandahar, later joined Aurangzeb in the Deccan, taking his side in the struggle for succession.[61] Abd-ul-Wahhab, the qazi of Patan in Gujarat, was also a supporter of the prince.[62] These figures represent a mix of ulama and Sufis, most of whom had personal ties to Aurangzeb.

Aurangzeb's camp was by no means a unified Sunni front against his brother. Ghauri identifies Hoshdar Khan, renowned as a superb shot, as a prominent Sunni figure. But the khan's primary role was that of a second-generation imperial servant whose father also served Aurangzeb—not a religious official.[63] Aurangzeb had Shias on his side as well, such as Iftikhar Khan Sultan Husain, who defected from Jaswant Singh's army to join him after Dharmat.[64] Indeed, though Sunni-Shia divisions existed in the seventeenth century, they did not play a defined role in the war of succession. Ethnicity, whether Afghan, Maratha, or Abyssinian, was a powerful marker of identity. Unlike Dara Shukoh, Aurangzeb had a significant number of Afghan nobles. Aurangzeb's household and army at Samugarh reflected the striking range and depth of his support across all levels. There is no evidence that Aurangzeb roused a widespread Sunni military revolt against his brother and the imperial army.

The battlefield at Samugarh thundered with artillery fire. Dara Shukoh's army discharged round after round at the opposing forces. They met with a surprisingly weak response; only a few rockets whizzed over to their side. Had the initial rounds inflicted sufficient damage? Manucci was one of the artillerymen operating the cannons under Barqandaz Khan, the former Jafar who had fought on Dara's side at Qandahar. The Italian gunner noticed that Aurangzeb's army seemed far enough away to remain relatively unscathed. The orders from above, though, pressed the men to keep firing. The enemy then sent out three shots. Was this a warning, a hidden message, or an exhausted army's last show of strength?[65]

Khalilullah Khan left his position in search of Dara. He advised the prince that now was an opportune moment to stop firing and directly attack the enemy. The artillery had achieved its goal, and now "little effort [remained] to gain a complete victory." Rustam Khan was summoned for a second option. He hesitated, preferring to wait for the enemy to attack first. Khalilullah Khan mocked Rustam Khan's courage. Dara Shukoh decided to go with Khalilullah Khan's advice. Rustam Khan attacked Aurangzeb's wing, and Khalilullah Khan led his troops toward Murad's army. Dara Shukoh himself marched forward on his elephant.[66]

As the men of the imperial army approached, Aurangzeb's army suddenly released a relentless torrent of bullets and cannonballs, like the April rains, says Masum.[67] Dara's own artillery had been left behind, advancing only belatedly. Rustam Khan was brutally wounded and would succumb to his injuries. Rao Satarsal Hada, too, lost his life.[68] Dara fought on, firm on his elephant, clearing a path through Aurangzeb's men. Aurangzeb sent reinforcements under Shaikh Mir. But as Manucci recalls, the enemy was taken aback by Dara's valor and, seeing themselves all but abandoned, "were forced to retreat."[69]

Dara Shukoh's goal was to advance far enough to fell one of his brothers. Manucci reports that he paused for a rest, when Khalilullah Khan, who had conveniently stayed out of danger, made an appearance. They could still reach Aurangzeb, the khan urged, if Dara were to dismount his elephant and proceed on a horse.[70] But in Masum's account, the prince found himself surrounded on all sides and feared that his height on the elephant would make him an easy target.[71] Whether or not the disloyal khan deceived him, when the prince slipped off the elephant, he was now lost in the throng, no longer visible from afar. His men scattered and fled, thinking that he had been killed. Aurangzeb's army beat the drums of victory. The battle ended swiftly.

A tinted drawing from the time survives, illustrating this final episode at Samugarh. Dara Shukoh, thinly encircled by his soldiers, descends his kneeling elephant using a ladder. Around them, bodies are splayed, cannons abandoned, horsemen and an elephant ride amok. The arrow-pierced body of Rustam Khan lies slumped on his dead horse. Opposite Dara, on the right, Aurangzeb perches aloft his elephant amid a solid barrier of horsemen and fiercely armed soldiers on elephants. Before them, a formidable wall of cannons discharges toward Dara's side. In the far right corner, Murad hastens from the battlefield on his elephant. This drawing is attributed to Payag, who worked at Shah Jahan's court and painted other battle scenes as well as portraits of Dara Shukoh conversing with his Sufi teachers. We

Battle of Samugarh.

do not know if the drawing was commissioned (by Aurangzeb, perhaps), or if the artist decided on his own volition to memorialize this momentous event, as did so many writers of the age.[72]

Masum relates that as Dara escaped, Sipihr Shukoh came up to him, breaking down in shuddering sobs and clawing at his face. Dara Shukoh managed outwardly to hold himself together as he consoled his son. They left on horseback with a few close servants. A few miles out they stopped by a shady tree. The exhaustion of the battle and the fierce heat had caught up with them. They sat down, planning to rest for an hour or so. Just then, they heard the sound of kettledrums. Some of Dara's stirrup attendants implored him to leave immediately. The prince, utterly debilitated, was unwilling to move. "How much better it would be," he said, "if someone were to come and liberate me from the abjectness of this life." With much effort, he was persuaded to get up, and the small party set forth toward Agra.[73] At some point in this story, Masum's informant Muhammad Said must have stayed behind. He later joined Aurangzeb's son, Muhammad Sultan, in the same role of paymaster that he held under Sipihr Shukoh.[74]

Dara Shukoh went straight to his mansion, declining his father's entreaty to join him inside the fort. He gathered up the members of the household: Nadira and other women of his family along with the "secluded ones" of his harem, including, according to Manucci, two other wives and his daughter Jani Begam and son Sipihr Shukoh. Then they all fled to Shahjahanabad.[75]

Shah Jahan made generous reconciliatory overtures to Aurangzeb. He sent letters and splendid gifts through Fazil Khan, the same chamberlain who years before had been involved with the fatwa against Mulla Shah.[76] Aurangzeb thought it prudent to disregard them.[77] The prince moved to surround the fort at Agra, cutting off its water supply.[78] Shaista Khan and Khalilullah Khan defected to Aurangzeb's side. The prince coerced Shah Jahan into complying with his wish to replace all the fortress's officials with his own.[79] He had effectively taken his father prisoner.

With his father safely under guard, relates Masum, Aurangzeb summoned Jafar Khan and subjected him to a tirade about Dara Shukoh's heresies. Dara, he claimed, "tempted by heresy-purveyors of the drunken persuasion, deviated and severed [himself] from the straight path of the Prophet's *shariat* and the creed of the lofty way of the Mustafian (i.e., Muhammadan) order." Day and night, the prince consorted with "a group of shameless, apostasy-dispositioned ones," brazenly drinking alcohol with them in public. He would openly tell people that it was permissible to imbibe the Indian arrack made of sugar, though fermented grape wine was prohibited. It was thus expedient, Aurangzeb argued, to deal with the prince. Surely the emperor would also wish to save the empire from falling into infidelity.[80]

In Masum's portrayal of Aurangzeb's accusations at Agra, Dara Shukoh's actual religious explorations find no description. If drinking alcohol was indeed his main sin, he was in the fine company of his brothers Murad and Shuja, not to mention his grandfather and several other ancestors. And if Shah Jahan once renounced alcohol as a prince, only the previous year, in 1657, he had a wine cup carved out of translucent white jade, its handle a ram's head that curved gracefully into a fluted bowl.[81] This account certainly reflects what Masum thought to be striking and important, probably filtered through his brother's reports. But Aurangzeb now had good reason to publicly bring up accusations of unbelief and apostasy. At this point, he could hardly criticize Dara Shukoh's injustice toward their father and brothers. After all, he himself had just imprisoned Shah Jahan and forced Dara to become a fugitive.

Jahanara once more attempted to plead with Aurangzeb. She came to meet him in the harem of his mansion, bearing Shah Jahan's solution for his four warring sons: Dara Shukoh would keep his Punjab assignment, Murad would look after Gujarat, and Shuja would remain in Bengal. Muhammad Sultan, Aurangzeb's son, would govern the Deccan. And Aurangzeb, instead of Dara, would get the title of "Buland Iqbal," as well as all the other lands of the empire not mentioned above.[82] Shah Jahan's proposal recalled the old Timurid model of furnishing each prince with his own territory rather than preserving an undivided kingdom. Shah Jahan also entreated Aurangzeb to have an audience with him. The prince, advised by Shaikh Mir and Shaista Khan, decided against even meeting his father.[83]

Bihishti corroborates Masum's account that Aurangzeb denounced Dara's religious leanings after securing the Agra Fort: "As Dara has strayed far from the path of sharia / By God's decree, he is subject to jihad." This version, too, skips the details of Dara's heresies. The poet also describes Aurangzeb's fear that Dara would escape to Iran and the shame that this would entail for the Mughals, "If he manages to turn his face to Iran / He would throw to the air the name of this lineage."[84]

Dara Shukoh now had to swiftly plot his future course. He was guided by Shah Jahan, who pleaded with Mahabat Khan, son of the general who had helped him in his own path to the throne, to assist the prince at Lahore. "Can it possibly happen, that Mahabat Khan, at dread of whom mortals tremble, while his sovereign Shah Jahan is in the hands of traitors, will not fly to his relief, bring the two undutiful rebels (Aurangzeb and Murad) to the deserved punishment of their actions, and rescue his master from a prison?[85] The letter was intercepted by Aurangzeb. Dara and his family hastily proceeded toward Lahore via Shahjahanabad, where he raised a small army with the help of his father's governor. As he traveled, he released a flood of letters to Jai Singh, informing him of the defeat, summoning him to court, and at least twice sending him ceremonial cloaks (*khilat*s).[86]

Dara tried to ally with Shuja after Samugarh, roping in Murad and Jaswant Singh as well; the brothers together might have had a shot at vanquishing Aurangzeb.[87] In the heat of the moment, though, Shah Jahan and Dara reckoned it would be most judicious to rely on the allies they still had in the empire's west. If Dara suffered more failure in battle, he could still hold out the hope of escaping to Iran.

Nevertheless, Shah Jahan also tried to enlist Murad against Aurangzeb, even writing to promise him the throne. The emperor instructed him to invite Aurangzeb to a banquet and then to do away with him. Murad was so disturbed and bewildered when he read his father's letter, writes Masum, that he did not know whether to rip it to shreds or hide it.[88] He had come to suspect Aurangzeb of not honoring his pledge, reports Bihishti.[89] But while Aurangzeb was capturing Agra, Murad had built up his army, luring men with good salaries. Through assurances laced with a tempting share of the spoils from Agra, Aurangzeb persuaded Murad to accompany him to Shahjahanabad in Dara's pursuit.[90]

The brothers pitched camp near Mathura but did not meet in person. Murad was still wary of his brother's intentions. They had been there for a few days when Murad's servant Nuruddin rushed with an urgent message: Aurangzeb was ill with dysentery and had been calling out for Murad. The prince went to his brother, forgetting his earlier apprehensions. He was led into a private enclosure in the tent complex. Aurangzeb was clearly well enough to welcome him warmly.[91]

An opulent feast was laid out. Did Aurangzeb also offer alcohol? Some chroniclers mention that he did. Masum describes jewel-encrusted pitchers brimming with the purest wine. The cup-bearer was surreptitiously instructed to refill Murad's goblet more generously than usual, he says. These details do not feature prominently in the accounts of Bihishti and Razi, though Bihishti does describe ruby-hued betel cones being consumed, staining mouths coral red. Out of etiquette, Murad was reluctant to imbibe before his elder brother, says Masum, but Aurangzeb persuaded him to do so.

After the repast, Murad rested in a bed prepared for him, making sure to keep his weapons by his side. Bihishti adds that a beautiful slave girl gently massaged Murad's feet, sending him into sleep's warm intoxication.[92] Finally, "the wine of action had fermented (*mukhammar shud*)," pronounces Aqil Khan Razi.[93] The comatose Murad was skillfully stripped of his weapons. In Manucci's account, Aurangzeb bribed his four-and-a-half-year-old son Sultan Azam with a shiny jewel to retrieve the arms.[94]

Murad awoke only to discover that he was a weaponless prisoner. Ac-cording to Masum, the prince wailed, "What a calamity that the covenants and agreements of Muslims can be dissolved all at once!" He declared that since life was as transient as a bonfire of twigs, it is best that people seek to please God and do good to others. One should not, he went on, just for the sake of acquiring more worthless worldly ephemera, break off from not only the path of Islam but also blood relatives linked by the same womb and oaths sworn on the Quran, only to perpetrate acts despised by all reli-gions and minds. In reply, Aurangzeb's servants pronounced that he had brought his fate upon himself.[95]

Eventually Aurangzeb seized Murad's property and army and incarcer-ated him and his family in Shahjahanabad's Salimgarh Fort. He had been holding off his own claim to the throne, but now was an opportune time. The astrologers agreed, fixing the thirty-first of July as the auspicious date. Aurangzeb held a hasty coronation in the Aizzabad Gardens outside Delhi.[96]

In mid-July, Dara Shukoh reached Lahore, where he attempted to raise a new army. His son Sulaiman was still far away. He received a long overdue letter from Jai Singh, full of excuses about how his return was delayed and he had to stop in Chetpur, an outpost in Bengal.[97] In contrast, Manucci braved roads beset by thieves to come to him. Dara was moved to tears upon meeting the Italian gunner. "See the loyalty of this firangi boy," he exclaimed.[98]

A glimmer of hope crept in when the Jammu ruler Raja Rajrup came to see Dara and offered to raise an army of Rajputs if the prince provided the funds. Nadira played her part in sealing the bond between the two men, by making them into milk kin. She was well past nursing children at this time, but she had Rajrup sip water that she had used to wash her breasts. This ritual ensured that Rajrup was now Dara and Nadira's milk child and Su-laiman Shukoh's milk brother. Manucci reports that "drinking with tremen-dous gratitude, he swore to always be loyal and to never fail in the duties of a son." With that, Rajrup took off back to his own kingdom.[99] The army never materialized.

There was not much time to build support in Lahore, because Aurang-zeb's pursuing forces were drawing close. For the next year, Dara and his family became fugitives on the run. His surviving children with Nadira, apart from Sulaiman Shukoh, included their son Sipihr Shukoh, not yet fourteen in mid-1658, as well as their daughters Paknihad Bano, in her late teens, and little Jahanzeb Bano.[100] Also in Dara's care were Sulaiman Shu-koh's children.[101] Masum records that Dara found it hard to keep up his morale. He vacillated between staying in Lahore and leaving. Sometimes, he would lament, "because no good scent wafts to my nose from any side, it is better that I take this half-life, which has remained safe from fate's claws, to a place where I won't see my wife and children killed before my eyes." Daud Khan, his longtime servant, consoled him, saying that despair was associated with unbelief. Eventually they decided to send young Sipihr Shukoh east to Sultanpur with Daud Khan to try to fend off Aurangzeb's army, led by Bahadur Khan and the turncoat Khalilullah Khan. With both her sons thrown to an uncertain fate, Nadira spent her days and nights in restless anguish and lamentation. Masum describes Sipihr Shukoh's absence as a dripping wound in Dara's heart.[102]

Masum and Manucci recount that Dara came by a letter purportedly written by Aurangzeb to Daud Khan.[103] According to Masum, it praised Daud Khan for his loyalty to Aurangzeb and promised that Sipihr Shukoh and other "deniers of the straight path" would become the prisoners of "Islam's holy warriors."[104] The letter was a ruse that Aurangzeb engineered, meant to spark Dara's distrust of Daud Khan. Despite the khan's remonstrations, the ploy drove a wedge between the two. Dara Shukoh had to flee Aurangzeb's advancing forces, his army shedding soldiers as he left. He headed with his family for the fort of Bhakkar, also taking along Sipihr Shukoh, whom he recalled from Sultanpur. Daud Khan insisted on coming with him until the prince finally made him leave.[105] Dara Shukoh had to keep traveling south to stay ahead of the imperial army.

Aurangzeb reached as far as Multan before departing abruptly to deal with another imminent threat: Shuja and his forces were approaching Agra from the east.[106] Aurangzeb appointed Shaikh Mir and Bahadur Khan to hunt down Dara and turned back. En route, he crossed paths with Jai Singh, who was finally returning to his kingdom. The two had already been corresponding, and Manucci notes that Aurangzeb quickly won the raja over by promising him the governorship of Delhi and a lucrative land assignment.[107]

Aurangzeb's army drove Dara Shukoh farther and farther south. Dara eventually ended up in Gujarat via Sindh. There, he found hospitality with the local elites—the governor, Shahnawaz Khan, father of Aurangzeb's late wife Dilras Bano, virtually handed him the city. Manucci observes that the khan did this out of deference to Dara's superior status as a prince and as heir to the empire. Further, Manucci rejects the rumor, later circulated by the likes of Bernier, that Shahnawaz Khan merely feigned loyalty to Dara, all the while secretly keeping Aurangzeb, his son-in-law, abreast of Dara's moves.[108] In Gujarat, Dara acquired an army of ten to fifteen thousand cavalry, according to Masum's count.[109] Suddenly it seemed as though he might be able to turn his fortunes around if only he could drum up some allies.

Jaswant Singh wrote Dara while the prince was in Gujarat. He encouraged Dara to march toward Hindustan's northwest, so that he could serve him by putting a Rajput army at his disposal. Dara headed back north to Ajmer. But meanwhile, Jai Singh warned Jaswant Singh not to ally with Dara.[110]

Dara penned a hopeful letter to Rana Raj Singh as he approached Ajmer. "I've thrown my honor in with all descendants of Rajputs. I've come as the guest of all Rajputs." He mentioned, too, that Jaswant Singh, the "cream of Rajput rulers," was supporting him.[111] There was no movement from Raj Singh's side.

As Dara Shukoh drew near, he sent a messenger to Jaswant Singh in Jodhpur. The Rajput ruler gave an evasive reply, so the prince waited longer. Eventually, he sent Sipihr Shukoh to meet Jaswant Singh. The raja finally, eyes averted, gave a clear answer: "I'm a loyal servant in the court of the World's Refuge and it would be beyond reason and wisdom to expect any help from me."[112]

By now, Dara Shukoh was a seasoned warrior. He secured his army in trenches protected on either side by a long, narrow mountain range.[113] Eventually, though, his troops proved no match for a constellation of Mughal India's powerful commanders: Aurangzeb, fresh from a victory over Shuja; Shaista Khan; Mirza Raja Jai Singh; Raja Rajrup; and Shaikh Mir, who lost his life to Dara's men. The empire's most prominent Hindu nobles now either joined Aurangzeb or, like Raj Singh and Jaswant Singh, stayed away from the fray. After Dara's defeat, the imperial army looted his soldiers and raided his coffers. He fled west and then south, traveling separately with Sipihr Shukoh before meeting up with the women in his family.

They kept going, with Jai Singh and others in swift pursuit, but they had nowhere to find refuge. Dara had less than two thousand soldiers to begin with. Bandits attacked the men, and their animals, famished and dehydrated, dropped dead along the way. Near Ahmedabad, Dara ran into the French physician Francois Bernier, who had only reached India earlier that year. Dara persuaded Bernier to join them, as they were without a medical doctor. The prince insisted that Bernier sleep in his caravanserai. There, the physician noticed that the women of his household did not even have a tent. These princesses, who would ordinarily maintain strict seclusion, now slept behind flimsy fabric screens tied to the wheels of their cart. The next morning, they discovered that the governor had barred them from entering Ahmedabad, where they had only recently found welcome. When these women heard this news, "they broke out at once into cries and lamentations so strange and pitiful that they brought tears to the eyes," recalls Bernier.[114] The party headed northwest, toward Sindh. Dara's army shrank rapidly to a few hundred soldiers. The desert sun blazed so fiercely, it killed an ox pulling Bernier's cart. Dara pressed Bernier to stay—one of his wives,

Nadira, perhaps, had a festering wound on her leg—but could find no mount for his transport. Bernier parted ways with them. With that, he would have no more direct contact with Dara and his family.

The royal entourage traveled farther west, losing more men along the way. By now Nadira was gravely ill with dysentery. Her body succumbed, Masum reports, to "grief from the separation from her older son, Sulaiman Shukoh, and other endless tribulations." Young Sipihr Shukoh, whose recent life was a rude departure from his upbringing in an atmosphere of privilege and abundance, was beside himself with worry. He wanted to stay put so that they could adequately treat his mother's illness, but fate did not cooperate. "Agonized and stupefied," the small group straggled toward the general direction of Iran.[115]

Between Multan and Qandahar as the crow flies, near the Bolan pass cleaving Mughal Baluchistan from the Iranian dominions, lay a territory ruled by a landowner called Malik Jivan. A while before, Jivan, after being convicted of a crime, was sentenced to a gory death under the feet of stampeding elephants. Jivan knew someone who was very close to one of Dara Shukoh's servants and managed, through him, to elicit the prince's sympathy. Dara intervened with the emperor and saved the landowner's life. He thought that perhaps now Jivan would be able to repay his obligation. As they drew close to Jivan's lands, Nadira, "out of misery and illness, became veiled by the curtain of God's forgiveness." She had breathed her last. Dara Shukoh's "light-filled eyes clouded over with darkness," and he grew crazed with grief.[116]

Jivan learned of Dara Shukoh's arrival and invited him to be his guest for a short while, so that he could recover from the fatigue of his journey, and figure out his next steps. Nadira's death had "broken the back" of Dara's "forbearance and strength." Sipihr Shukoh and the prince's well-wishers in his group tried to talk him out of accepting Jivan's invitation, saying that the landowner was a notorious villain. Dara Shukoh stubbornly insisted on taking him up on it. He sent Nadira's body back to be buried in Lahore and allowed his few remaining servants to go. His other wives may also have gone with them, because we do not hear about them staying with Jivan. Dara was left with his son and two daughters. Jivan promptly dispatched a fast courier with a message to Jai Singh and Bahadur Khan: "I've trapped the golden-winged bird."[117]

The next day, the pursuing army arrived and surrounded Jivan's home. When Dara was captured, writes Bihishti, his daughter tore out: "When that flower blown onto the dirt by the wind/Fell, in that manner, at Jivan's feet." She begged the "stone-hearted" landowner to free her father. Even if that meant enslaving her:

> Bring me, with countless gold and jewels
> Into the train of maidservants in your kitchen
> My mother is the daughter of Parwez Shah
> My father is Timur's descendant, possessor of glory
> Exhibit me to the world in the position of a maidservant
> Release the fetters from Dara's legs.[118]

Malik Jivan remained unmoved. Dara's elder daughter, Paknihad Bano, may indeed have pleaded with Jivan thus, though for Bihishti this anecdote has a function beyond veracity. By giving this unnamed daughter a voice and filling it with verse, Bihishti accentuates the pathos of Dara's capture.

Jivan, newly rewarded with the title Bakhtiyar Khan, together with Bahadur Khan hustled Dara Shukoh and his family to Shahjahanabad. It was thought that Dara might thereafter be imprisoned in Gwalior's infamous fort, just like his brother Murad, who still languished there.[119] First, in a display of the new dispensation's power, Dara Shukoh and Sipihr Shukoh, their clothes in tatters, were paraded around the city on a filthy elephant.[120] Bernier found a place where he could have a good view. The spectacle triggered widespread mourning and protest. He remarks that Dara "was very much beloved by the masses (*du menu peuble*) who cried forcefully against the cruelty and tyranny of Aurangzeb for imprisoning his father, his own son Sultan Mahmoud (sic), and his brother Morad-Bakche." Wailing and heaving, the crowd of onlookers swelled. Bernier, who expected to witness an execution, reports that some "*fakires* and poor people from the Bazaar" began hurling stones at Jivan and cursing him, but none found the courage to draw a sword. Aurangzeb's advisors warned of a dangerous insurrection.[121]

In Bihishti's lament on Hindustan, it is precisely the public outpouring of sympathy for the captive prince and the anger at Jivan that swayed Aurangzeb's decision to put his brother to death:

> In this way, inside the capital it happened thus
> The ill fated Jivan had his face blackened
> From every quarter, roof and door without pause
> They caught him with curses and stones
> From every corner the loud mayhem arising
> Threw the emperor into apprehension
> He asked, "What is this noise and rioting?
> Who is the weaver of this sedition?"
> It was submitted to him, "O ruler,
> This chaos and evil has become manifest because of Dara"
> The people are all praising him
> They are badmouthing the emperor
> When Aurang Shah heard these words

> He trembled with zeal for himself
> He said to himself, As long as Dara lives
> Our world-rulership will not have stability
> He wiped off the reflection of affection and loyalty from his heart
> That moment he signaled for his (Dara's) killing.[122]

In contrast to the rioting throngs of Bihishti's lamentation, Masum's narrative does not mention the public protests. Instead, it lays the blame on Roshanara and other well-wishers who encouraged Aurangzeb to eliminate Dara for good.[123] But it is Bernier who gives us the idea of an actual assembly convened to decide Dara's fate. Though he could not have possibly been at the events as he describes them for he was far from inner Aurangzeb's inner circle, Bernier brings us close into deliberations of the council. Here, he says, Shaista Khan, Khalilullah Khan, and Roshanara were present. It would be unusual, though, if she had been physically there with the other men. In Bernier's version, by far the most strident voice against Dara was that of Shah Jahan's former physician, Hakim Daud, also known by his title Taqarrub Khan. In his telling, Hakim Daud, a "villainous man (*méchant homme*)," rose up before the full assembly, shouting that it was "expedient for the safety of the State to put [the prince] to death immediately." The Hakim argued that Dara's death was warranted, for he "had ceased to be a Musulman" having rather "long since become a Kafier, an idolater, without religion."[124] Taken together, these accounts go some measure in exonerating Aurangzeb from the singular responsibility of ordering his brother's death. They shift the blame to his sister or the Iranian physician. Surely, Aurangzeb would benefit from the idea that Dara's execution was a considered decision, made under the guidance of the emperor's close advisors.

In Bernier's report of Hakim Daud's words lie the tiniest seeds of the stories that later took root: that a council of ulama determined the firstborn prince's fate and even that they tried him for heresy and proclaimed him guilty. It would take a while for the murmurs about Dara's heresy and apostasy to turn into a detailed indictment. Almost thirty years later, Aurangzeb's official historian, Muhammad Kazim, would write the following condemnation of Dara Shukoh:

[N]ot content with displaying the degrees of permissiveness and apostasy that were fixed in his nature, which he named *tasawwuf,* he developed an inclination for the religion (*din*) of the Hindus, and the traditions and institutions of those people of bad faith. He always had affection for brahmins, jogis and sanyasis, and considered that wayward, misleading and false group to be perfect spiritual guides and gnostics united with the truth. He thought that their books, which they call Veda (*bed*) were the word of God revealed in heaven, and he called them "eternal codex" and "noble book."[125] Because of the false belief he reposed in the fruitless Veda, he gathered together sanyasis and brahmins from various areas for a mammoth effort, and with great patronage, to help in translating it. His time was constantly spent on this immoral task and in thinking and meditating on the misguided contents of this book. Instead of the Beautiful Names of God, he etched a Hindu name, which Hindus called Prabhu, on his ringstones of diamond, ruby, emerald and other gems, which he wore.[126]

Kazim objects to Dara Shukoh's (in his view blasphemous) engagement with Indic thought, but not to Sufism as such. He refers to the prince's project of translating the Upanishads, which he represents as Dara's main preoccupation. In reality, of course, this translation capped a lifetime of diverse activities and spiritual endeavors. Kazim also cites Dara's rings inscribed with the name "Prabhu." The prince does not mention these rings in his own writings, but if he did have them made, they would not have been such a radical innovation in the Mughal court. Akbar, the great-grandfather of both Dara and Aurangzeb, commissioned rings on which "Allahu akbar" was carved. This phrase signified not merely divine praise uttered during ritual devotion affirming the transcendence of God, for it also was a play on words hinting at the emperor's own divinity. These rings were then bestowed on the emperor's select disciples.[127] Seen in this context, Dara's rings, alluded to here, could well invoke Akbar's earlier tradition of elect discipleship. The prince may have given them to a chosen few who would understand that "Prabhu" was only a different name for the one God.

Despite these more specific accusations against Dara Shukoh, Kazim's account, too, acknowledges the role of the crowds in the prince's subsequent execution. Dara's heresies provided justification enough for his death—he was a "barren date-palm" whose only fruits were "leaves of sedition and corruption" and "thorns of deviance and apostasy." But "the flame of corruption was about to flare up" when the masses rose up to attack Bakhtiyar Khan (Jivan) with sticks and stones, and Aurangzeb had to take quick action for the sake of the empire's "peace and security (*amn o aman*)."[128]

It is Kazim's account that endures—not the vague stabs at pinning the label "heretic" or "apostate" on Dara that we see through the unofficial chronicles of the succession war. Modern writers, novelists, and playwrights often quote this first passage from Kazim's *Alamgir-nama* almost verbatim, as though it is an open window onto Dara's inner life and not a retrospective spin to justify the prince's murder. But while Dara Shukoh was alive, these aspersions had yet to coalesce into a coherent narrative.

The accounts of Masum, Bihishti, and other observers of the battle for succession, as well as Aurangzeb's correspondences with his family, reveal a rich, complex set of ideas about what it meant to live as a Muslim. In these texts, Islam is not merely a checklist of religious observances. Islam is also how you treat your parents and siblings—recall Jahanara's admonishment of Aurangzeb. To be a Muslim is to honor your agreements, as Masum has Murad Bakhsh declare. To be religious is to have hope in adverse times, as Daud Khan reminds Dara in Masum's narration. And, Bihishti informs us, contrary to what Aurangzeb's chroniclers would write, that Dara Shukoh, till his dying breath, never renounced Islam: "When his killer brought the cup of poison/saying, 'Quaff it by the order of the emperor of the age'//He refused and said, 'First of all/I've had true faith in God//I'm a Muslim and a follower of Mustafa (the Chosen Prophet)/why sacrifice myself like the unbelievers?/My heart has grown cold to life/by whatever means you know, slaughter me.'"[129]

Masum has a more intricate description of the prince's final hours. Once Aurangzeb decided that Dara must die, the emperor summoned Saif Khan, his *chela*, an Indic word meaning "a guru's disciple." Ever since Akbar's reign, an emperor's close servants were called chelas, explains Masum, though it was more common in the Mughal court to call them *murid*s, disciples of a Sufi shaikh. Saif Khan's father Tarbiyat Khan had a distinguished record of imperial service and had been Shah Jahan's paymaster. "Go at this instance," commanded Aurangzeb, "and separate Sultan Dara Shukoh's son from his father." After that, Aurangzeb continued, Saif Khan was to carry out God's will.

The chelas reached the place where Dara was held. When he saw them, he sprang up. "Have you been sent to kill?" he asked. "We really know nothing about killing anyone," they replied. "The order has come that your son be separated from you and kept under guard in another place. We've come to take him." Sipihr Shukoh and his father were sitting close to each other. "Get up," ordered Nazar Beg, harshly. Sipihr Shukoh lost his mind, and sobbing and wailing, clutched hold of his father's legs. Father and son embraced tightly, weeping. "Get up," the chelas ordered Sipihr Shukoh, threatening to drag him away otherwise.

Dara Shukoh wiped his tears and pleaded with the chelas that they ask Aurangzeb to spare his own nephew. In Masum's account, Dara recited a verse by the Persian poet and moralist Saadi, which he hoped would inspire Aurangzeb's future actions: "It's easy to retaliate with bad for bad/If you're a man, 'Do good to the one who harms you.'"[130] The verse is from a story in Saadi's *Bustan* about a magnanimous king, and it weaves in an Arabic quote from the Prophet's nephew Ali ibn Abi Talib.

"We're nobody's messengers," the chelas replied. "We need to carry out our orders." Saying this, they violently snatched Sipihr Shukoh from his father's arms and took him away. Earlier Dara, having realized that his end was near, had hidden in a pillow a small folding penknife used for sharpening reed pens. He whipped it out of the pillow cover and stabbed the chela who was about to seize him. The tiny knife got stuck in his victim's bone. Dara tried unsuccessfully to pull it out. He then used his fist to land some blows. The chelas, acting in unison, pounced on the prince. Sipihr Shukoh was being held nearby. The last sounds Dara Shukoh heard were his son's piercing cries.[131]

The story soon circulated that Dara's severed head uttered the Muslim declaration of faith (*shahada*), the miraculous sign of a righteous martyr (*shahid*), who even after death bears witness to the oneness of God. The chelas brought the head to Aurangzeb, who appeared reluctant to actually look at it. "I never saw the face of that faith-forsaker when alive and have no wish to do so now," Masum quotes him saying.[132] Here Aurangzeb is permitted some reticence, and revulsion, to distance himself from the act. The new emperor did order that Dara's head be reattached to his body, so that he could be interred.

But Manucci's account is gorier—the emperor stabs his dead brother's face thrice, the head laughs eerily, and he then sends it to Shah Jahan as though offering a gift, leaving his father, the former emperor, shocked and his eldest daughter utterly distraught. To memorialize this gruesome event, Manucci included among the miniatures he had commissioned in India a painting of Aurangzeb receiving Dara's severed head—a scene which is otherwise absent from the repertoire of the imperial atelier. Just as with Masum, there are reasons to be a bit suspicious of Manucci, despite his abiding sympathies for the prince. On Manucci's page, Dara dies a Christian martyr, by rejecting the Prophet while steadfastly professing devotion to Christ in the face of certain death. Here Dara calls out for a priest to hear his last words, but to no avail, "Muhammad kills me and the son of God will give me life."[133] But this version, which is meant to endear Dara to Manucci's Christian readers, serves a very practical purpose: it lends even greater tragedy to the events, while accentuating the tyranny of Aurangzeb, a figure who Manucci consistently vilifies as a duplicitous zealot.

The new emperor made sure to stifle all remaining potential threats after Dara Shukoh's execution. Murad remained imprisoned in Gwalior, until Aurangzeb charged him with the murder of Ali Naqi. He was then swiftly executed in December 1661. Sulaiman Shukoh took refuge with the raja of Srinagar while on his journey westward to join his father. Jai Singh applied pressure to induce the raja to betray him. In January 1661, Sulaiman

Portrait of Dara Shukoh's head brought to
Aurangzeb.

Shukoh, too, was incarcerated in Gwalior, and, after a year, strangled to
death. After Aurangzeb defeated Shuja at Khajua, near Agra, the prince
had retreated eastward until he crossed the boundaries of the Mughal empire into the kingdom of Arakan. There, Shuja sought refuge at the court
of the Mrauk-U ruler Candasudhammaraja, but died mysteriously around
1660. His daughter, Gulrukh Bano, Aurangzeb's daughter-in-law and Muhammad Sultan's wife, joined him in death. Only Sipihr Shukoh, sent to
the Gwalior jail after his father's execution, managed to survive.[134]

Yet, Aurangzeb consciously ensured that the bloodlines of his and Dara
Shukoh's descendants mingled in successive generations. He eventually had
Sipihr Shukoh released in early 1673 and married to Aurangzeb's daughter
Zubdat-un-Nisa. Jahanara may have played a role in this reconciliation.[135]
Around the same time, the emperor freed his eldest son Muhammad Sultan
and wed him to Murad Bakhsh's daughter.[136] Sulaiman Shukoh's daughters
were raised in Gauharara's care. One married Aurangzeb's youngest son,
Muhammad Akbar.[137] Dara Shukoh's youngest daughter, Jahanzeb or Jani

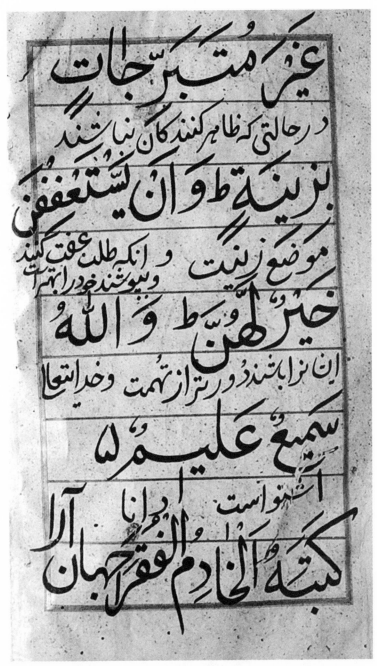

Colophon of Jahanara, *Ayat-ul-bayyinat*, dated 1663, autograph copy.

Begam, brought up by Jahanara, wed Aurangzeb's third son Muhammad Azam.[138]

Jahanara tended to her father in his last years, until his death in 1666. A material remnant of her life survives from this time—an autograph manuscript completed in 1663, which contains select Quranic verses with interlinear translations in Persian and short glosses on piety, devotion, and forbearance. It is written in her generous, clear hand, matching that of her copy of the *Munis-ul-arwah*. She signs it as a humble servant (*khadim*) and faqir. One of the passages includes this Quranic admonition about treating family elders with respect: "Your Lord has decreed that you worship none other than Him, and that you be kind to your parents. If either one or both of them grow with you, do not speak disrespectfully to them nor repulse them, but speak to them with kind words."[139] Amidst an array of verses on other topics—exhorting believers to patience, for instance, or describing the divine attributes—the princess slips in a subtle critique of her brother's actions.

CONCLUSION

I F DARA SHUKOH HAD SURVIVED and managed to rule, he would have
had his own mausoleum. He would have built it in Lahore, perhaps,
alongside Nadira's tomb, close to the resting place of his late pir, Miyan
Mir. The sources are unanimous in saying that Dara Shukoh was buried in
the precincts of Humayun's magnificent red sandstone tomb. But he was
neither conferred the dignity of a ceremonial washing and burial rites nor
granted a marked grave.[1] No inscription identifies his gravestone. According
to the *Alamgir-nama* of the court chronicler Muhammad Kazim, Dara
Shukoh was interred in the vaulted plinth (*tahkhana*) of the tomb complex.[2]
His is only one of many marble cenotaphs strewn across the area, including
those of Emperor Akbar's sons, Murad and Daniyal. Unlike the tomb of
the mystic Sarmad near the congregational mosque of Delhi, which today
attracts throngs of devotees, Dara's grave would not become a popular
shrine.

There is no consensus on precisely where Dara Shukoh is buried. One
grave is popularly considered to be his—its cenotaph has a deliberate
cleavage along its width, suggesting that it shelters a body split asunder.[3]
But according to another view, his grave is one of three grouped together,
each adorned with Quranic inscriptions.[4] We cannot, of course, definitively
identify that either grave is that of the prince. Moreover, a nineteenth-
century account in the *Tarikh-i Farah Bakhsh,* claiming to be based on

reliable sources, states that a Quranic verse was carved on Dara's grave: "So learn a lesson, O you who have insight!"[5]

Some of those who were Dara Shukoh's closest associates carefully proclaimed their allegiance to the new emperor. Mulla Shah sent Alamgir a poem. Once again, murmurs of blasphemy arose against the Sufi, just as they had after Shah Jahan's accession. Alamgir ordered the governor of Kashmir to dispatch Mulla Shah to court in Delhi. The governor pleaded for lenience on account of the Sufi's age and declining health. Jahanara also intervened. Mulla Shah sent these lines of verse, which include a chronogram for the date of Alamgir's accession:

> At dawn my heart bloomed like a sunflower
>   Truth has manifested, purging the dust of falsehood.
> The chronogram of my Shah of the Throne (aurang)
>   It coined "Shadow of Divine Truth," it said; indeed, it spoke the truth (haqq).

The quatrain suggests that the chronogram came to Mulla Shah in a burst of divine inspiration; the term "haqq" in the last line is also synonymous with Divine Truth, so it could also mean "Divine Truth said this." According to Tawakkul Beg, Alamgir was well pleased with the verse.[6] The emperor asked the Sufi to go to Lahore instead, where Mulla Shah lived briefly until his passing in 1661–1662.

The prince's household superintendent, Munshi Chandarbhan Brahman, twice wrote the new emperor. Once to convey his praises after Aurangzeb acceded to the throne and then again to beg for leave to retire, on account of his advancing years.[7] Toward the end of Shahjahan's reign, Chandarbhan had begun to compose his magnum opus of Persian prose, called the *Chahar Chaman,* or Four Meadows. This work takes the reader on an elegant stroll through Shahjahan's empire and Chandarbhan's inner self. It describes Shahjahan's sublime court and the emperor's daily routine, along with the wonders, delights, and characteristics of the empire's regions; it also includes, among other matters, the author's memoirs and spiritual autobiography as well as scholarly and ethical advice to his son.

During Dara Shukoh's last years, Chandarbhan played an important role in the prince's quotidian life and very likely aided his religious explorations. The *Chahar Chaman* refers to the Mughal princes, collectively and individually, by name, but there is not a single mention of Dara Shukoh. Chandarbhan made sure that if Dara made any appearances in the *Chahar Chaman,* not one remained.[8]

The munshi was a seasoned Mughal bureaucrat, experienced enough to take in his stride the vicissitudes of imperial power. We do not have insight into his personal feelings about Dara Shukoh. After Aurangzeb came to the throne, he was happy enough to take a post-retirement position overseeing Mumtaz Mahal's tomb in Agra.[9] But our knowledge that the *Chahar Chaman* must have been reworked under Aurangzeb's rule potentially changes how we see it. It can no longer remain just a celebration of Shah Jahan's court at its pinnacle. It now also reads like an elegy to a time suddenly gone. Its injunctions to look inward, to further refine the self the way Chandarbhan polishes his exquisite prose, are part of an ideal munshi's ethical shaping. But they might also point to a refuge from the turmoil of the troubled years after Shah Jahan's illness.

Unlike Chandarbhan and Mulla Shah, Sarmad Kashani paid dearly for his brazenness. Regardless of how close he was or was not to Dara Shukoh, he was a symbol of the profligate age Alamgir sought to stamp out. Aqil Khan Razi approvingly records Sarmad's execution. He notes that the guardians of the sharia "denuded" Sarmad of "life's garment" because of his nakedness. Without a trace of sorrow, Sarmad laid his neck down, says Razi, and then recited this verse: "The body's nudity is dust on the path to the Friend / This too they severed from my head with the blade." Razi also mentions Dara Shukoh's arrest but not his killing. Here, Sarmad, the naked faqir, stands in for the ill-starred prince.[10]

Alamgir managed to stain his brother's image for posterity. This stain was long-lasting but not indelible. The *Alamgir-nama*'s portrait of Dara Shukoh as a scheming, power-hungry infidel bent on destroying his brothers became quite influential. It informs several late seventeenth- or eighteenth-century chronicles composed toward the end of Aurangzeb's reign or after his death. Bakhtawar Khan's *Mirat-i Jahan-numa* (World-Revealing Mirror) reiterates the *Alamgir-nama*'s phrasing while discussing Dara Shukoh. The widely read *Khulasat-ut-tawarikh* (Epitome of History) attributed to the Hindu writer Sujan Rai Bhandari, is more favorable to Aurangzeb than to Dara Shukoh. Khafi Khan's *Muntakhab-ul-lubab* (Selections of the Pure) takes a similar line.[11]

Some of the earliest portrayals of Dara Shukoh crystallized a little more than a decade after his death. Francois Bernier had only that one encounter with Dara in Gujarat, when the prince was in a miserable and desperate state. But Bernier stayed on in India after Alamgir's accession, in the service of the nobleman Danishmand Khan. During his years in the subcontinent, he sent regular dispatches to Europe about his travels and adventures. These he later compiled into four volumes, which included an account of the war of succession. Here, he assesses the prince's character: Dara Shukoh, though "not deficient in good qualities," had a rather "high opinion of himself," was not amenable to taking advice from others, and often grew

quickly irritable.[12] Bernier's assessment of Dara gained currency. It is repeated, almost verbatim, in the travelogue of Niccoló Manucci and reap-
pears in the early twentieth century, in the Indologist Vincent Smith's *History of India.*[13]

Such representations of Dara, both European and Indian, eventually fed
the modern memory of the prince, especially when taken up by nineteenth-
century colonial historians. This memory—forming the portraits of Dara
Shukoh today etched in the public imagination—is powerful and, of course,
still mutable. But there is a difference between memories that are alive and
memories that have been archived.[14] If traces survive of lesser-known people
who wrote about the prince before the modern period or who engaged with
him and his works in some way, chances are they remain buried in the stacks
of a library or in the internet's ether.

Alamgir's long rule guided the erasure of Dara Shukoh's memory in very
tangible ways. The new emperor was likely responsible for having his
brother's name scratched or blotted out from the valuable manuscripts that
bore his autograph, including the jewel-like album that Dara Shukoh gifted
Nadira and calligraphy panels that Dara himself inscribed. Though a manuscript of Dara's earliest work, the *Safinat-ul-auliya,* still survives, written
and corrected in the prince's distinctive hand, there do not seem to be any
remaining autographed manuscripts of Dara's *Majma-ul-bahrain* or *Sirr-i
akbar.* Of course, vast numbers of Persian manuscripts in collections across
South Asia and the world remain inadequately catalogued. A *Majma* or
Sirr-i akbar manuscript from Dara's lifetime might well exist somewhere.
If Alamgir had anything to do with the loss of the imperial copies, he certainly did not halt their circulation beyond the court.

But for all the chronicles, travelogues, and other writings that show the
prince in a somewhat negative light, the archive holds no dearth of sympathetic and affectionate portrayals. In contrast to works like the *Khulasat-
ut-tawarikh,* the later *Tarikh-i Farah Bakhsh* (Joy-Granting History) by
the Muslim author Muhammad Faiz Bakhsh, criticizes Alamgir for his hy-
pocrisy: "that one who clothed himself as Aurangzeb did, with a cloak of
godly reverence, piety, devotion, consistency, sanctity and moderation,
should treat his own father and brothers so foully as he did; should murder
Dara Shikoh pleading the law of the Muslim faith as his authority . . . all
this is certainly inconsistent with piety and the love of God."[15] The religious identities of these chroniclers did not alone predict their attitudes
toward Aurangzeb Alamgir and Dara Shukoh.

Ironically, Alamgir's administrative policies may have inadvertently
helped more people gain access to his brother's writings. The emperor's
expansion of the bureaucracy greatly increased the number of Hindus

working for the imperial government.[16] These Hindus cultivated Persian learning and often accessed their own devotional texts through the medium of the Persian language. Many were interested in improving themselves ethically and spiritually while also conducting the duties that bound them to this world. Questions that absorbed a would-be king were relevant to others as well: How can I be liberated? How ought I to live in this world? Short tracts detailing steps to liberation were a popular genre. The flourishing of Persian among Mughal Hindus generated a demand for works in the very fields that Dara explored.[17]

Dara Shukoh's prolific writings thrived after his death, taking on lives of their own as they acquired new readers outside his own circles. All the works that can be clearly attributed to him are available in multiple manuscript copies. The wide circulation of these manuscripts before, and even during, the age of print points to the enduring centrality of Dara's project in the arena of Indo-Persian letters.[18] These hand-copied texts are material testaments to the diverse range of readers that the prince posthumously acquired. They offer us clues about their production and context of use.

One Persian copy of the *Majma-ul-bahrain* finds its way into an eclectic collection of texts compiled by a Hindu only shortly after Dara's death. Debi Das, a Kayasth from Sandila writing in Persian, with apparently no direct connection to the court or to Dara, included the *Majma* along with a version of the Dara Shukoh's dialogues with Baba Lal in a compendium of Indic knowledge that Sandilwi called *Khulasat-ul-khulasa,* or Quintessence of the Quintessence. The author completed this work in the thirteenth year of Aurangzeb's reign. In an autobiographical sketch, Debi Das relates that in his youth he sought the company of "pure Brahmans" and studied the Puranas, Vedas, Smriti, and Shastras. He finally achieved a thisworldly liberation under the guidance of his spiritual teacher Swami Nand Lal. Debi Das is only one of several Hindus who composed Persian works on Hindu themes while Aurangzeb ruled.[19]

Another example is a manuscript of the *Majma-ul-bahrain* in an Arabic translation. A date on its frontispiece informs us that it was sold in March or April 1771 to one Hajji Salih Effendi Qadiri Naqshbandi.[20] We can infer from the owner's name that he had been to Mecca for the pilgrimage—a significant journey in those days—that he had some Turkish or Ottoman connection or ancestry, due to the title of "effendi," and that he had both Qadiri and Naqshbandi Sufi affiliations. Other inscriptions on this page, as well as on the end flyleaves, record more names of the manuscript's owners, indicating that it had been passed down through a lineage of Qadiri-affiliated Sufis.[21] The marginal notes also include prayers, recipes for healing potions, a hadith on the permissibility of striking a drum, and much else, all in Arabic. This Arabic translation reflects the transregional reach of Dara's reputation among early modern Qadiris. The text must have fed the curiosity of Arabic-speaking migrants or travelers to India about Indic religious thought, as its readers or their forebears would have arrived from outside the subcontinent.

The *Sirr-i akbar* enjoyed an impressive audience in the Indian subcontinent, especially among Hindus for whom Persian was the main language they used for reading. I have encountered nearly eighty manuscript copies of the text, which, for a manuscript, would make it a veritable bestseller.[22] My own enumeration is hardly exhaustive and is only an indication of what its actual circulation might have been.

Some of the *Sirr-i akbar*'s scribes were Muslim, but they might have had Hindu patrons. Such is the case with one Ashraf Ali who copied the text for Rai Sankat Prasad, the rais of Benares in 1875.[23] At times, the manuscripts are marked with signs of Hindu scribes or readers, such as the opening invocation to the elephant-headed deity Ganesha, "Om Shri Ganeshaya namah," seen in multiple copies.[24] The *Sirr-i akbar* was especially widespread in Kashmir. Several manuscripts are either located in libraries there or bear the names of Kashmiri Pandit copyists. The figure produced in this chapter depicts Dara Shukoh with Sanskrit scholars in the style of Kashmiri painting under Afghan rule (1753–1819).[25]

The text's reach goes beyond its manuscripts. We hear, for instance, that Nand Lal, a prominent nineteenth-century poet in Kashmiri, first cultivated his interest in Vedanta through reading Dara Shukoh's Persian Upaniṣads.[26] By virtue of being in Persian, the *Sirr-i akbar* also gave non-Brahmins, who would not typically learn Sanskrit, access to the Upanishads.

Dara's *Sirr-i akbar* introduced Europe to the Upanishads. Its first translator was the British orientalist, Nathaniel Brassey Halhed. He initially encountered the text while working for the East India Company in Bengal. After returning to England, armed with two copies of the *Sirr-i akbar,* Halhed completed in 1787 a full English translation of the work, which he never managed to publish.[27] In a short piece on Vedic horse-sacrifice, drawn from his Upanishad translation, he equates this ritual to the scapegoat ceremonies recorded in the Hebrew Bible.[28] Halhed's basic assumption underpinning this comparative activity was the superiority of Christianity and European civilization.

Soon after Halhed completed his translation, many British orientalists came to see Mughal Persian translations of Hindu works as derivative and impure. The scholar and pioneer Sanskritist William Jones (d. 1794) warns against following "the muddy rivulets of Muselman writers on India, instead of drinking from the pure fountain of Hindu learning."[29] Such a scant appreciation for these texts led Jones's good friend Sir John Shore, governor general of India (1793–1798), to destroy his own three-volume translation of the Persian *Jog Basisht,* which he had so painstakingly prepared.[30]

The French orientalist, Abraham Hyacinth Anquetil-Duperron (d. 1805), had a more sympathetic view of the Persian Upanishads and of Dara Shukoh's project. He spent nearly two and a half decades working on his translation of the *Sirr-i akbar.* Anquetil first rendered it into French but then found that version to be not literal enough for his tastes. He then retranslated it into Latin, publishing the latter in 1801. Anquetil's view of the Persian language accorded with the manner that learned Indians used it— transcending both region and religion. For Anquetil, Persian's status was akin to that of Latin within European letters, as the language of the intellectual elite.[31]

Remarkably, Anquetil's writings take aim at a widespread conception of his time—that "Orientals" could only produce despotic systems of rule.[32] He argues that one should not impute Aurangzeb's zeal to the rest of the Mughal rulers. He adds that the nawabs and subadars of India were all very tolerant.[33] Anquetil also advances the point that the Mughals took an interest in Indian religions. Were it not for Akbar and Dara, he concludes, "we would have no translation of Indian books."[34]

Like Dara, Anquetil thought the Upanishads to be a font of truth. Though his introductory remarks to the translation subtly privilege Christianity, he emphasizes the common origins of all sacred texts.[35] He sees the "Solomonic books" [Proverbs, Ecclesiastes, and Canticle of Canticles], the "Chinese Kims" [Shu Jing or "The Classic of History"], the "Zend-avesta" [Zand-Avesta] of the Persians, and the "Beids" [Vedas] of the Indians as all sharing "the same dogma, the same universal parent, and the same spiritual beginning."[36]

Anquetil's *Oupnek'hat* would soon lose its relevance as a means of accessing the Upanishads, as European orientalists, such as English Sanskritist Henry Thomas Colebrooke (d. 1837) came to gain direct access to the Sanskrit works. Anquetil's translation itself, a mammoth project of over seventeen hundred pages, replete with digressions and commentaries, was ridiculed in its earliest reception as a bizarre disfiguration of the original text.[37] Yet, as an inspired work of translation blended with theology, the *Oupnek'hat* played a significant role in framing the "wisdom of India" as part of a universal history of monotheism. Its profound influence on the German philosopher Arthur Schopenhauer (d. 1860) is a well-known aspect of its European reception.[38] Others, too, like Schopenhauer's contemporary, the orientalist and scholar of religion Friedrich Majer (d. 1818), came to see the Upanishads as a primeval source for all religions.[39]

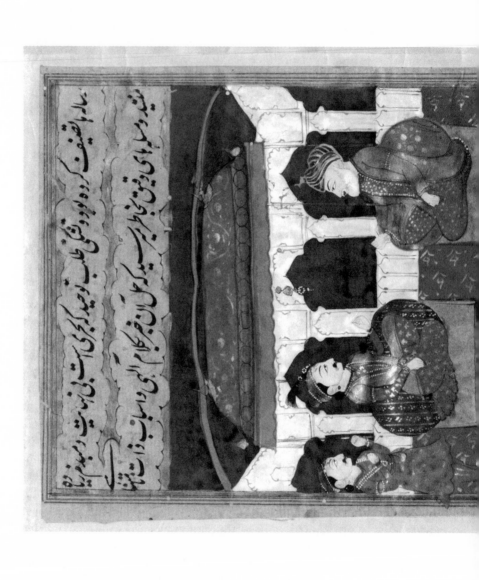

Dara Shukoh with pandits, in *Sirr-i akbar* manuscript.

Back in Hindustan, Dara Shukoh's writings continued to spark engagements between different languages and interpretive communities. The prince's works left a pervading influence on the idiom of various Persian writings on mysticism and Hindu religious topics. For instance, in 1767, a Hindu Kayasth named Sita Ram penned a commentary on the *Jnanasara* composed by Dara's pandit interlocutor Kavindracharya. Sita Ram interspersed his explanations of its couplets with lines from Persian mystical poetry as well as Arabic verses from the Quran and sayings of the prophet Muhammad. His stated intention here was, in fact, to continue Dara Shukoh's work in the *Majma-ul-bahrain*. The *Majma,* he felt, was too succinct and had left many problems unresolved. Sita Ram wanted to show that all paths, "Muslim, Jew, Christian, Magian, Hindu, seek God, the Glorious and Exalted." Unfortunately, after the scholar Tara Chand described this manuscript in 1944, it has since been lost.[40]

One way in which Indo-Persian authors forged connections to Dara is by citing the same verses that he did or by using similar vocabulary to convey the secrets of divine unity. The couplet with which the *Majma-ul-bahrain* opens proved popular: "In the name of the One who has no name/ by whatever name you call Him, He raises His head."[41] This evocation of a nameless divine being features in the *Khulasat-ul-khulasa*. It also appears in a prose work called *Nazuk khayalat* (Subtle Imaginings), purporting to be a translation of the eighth-century philosopher Shankara's *Atma Vilasa* on the essence of the Vedas and Puranas. This latter work is attributed to Chandarbhan Brahman, but its internal contents and date (circa 1710) reveal that the actual author was one Chaturman Kayasth.[42]

Banwalidas, the prince's erstwhile secretary who stayed on in Kashmir as a disciple of Mulla Shah, translated the allegorical play *Prabodhachandrodaya* into Persian. It was originally composed in Sanskrit in the twelfth century, with several Hindavi translations appearing later. Banwalidas called it *Gulzar-i hal* (Rose Garden of Ecstatic States). It was exactly the kind of project that would have delighted Dara Shukoh, though it cautiously avoids mention of either the late prince or the reigning Emperor Alamgir. The story, hinging on a realization of oneness, is framed in the Sufi terms used to portray the ultimate goals of the spiritual path. Banwalidas adds to the text lashings of Persian poetry, both his own verses and those composed by other canonical poets of India and Iran. Their inclusion serves to imply a mutual equivalence between Indic and Persianate or Muslim vocabularies of non-dualism. Indeed, through the repetitive, universalizing tenor of Banwalidas's poetry on unity, he invokes the interpretive moves that Dara Shukoh had made only a few years earlier in his *Majma-ul-bahrain*.

Dara Shukoh's name was also frequently attached to books that he probably never wrote. These works tend not to have the introductions with which he prefaced his writings. They also do not circulate in as many copies as his other, more famous works. The *Tariqat-ul-haqiqat* (Path of Spiritual Reality), is one such example. Here, through a series of guided steps, thirty in all, the seeker is led along the path of liberation. These stages detail such topics as purifying the heart and the mystical state of the adept.[43] Another example is *Rumuz-i tasawwuf* (Mysteries of Mysticism), which compiles several aphoristic riddles relating to the concepts of divine law, the Sufi lineage, spiritual reality, and divine gnosis.[44] A certain Mirza Nek Akhtar Timur Dihlavi composed a Persian translation of what was purportedly an Arabic work by Dara Shukoh called *Sirat-i Wahdat* (Path of Divine Unity).[45] Another curious work attributed to the prince is *Ima-ul-muhaqqiqin* (Allusions of the Truth-Seekers). This presents itself as the prince's renderings of the poetry of Mulla Shah and Miyan Mir. This slim text brings together Hindavi and Persian poetry, which it intersperses with Quranic verses.[46]

Later on, in the age of print, as colonial rule sunk its grip deeper into the subcontinent, Dara Shukoh's writings acquired an expanded audience. Hindus who sought to recover a tradition of their own found in his later writings a way to access key sacred texts. Persian continued to be an important literary language across religious lines in Punjab, Bengal, and other parts of northern India. The pioneering Hindu reformer, Rammohun Roy (d. 1833), who espoused a strict monotheism, composed his initial works in Persian and must have been exposed to the prince's writings.[47] Like Dara Shukoh, he set great store by the Upanishads, even translating five of them into Bengali and English.[48]

Another nineteenth-century reformer, Kanhaiyalal Alakhdhari, indefatigably published several editions of Dara Shukoh's *Jog Basisht* and Upanishad translations, rendered in Urdu. Alakhdhari wished for Hindus to draw on the *Sirr-i akbar* for a monotheistic scripture of their own. Divested of its inscrutable Sanskrit garb, it was now accessible to the masses. Alakhdhari, who helped pave the way for the Arya Samaj's spread in the Punjab, could be bitterly critical of Muslims. Dara Shukoh, for him, was an exception who "laid out the tablespread of universal peace for the sake of commoners and the elites."[49] A twentieth-century publisher, Hira Lal of Jaipur, used his press to print the *Sirr-i akbar*. Here, Dara's equivalence between Om and Allah mentioned in the *Sirr-i akbar*'s glossary adopts a striking visual form. The calligraphy resembles Om in the Nagari script if viewed vertically, and when turned horizontally, it echoes Allah written in the Arabic script. In a seemingly incongruous twist of fate, the religious wanderings of a

Om/Allah, opening to early twentieth-century lithograph edition of Dara Shukoh, *Sirr-i akbar*.

seventeenth-century Muslim prince fed currents that would eventually shape modern Hinduism.

A popular thought experiment in the subcontinent today involves asking what might have happened if Dara Shukoh had actually managed to become emperor. How would he have ruled? Would South Asian history have taken a markedly different turn? Would its population have suffered the same interreligious conflicts between Hindus and Muslims that we see today? Would Pakistan ever have been created?

There are many ways of writing this alternate history. But encoded in this very question is the modern assumption that Alamgir's bigotry was somehow responsible for the empire's decline. Who could predict in the mid-1600s that half a century later, weak princes would tumble one after the other, so that twelve years after Alamgir's death, six rulers had already sat on Shah Jahan's bejeweled throne? Or foresee the groaning repercussions of Alamgir's costly Deccan expansion? The causes of the Mughal empire's decentralization and of British colonialism's swift inroads into the subcontinent are much debated and beyond the scope of this book. But they were far more complex than an explanation based on Alamgir's religious policies allows.

We do not have to go far to wonder what kind of emperor Dara Shukoh would have been. We do not need to speculate, because in his father's court, he was already a ruler. For a handful of years in the 1650s, the two governed in tandem. They hosted scholars, prosecuted a war, managed allies, and subdued threats. If Dara had come to power, he too would have had to reproduce the very fratricidal violence that had brought his father to the throne. Aurangzeb would not necessarily have been turned into an unbeliever. He would, though, have become the rebel prince, who excited sedition and deserved to have his worldly existence effaced.

DRAMATIS PERSONAE

Mughal Imperial Family

Asaf Khan (d. 1641): Father of Arjumand Bano, brother of Nur Jahan, served Jahangir and Shah Jahan.

Arjumand Bano / Mumtaz Mahal (1593–1631): An Iranian noblewoman and Shah Jahan's second wife, confidante, and advisor. Mother of fourteen children, seven of whom survived her.

Aurangzeb (1618–1707): The third son of Shah Jahan and an experienced administrator and general in the Deccan who led an unsuccessful campaign to Qandahar in 1652.

Dara Shukoh (1615–1659): Shah Jahan's eldest son and heir, a Qadiri Sufi, who drew on earlier Mughal traditions to fashion himself as a philosopher-king.

Dawar Bakhsh (d. 1628): Son of Khusrau, a hapless puppet emperor installed for a brief period to keep the throne for Shah Jahan.

Khurram / Shah Jahan (1592–1666): Jahangir's third son, who succeeded him to the throne.

Khusrau Mirza (1587–1622): Jahangir's eldest son, and competitor for the throne, who was eventually blinded by his father and murdered at his brother's behest.

Jahanara (1614–1681): Shah Jahan's eldest daughter, author of Sufi works, patron of architecture, and family mediator.

Jahangir (1569–1628): The fourth Mughal emperor of Hindustan, a memoirist, and a patron of art.

Muhammad Sultan (1639–1676): Aurangzeb's eldest son by his second wife, Nawab Bai, who supported his uncle and father-in-law Shuja in the war of succession.

Murad Bakhsh (1624–1661): The fourth son of Shah Jahan, a governor of Gujarat, who led an ultimately unsuccessful campaign to Central Asia.

Nadira Bano (1618–1659): Dara Shukoh's wife, whom he called his "most intimate companion and sharer of secrets."

Nur Jahan (1577–1645): The Iranian-born former Mihr-un-Nisa, Jahangir's consort and co-ruler.

Shah Shuja (1616–1661): The second son of Shah Jahan, a governor of Bengal, a patron, and an aesthete.

Sipihr Shukoh (1644–1708): Dara Shukoh's younger son who later married Aurangzeb's daughter.

Sulaiman Shukoh (1635–1662): Dara Shukoh's eldest son who served as governor of Kabul and led the campaign against Shuja in the war of succession.

Scholars, Sufis, and Sages

Abd-ul-Hakim Siyalkoti (d. 1656): A scholar and philosopher in Shah Jahan's service.

Abd-ul-Haqq Dihlawi (d. 1642): A scholar, Qadiri Sufi, and prolific author of works on prophetic traditions, saints' biographies, and theology.

Abd-ur-Rahman Chishti (d. 1683): A Sabiri Chishti Sufi and prolific author who creatively engaged with Indic religious thought in some of his writings.

Ahmad Sirhindi (d. 1624): An influential Naqshbandi Sufi whose followers controversially anointed him as "the Renewer" of the second Islamic millennium.

Baba Lal (fl. 1653): A Hindu ascetic who held a series of conversations with Dara Shukoh.

Chandarbhan Brahman (d. circa 1670): Persian poet and author in the employ of the Mughal court, he was Dara Shukoh's master of works in the 1650s.

Chidrup (d. circa 1637): A Hindu ascetic who enjoyed good relations with Akbar and Jahangir.

Kavindracharya Saraswati (fl. 1650s): A renowned scholar and poet from Benares sponsored by Shah Jahan's court.

Miyan Mir (d. 1635): A prominent Sufi teacher of the Qadiri order, based in Lahore.

Muhibb-ullah Ilahabadi (d. 1648): A Chishti Sufi and noted interpreter of the dense works authored by the Andalusian mystic Ibn Arabi (d. 1240), he also corresponded with Dara Shukoh.

Mulla Shah (d. 1661): A Qadiri Sufi and disciple of Miyan Mir, as well as a spiritual teacher of Dara Shukoh and Jahanara, who became increasingly close to the imperial family, including Shah Jahan, in the 1640s and 1650s.

Sarmad (d. 1661): An Armenian Jewish merchant who journeyed to Shahjahanabad via Sindh and the Deccan with his lover Abhai Chand. He converted to Islam, composed Persian mystical poetry, and reportedly shunned clothing. Aurangzeb executed him after gaining the throne.

Nobles and Imperial Servants

Hakim Daud (d. circa 1662): Iranian physician at the Mughal court who came from a family of Safavid physicians.

Jai Singh (d. 1667) Mughal general and ruler of Amer, reluctant supporter of the imperial army during the war of succession.

Jaswant Singh (d. 1678): Ruler of Marwar and author of several religious works in Brajbhasha. Defeated by Aurangzeb at Dharmat during the struggle for succession in 1658, he subsequently held back from supporting Dara Shukoh's bid for victory.

Mir Askari/Aqil Khan Razi (d. 1696): Aurangzeb's equerry in the Deccan, disciple of the Chishti-Shattari Sufi Burhan-ud-Din Raz-i Ilahi (d. 1673), and skilled Persian litterateur.

Raj Singh (d. 1680): Ruler of Mewar and grandson of Shah Jahan's ally Karan Singh. Both Aurangzeb and Dara Shukoh courted him before the war of succession.

Chroniclers and Poets

Abd-ul-Hamid Lahori (d. 1654): The official historian of over two decades of Shah Jahan's rule.

'Bihishti, Shirazi (fl. 1658): A Persian poet from Iran in Murad's employ, who wrote a versified account of the war of succession.

Inayat Khan (fl. 1658): Son of Zafar Khan, governor of Kashmir, he produced an abridgment of the *Padshah-nama* of Lahori and Waris.

Jalaluddin Tabatabai (fl. 1630s): An Iranian émigré to Shah Jahan's court, and early chronicler of his reign.

'Kalim' Kashani (d. 1651): A Persian poet who initially migrated from Iran to the Deccan and eventually served as Shah Jahan's poet laureate.

Mirza Nathan (Shitab Khan) (fl. 1620s): An imperial servant of Jahangir, who came into contact with Shah Jahan during the latter's rebellion. Wrote a sprawling history of Mughal involvement in Bengal and neighboring regions.

Muhammad Amin Qazwini (fl. 1630–1645): The official chronicler of the first decade of Shah Jahan's reign.

Muhammad Masum (fl. 1660): Shuja's retainer, who chronicled the war of succession using a mixture of reports and his own eyewitness observations. One of his informants was his brother-in-law, a servant of Sipihr Shukoh who later defected to work for Aurangzeb's son, Muhammad Sultan.

Muhammad Salih Kamboh (d. circa 1675): A court chronicler late in Shah Jahan's reign, he oversaw the tumultuous transition to Aurangzeb's enthronement.

Muhammad Waris (fl. 1650s): The official court chronicler and author of the last part of the *Padshah-nama*, who took over from Lahori after the latter's death in 1654.

Mutamad Khan (Muhammad Sharif) (d. circa 1639): Paymaster of the imperial cavalry and chronicler of Jahangir's reign.

Rashid Khan (Muhammad Badi) (fl. 1650s): Servant of the second Mahabat Khan, he wrote a detailed account of Dara Shukoh's 1653 Qandahar expedition.

'Saib' Tabrizi (1592–1676): A noted Persian poet from Iran who spent seven years in India serving the Mughal nobleman Zafar Khan and later returned to Iran, attaching himself to the Safavid court.

Tawakkul Beg (fl. 1630s–1660s): A disciple of Mulla Shah, he later joined imperial service under Dara Shukoh. He wrote an account of Mulla Shah's life and relationship with the imperial family.

'Qudsi' Mashhadi (1582–1646): A renowned Persian poet from Iran who spent his advanced years at Shah Jahan's court and became poet laureate.

European Writers on India

Abraham Hyacinthe Anquetil-Duperron (d. 1805): French orientalist, who rendered Dara Shukoh's translation of the Upanishads into French and Latin.

Thomas Coryate (d. 1617): An English adventurer who traveled by land to the Mughal court.

Francisco Pelsaert (d. 1630): A merchant in the employ of the Dutch East Indies Company.

Niccolò Manucci (d. circa 1720): A Venetian adventurer and artilleryman in Dara Shukoh's employ.

Peter Mundy (d. 1667): An author in the employ of the East India Company.

Thomas Roe (d. 1644): Ambassador of King James to Jahangir's court.

Heinrich Roth (d. 1668): Jesuit missionary as well as scholar of Sanskrit and Indian philosophy.

NOTES

Introduction

1. According to the play, this scene occurs on August 27. Tanya Ronder and Shahid Nadeem, *Dara* (London: Bloomsbury, 2017). Ronder mentions that she added the trial scene for dramatic effect. My use of these examples from the play is not intended in any way to disparage Nadeem and Ronder's work. Rather, it aims to illustrate the modern memory of Dara Shukoh.

2. Mohsin Hamid, *Moth Smoke* (New York: Farrar, Strauss, and Giroux, 2000); Akbar Ahmed, *Two Plays: The Trial of Dara Shikoh, Noor* (London: Saqi, 2009); Ishtiaq Husain Qureshi, *The Administration of the Mughal Empire* (Karachi: University of Karachi, 1966), 196–197.

3. *"Tukhm-i ilhadi kih Akbar parwarid / baz andar fitrat-i Dara damid / shama-i dil dar sina-ha raushan nabud / millat-i ma az fasad aiman nabud,"* Muhammad Iqbal, *Ashar-i Farsi-i Iqbal Lahuri,* ed. Muhammad Darvish (Tehran: Sazman-i Intisharat-i Javidan, 1991), 149.

4. *"Haqq guzid az Hind Alamgir ra / an faqir sahib-i shamshir ra / az pay-yi ihya-yi din mamur kard / bahr-i tajdid-i yaqin mamur kard,"* Iqbal, *Ashar,* 149.

5. Ishtiaq Husain Qureshi, *Muslim Community of the Indo-Pakistan Subcontinent* (The Hague: Mouton, 1962), 180.

6. Ashok Malik, "The Month We Lost Dara," *Daily Pioneer,* August 11, 2009, accessed October 8, 2018, archived at www.defence.pk/pdf/threads/the-month-we -lost-dara-shikoh.31550.

7. Maulana Abul Kalam Azad, *Sufi Sarmad Shahid* (Hyderabad: Abul Kalam Azad Oriental Research Institute, 1986), 20.

8. Kenneth W. Jones, "Two Sanatan Dharma Leaders and Swami Vivekananda: A Comparison," in *Swami Vivekananda and the Modernisation of Hinduism,* ed. William Radice (New Delhi: Oxford University Press, 1999), 224–243, 227.

9. Cross-reference the Epilogue.

10. Saeed Naqvi, *Being the Other* (New Delhi: Aleph, 2016), 114.

11. Roland Barthes, *Mythologies,* trans. Annette Lavers (New York: Hill and Wang, 1975), 151. For myth as ideology in narrative form, see Bruce Lincoln, *Theorizing Myth* (Chicago: University of Chicago Press, 1999), xii .

12. Shahid Nadeem, foreword in Nadeem and Ronder, *Dara.*

13. Adrija Roychowdhury, "Dalhousie Road Renamed after Dara Shikoh: Why Hindutva Right Wingers Favour a Mughal Prince," *Indian Express,* February 7, 2017, www.indianexpress.com, accessed October 8, 2018.

14. Kalika Ranjan Qanungo, *Dara Shukoh* (Calcutta: S.C. Sarkar, 1952); Bikrama Jit Hasrat, *Dārā Shikūh: Life and Works* (Calcutta: Visvabharati, 1953).

15. Hasrat, *Dārā Shikūh,* 103.

16. Qanungo, *Dara Shukoh,* 271.

17. Hasrat, *Dārā Shikūh,* 6–7.

18. A recent study of Mughal sacred sovereignty is Azfar Moin, *The Millennial Sovereign* (New York: Columbia University Press, 2015).

19. An overview of Persian translations in South Asia, including during the Sultanate period, can be found in Carl Ernst, "Muslim Studies of Hinduism? A Reconstruction of Arabic and Persian Translations from Indian Languages," *Iranian Studies* 36.2 (2003): 173–195. For a recent study of the Mughal court's engagement with Sanskrit knowledge, see Audrey Truschke, *Culture of Encounters* (New York: Columbia University Press, 2016). See also Abu-l-Fazl, *Ain-i Akbari,* ed. Heinrich Blochmann, 2 vols. (Calcutta: Calcutta Baptist Mission Press, 1872–1877), 1: 51–52; translated as *The Ā'in-i Akbarī,* trans. Heinrich Blochmann, ed. Douglas Craven Phillott, 3 vols. (Calcutta: Asiatic Society of Bengal, 1927–1949), vol. 3.

20. Svevo D'onofrio and I have been independently researching Shaikh Sufi's writings. I am grateful to him for sharing details of his unpublished research on Shaikh Sufi.

21. Kalika Ranjan Qanungo, *Historical Essays* (Agra: Shiva Lal Agarwala, 1968), 129.

1. Empire, 1615–1622

1. Nur-ud-Din Muhammad Jahangir, *Jahangir-nama (Tuzuk-i Jahangiri),* ed. Muhammad Hashim (Tehran: Fahrang, 1980/1), 144–145; translated as *The Jahangirnama: Memoirs of Jahangir, Emperor of India,* trans. Wheeler M. Thackston (New York: Oxford University Press, 1999), 153.

2. Catherine Ella Blanshard Asher, *Architecture of Mughal India* (Cambridge: Cambridge University Press, 2008), 122.

3. See the observations of the English merchant William Finch (d. 1613) in Samuel Purchas, *Purchas his Pilgrimes: In Fiue Bookes* (London: Henry Fetherston, 1625), 1: 428 (bk. 4, ch. 4, §5); quoted in Sayyid Akbarali Ibrahimali Tirmizi,

Ajmer through Inscriptions (New Delhi: Indian Institute of Islamic Studies, 1968), 17–18.

4. The submission of the Rana Amar Singh to Prince Khurram is illustrated by Lalchand in Abd-ul-Hamid Lahori (d. 1654), *Padshah-nama*, Royal Collection Trust, MS 1367, fol. 46b; reproduced in Milo Cleveland Beach and Ebba Koch, *King of the World. The Padshahnama: An Imperial Mughal Manuscript, the Royal Library, Windsor Castle* (London: Thames and Hudson, 1997), plates 6–7.

5. Jahangir, *Tuzuk,* 147; translation, 167.

6. Anand Pandian, "Predatory Care: The Imperial Hunt in Mughal and British India," *Journal of Historical Sociology* 14.1 (2001): 79–107, 89–100.

7. Jahangir, *Tuzuk,* 164; translation, 174.

8. Indian Museum, Calcutta, Indian Museum Art Section, No. 316. Printed and discussed in Asok Kumar Das, "Mughal Royal Hunt in Miniature Paintings," *Indian Museum Bulletin* 2.1 (1967): 19–23.

9. Mirza Amin Qazwini, *Padshah-nama*, British Library, MS Or. 173, fols. 42a–43a. I have benefited greatly from the unpublished edition prepared by the late Dr. Yunus Jaffery, kindly shared with me by the late Dr. Majid Ahmady. As the basis for his unpublished edition, Dr. Jaffery took the British Library manuscript and a handwritten copy made in Aligarh of Rampur Raza Library MS 2091/495m. I have also benefited from discussing the text's provenance with Stephan Popp, who is preparing a partial translation of the text. For the two copies in the British Library, see Charles Rieu, *Catalogue of the Persian Manuscripts in the British Museum*, 1: 258–259. For the Rampur copy, see *Fihrist-i nuskha-i khatti-i farsi-i kitabkhana-i Raza Rampur*, 3 vols. (Delhi: Diamond Printers, 1996), 1: 621.

10. Jahangir, *Tuzuk,* 160; translation, 172.

11. See also chap. 4, 103.

12. Avner Giladi, *Infants, Parents and Wet Nurses: Medieval Islamic Views on Breastfeeding and Their Social Implications* (Leiden: Brill, 1999), 21, 55.

13. Jahangir, *Tuzuk,* 151; translation, 161.

14. Qazwini, *Padshah-nama*, fol. 233a.

15. Qazwini, *Padshah-nama*, fol. 47a.

16. Qazwini, *Padshah-nama*, fol. 47b.

17. Jahangir, *Tuzuk,* 70–71; translation, 84; for a discussion of the plot, see Beni Prasad, *History of Jahangir* (London: Oxford University Press, 1922), 164–165; Fergus Nicoll, *Shah Jahan: The Rise and Fall of the Mughal Emperor* (London: Haus, 2009), 69; Munis Faruqui, *The Princes of the Mughal Empire, 1504–1719* (Cambridge: Cambridge University Press, 2012), 221–223.

18. Qazwini, *Padshah-nama*, fol. 47a.

19. Ellison Banks Findly, *Nur Jahan: Empress of Mughal India* (Oxford: Oxford University Press, 1999), 36.

20. Jahangir, *Tuzuk,* 181; translation, 190.

21. Jahangir, *Tuzuk,* 148; translation, 157.

22. Jahangir, *Tuzuk,* 31; translation, 49.

23. Hakim Nizami Ganjawi, *Sharaf-nama*, ed. Hasan Wahid Dastgirdi (Tehran: Armaghan, 1937), 181, lines 1–3. For a recent account of the Alexander romance

in Persian letters, see Haila Manteghi, *Alexander the Great in the Persian Tra-dition: History Myth and Legend in Medieval Iran* (London: I. B. Tauris, 2018), esp. 71–127.

24. For a royal copy of the collection originally produced in Central Asia with seals from the Mughal holdings of Jahangir's court, see Nizami, *Khamsa,* National Library, Kolkata, Buhar Collection, MS 296, dated 940 AM (1534/5). This may well be the gift to Jahangir of an illuminated copy of the *Khamsa* done by "the masters," referred to in Jahangir, *Tuzuk,* 392; translation, 378. For an exquisite copy already in the court of Jahangir during this period, see British Library, MS Or. 6810, discussed in Rochelle Kessler, "In the Company of the Enlightened: Portraits of Mughal Rulers and Holy Men," *Studies in Islamic and Later Indian Art from the Arthur M. Sackler Museum* (Cambridge: Harvard University Art Museums, 2002), 17–41, 19–21.

25. As recorded in the anonymous collection entitled *Intikhab-i Jahangirshahi,* written by a courtier, translated in Henry Miers Elliot and John Dowson, *The History of India, as Told by its Own Historians,* 8 vols. (London: Trübner and Co., 1867–1877), 6: 448. The differing European accounts of the blinding epi-sode and the variants are treated in Findly, *Nur Jahan,* 33–34. For the blinding of Kamran Mirza, see Gulbadan Begam, *Humayun-nama,* in *Three Memoirs of Humáyun,* ed. and trans. Wheeler Thackston (Costa Mesa, CA: Mazda Publishers, 2009), 73 (Persian), 67 (translation); Jawhar Aftabchi, *Tazkirat-ul-vaqiat,* in *Three Memoirs of Humáyun,* 193 (Persian), 158 (translation). The ongoing unpublished research of Emma Flatt treats the topic of fragrances and sociability in Persianate South Asia.

26. *Letters Received by the East India Company from Its Servants in the East,* ed. William Foster et al., 6 vols. (London: Sampson Low, Martson and Company, 1896–1902), 2: 297, letter of Thomas Keridge, January 20, 1614.

27. Thomas Coryate, *Traueller for the English Wits: Greetings from the Court of the Great Mogul* (London: William [J]aggard and Henry Fetherton, 1616), b 1. See, broadly, Dom Moraes and Sarayu Srivats, *The Long Strider: How Thomas Coryate Walked from England to India in the Year 1613* (Delhi: Penguin, 2003).

28. Coryate, *Traueller,* 18–19; Purchas, *Pilgrimes,* 1: 593–594 (bk. 4, ch. 17).

29. For a brief account of Thomas Coryate's life and travels in India, see William Foster's note in Thomas Roe, *The Embassy of Sir Thomas Roe to the Court of the Great Mogul,* ed. William Foster, 2 vols. (London: Hakluyt Society, 1899), 1: 103–5n3.

30. Coryate, *Traueller,* 35; Purchas, *Pilgrimes,* 1: 595 (bk. 4, ch. 17).

31. *Letters Received,* 1: 256, letter of Thomas Keridge, March 12, 1612.

32. In 1612 and again in 1615, the East India Company withstood pitched naval battles at the port of Surat against the Portuguese.

33. Roe, *Embassy,* 1: 103–105.

34. *Letters Received,* 4: 13–14, letter of Roe, January 25, 1616; cited in Findly, *Nur Jahan,* 157.

35. Roe, *Embassy,* 1: 43–44, 67–68. On the episode at Surat, see Michael Brown, *Itinerant Ambassador, The Life of Sir Thomas Roe* (Lexington: The University Press of Kentucky, 1970), 39–44.

36. Description drawn from Francisco Pelsaert (d. 1630), *Remonstrantie*, edited in *De Geschriften van Francisco Pelsaert over Mughal Indië, 1627: Kroniek en Remonstrantie*, eds. D. H. A. Kolff and H. W. Van Santen (The Hague: Nijhoff, 1979), 245–335, 310–311; translated as *Jahangir's India, the Remonstrantie of Francisco Pelsaert*, trans. W. H. Moreland and P. Geyl (Cambridge: W. Heffer and Sons, 1925), 62. For more on Pelsaert, see chap. 2, note 6.

37. See William Harrison, *India at the Death of Akbar: An Economic Study* (London: Macmillan and Co., 1920), 14–15; Shireen Moosvi, *The Economy of the Mughal Empire c. 1595*, rev. ed. (New Delhi: Oxford University Press, 1987), 405–416. Moosvi reviews several attempts, including Harrison's, at calculating the population for the region, and produces an estimate of roughly ninety-five million for the Mughal empire during the reign of Akbar and a hundred forty-five million for the entire subcontinent. See, however, Prabhat Patnaik, "Review: Shireen Moosvi, *The Economy of the Mughal Empire*," *Studies in People's History* 3.1 (2016): 100–106, 102.

38. Figures from Athar Ali, *The Apparatus of Empire: Awards of Ranks, Offices and Titles to the Mughal Nobility, 1574–1658* (Delhi: Oxford University Press, 1985), xiii (table showing mansabs in Akbar's reign); 3–33 (list of Akbar-era nobility); and 41–90 (list of Jahangir-era nobility).

39. Shireen Moosvi, "The Evolution of the Manṣab System under Akbar until 1596–7," *Journal of the Royal Asiatic Society* 113.2 (1981): 173–185.

40. Masashi Haneda, "Emigration of Iranian Elites to India during the 16th–18th Centuries," in *L'heritage timouride: Iran, Asie Centrale, Inde, XVIe–XVIIIe siècles*, ed. Maria Szuppe (Aix-en-Provence: Édisud, 1997), 129–143.

41. Quote from Iqtidar Alam Khan, "The Middle Classes in the Mughal Empire," *Social Scientist* 5.1 (1976): 28–49, 29. See also Muzaffar Alam and Sanjay Subrahmanyam, *Writing the Mughal World: Studies on Culture and Politics* (New York: Columbia University Press, 2015), 397.

42. Muzaffar Alam and Sanjay Subrahmanyam, "Frank Disputations: Catholics and Muslims in the Court of Jahangir (1608–11)," *Indian Economic and Social History Review* 46.4 (2009): 457–511.

43. Jahangir, *Tuzuk*, 153; translation, 162–163.

44. Pelsaert, *Remonstrantie*, 297n373; translation, 48.

45. On the institution of the *abdar-khana*, see Abu-l-Fazl (d. 1602), *Ain-i Akbari*, ed. Heinrich Blochmann, 2 vols. (Calcutta: Calcutta Baptist Mission Press, 1872–1877), 1: 51–52; translated as *The Ā'in-i Akbarī*, trans. Heinrich Blochmann, ed. Douglas Craven Phillott, 3 vols. (Calcutta: Asiatic Society of Bengal, 1927–49), 1: 57–59.

46. Pelsaert, "Remonstrantie," 321; translation, 72.

47. For the original Persian transcription followed by translation and commentary of the speech, see Thomas Coryate, *Mr. Thomas Coriat to his Friends in England* (London: J. Beale, 1618), B2a–B3a, B3b–4b (paginated by alphabetized quire signatures). The following is a modernized re-transcription of the phrasing quoted above from Coryate's introduction to his Persian speech: "*faqir darwesh wa jahan-gashta hastam ke man amadam az wilayat-i dur yani az mulk-i Inglizan . . .*"

48. Roe, *Embassy,* 1: 108; Purchas, *Pilgrimes,* 1: 542 (bk. 4, ch. 16, §2); cited in Jonathan Gill Harris, "Becoming Indian," in *Modern Theatricality,* ed. Henry Turner (Oxford: Oxford University Press, 2017), 442–459, 447.
49. Edward Terry, *A Voyage to East India* (London: John Martin and James Alles-trye, 1655), 58–59, 270–271.
50. Coryate, *Thomas Coriat,* D1b.
51. Terry, *Voyage,* 271; compare with Purchas, *Pilgrimes,* 2: 1476 (bk. 5, ch. 6, §3).
52. Coryate, *Traueller,* 23; Roe, *Embassy,* 2: 313–314; *Letters Received,* 6: 184–185, letter of Joseph Salbank to the East India Company, November 22, 1617.
53. Purchas, *Pilgrimes,* 1: 564 (bk. 4, ch. 16, §7).
54. Roe, *Embassy,* 1: 137.
55. Pramod Nayar, "Colonial Proxemics: The Embassy of Sir Thomas Roe to India," *Studies in Travel Writing* 6 (2002): 9–53.
56. For reference to the famed Mercator map presented by Roe, see Roe, *Embassy,* 2: 413–414, 416–417; Purchas, *Pilgrimes,* 1: 569–570 (bk. 4, ch. 16, §8); Terry, *Voyage,* 368. For further information, see Irfan Habib, "Cartography in Mughal India," *Proceedings of the Indian History Congress* 35 (1974): 150–162, 154–155; Sanjay Subrahmanyam, *Europe's India: Words, People, Empires, 1500–1800* (Cambridge, MA: Harvard University Press, 2017), 300–301. See also Simon Digby, "Beyond the Ocean: Perceptions of Overseas in Indo-Persian Sources of the Mughal Period," *Studies in History* n.s., 14.2 (1999): 247–259, 255–256.
57. Colophon of Jamal-ud-Din Inju, *Farhang-i Jahangiri,* 2 vols. (Mashad: Dan-ishgah-i Mashhad, 1972–1973), 2: 699–700. For more on this work, which was originally composed for Akbar, and the broader context of Persian philology in the Mughal court, see Rajeev Kinra, "Cultures of Comparative Philology in the Early Modern Indo-Persian World," *Philological Encounters* 1 (2016): 225–287, 263–278.
58. Roe, *Embassy,* 2: 334; Purchas, *Pilgrimes,* 1: 558 (bk. 4, ch. 16, §6); cited in Harris, "Becoming Indian," 449.
59. On the phenomenon, see Ebba Koch, "Jahangir and the Angels: Recently Dis-covered Wall Paintings under European Influence in the Fort of Lahore," in *India and the West,* ed. Joachim Deppert (Delhi: Manohar, 1983), 173–195; Koch, "*Diwan-i 'amm* and Chihil Sutun: The Audience Halls of Shah Jahan," *Muqarnas* 11 (1994): 143–165.
60. Drawn from his section on foreign words: Jamal-ud-Din, *Farhang,* 2: 625–699; on the *pairuj,* see 693. In Goa, Muqarrab Khan bought for Jahangir rare ani-mals that the Franks had brought from their travels, including turkeys from America. Jahangir was so impressed by the strange rarity of the bird, "whose name no one knows," that he dedicated several lines to its description in his memoirs: Jahangir, *Tuzuk,* 123; translation, 133, with a print of Victoria and Albert Museum, IM 135–1921.
61. Jamal-ud-Din, *Farhang,* 2: 553–623, with equivalents in Book Pahlavi given in the marginal notes.

62. See Akbar portrayed as Alexander visiting a sage: Nizami, *Sharaf-nama,* School of Oriental and African Studies, London, MS 24952, fol. 48b; reproduced in Gregory Minissale, "Piecing Together the Emperor Akbar's Lost *Sharaf-nāme,*" *Oriental Art* 44.1 (1998): 67–71, 70, fig. 4. For more on the Alexander Romance in the Indian context, see Sanjay Subrahmanyam, "Connected Histories: Notes toward Reconfiguration of Early Modern Eurasia," *Modern Asian Studies* 31.3 (1997): 735–762, 755–757. See also Blain Auer, *Symbols of Authority in Medieval Islam: History, Religion, and Muslim Legitimacy* (London: I. B. Tauris, 2011), 29, 123–124.

63. Nizami, *Sharaf-nama,* 70, lines 11–12; 71, lines 1–3.

64. See Coryate, *Traueller,* 29; Roe, *Embassy,* 1: 102–103n2; Purchas, *Pilgrimes,* 1: 541, 579 (bk. 4, ch. 16, §§1, 10); Terry, *Voyage,* 81–82; Joannes De Laet (d. 1649), *De imperio Magni Mogolis* (Leiden: Elzeviriania, 1631), 53–54; translated as *The Empire of the Great Mogol,* trans. J. S. Hoyland (Bombay: D. B. Taraporevala Sons, 1928), 48n64. See also B. Finbarr Flood, "Pillars, Palimpsests, and Princely Practices: Translating the Past in Sultanate Delhi," *RES: Anthropology and Aesthetics* 43 (2003): 95–116, 111n62.

65. Jahangir, *Tuzuk,* 185; translation, 194.

66. Jahangir, *Tuzuk,* 185–186; translation, 195.

67. Jahangir, *Tuzuk,* 281–282; translation, 281. For a useful, if at times simplistic, overview of this episode, see Ellison Findly, "Jahāngīr's Vow of Non-Violence," *Journal of the American Oriental Society* 107.2 (1987): 245–256.

68. Jahangir, *Tuzuk,* 186; translation, 196.

69. Roe, *Embassy,* 1: 201.

70. Jahangir, *Tuzuk,* 202–203; translation, 209.

71. *"Ilm-i bedant kih imroz murad az tasawwuf bashad"* and *"mustalihat-i tasawwuf-i ahl-i islam ra ba tariq-i tasawwuf khud tatbiq dada,"* Mutamad Khan, *Iqbal-nama-i Jahangiri,* ed. Abd-ul-Hayy and Ahmad Ali (Calcutta: Asiatic Society of Bengal, 1865), 95–96. For the argument that in Mutamad Khan's use of the term *imroz* (i.e., currently), the notion of making an equivalence between *tasawwuf* and Vedanta was starting to take root in Mughal circles), see Shireen Moosvi, "The Mughal Encounter with Vedanta: Recovering the Biography of Jadrup," *Social Scientist* 30.7/8 (2002): 13–23, 16. Following Moosvi, I take Chidrup to be the basis of the name transcribed in Persian as Jadrup.

72. See M. Abdullah Chaghtai, "Emperor Jahangir's Interviews with Gosāin Jadrūp and His Portraits," *Islamic Culture* 36.2 (1962): 119–128; and Sajida S. Alvi, "Religion and State during the Reign of Mughal Emperor Jahāngīr (1605–27): Nonjuristical Perspectives," *Studia Islamica* 69 (1989): 95–119, 113–114.

73. Jahangir and Chidrup, Paris, Musée national des arts asiatiques Guimet, accession 85EE1944; reproduced in Thackston (trans.), *Jahangirnama,* 312. Compare this with the painting in the National Gallery of Australia, Gayer-Anderson Gift, accession 91.1360; reproduced in S. A. A. Rizvi, "Mughal Paintings in the Australian National Library," *Hemisphere* 14 (March 1970): 18–25, 23.

74. For more on the allegorical dimensions of this motif in figural representations, see the chapter "Alexander's Cave," in Michael Barry, *Figurative Art in Medieval Islam and the Riddle of Bihzâd of Herât* (Paris: Flammarion, 2004), 253–385.

75. For the "museological character" of Jahangir's power, see Corinne Lefèvre, "Recovering a Missing Voice from Mughal India: The Imperial Discourse of Jahāngīr (r. 1605–1627) in His Memoirs," *Journal of the Economic and Social History of the Orient* 50.4 (2007): 452–489.

76. Painting of Akbar and Chidrup in the Arthur M. Sackler Museum of the Harvard Art Museums, accession 1937.20.1; reproduced in Kessler, "In the Company of the Enlightened," 24–25, 34–35 (fig. 3).

77. The *Yoga Vasishta* in question was translated into Persian by Nizam Panipati with the aide of two pandits. *Jog Basisht*, eds. Tara Chand and S. A. H. Abidi (Aligarh: Aligarh Muslim University, 1978).

78. *Yog Vashisht*, Chester Beatty Library, MS 5. For a detailed description of the manuscript and several reproductions from it, see Linda Leach, *Mughal and Other Indian Paintings from the Chester Beatty Library*, 2 vols. (London: Scorpion Cavendish, 1995), 1: 155–195. For confirmation that this manuscript was prepared for Akbar's use, though it carries a note in Jahangir's hand, see Heike Franke, "Akbar's Yogavāsiṣṭha in the Chester Beatty Library," *Zeitschrift Der Deutschen Morgenländischen Gesellschaft* 161.2 (2011): 359–375.

79. Jahangir, *Tuzuk*, 225; translation, 228–229.

80. See the two-volume illuminated translation in the Arthur M. Freer Gallery, Washington, DC, F1907.271.1–172 (vol. 1), F1907.271.173–346 (vol. 2). For further information, see John Seyller, *Workshop and Patron in Mughal India: The Freer Rāmāyaṇa and Other Illustrated Manuscripts of ʿAbd al-Raḥīm* (Washington, DC: Artibus Asiae, 1999). For more on Rahim's artistic and literary patronage, see Sunil Sharma, *Mughal Arcadia: Persian Literature in an Indian Court* (Cambridge, MA: Harvard University Press, 2017), 47–49; Corinne Lefèvre, "The Court of Abd-ur-Rahim Khan-i Khanan as a Bridge between Iranian and Indian Cultural Traditions," in *Culture and Circulation: Literature in Motion in Early Modern India*, eds. Thomas de Bruijn and Allison Busch (Leiden: Brill, 2014): 75–106. See also the portrait of Abd-ur-Rahim held in the Yale University Art Gallery, 1983.94.11, discussed by Kishwar Rizvi, "Introduction," in *Affect, Emotion, and Subjectivity in Early Modern Muslim Empires: New Studies in Ottoman, Safavid, and Mughal Art and Culture*, ed. Kishwar Rizvi (Leiden: Brill, 2018), 1–20, 11–12.

81. Qazwini, *Badshah-nama*, Raza Rampur Library, MS 2091/495m, fol. 80b.

82. Corinne Lefèvre, "Europe–Mughal India–Muslim Asia: Circulation of Political Ideas and Instruments in Early Modern Times," in *Structures on the Move: Technologies of Governance in Transcultural Encounter*, eds. A. Flüchter and S. Richter (Heidelberg: Springer, 2012), 127–145, 141–142.

83. Jahangir, *Tuzuk*, 283; translation, 282. See also the birth commemorated in Sujan Rai Bhandari (d. 1689), *Khulasat-ut-tawarikh*, ed. Muhammad Irshad Alam (published PhD diss., Aligarh Muslim University, 2013), 635–636.

84. Mutamad Khan, *Iqbal-nama*, 129–130.

85. Jahangir, *Tuzuk*, 317; translation, 313.

86. See Mirza Muhammad Inayat Khan (d. 1670), *Mulakhkhas-i Shahjahan-nama*, ed. Jamil-ur-Rahman (Delhi: Rayzani-i Farhangi-i Jumhuri-i Islami-i Iran, 2009), 53; translated as *The Shah Jahan nama of 'Inayat Khan: An Abridged History of the Mughal Emperor Shah Jahan*, trans. Wayne Edison Begley and Ziya-ud-Din A. Desai (Delhi: Oxford University Press, 1990), 9.

87. See Art and History Trust, Arthur M. Sackler Gallery, Smithsonian Institution, accession LTS 1995.2.98. Printed in Thackston (trans.), *Jahangirnama*, 336.

88. Painting of Young Dara Shukoh, Metropolitan Museum of Art, accession 55.121.10.36; reproduced in Stuart Cary Welch et al., *The Emperors' Album: Images of Mughal India* (New York: The Metropolitan Museum of Art, 1987), 194–195, plate 55.

89. Victoria and Albert Museum, IS. 90–1965. Printed in Rosemary Crill et al., *Arts of India: 1550–1900* (London: Victoria and Albert Publications, 1990), 93, no. 70.

90. Jahangir, *Tuzuk,* 174; translation, 184.

91. For the later continuation of these associations within the Qajar Iran, see Afsaneh Najmabadi, *Women with Mustaches and Men without Beards: Gender and Sexual Anxieties of Iranian Modernity* (Berkeley: University of California Press, 2005), 11–25.

92. See André Wink, *Akbar* (Oxford: Oneworld, 2009), 109–110.

93. Jahangir, *Tuzuk,* 318–319; translation, 314–316.

94. Scott Kugle "'Abd al-Ḥaqq Dihlawī, an Accidental Revivalist: Knowledge and Power in the Passage from Delhi to Makka," *Journal of Islamic Studies* 19.2 (2008): 196–246, 205.

95. Abd-ul-Haqq Dihlawi, *Akhbar-ul-akhyar fi asrar-ul-abrar*, ed. Alim Ashraf Khan (Tehran: Danishgah-i Tihran, 2005), 595–616. For a persuasive challenge to the commonly held notion that Abd-ul-Haqq was critical of Akbar's "heretical" innovations, see Kugle, "'Abd al-Ḥaqq," 209–210, 212.

96. For an overview of this text, see Bruce Lawrence, "*Akbār al-akyār*," *Encyclopaedia Iranica*, ed. Ehsan Yarshater, 15 vols. (London: Routledge, 1982–), 1: 711–712.

97. Jahangir, *Tuzuk,* 320; translation, 316.

98. See Sushmita Banerjee, "Conceptualising the Past of the Muslim Community in the Sixteenth Century: A Prosopographical Study of the *Akhbār al-akhyār*," *The Indian Economic and Social History Review* 54.4 (2017): 423–456.

99. "*Maqsud-i ahl-i zauq zi zikr-i guzashtigan/tanbih-i ibrat ast chih miskin chih padshah,*" cited in Khaliq Ahmad Nizami Dihlavi, *Hayat-i Shaikh Abd-ul-Haqq* (Delhi: Nadwat-ul-Musannifin, 1964), 190; translated in Dihlavi, *On History and Historians of Medieval India* (New Delhi: Munshiram Manoharlal, 1983), 45. See also, Abd-ul-Haqq, *Risala-i nuriya-i sultaniya*, ed. Muhammad Salim Akhtar (Islamabad: Markaz-i Tahqiqat-i Farsi-i Iran va Pakistan, 1985).

100. For further information, see Yohanan Friedmann, *Shaykh Ahmad Sirhindi: An Outline of His Thought and a Study of His Image in the Eyes of Posterity* (Montreal: McGill University, 1971); J. G. J. ter Haar, *Follower and Heir of the Prophet: Shaykh Ahmad Sirhindi (1564–1624) as Mystic* (Leiden: Het Oosters Instituut, 1992).

101. Jahangir, "*Az maqam-i khalifa dar guzashta ba ali martabat-i uruj*," *Tuzuk,* 309; translation, 304. See Shaikh Ahmad Sirhindi, *Maktubat-i Imam-i Rabbani,* ed. Nur Ahmad, 3 vols. (Karachi: Educational Press, 1977), 23–30, 25–26, letter 11; selections translated as *The Revealed Grace: The Juristic Sufism of Ahmad Sirhindi (1564–1624),* trans. Arthur Buehler (Louisville, KY: Fons Vitae, 2011), 117–124, 119.

102. Jahangir, *Tuzuk,* 363–364; translation, 352–353.

103. Qazwini, *Padshah-nama,* fols. 89a–90a.

104. "*Zi mai pir dast-i tamanna kashid/na az tauba, az sharm-i muy-i safid,*" Abu Talib Kalim Kashani (d. 1652), *Masnawi-i Padshah-nama,* ed. Muhammad Yunus Jaffery (Delhi: Rayzani-i Farhangi-i Jumhuri-i Islami-i Iran, 2016), 225.

105. Kalim, *Masnawi,* 225–227.

2. Dynasty, 1622–1628

1. See Beni Prasad, *History of Jahangir* (London: Oxford University Press, 1922), 336–338, n. 4, with sources given. For the minority view that Khurram did not engineer Khusrau's death, see Henry Beveridge, "Sultan Khusrau," *Journal of the Royal Asiatic Society of Great Britain and Ireland* (1907): 597–609, 591–601; B. B. L. Srivastava, "The Fate of Khusrau," *Journal of Indian History* 42.2 (1964): 479–492.

2. For instance, see Nicholas Bangham's letter from Burhanpur to the Surat Factory in *The English Factories in India,* ed. William Foster, 13 vols. (Oxford: Clarendon Press, 1906–1927), 2: 30.

3. Nur-ud-Din Muhammad Jahangir, *Jahangir-nama (Tuzuk-i Jahangiri),* ed. Muhammad Hashim, (Tehran: Farhang, 1980/1), 390; translated as *The Jahangirnama: Memoirs of Jahangir, Emperor of India,* trans. Wheeler M. Thackston (New York: Oxford University Press, 1999), 376.

4. Muhammad Salih Kamboh, *Amal-i Salih,* ed. Ghulam Yazdani, 3 vols. (Lahore: Majlis-i Taraqqi-i Adab, 1958–1960), 1: 133.

5. William Methworld et al., two dispatches from Masulipatam to Surat, March 10, 1622, and June 30, 1622, in *English Factories,* 2: 59, 98.

6. Francisco Pelsaert, the chief Dutch factor in Agra, is associated with two manuscripts that give a description of Khusrau's murder, offering long and short versions: National Archives of The Hague, MSS VOC 4905 and 4906, respectively. The long version is preserved in the *Kroniek,* an anonymous chronicle of Mughal rule that extends to February 1627. The haphazard collection of historical accounts and documents is based on the writings of a *munshi* in the Dutch employ. While Pelsaert's name is associated with the text, his exact role in the redaction of the chronicle remains uncertain. This account contains more details of the murder, such as "*een astave ofte water-pott.*" A shorter version appears in Pelsaert's *Remonstrantie,* a memorandum of information on India for Dutch trading interests. Both manuscripts have been edited and published together in a single volume: Francisco

Pelsaert, *De Geschriften van Francisco Pelsaert over Mughal Indië, 1627: Kroniek en Remonstrantie,* eds. D. H. A. Kolff and H. W. Van Santen (The Hague: Nijhoff, 1979), 157–159, 320. An abbreviated Latin translation of the *Kroniek* appears in Joannes De Laet (d. 1649), *De imperio Magni Mogolis* (Leiden: Elzeviriania, 1631), 243, 266; translated as *The Empire of the Great Mogol,* trans. J. S. Hoyland (Bombay: D. B. Taraporevala Sons, 1928), 198–199, 219. The *Kroniek* was translated as *A Contemporary Dutch Chronicle of Mughal India,* trans. Brij Narain and Sri Rama Sharma (Calcutta: Susil Gupta, 1957), 53–55; Pelsaert's *Remonstrantie* was translated as *Jahangir's India. The Remonstrantie of Francisco Pelsaert,* trans. W. H. Moreland and P. Geyl (Cambridge: W. Heffer and Sons, 1925), 70–71. For more on the textual history, see the introduction to Kolff and Van Santen's Dutch edition (45–49).

7. Kamboh, *Amal-i Salih,* 1: 133.

8. Robert Hughes, *English Factories,* 2: 94, letter dated June 20, 1622.

9. Pietro Della Valle (d. 1652), *The Travels of Pietro della Valle in India: From the Old English Translation of 1664,* ed. Edward Grey (London: Hakluyt Society, 1892), iv.

10. For the embalming of Timur, see Sharaf-ud-Din Ali Yazdi (d. 1454), *Zafarnama,* ed. Mawlavi Muhammad Ilahdad, 2 vols. (Calcutta: Baptist Mission Press, 1887–1888), 2: 666. For a medical treatment of embalming, see Emilie Savage-Smith, "Attitudes Toward Dissection in Medieval Islam," *Journal of the History of Medicine and Allied Sciences* 50.1 (1995): 67–110, 78–79. For an early example of the Hanafi distaste for the transference of corpses over long distances, see Muhammad Sarakhsi (d. c. 1090), *Sharh al-Siyar al-kabir,* ed. Abu Abdullah Shafii, 5 vols. (Beirut: Dar-ul-Kutub il-Ilmiya, 1997), 1: 164.

11. Kamboh, *Amal-i Salih,* 1: 164. See Pelsaert, *Remonstrantie,* 320–321; translation, 71–72.

12. Abd al-Hamid Lahauri, *Padshah-nama,* eds. Kabir-ud-Din Ahmad, Abd-ur-Rahim, and William Nassau Lees, 2 vols. (Calcutta: Asiatic Society of Bengal, 1866–7), 1: 392.

13. Munis Faruqui, *The Princes of the Mughal Empire, 1504–1719* (Cambridge: Cambridge University Press, 2012), 77; Stephen Blake, *Time in Early Modern Islam: Calendar, Ceremony, and Chronology* (Cambridge: Cambridge University Press, 2017), 101.

14. Compare this to Khurram's ceremony described in Fergus Nicoll, *Shah Jahan: The Rise and Fall of the Mughal Emperor* (London: Haus, 2009), 28. See also Binode Kumar Sahay, *Education and Learning under the Great Mughals, 1526–1707 A.D.* (Bombay: New Literature, 1968), 7–8.

15. For classical juridical attitudes about teaching children Islamic norms, see Avner Gil'adi, *Children of Islam: Concepts of Childhood in Medieval Muslim Society* (London: Macmillan, 1992), 42–67.

16. Jahangir, *Tuzuk,* 372; translation, 369; Mutamad Khan, *Iqbal-nama,* 187.

17. Jahangir, *Tuzuk,* 390; translation, 376.

18. Appendix added by eighteenth-century historian Muhammad Hadi Kamwar Khan in Jahangir, *Tuzuk,* 466; translation 423.

19. Jahangir, *Tuzuk,* 391; translation, 377.

20. Jahangir, *Tuzuk*, 392; translation, 378.
21. Mutamad Khan, *Ahwal-i Shahzadagi-i Shah Jahan*, British Library MS Or. 3271, fols. 46–138, fols. 96a–b; also cited in Nicoll, *Shah Jahan*, 122. Nicoll, however, seems to use a different pagination system.
22. Jahangir, *Tuzuk*, 393–394; translation, 379.
23. Jahangir, *Tuzuk*, 403; translation, 387. See also *Kroniek*, 231; translation, 92.
24. Jahangir, *Tuzuk*, 401–402; translation, 386.
25. Syed Moinul Haq, "An Unpublished Letter of Jahangir Addressed to Prince Khurram," *Journal of the Pakistan Historical Society* 2.4 (1954): 302–311, 302–303. Moinul Haq makes a case for the letter's authenticity, which is found in an unpublished manuscript of *insha* copied in 1819, entitled *Majmua-i maktubat*, originally compiled by a certain Dud-Raj. The letter, however, may well be spurious. I have in some cases adapted Haq's translations here.
26. Mutamad Khan, *Iqbal-nama*, 193.
27. Mutamad Khan, *Iqbal-nama*, 194.
28. Letter from Shah Abbas in Jahangir, *Tuzuk*, 397–398; translation, 383–384.
29. Mutamad Khan, *Iqbal-nama*, 198.
30. Jahangir, *Tuzuk*, 407; translation, 391–393.
31. On the Mughal practice of traveling through India as a means of "ruling India," see Jos Gommans, *Mughal Warfare, Indian Frontiers and High Roads to Empire, 1500–1700* (London: Routledge, 2002), 99.
32. These sources include the *Amarkavya Vanshavali*. For further information, see Gopi Nath Sharma, *Mewar and the Mughal Emperors, 1526–1707 AD* (Agra: Shiva Lal Agarwala, 1954), 144n11.
33. For doubt cast on this claim, see Giles Tillotson, *The Rajput Palaces: The Development of an Architectural Style, 1450–1750* (Delhi: Oxford University Press, 1999), 116–117.
34. Gopi Nath Sharma, *Mewar and the Mughal Emperors*, 144–146. The turban said to belong to Khurram is on display at the City Palace Government Museum of Udaipur.
35. Jahangir, *Tuzuk*, 424; translation, 407.
36. Jahangir, *Tuzuk*, 424–425; translation, 407.
37. Mutamad Khan, *Iqbal-nama*, 215; Jahangir, *Tuzuk*, 432; translation, 414.
38. Thomas Mills and John Dod, "From Masulipatam to Surat," November 12, 1623, *English Factories*, 2: 314.
39. Mutamad Khan, *Iqbal-nama*, 217; Jahangir, *Tuzuk*, 437; translation, 419.
40. For the seminal study on the Islamization of Bengal, see Richard Eaton, *The Rise of Islam and the Bengal Frontier, 1204–1760* (Berkeley: University of California Press, 1993).
41. On nose piercing in the Indian context, see Narendra Nath Bhattacharyya, *Indian Puberty Rites* (Calcutta: Indian Studies, 1968), 45.
42. For Shitab Khan in a broader discussion of imperial discipleship, see John Richards, *The Mughal Empire* (Cambridge: Cambridge University Press, 1993), 108.
43. Ali Anooshahr examines how Shitab Khan negotiated his tricky position of being the emperor's servant, as well as that of Jahangir's rebel son, Khurram. See Ali Anooshahr, "No Man Can Serve Two Masters: Conflicting Loyalties in

Bengal during Shah Jahan's Rebellion of 1624" in Ebba Koch with Ali Anooshahr (eds.), *The Mughal Empire from Jahangir to Shah Jahan: Art, Architecture, Politics, Law and Literature*, Mumbai: The Marg Foundation, Vol. 70 Nos. 2 & 3, (December 2018-March 2019), 54–63. I am grateful to Ali Anooshahr for sharing a pre-publication version of this article with me.

44. Shitab Khan Mirza Nathan Ala-ud-Din Isfahani (fl. 1624), Bibliothèque nationale de France, Paris, MS Persan suppl. 252. Translated as *Bahāristān-i-Ghaybī: A History of the Mughal Wars in Assam, Cooch Behar, Bengal, Bihar and Orissa during the Reigns of Jahāngīr and Shāhjahān*, 2 vols., trans. Moayyidul Islam Borah and Suryya Kumar Bhuyan (Gauhati, Assam: Narayani Handiqui Historical Institute, 1936), 2: 691.

45. Shitab Khan, *Baharistan*, fols. 306b–307a; translation, 2: 728.

46. Shitab Khan, *Baharistan*, fol. 308b; translation, 2: 733.

47. Shitab Khan, *Baharistan*, fols. 309a–309b; translation, 2: 735.

48. Ghulam Husain Salim Zaidpuri (d. 1765), *Riyazu-s-Salāṭīn: A History of Bengal*, trans. Abd-us-Salam (Calcutta: The Asiatic Society, 1902), 198–199.

49. Shitab Khan, *Baharistan*, fol. 319a; translation, 2: 762.

50. Shitab Khan, *Baharistan*, fol. 309b; translation, 2: 735–736.

51. Jawhar Aftabchi, *Tazkirat-ul-vaqiat* in *Three Memoirs of Humáyun*, ed. and trans. Wheeler Thackston (Costa Mesa, CA: Mazda Publishers, 2009), 127 (Persian); 111 (translation).

52. Mirza Nathan, *Baharistan*, fol. 319b; translation, 2: 763.

53. Mirza Nathan, *Baharistan*, fol. 320a; translation, 2: 764. Nawab Shahnawaz Khan (d. 1758), *Maasir-ul-umara*, ed. Maulvi Abd-ur-Rahim, 2 vols. (Calcutta: Asiatic Society of Bengal, 1888), 1: 811.

54. Muhammad Hadi in Jahangir, *Tuzuk*, 469; translation, 425.

55. Mirza Nathan, *Baharistan*, translation, 2: 780.

56. Muhammad Hadi Kamwar Khan in Jahangir, *Tuzuk*, 479–480; translation, 434.

57. Findly, cited in note 58, argues that this was at Nur Jahan's instance.

58. "*Dar an asna Mahabat Khan fusun kard/hama-yi farman-i shah az dil birun kard*," Kami Shirazi, in *Waqai-uz-zaman (Fath nama-i Nur Jahan Begam): A Contemporary Account of Jahangir*, ed. and trans. W. H. Siddiqi (Rampur: Rampur Raza Library, 2003), 103. I have slightly adapted Siddiqi's translation. For a diametrically opposed view, see *Kroniek*, 200–202, 230, 238; translation, 75–77, cf. 91, 96. The "Indian historian" at the basis of the anonymous Dutch *Kroniek* was a partisan of Mahabat Khan. The entire episode features in Findly, *Nur Jahan*, 260–274, though she does not draw upon Shirazi. Munis Faruqui offers the most extensive analysis so far of Kami Shirazi's poem, and the poet's own positionality in the context of the erosion of Jahangir's power. See Munis Faruqui, "Erasure and Exaltation: The Coup of 1626 and the Crisis of Mughal Imperial Authority," in Ebba Koch with Ali Anooshahr (eds.), *Mughal Empire*, 64–81.

59. Thomas Roe, *The Embassy of Sir Thomas Roe to the Court of the Great Mogul*, ed. William Foster, 2 vols. (London: Hakluyt Society, 1899), 1: 262; also cited in Findly, *Nur Jahan*, 263.

60. Muhammad Hadi in Jahangir, *Tuzuk*, 485; translation, 438.

61. Kami Shirazi, *Waqai*, 107.

62. "*Wali chun waqt nazuk bud an dam/nakard izhar shah az besh w-az kam*," Kami Shirazi, *Waqai*, 129.

63. Kami Shirazi, *Waqai*, 137.

64. "*Pas an kih az ghazab chun sher-i ghurran/rawan shud fil-i Begam ru ba maidan*," Kami Shirazi, *Waqai*, 158–159. I have altered Siddiqi's translation here.

65. Kami Shirazi, *Waqai*, 153.

66. Mutamad Khan, *Iqbal-nama*, 273; Muhammad Hadi in Jahangir, *Tuzuk*, 479–480; translation, 434.

67. Account drawn from Muhammad Hadi in Jahangir, *Tuzuk*, 494–495; translation, 445–446. For an account using Mutamad Khan's *Ahwal*, see also Nicoll, *Shah Jahan*, 144.

68. Mutamad Khan, *Iqbal-nama*, 273–274.

69. "*Kih hasti tu sharik-i man ba shahi*," Kami Shirazi, *Waqai*, 211. For a fresh and in-depth study of Nur Jahan, arguing that she should be seen as Jahangir's co-ruler in her own right see Ruby Lal, *Empress: The Astonishing Reign of Nur Jahan* (New York: W.W. Norton, 2018).

70. Mutamad Khan, *Iqbal-nama*, 273–274.

71. Muhammad Hadi in Jahangir, *Tuzuk*, 496; translation, 447–448.

72. Faruqi, *Princes*, 254.

73. Muhammad Hadi in Jahangir, *Tuzuk*, 500; translation, 449–450.

74. Lahauri, *Badshah-nama*, 1: 393.

75. Muhammad Hadi in Jahangir, *Tuzuk*, 500; translation, 450, also Nicoll, *Shah Jahan*, 144.

76. Muhammad Hadi in Jahangir, *Tuzuk*, 499; translation, 448. Cf. *Kroniek*, 216–217; translation, 84.

77. Muhammad Hadi in Jahangir, *Tuzuk*, 505; translation, 453.

78. William Foster, *Early Travels in India, 1583–1619* (London: Oxford University Press, 1921), 243.

79. Muhammad Hadi in Jahangir, *Tuzuk*, 501; translation, 450.

80. The Arabic term given is *da-uth-thalab*, "the ailment of the fox," from the Greek *alopecia*. Mutamad Khan, *Iqbal-nama*, 291–292; Muhammad Hadi in Jahangir, *Tuzuk*, 508; translation, 455–456. For the identification with syphilis (*atishak*), see Shahnawaz Khan, *Maasir*, 1: 155.

81. Muhammad Hadi in Jahangir, *Tuzuk*, 509; translation, 456. See also the description of Jahangir's death in *Kroniek*, 226–227; translation, 89.

82. Mutamad Khan, *Iqbal-nama*, 297–298; Qazwini, *Badshah-nama*, British Library, MS Or. 173, fol. 113b.

83. Qazwini, *Badshah-nama*, fol. 115b.

84. The above account draws on Qazwini, *Badshah-nama*, fols. 116a–116b; Abd-ul-Hamid Lahori (d. 1654), *Badshah-nama*, ed. Maulvi Kabir-ud-Din Ahmad, Maulvi Abd-ur-Rahmin, and W. Nassau Lees, 3 vols. (Calcutta: Bibliotheca Indica, 1867–1872), 1: 74–75; Mutamed Khan, *Iqbal-nama*, 296–297; Muhammad Hadi in Jahangir, *Tuzuk*, 511; translation, 458.

85. *A Descriptive List of Farmans, Manshurs, and Nishans addressed by the Imperial Mughals to the Princes of Rajasthan*, ed. and trans. Nathu Ram Khadgawat (Bikaner: Directorate of Archives, Rajasthan, 1962); translation, 69, no. 63. Also, Sayyid Akbarali Ibrahimali Tirmizi, *Mughal Documents*, 2 vols. (New Delhi: Manohar, 1989–1995), 1: 137.

86. Mutamad Khan, *Iqbal-nama*, 303.

87. Mutamad Khan, *Iqbal-nama*, 303; also Muhammad Hadi in Jahangir, *Tuzuk*, 514; translation, 460.

88. "*Shudash lauh-i khatir zi andesha pak / k-az zada-yi sher shud besha pak*," Hadi Hasan quotes an excerpt from Qudsi's unpublished *Zafarnama-i Shahjahani* in *Mughal Poetry: Its Cultural and Historical Value* (Delhi: Aakar Books, 2008), 41–42. I have altered his translation.

89. Shahnawaz Khan, *Maasir*, 1: 812.

90. Munis Faruqui's *Princes* looks comprehensively at the princely institution in Mughal India, arguing that its pattern of open-ended succession was a source of strength for the empire.

91. Shah-Jahan receives his three eldest sons and Asaf Khan during his accession ceremonies, Rajab 1, 1037 (March 7, 1628), Abd-ul-Hamid Lahori, *Padshahnama*, Royal Collection Trust, Royal Library, Windsor Castle, MS 1367, f. 50b; reproduced in Milo Cleveland Beach and Ebba Koch, *King of the World. The Padshahnama: An Imperial Mughal Manuscript, the Royal Library, Windsor Castle* (London: Thames and Hudson, 1997), plates 10–11.

3. Youth, 1628–1634

1. For a brief account of the Khan-i Khanan's architectural legacy in Burhanpur, see George Mitchell and Mark Zebrowski, *Architecture and Art of the Deccan Sultanates* (Cambridge: Cambridge University Press, 1999), 53. For Abd-ur-Rahim's circle of patronage, see Chhotubhai Ranchhodji, *'Abdu'r-Rahīm Khān-i-Khānān and His Literary Circle* (Ahmedabad: Gujarat University, 1966).

2. Mughal princes generally moved into their own quarters upon reaching their early teens. See Munis Faruqui, *Princes of the Mughal Empire* (Cambridge: Cambridge University Press, 2012), 70.

3. See Francisco Pelsaert, *Remonstrantie*, in *De Geschriften van Francisco Pelsaert over Mughal Indië, 1627: Kroniek en Remonstrantie* (The Hague: Nijhoff, 1979), 285; translated in *Jahangir's India, the Remonstrantie of Francisco Pelsaert*, trans. W. H. Moreland and P. Geyl (Cambridge: W. Heffer and Sons, 1925), 38.

4. Mirza Amin Qazwini, *Padshah-nama*, British Library, MS Or. 173, fol. 175a; Abd-ul-Hamid Lahori, *Badshah-nama*, ed. Maulvi Kabir-ud-Din Ahmad, Maulvi Abd-ur-Rahmin, and W. Nassau Lees, 3 vols. (Calcutta: Bibliotheca Indica, 1867–1872), 1: 259.

5. Fergus Nicoll, *Shah Jahan: The Rise and Fall of the Mughal Emperor* (London: Haus, 2009), 177.

6. Lahori, *Badshah-nama*, 1: 385.

7. Qazwini, *Padshah-nama*, fol. 233b. While my translation is independent, it resembles the one in *Taj Mahal: The Illumined Tomb: An Anthology of Seventeenth-Century Mughal and European Documentary Sources*, ed. and trans. Wayne Begley and Ziya-ud-Din Desai (Cambridge: Aga Khan Program for Islamic Architecture, 1989), 15.
8. Lahori, *Badshah-nama*, 1: 386.
9. Lahori, *Badshah-nama*, 1: 386–388.
10. Mumtaz Mahal, *Khulasa-i ahwal-i Bano Begam*, Harvard University, Houghton Library, MS Persian 90, fol. 8b.
11. Mumtaz Mahal, *Khulasa-i ahwal*, fol. 13a.
12. Sayyid Akbarali Ibrahimali Tirmizi, *Mughal Documents*, 2 vols. (New Delhi: Manohar, 1989–1995), 2: 54.
13. Qazwini, *Padshah-nama*, fol. 232b–233a.
14. Kalim, *Padshah-nama* in *Taj Mahal*, 34.
15. An imperial edict dated December 28, 1633, grants four properties to Jai Singh, *Taj Mahal*, 34, 169–171, and Tirmizi, *Mughal Documents*, 2: 53–54.
16. For instance, Jai Singh tried to hold up the transport to Agra of marble intended for the tomb's construction. See the imperial edict to Raja Jai Singh dated November 14, 1632, in Tirmizi, *Mughal Documents*, 2: 49.
17. Qazwini, *Padshah-nama*, fol. 240a. For extracts from the chronicles of Qazwini, Lahori, and Kamboh regarding the transport of Mumtaz Mahal's body and the initial foundations of the tomb, see *Taj Mahal*, 41–44.
18. See Begley and Desai's detailed discussion of the identifiable architects working on Mumtaz Mahal's mausoleum in *Taj Mahal*, xli–xlix. While Qazwini initially reported the tomb's projected cost of twenty lakhs, Kamboh, writing at the end of Shah Jahan's reign, provides the figure of fifty lakhs, which more accurately represents the actual cost.
19. The most comprehensive study of the tomb is Ebba Koch and Richard André Barraud, *The Complete Taj Mahal: And the Riverfront Gardens of Agra*, (London: Thames & Hudson, 2006).
20. Abd-ur-Rahman Chishti, *Mirat-ul-makhluqat*, Aligarh, MS 21/343, fol. 1b.
21. Abd-ur-Rahman Chishti, *Mirat*, fol. 3a.
22. Abd-ur-Rahman Chishti, *Mirat*, fol. 4a.
23. For translations of two treatises attributed to Muin-ud-Din Chishti, see Carl Ernst, "Two Versions of a Persian Text on Yoga and Cosmology," in *Sufi Meditation and Contemplation: Timeless Wisdom from Mughal India*, ed. Scott Kugle (New Lebanon, NY: Omega Publications, 2012), 167–169, 181–192.
24. Simon Digby, "Abd al-Quddus Gangohi (1456–1537 A.D.): The Personality and Attitudes of a Medieval Indian Sufi," *Medieval India: A Miscellany* 3 (1975): 1–66, 37.
25. Digby, "'Abd al-Quddus," 38–50.
26. For details of Khwaja Hasan's ties to Mirza Hakim, see Munis Faruqui, "The Forgotten Prince: Mirza Hakim and the Formation of the Mughal Empire in India," *Journal of the Economic and Social History of the Orient* 48.4 (2005): 487–523.

27. David Damrel, "The 'Naqshbandi Reaction' Reconsidered," in *Beyond Turk and Hindu: Rethinking Religious Identities in South Asia*, eds. David Gilmartin and Bruce Lawrence (Gainesville: University Press of Florida, 2000), 176–198, 185. See also Arthur Buehler, *Sufi Heirs of the Prophet: The Indian Naqshbandiyya and the Rise of the Mediating Sufi Shaykh* (Columbia: University of South Carolina Press, 1997).

28. Digby, "'Abd al-Quddus," 33, 36.

29. Buehler, *Sufi Heirs*, 68.

30. Muhammad Masum, *Maktubat*, lithograph (Karachi: Lala Muhammad Khan, n.d.), 170, letter 54.

31. Muhammad Masum, *Maktubat*, 36, letter 11.

32. Saiyid Athar Abbas Rizvi, *A History of Sufism in India*, 2 vols. (New Delhi: Munshiram Manoharlal, 1978–1983), 2: 288.

33. Abd-ur-Rahman Chishti, *Mirat al-Asrar*, fol. 508a. For a broader look at this work, and at Abd-ur-Rahman Chishti's relationship with the court, see Muzaffar Alam, "The Debate Within: A Sufi Critique of Religious Law, Tasawwuf and Politics in Mughal India," *South Asian History & Culture* 2 (2011): 138–59.

34. Mirza Muhammad Tahir Inayat Khan (d. 1670), *Mulakhkhas-i Shahjahan-nama*, ed. Jamil-ur-Rahman (Delhi: Rayzani-i Farhangi-i Jumhuri-i Islami-i Iran, 2009), 89.

35. Arthur Buehler, *Revealed Grace: The Juristic Sufism of Ahmad Sirhindi (1564–1624)* (Louisville, KY: Fons Vitae, 2012), 51.

36. Rizvi, *History of Sufism*, 2: 288–289.

37. Qazwini, *Padshah-nama*, fol. 260a.

38. For a redaction of Umar's letter and its use in formative Hanafi law, see Abu Yusuf (d. 798), *Kitab-ul-kharaj* (Beirut: Dar-ul-Marifa, 1979), 140–141. For a treatment of the so-called covenant, see A. S. Tritton, *The Caliphs and Their Non-Muslim Subjects* (London: Cass, 1930), 5–17, 37–38. For the early Arabic accounts on Umar, see also Heribert Busse, "'Omar b. al-Ḥaṭṭāb in Jerusalem," *Jerusalem Studies in Arabic and Islam* 5 (1984): 73–119.

39. Tirmizi, *Mughal Documents*, 2: 52–53, §§ 48 and 53.

40. The text introducing the album is printed in Dara Shukoh, "Muraqqa-i Dara Shukoh aur uska Muqaddima," ed. Muhammad Abdullah Chaghtai, *Oriental College Magazine* (Lahore) 13.3 (1937): 97–103. The album is held in the British Library, Add. Or. 3129. For an inventory of the album, see Toby Falk and Mildred Archer, *Indian Miniatures in the India Office Library* (London: Sotheby Parke Bernet, 1981), 72–81; see also Milo Beach, *The Grand Mogul: Imperial Painting in India, 1600–1660* (Williamstown, MA: Sterling and Francine Clark Art Institute, 1978), 77.

41. For a description of the dispersed *muraqqa* album dated 1611–1612, made for Prince Khurram before his accession as Shah Jahan, see Beach, *Grand Mogul*, 74. It is also possible that Dara Shukoh's siblings compiled albums that did not survive the ravages of time or have suffered neglect. An early twentieth-century source suggests that an album sponsored by Aurangzeb as a prince was housed in the collection of the Murshidabad nawabs. See Purna Chundra

Majumdar, *The musnud of Murshidabad (1704–1904) being a synopsis of the
history of Murshidabad for the last two centuries, to which are appended
notes of places and objects of interest at Murshidabad* (Murshidabad: Saroday
Ray, 1905), 83. As the library is currently closed to researchers, it has not been
possible to verify the manuscript's existence.

42. Stuart Cary Welch, *Emperor's Album: Images of Mughal India* (New York:
Metropolitan Museum of Art, 1987), 18–19.

43. Abu-l-Fazl (d. 1602), *Ain-i Akbari*, ed. Heinrich Blochmann, 2 vols. (Calcutta:
Calcutta Baptist Mission Press, 1872–1877), 1: 111–112; translated as *The
Ā'īn-i Akbarī*, trans. Heinrich Blochmann, ed. Douglas Craven Phillott, 3 vols.
(Calcutta: Asiatic Society of Bengal, 1927–1949), 1: 103, §34.

44. Dara Shukoh, "Muraqqa," 101.

45. See, for example, Shah Quli Khalifa Muhrdar (d. 1558), "Shah Tahmasp Album
İÜK F.1422," in Wheeler M. Thackston, *Album Prefaces and Other Documents
on the History of Calligraphers and Painters* (Leiden: Brill, 2001), 3.

46. Dara Shukoh, "Muraqqa," 102.

47. I follow the new dating of the album advanced by John Seyller, cited in Jeremiah P. Losty, "Dating the Dara Shikoh Album: The Floral Evidence," in *The
Mughal Empire from Jahangir to Shah Jahan: Art, Architecture, Politics, Law
and Literature*, eds. Ebba Koch and Ali Anooshahr (Mumbai: Marg Foundation, 2019), 246–87, 246n1.

48. Losty contends that Khurram and Salim's albums also had "relatively simple"
contents. Losty, "Dara Shikoh Album," 247.

49. According to Falk and Archer, "the entire contents are of a serene and feminine nature," *Indian Miniatures*, 73.

50. Dara Shukoh Album, British Library, Add. Or. 3129, fol. 2a.

51. See Jeremiah P. Losty, "The Dara Shikoh Album: A Reinterpretation," unpublished article, available on Academia.edu, delivered at the Institute for Iranian
Studies of the Austrian Academy of Sciences, Vienna, "The Mughal Empire
Under Shah Jahan (1628–58): New Trends of Research, Vienna" (May 2014),
1–30, 12–17.

52. For Chitarman, see Losty, "A Reinterpretation," 11–12.

53. For these interpretations, see Losty, "A Reinterpretation," 22–26.

54. Muhammad Tabatabai, *Shahjahan-nama*, ed. Muhammad Yunus Jaffery (Delhi:
Rayzani-i Farhangi-i Jumhuri-i Islami-i Iran, 2009), 80.

55. Peter Mundy (d. 1667), *Travels*, ed. Richard Carnac Temple, 4 vols. (London:
Hakluyt Society, 1907–1925), 2: 207–208.

56. For a reconstructed map of Agra's waterfront mansions in relation to the fort
and Mumtaz Mahal's mausoleum, see Ebba Koch, *Complete Taj Mahal*,
30–31.

57. Tabatabai, *Shahjahan-nama*, 82.

58. Inayat Khan, *Mulakhkhas*, 148.

59. Tabatabai, *Shahjahan-nama*, 97.

60. Lahori, *Badshah-nama*, 1: 453–454.

61. Ebba Koch, *Mughal Art and Imperial Ideology* (Delhi: Oxford University Press,
2001), 229–231.

62. Tabatabai, *Shahjahan-nama*, 96.

63. Lahori, *Padshah-nama*, Royal Collection Trust, Windsor Castle, RCIN 1005025.v (fol. 120b) and RCIN 1005025.w (fol. 121a).

64. Tabatabai, *Shahjahan-nama*, 97.

65. Francisco Pelsaert, *Remonstrantie*, 248; translation, 3; Joannes De Laet, *De imperio Magni Mogolis* (Leiden: Elzeviriania, 1631), 43–44; translated as *The Empire of the Great Mogol*, trans. J. S. Hoyland (Bombay: D. B. Taraporevala Sons, 1928), 39–40n51.

66. Tabatabai, *Shahjahan-nama*, 98.

67. Inayat Khan, *Mulakhkhas*, 146.

68. Tabatabai, *Shahjahan-nama*, 98–99.

69. Inayat Khan, *Mulakhkhas*, 146

70. Inayat Khan, *Mulakhkhas*, 147.

71. Tabatabai, *Shahjahan-nama*, 100.

72. Tabatabai, *Shahjahan-nama*, 114.

73. Tabatabai, *Shahjahan-nama*, 144.

74. This description is drawn from the illustration of the event in Lahori, *Padshah-nama*, Royal Collection, Windsor Castle, MS 1367, fol.134a; reproduced in Milo Cleveland Beach and Ebba Koch, *King of the World. The Padshahnama: An Imperial Mughal Manuscript, the Royal Library, Windsor Castle* (London: Thames and Hudson, 1997), plate 29.

75. Tabatabai, *Shahjahan-nama*, 146–147.

76. Tabatabai, *Shahjahan-nama*, 148.

77. Cited in note 74 above.

78. Ascribed to Hamid-ud-Din Khan (fl. 1660), *Ahkam-i Alamgiri*, ed. Jadunath Sarkar, 2nd ed. (Calcutta: Sarkar and Sons, 1926), 1–2; translated as *Anecdotes of Aurangzib*, trans. Jadunath Sarkar (Calcutta: Sarkar and Sons, 1912), 23–24.

79. "*Az an rakhna k-az naiza shud dar sarash/birun raft masti kih bud dar sarash,*" Tabatabai, *Shahjahan-nama*, 152.

80. "*Chu nabuwad pasandida-yi purdilan/kih girad yaki ra do tan dar miyan//zi ruy-i muruwwat azu dast dasht/ba chang ham awurd, khweshish guzasht//ba taklif-i fitrat daleri namud/ba sinni kih taklif bar way nabud,*" Tabatabai, *Shahjahan-nama*, 152–153.

81. Alexander Dow (d. 1779), *History of Hindostan*, 3 vols., 3rd ed. (London: John Murray, 1792), 3: 158–159.

82. Qazwini, *Padshah-nama*, fol. 299b.

83. Qazwini, *Padshah-nama*, fol. 302a.

84. Lahori, *Badshah-nama*, 2: 3.

85. Lahori, *Badshah-nama*, 2: 9.

86. Lahori, *Badshah-nama*, 2: 10.

87. Dara Shukoh, *Sakinat-ul-auliya*, ed. Tara Chand and Muhammad Riza Jalali-Naini (Tehran: Muassasa-i Matbuati-i Ilmi, 1965), 48.

88. This is mentioned in a biographical note on the saint and not the main chronology of the court events, Lahori, *Badshah-nama*, 1: 329–331.

89. Dara Shukoh, *Sakina*, 49.

90. Lahori, *Badshah-nama*, 1: 330.
91. Lahori, *Badshah-nama*, 1: 331.
92. "*Ham khuda mi khwahi ham dunya-i dun/in khiyal ast o muhal ast o junun*," Dara Shukoh, *Sakina*, 50.
93. Lahori, *Badshah-nama*, 1: 65, 334.
94. Qazwini, *Padshah-nama*, fols. 333b–334a.
95. Dara Shukoh, *Sakina*, 51–52.
96. "*An Shah Jahan o ma do kas shah [o] gada/yak roz nishastim bar do takht-i huda//u bar takht-i shah jahani binishast/ma bar takht-i marifat-i zat-i khuda*," Tawakkul Beg Kulabi, *Nuskha-yi ahwal-i shahi*, British Library, MS Or. 3203, fol. 12a.
97. "*Panja dar panja-yi khuda daram/man chih parway-i Mustafa daram*," Tawakkul Beg, *Nuskha*, fol. 29a. This is also cited in Fatima Zehra Bilgrami, "A Controversial Verse of Mulla Shah Badakhshi (a Mahdar in Shahjahan's Court)," *Journal of the Pakistan Historical Society* 34.1 (1986): 26–32, 27. The author also draws on Tawakkul Beg's *Nuskha* in her book reconstructing the details of the various Qadiri banches in early modern India. See Fatima Zehra Bilgrami, *History of the Qadiri Order in India: 16th-18th Century* (Delhi: Idarah-i Adabiyat-i Delli, 2005).
98. Tawakkul Beg, *Nuskha*, fol. 29a.
99. Bakhtawar Khan, *Mirat-ul-alam*, 2: 442.
100. Rafat Mashood Bilgrami, *Religious and Quasi-religious Departments of the Mughal Period, 1556–1707* (Delhi: Munshiram Manoharlal, 1984), 48.
101. Tawakkul Beg, *Nuskha*, fol. 30b.
102. Tawakkul Beg, *Nuskha*, fol. 31a.

4. Discipleship, 1634–1642

1. Muhammad Tabatabai, *Shahjahan-nama*, ed. Muhammad Yunus Jaffery (Delhi: Rayzani-i Farhangi-i Jumhuri-i Islami-i Iran, 2009), 148.
2. Mirza Amin Qazwini, *Padshah-nama*, British Library, MS Or. 173, fols. 310b–311a.
3. "*Saba dar damanash zan mi khiramad/kih natawanad ba balayash baramad . . . dar in rah murgh natawanad paridan/ba miqraz-i par in rah ra buridan*," cited in Qazwini, *Padshah-nama*, fol. 311a.
4. For the place of Kashmir in the Indo-Persian literary imagery, see Sunil Sharma, *Mughal Arcadia: Persian Literature in an Indian Court* (Cambridge, MA: Harvard University Press, 2017), esp. 125–166, and Anubhuti Maurya, "Of Tulips and Daffodils: Kashmir Jannat Nazir as a Political Landscape in the Mughal Empire," *Economic and Political Weekly* 52, no. 15 (2017): 37–44.
5. Qazwini, *Padshah-nama*, fol. 309b.
6. Qazwini, *Padshah-nama*, fol. 314b.
7. Qazwini, *Padshah-nama*, fol. 316a.
8. Tawakkul Beg Kulabi, *Nuskha-i ahwal-i shahi*, British Library, MS Or. 3203, fol. 31a.

9. For the religious and intellectual world of Mubad Shah's teacher Azar Kaiwan, see Daniel Sheffield "The Language of Paradise in Safavid Iran: Speech and Cosmology in the Thought of Āẓar Kayvān and His Followers." In Alireza Korangy and Daniel Sheffield (eds.) *There's No Tapping around Philology*, (Wiesbaden: Otto Harrassowitz Verlag, 2014), 161–183.

10. *Dabistan-i mazahib*, ed. Rahim Raza-zada Malik, 2 vols. (Tehran: Kitabkhana-i Tahuri, 1983), 1: 155. Here the *Dabistan* notes that Banwali travelled to Kashmir in 1044 AH (1634/5). For further details on the *Dabistan* and debates surrounding its authorship, see M. Athar Ali, "Pursuing an Elusive Seeker of Universal Truth: The Identity and Environment of the Author of the *Dabistān-i Mazāhib*," *Journal of the Royal Asiatic Society* 9.3 (1999): 365–373; Aditya Behl, "Pages from the Book of Religions: Comparing Self and Other in Mughal India," in *Notes from a Mandala: Essays in Honor of Wendy Doniger*, ed. Laurie Patton and David Haberman (Newark: University of Delaware Press, 2010), 113–148. A discussion of the complex codicological tradition of the *Dabistan* is included in Irfan Habib, "A Fragmentary Exploration of an Indian Text on Religion and Sects: Notes on the Earlier Version of the *Dabistan-i Mazahib*," *Proceedings of the Indian History Congress* 61.1 (2000/1): 474–491.

11. Tawakkul Beg, *Nuskha*, fols. 64b–65a. For more on Banwalidas, see Supriya Gandhi, "The Persian Writings on Vedānta attributed to Banwālīdās Walī" (forthcoming).

12. Dara Shukoh, *Sakinat-ul-auliya*, ed. Tara Chand and Muhammad Reza Jalali-Naini (Tehran: Muassasa-i Matbuati-i Ilmi, 1965), 54.

13. Dara Shukoh, *Sakina*, 55; and Abd-ul-Hamid Lahori (d. 1654), *Badshah-nama*, eds. Maulvi Kabir-ud-Din Ahmad, Maulvi Abd-ur-Rahmin, and W. Nassau Lees, 3 vols. (Calcutta: Bibliotheca Indica, 1867–1872), 1: 329.

14. Dara Shukoh, *Sakina*, 54.

15. On the canonical tradition of cleansing the Prophet's heart as part of the apocalyptic *miraj*-cycle, see Frederick Colby, *Narrating Muḥammad's Night Journey, Tracing the Development of the Ibn ʿAbbās Ascension Discourse* (New York: State University of New York Press, 2008), 58 n. 28, 197; see also Brannon Wheeler, *Moses in the Quran and Islamic Exegesis* (London: Routledge, 2002), 119, 181–182, notes 1, 5.

16. For a range of early exegetical opinions concerning the first revelations to the Prophet on Lailat-ul-Qadr, see, Abu Jafar Tabari, *Jami-ul-bayan an tawil-il-Quran*, ed. Abdullah Turki, 26 vols. (Cairo: Dar Hijr, 2001), 24:542–544, Quran 97:1.

17. Dara Shukoh, *Sakina*, 55.

18. Qazwini, *Padshah-nama*, fol. 317b.

19. Sunil Sharma kindly shared with me his unpublished translation of the *Sahibiya*. All translations are my own, unless otherwise stated. See Jahanara, "Risala-i Sahibiya," ed. (with Urdu translation) Muhammad Aslam, *Journal of Research Society of Pakistan* 16 (1979): 78–110.

20. Tabatabai, *Shahjahan-nama*, 380.

21. On Jahangir's throne, see Catherine Asher, *Architecture of Mughal India* (Cambridge: Cambridge University Press, 1992), 101–102.

22. Tabatabai, *Shahjahan-nama*, 379–380.

23. "*Zihi farkhunda takht-i padshahi/kih shud saman ba tayid-i ilahi/falak rozi kih mikardash mukammal/zar-i khurshid ra bigudakht awwal,*" Tabatabai, *Shahjahan-nama*, 380. Also quoted in Hadi Hasan, *Mughal Poetry*, 58. I have adapted Hasan's translation.

24. See the introduction to the translation of Mirza Muhammad Tahir Inayat Khan, *The Shah Jahan Nama of 'Inayat Khan*. trans. A.R. Fuller, ed. W. E. Begley and Z. A. Desai (Delhi: Oxford University Press, 1990), xvii–xix.

25. Tabatabai, *Shahjahan-nama*, 396–397.

26. Lahori, *Padshah-nama*, 1: 121–122. For a description of the temple, see Heidi Pauwels, "A Tale of Two Temples: Mathura's Kesavadeva and Orchha's Caturbhujadeva," *South Asian History and Culture* 2.2 (2011): 278–299, esp. 282–284.

27. Asher, *Architecture*, 164.

28. Tabatabai, *Shahjahan-nama*, 429.

29. Tabatabai, *Shahjahan-nama*, 431.

30. Sayyid Akbarali Ibrahimali Tirmizi, *Mughal Documents*, 2 vol. (New Delhi: Manohar, 1989–1995), 2: 56.

31. Tirmizi, *Mughal Documents*, 2: 57.

32. Mirza Muhammad Tahir Inayat Khan, *Mulakhkhas-i Shahjahan-nama*, ed. Jamil-ur-Rahman (Delhi: Rayzani-i Farhangi-i Jumhuri-i Islami-i Iran, 2009), 280–281.

33. Jigar Mohammed, "Mughals and the Jammu Hill States (1556–1707)," *Proceedings of the Indian History Congress* 64 (2003): 450–465, 454. Jigar Mohammad erroneously dates Aurangzeb's marriage to 1644. It has to have occurred prior to 1639, as his son with Nawab Bai, Muhammad Sultan, was born then.

34. Lahori, *Padshah-nama*, 2: 101.

35. Dara Shukoh, *Safinat al-auliya*, lithograph (Lucknow: Nawal Kishore, 1872), 216.

36. My discussion of the books that Jahanara read is based on Jahanara's *Munis-ul-arwah*, an edition of which is included in Qamar Jahan Begam, *Princess Jahān Ārā Begam: Her Life and Works* (Karachi: S. M. Hamid Ali, 1991), 2–93.

37. For example, see Yedda Godard, "Un Album de portraits des princes timurides de l'Inde," *Athar-e Iran* 2 (1937): 179–281, fig. 19. The image, now located in the Gulistan Palace of Tehran, was painted by Govardhan. It features a princess and attendants studying with a bearded religious scholar. It is part of an album compiled by the Iranian ruler Nasir-ud-Din Shah from miniatures brought by Nadir Shah after his sack of Delhi in 1739.

38. Jahan Begam, *Princess*, 5. For Huri Khanam as Jahanara's "nurse" and her powerful status at the court, see the description in *The English Factories in India*, ed. William Foster, 13 vols. (Oxford: Clarendon Press, 1906–1927), 10: 74–3, letter to Surat from William Jesson, English factor in Agra, December 4, 1654.

39. Jahanara, *Sahibiya*, 98.

40. Jahanara, *Sahibiya*, 97–98. This quoted excerpt draws on Sunil Sharma's unpublished translation of the text.

41. For an examination of the omissions, with regard to Dara Shukoh's treatment of Qadiris, see Bruce Lawrence, "Biography and the Seventeenth Century Qadiriyya of North India," in *Islam and Indian Regions*, eds. Anna Dallapiccola and Stephanie Zingal-Avé Lallemant (Stuttgart: Steiner, 1993), 399–414.

42. Dara Shukoh, *Safina*, 12–13.

43. The title page has "*qabalahu Muhammad Dara Shukoh*" and the manuscript contains glosses in his hand. Dara Shukoh, *Safinat-ul-auliya*, Khuda Bakhsh Library, Patna, MS HL 200, fol. 1a.

44. Jahanara, *Munis-ul-arwah*, British Library, Or. 5637, fols. 122b–123a.

45. Lahori, *Padshah-nama*, 1: 10.

46. See, for instance, Stephen Blake, *Time in Early Modern Islam: Calendar, Ceremony, and Chronology in the Safavid, Mughal and Ottoman Empires* (Cambridge: Cambridge University Press, 2013), 131.

47. Ebba Koch, "The Hierarchical Principles of Shah-Jahani Painting," in *The King of the World. The Padshahnama: An Imperial Mughal Manuscript from the Royal Library, Windsor Castle*, ed. Milo Cleveland Beach and Ebba Koch (London: Thames and Hudson, 1997), 130–142, 132.

48. Jahanara, *Sahibiya*, 23. I have adapted Sunil Sharma's unpublished translation here.

49. Tawakkul Beg, *Nuskha*, fols. 38a–38b. Lahori corroborates the fact of their meeting in *Padshah-nama*, 2: 333.

50. Tawakkul Beg, *Nuskha*, fols. 39a–39b.

51. Tawakkul Beg, *Nuskha*, fol. 39b.

52. Tawakkul Beg, *Nuskha*, fols. 39b–40a. Dara Shukoh, *Sakina*, 5. Dara mentions a special spiritual experience on the night of Dhu-l-Hijja 12 (April 4).

53. Jahanara, *Sahibiya*, 101; Tawakkul Beg, *Nuskha*, fols. 41b–42a. Tawakkul Beg also refers to Jahanara's composition of the *Sahibiya* here. While some have doubted the *Sahibiya*'s authenticity, this corroborates Jahanara's authorship.

54. Album of Mughal portraits housed in Royal Collection Trust, Windsor Castle, RCIN 1005038.bb (fol. 54a). There is also a portrait of a standing Mulla Shah in the Musée national des arts asiatiques Guimet, MA 1651.

55. For a discussion of this particular portrait and a different interpretation of Jahanara's visual engagement with Mulla Shah's painted image, see Afshan Bokhari, "Masculine Modes of Female Subjectivity: The Case of Jahanara Begam," in *Speaking of the Self: Gender, Performance, and Autobiography in South Asia*, ed. Anshu Malhotra and Siobhan Lambert-Hurley (Durham, NC: Duke University Press, 2015), 166–202, 182–187.

56. Often, in paintings with both Mulla Shah and Miyan Mir, it is Miyan Mir, the older pir of the former, who uses the *yogapatta* or ascetic's sash.

57. Jahanara, *Sahibiya*, 103.

58. Jahanara, *Sahibiya*, 106–107. For the painting, see British Museum, 1949,0212,0.5. The tree here resembles a plane tree, commonly featured in Mughal paintings, rather than a mulberry tree.

59. Dara Shukoh, *Sakina*, 167–168.

60. Dara Shukoh, *Sakina*, 5.
61. "*Shah Jahan-i alam-i tan nist shahi/Shah-i Jahanast ku shuda shah jahan-i dil/Sahibqiran-i awwal o sani qarin-i chist/Dara Shukoh-i ma shuda sahibqiran-i dil*," Dara Shukoh, *Sakina*, 179–180.
62. Dara Shukoh, *Sakina*, 177.
63. Dara Shukoh, *Sakina*, 178.
64. Quoted in Bikrama Jit Hasrat, *Dārā Shikūh: Life and Works* (Calcutta: Visvabharati, 1953), 91.
65. Dara Shukoh, *Sakina*, 190.
66. Dara Shukoh, *Sakina*, 186.
67. Jahanara, *Sahibiya*, 109. The date is Ramazan 27, 1051 (December 30, 1641).
68. "*Baz chun jan o dilam betab hast/baz chun chashman-i man bekhwab hast//ishq-i Panjabam namuda be qarar/zankih naqsh-i dost dar Panjab hast//chun ba pa dakhil shawam dar shahr-i u/sakhtan az sar qadam zih adab hast//Kaaba-i man jannat-i Lahaur dan/sajda-i man suy-i an mihrab hast//ta kunam anja tawaf-i pir-i khwesh/jan-i be aram chun simab hast//Qadiri ra Kaaba Darapur shud/k-andar an bisyar fath-ul-bab hast*," Dara Shukoh, *Diwan*, ed. Ahmad Nabi Khan (Lahore: Research Society of Pakistan, 1969), 71–72, §41. A note by the editor states that according to one manuscript Darapur is glossed as the place in which Miyan Mir's tomb was located.
69. "*Chun khuda o sahib-i man pir hast/Kaaba-i man hazrat-i Kashmir hast/har kih Shah ra did Kaaba ra na just/dar nigah-i ruyash in tasir hast/daman-i Shah ra bigir ai Kaaba ro/Kaaba ra pas chun tu daman gir hast*," Dara Shukoh, *Divan*, 67. The word *khuda*, which in classical Persian literally means "lord," is also often used as an epithet for God.
70. Lahori, *Padshah-nama*, 1: 291.
71. Quran 8: 17. Dara Shukoh, *Sakina*, 185–186.
72. Jalal-ud-Din Suyuti (d. 1505) and Jalal-ud-Din Mahalli (d. 1459), *Tafsir-ul-Jalalain*, 3rd ed. (Beirut: Dar-ul-Khair, 2002),179. For more, see Tabari, *Jami*, 11:82–87.
73. Dara Shukoh, *Sakina*, 193.
74. Lahori, *Padshah-nama*, 292–295.
75. Lahori, *Padshah-nama*, 297.
76. Dara Shukoh, *Sakina*, 185–186.
77. Roger Savory, *Iran under the Safavids* (Cambridge: Cambridge University Press, 1980), 231.
78. Lahori, *Padshah-nama*, 301.
79. Lahori, *Padshah-nama*, 308.
80. Dara Shukoh, *Sakina*, 5–6.
81. Dara Shukoh, *Sakina*, 6. The prince refers to the Platonic and Sufi conception of the soul as a prisoner in the cage of the body.
82. Dara Shukoh, *Sakina*, 47.
83. Dara Shukoh, *Sakina*, 115.
84. For a critique of modern nationalist and reformist readings of Sirhindi, see Yohanan Friedmann, *Shaykh Ahmad Sirhindi: An Outline of His Thought and*

a Study of His Image in the Eyes of Posterity (New Delhi: Oxford University Press, 2001).

85. For a translation and analysis of this incident, see Carl Ernst, "Lives of Sufi Saints," in *Religions of India in Practice,* ed. Donald S. Lopez (Princeton, NJ: Princeton University Press, 1995), 495–512, 507–508.

86. Dara Shukoh, *Sakina,* 47–48.

87. Nur-ud-Din Muhammad Jahangir, *Jahangir-nama (Tuzuk-i Jahangiri),* ed. Muhammad Hashim (Tehran: Farhang, 1980/1), 325; translated as *The Jahangir-nama: Memoirs of Jahangir, Emperor of India,* trans. Wheeler M. Thackston (New York: Oxford University Press, 1999), 320.

5. The Chosen, 1642–1652

1. Catherine Asher, *Architecture of Mughal India* (Cambridge: Cambridge University Press, 1992), 212.

2. Abdul-Hamid Lahori, *Badshah-nama,* eds. Maulvi Kabir-ud-Din Ahmad, Maulvi Abd-ur-Rahim, and W. Nassau Lees, 3 vols. (Calcutta: Bibliotheca Indica, 1867–1872), 2: 346.

3. Tawakkul Beg Kulabi, *Nuskha-i ahwal-i shahi,* British Library, MS Or. 3203, fol. 48a.

4. Tawakkul Beg, *Nuskha,* fol. 48b. As Tawakkul Beg had earlier served under Shuja, he may have had a hand in the prince's entrance into Mulla Shah's order.

5. Tawakkul Beg, *Nuskha,* fol. 50a. For Mutaqid Khan's relation to Dara Shukoh's network and his closeness to Iraj Khan, a close associate of Dara, see Nawab Shahnawaz Khan, *Maasir-ul-umara,* ed. Maulvi Abd-ur-Rahim, 2 vols. (Calcuta: Asiatic Society of Bengal, 1888), 2: 268–272. For a discussion of the *khanazad* (house-born) imperial servants, see John Richards, "Norms of Comportment among Mughal Imperial Officers," in *Moral Conduct and Authority: The Place of Adab in South Asian Islam,* ed. Barbara Daly Metcalf (Berkeley: University of California Press, 1984), 255–289.

6. Tawakkul Beg, *Nuskha,* fol. 50b.

7. Tawakkul Beg, *Nuskha,* fols. 50b–51a.

8. For recent scholarship examining how Mughal emperors appropriated Sufi authority, see A. Azfar Moin, *The Millennial Sovereign: Sacred Kingship and Sainthood in Islam* (New York: Columbia University Press, 2012), 94–170; John Richards, *The Mughal Empire* (Cambridge: Cambridge University Press, 1993), 105.

9. Tawakkul Beg, *Nuskha,* fol. 52a.

10. Tawakkul Beg, *Nuskha,* fol. 50a.

11. On this custom, see Richards, "Norms of Comportment."

12. Lahori, *Badshah-nama,* 2: 363.

13. Lahori, *Badshah-nama,* 2: 363–364.

14. Tawakkul Beg, *Nuskha,* fols. 51a–51b.

15. Lahori, *Badshah-nama,* 2: 367–368.

16. Lahori, *Badshah-nama*, 2: 369.
17. Lahori, *Badshah-nama*, 2: 379–380.
18. Tawakkul Beg, *Nuskha*, fol. 52a.
19. Tawakkul Beg, *Nuskha*, fol. 52b.
20. Tawakkul Beg, *Nuskha*, fols. 52b–53a.
21. Lahori, *Badshah-nama*, 2: 376.
22. Mirza Muhammad Tahir Inayat Khan, *Mulakhkhas-i Shahjahan-nama*, ed. Jamil-ur-Rahman (Delhi: Rayzani-i Farhangi-i Jumhuri-i Islami-i Iran, 2009), 388; translated as *The Shah Jahan Nama of 'Inayat Khan*, trans. A. R. Fuller, eds. W. E. Begley and Z. A. Desai (Delhi: Oxford University Press, 1990), 313.
23. Lahori, *Badshah-nama*, 2: 397–398, 411 (on the Gujarat assignment).
24. Sipihr Shukoh was born on Shaban 11, 1054 AH (October 13, 1644), noted in Lahori, *Badshah-nama*, 388.
25. Lahori, *Badshah-nama*, 408–409.
26. Johann Albrecht von Mandelslo, *Des Hoch Edelgebornen Johan Albrecht von Mandelslo Morgenländische Reyse-Beschreibung* (Schleswig, Germany: Johan Holwein, 1658), 60–61; translated in *The Voyages and Travels of the Ambassadors sent by Frederick, Duke of Holstein . . . Whereto are added The Travels of John Albert de Mandelslo*, trans. John Davies, 2 vols. (London: Thomas Dring and John Starkey, 1662), 2: 30. See also Johann Albrecht von Mandelslo, *Voyage en Perse et en Inde de Johann Albrecht von Mandelslo, 1637–1640*, trans. Françoise de Valence (Paris: Chandeigne, 2008), 96–97, 240–241.
27. "*Qui de tout tems a fait profession d'une devotion affectée,*" Jean de Thévenot (d. 1667), *Les Voyages aux Indes Orientales*, ed. Françoise de Valence (Paris: Honoré Champion, 2008), 53–54; translated in *Indian Travels of Thevenot and Careri*, trans. Surendranath Sen (Delhi: National Archives of India, 1949), 13–14.
28. See chap. 3, 101.
29. Tawakkul Beg, *Nuskha*, fol. 53a.
30. Tawakkul Beg, *Nuskha*, fols. 53a–53b.
31. Tawakkul Beg, *Nuskha*, fols. 54a–54b.
32. See B. G. Gokhale, "Tobacco in Seventeenth-Century India," *Agricultural History* 48.4 (1974): 484–492.
33. Tawakkul Beg, *Nuskha*, fol. 54a.
34. Quran 9:36. See also Meir Jacob Kister, "'Rajab Is the Month of God': A Study in the Persistence of an Early Tradition," *Israel Oriental Studies* 1 (1971): 191–223.
35. Dara Shukoh, "*Risala-i Haqqnuma,*" in *Muntakhabat-i asar: Risala-i Haqqnuma, Majma-ul-bahrain, Upankihat Mundak*, ed. Muhammad Raza Jalali Naini (Tehran: Taban, 1956/7), 2–3.
36. Lahori, *Badshah-nama*, 2: 444.
37. Among Muhibbullah's many works are: the *Tarjumat-ul-kitab*, an Arabic commentary on the Quran, manuscripts of which are located in the British Library, MS India Office Islamic, 1369, and Maulana Azad Library, Tonk, MS 123/78; a Persian treatise outlining twenty-seven *manazir* for the Sufi seeker, the *Manazir-i akhass-ul-khawass*, ed. Hafiz Muhammad Tahir Ali (Santiniketan,

Bengal: Visva Bharati Research Publications, 1993); and an Arabic commentary on Ibn Arabi's *Fusus*, couched in the philosophical idiom of Avicennian Neoplatonism, *at-Taswiya bayn-al-ifada wa-l-qabul* (The Equivalence Between Giving and Receiving), translated in G. A. Lipton, *"The Equivalence" (Al-Taswiya) of Muhibb Allah Ilahabadi: Avicennan Neoplatonism and the School of Ibn 'Arabi in South Asia* (Saarbrücken, Germany: VDM Verlag Dr. Müller, 2009). In addition to Lipton, for a list of more of Muhibbullah's writings, see Yusuf Husain Khan, "Shah Muhibbullah of Allahabad and His Mystical Thought," *Islamic Culture* (Hyderabad) 34 (1964): 315–322, 318–319. See also the treatment of Muhibbullah in Shankar Nair, *Philosophy in Any Language: Interaction Between Arabic, Sanskrit and Persian Intellectual Cultures in Mughal South Asia* (PhD thesis, Harvard, 2014).

38. An epistolary correspondence between Muhibbullah and Abd-ur-Rahman can be found in the collected letters of Muhibbullah, *Maktubat-i Shaikh Muhibbullah Ilahabadi*, Aligarh Muslim University, Subhanallah collection, MS 297071/13.

39. First letter from Dara Shukoh to Muhibbullah, *Maktubat*, Staatsbibliothek, Berlin, MS Sprenger 1972, fols. 14b–15a (correspondence dated 1055/1645-6). The exchange is abbreviated in *Fayyaz-ul-qawanin*, British Library, MS Or. 9617, fols. 37a–39a. I am indebted to Carl Ernst, who kindly shared with me his unpublished paper, "Some Notes on the Correspondence between Dara Shikuh and Shah Muhibb Allah Allahabadi," originally presented at a conference of The Indian History and Culture Society, New Delhi, February, 1979. Here Ernst provides a useful summary of the codicological and bibliographic record of the epistolary exchange.

40. See chap. 4, 115.

41. First response from Muhibbullah to Dara Shukoh, *Maktubat*, Berlin MS, fols. 15a–31a; also recorded, without Dara Shukoh's epistles, in Muhibbullah, *Maktubat*, Aligarh MS, fols. 193b–213b.

42. Second letter from Dara Shukoh to Muhibbullah, *Maktubat*, Berlin MS, fol. 31a; see *Fayyaz*, fol. 39a. The key expression in the letter is *"wajdi kih muwafiq nayuftad ba-qaul-i khuda o rasul basi bihtar-i anast."* The line of verse quoted at the end of the passage runs: *"mara hech kitabi digar hawala makun/kih man haqiqat-i khud ra kitab midanam."*

43. Second response from Muhibbullah to Dara Shukoh, *Maktubat*, Berlin MS, fols. 31b–33b; and in Muhibbullah, *Maktubat*, Aligarh MS, fols. 214a–217b.

44. Lahori, *Badshah-nama*, 2: 543.

45. M. Athar Ali, "The Objectives behind the Mughal Expedition into Balkh and Badakhshan 1646–47," *Proceedings of the Indian History Congress* 29 (1967): 162–168.

46. On this title, which was used at various times by Timurid, Safavid, Ottoman, and Mughal dynasts, see Lisa Balabanlilar, "Lords of the Auspicious Conjunction: Turco-Mongol Imperial Identity on the Subcontinent," *Journal of World History* 18.1 (2007): 1–39; Corinne Lefèvre, "In the Name of the Fathers: Mughal Genealogical Strategies from Bābur to Shāh Jahān," *Religions of South Asia* 5.1/2 (2011): 409–442; Moin, *Millennial Sovereign*, 23–55; for its earlier

use, see also Naindeep Singh Chann, "Lord of the Auspicious Conjunction: Origins of the Ṣāḥib-Qirān," *Iran and the Caucasus* 13.1 (2009): 93–110.

47. Irfan Habib, "Timur in the Political Tradition and Historiography of Mughal India," *Proceedings of the Indian History Congress* 57 (1996): 289–303, esp. 296–299.

48. Ahmad Rabbani, "'Haran Munara' at Sheikhupura (Punjab) and Some Problems Connected with It," in *Armughan-i Ilmi: Professor Muhammad Shafi' Presentation Volume,* ed. S. M. Abdullah (Lahore: The Majlis-e-Armughan-e Ilmi, 1955), 181–199, p. 181.

49. Lahori, *Badshah-nama,* 2: 634. For the observation, on the other hand, that Dara's children were unwell rather than their mother, see Tawakkul Beg, *Nuskha,* fol. 54b.

50. Dara Shikoh Album, British Library, Add. Or. MS 3129.

51. Dara Shukoh, *Haqqnuma,* 3.

52. Dara Shukoh, *Haqqnuma,* 3–4.

53. "*Tu batin-i shar gar na-dani ba-khusus/w-ar ham na-kuni nazar tu bar naqd-i nusus//yak dan o ma-dan tu ghair-i u dar do jahan/in ast haqiqat-i Futuhat o Fusus,*" Dara Shukoh, *Haqqnuma,* 4. The translation of the verse is taken from the English translation of the *Haqqnuma* in Dara Shukoh, "The Compass of Truth," in *Sufi Meditation and Contemplation: Timeless Wisdom from Mughal India,* trans. Scott Kugle and Carl Ernst (New Lebanon, NY: Omega Publications, 2012), 129–164, 134.

54. Dara Shukoh, *Haqqnuma,* 4.

55. While Ibn Arabi puts forth a typology of three worlds, other Sufi thinkers such as Ala ud-Dawla Simnani present a fourfold division of the realms of existence, such as that depicted in the *Haqqnuma* and the *Majma-ul-bahrain.* See Jamal Elias, *Throne Carrier of God, The Life and Thought of 'Alā' Ad-Dawla As-Simnānī* (Albany: State University of New York Press, 1995), 61.

56. Dara Shukoh, *Haqqnuma,* 5–6.

57. Sayyid Murtaza died in 1661. The edition of the *Yoga Qalandar* is included in *Banglara Suphi Sahitya,* ed. Ahmad Sharif (Dhaka: Bangla Academy, 1969), 87–116. Another Bengali work treating yoga that appears to have drawn considerably on the *Yoga Qalandar* is the *Cari Mokamer Bhed,* attributed to Abd-ul-Hakim. This is the subject of a detailed study and translation by David Cashin, *Middle Bengali Sufi Literature and the Fakirs of Bengal* (Stockholm: Association of Oriental Studies, Stockholm University, 1995), 116–157.

58. Dara Shukoh, *Haqqnuma,* 9. I have used my own translation to more literally reflect the text, though it shares the phrase "gathers into unity" with Kugle and Ernst's translation, 144.

59. Dara Shukoh, *Haqqnuma,* 9–10.

60. Dara Shukoh, *Haqqnuma,* 13.

61. These are described, for instance, in the *Hathayogapradipika* (c. 1400), the *Shivasamhita* (c. 1300–1500), and the later *Gherandasamhita* (c. 1700).

62. Verses 5:36–37 and 5:42–43 in *The Shiva Samhita,* ed. and trans. James Mallinson (Woodstock, NY: YogaVidya, 2007), 112–113. See also a roughly sim-

ilar account in verses 5:73–76 of the *Gheranda Samhita,* trans. James Mallinson (Woodstock, NY: YogaVidya, 2004), 107–108. Craig Davis also notes this similarity. See Craig Davis, "The Yogic Exercises of the 17th-Century Sufis," in *Theory and Practice of Yoga: Essays in Honour of Gerald James Larson,* ed. Knut A. Jacobsen (Leiden: Brill, 2005), 303–317.

63. For instance, manuscript copies of the Arabic text on *hatha* yoga, the *Hauz-ul-hayat* (Pool of Nectar), are sometimes attributed to Ibn Arabi, while other manuscripts of a treatise on yoga claim the authorship of Muin-ud-Din Chishti. See Carl Ernst, "Two Versions of a Persian Text on Yoga and Cosmology Attributed to Shaykh Mu'in al-Din al-Chishti," *Elixir* 2 (2006): 69–76, 124–125.

64. Rajeev Kinra, *Writing Self, Writing Empire: Chandar Bhan Brahman and the Cultural World of the Indo-Persian State Secretary* (Oakland: University of California Press, 2015), 39.

65. For a discussion of Malajit Vedangaraya's lexicon entitled *Parasiprakasha,* see Sreeramula R. Sarma, "Persian-Sanskrit Lexica and the Dissemination of Islamic Astronomy and Astrology in India," in *Kayd: Studies in History of Mathematics, Astronomy and Astrology in Memory of David Pingree,* eds. Gherardo Gnoli and Antonio Panaino (Rome: Istituto Italiano per l'Africa e l'Oriente, 2009), 129–150; and more broadly, Audrey Truschke, "Defining the Other: An Intellectual History of Sanskrit Lexicons and Grammars of Persian," *Journal of Indian Philosophy* 40.6 (2012): 635–668.

66. Waris, *Padshah-nama,* British Library, I.O. Islamic 324, fol. 112a; Muhammad Waris, *Badshahnamah of Muhammad Waris,* trans. Ishrat Husain Ansari and Hamid Afaq Qureshi (Delhi: Idara-i Adabiyat-i Dehli, 2017), 132.

67. Kavindracharya Sarasvati, *Kavindrakalpalata,* ed. Lakshmikumari Chundavat (Jaipur: Puratattvanveshana Mandir, 1958), 4.

68. "*Indra sam, chandra sam, yogamen Macchindra sam,*" Kavindracharya, *Kavindrakalpalata,* 48.

69. "*Dara Nadir yaun vane, jaise Sitaramu / kiratimurati mati sumati, paramanand ke dham,*" Kavindracharya, *Kavindrakalpalata,* 54.

70. "*Aur aur kaha kahe, jagat vahe hai brahm,*" Kavindracharya, *Kavindrakalpalata,* 41.

71. See, for instance, Qazwini, *Padshah-nama,* fols. 64a, 145b, 233b, and 433b.

72. The collection is also known as *Tibb-i Dara-shukohi* (Medicine of Dara Shukoh). For a description of the work and its author, see Fabrizio Speziale, "The Encounter of Medical Traditions in Nūr al-Dīn Šīrāzī's "*Ilājāt-i Dārā Šikōhī,*" *eJournal of Indian Medicine* 3.1 (2010): 53–67.

73. Nur-ud-Din Shirazi, *Ilajat-i Dara-shukohi,* Majlis Library of Tehran, MS 6226, 3–6.

74. "*Ma mashrab-i sulh-i kull girifta,*" Shirazi, *Ilajat,* 6.

75. For more information, see Saiyid Athar Abbas Rizvi, "Dimensions of *Sulh-i kul* (Universal Peace) in Akbar's Reign and the Sufi Theory of Perfect Man," in *Akbar and His Age,* ed. Iqtidar Alam Khan (New Delhi: Northern Book Centre, 1999), 3–21; and Rajeev Kinra, "Handling Diversity with Absolute Civility: The

Global Historical Legacy of Mughal *Ṣulḥ-i Kull,*" *The Medieval History Journal* 16.2 (2013): 251–295.

76. For instance, the opening to Abu-l-Fazl, *Ain-i Akbari,* ed. Heinrich Blochmann, 2 vols. (Calcutta: Baptist Mission Press, 1872–1877), 1: 3; translated as *The Āʾin-i Akbarī,* trans. Heinrich Blochmann, ed. Douglas Craven Phillott, 3 vols. (Calcutta: Asiatic Society of Bengal, 1927–1949), 1: 4.

77. Abd-ul-Hayy Lakhnawi, *Nuzhat-ul-khawatirwa-bahjat-ul-masami wa-n-nawazir,* 8 vols. (Beirut: Dar Ibn Hazm, 1999), 5: 654, §671.

78. See for instance, Shirazi, *Ilajat,* 3, 1454ff, 1555ff. For more on the *Zakhira-i Iskandarani,* see chap. 6, 161.

79. Muhammad Salih Kamboh, *Amal-i Salih,* ed. Ghulam Yazdani, 3 vols. (Lahore: Majlis-i Taraqqi-i Adab, 1958–1960), 2: 493; Mohammad Quamruddin, *Life and Times of Prince Murād Bakhsh (1624–1661),* (Calcutta: M. Quamruddin, 1974), 73.

80. Salih Kamboh, *Amal-i Salih,* 2: 494; Quamruddin, *Life and Times,* 76.

81. Tawakkul Beg, *Nuskha,* fol. 56b.

82. Quamruddin, *Life and Times,* 84.

83. Arthur Neve, *Picturesque Kashmir* (London: Sands & Co., 1900), 100–101.

84. For instance, see Krishan Lal Kalla, *Kashmir Panorama* (Delhi: Raj Publications, 1997), 110.

85. There are some missing pieces in Tawakkul Beg's report, however. Engraved upon the gateway to the complex built at the lower spring, now known as *Chashma-i Shahi,* is a chronogram that dates it to 1042 AH (1632/3). This suggests that some sort of complex had been constructed there for Shah Jahan before his trip to Kashmir in 1634. In a further twist to this puzzle, another verse in the same inscription is thought to refer to Ali Mardan Khan, who entered Mughal service only in 1638. For details of the verses, see Anand Koul, *The Kashmiri Pandit* (Calcutta: Thacker and Spink, 1924), 136.

86. Neve, *Picturesque Kashmir,* 101.

87. Tawakkul Beg, *Nuskha,* fols. 56a–56b.

88. Tawakkul Beg, *Nuskha,* fol. 58a.

89. Tawakkul Beg, *Nuskha,* fol. 58b.

90. Tawakkul Beg, *Nuskha,* fol. 59b. Compare with the forty thousand rupees for mosque and twenty thousand for homes for faqirs in Inayat Khan, *Mulakh-khas,* 534–535; translation, 458.

91. For an account of the mosque's architectural features and inscriptions, see Afshan Bokhari, "The 'Light' of the Timuria: Jahan Ara Begam's Patronage, Piety, and Poetry in 17th-Century Mughal India," *Marg* 60.1 (2008): 52–61.

92. Tawakkul Beg, *Nuskha,* fol. 60b.

93. Mulla Shah, *Masnawiyat-i Mulla Shahi,* British Library, MS India Office Islamic, 578. Attached to the frontispiece is a tinted drawing (*nim qalam*) signed by the artist Miskin Muhammad, depicting the pir Mulla Shah in dialogue with his master, Miyan Mir. This was probably added later. It is quite possible that this manuscript was in Dara Shukoh's possession. As for his familiarity with Mulla Shah's poetry, it is evident in his quotations of excerpts from it in Dara Shukoh, *Sakina,* 195–204.

94. "*Ay tu Shah Jahan o tu Dara!/way tu Dara o tu Jahanara!//ba-tu Shah Ja-hani-yi qaim/ba-tu Daray-i jahan daim//hama Shah-i Jahaniyat, Dara/ba-tu Daray-i har Jahanara*," Mulla Shah, *Masnawiyat*, fol. 226b.

95. This painting is reproduced in Linda Leach, *Mughal and Other Indian Paintings from the Chester Beatty Library* (London: Scorpion, 1995), 447, fig. 3.58.

96. Tawakkul Beg, *Nuskha*, fol. 61b.

97. Tawakkul Beg, *Nuskha*, fol. 62a.

98. See Munshi Shaikh Abu-l-Fath Qabil Khan (d. 1662), "Correspondence with Jahanara Begam," *Adab-i Alamgiri*, ed. Abd-ul-Ghafur Chaudhari, 2 vols. (Lahore: Idara-i Tahqiqat-i Pakistan, 1971), 2: 800–832, 813–814, §11. On the quality of this edition, see Vincent Flynn, *An English Translation of the Ādāb-i-ʿĀlamgīrī. The Period before the War of Succession* (PhD thesis, Australian National University, 1974), xvi–xviii.

99. Qabil Khan, *Adab-i Alamgiri*, 2: 817–818, §17; also 824, §22.

100. Qabil Khan, *Adab-i Alamgiri*, 2: 815–817, §16.

101. Qabil Khan, *Adab-i Alamgiri*, 2: 818, §17. I use the first person in the quote from Aurangzeb's letter, though out of convention he uses the third person.

102. Qabil Khan, *Adab-i Alamgiri*, 2: 811–812, §9.

103. "*Az sang sakht Begam Sahib imarati/farzand-i nek-i Shah Jahan-i din panah*," Mulla Shah, *Kulliyat-i Mulla Shah*, Khuda Bakhsh Library, MS HL 688, fol. 129a.

104. "*Tarikh-i khanqah-i mara Khanqah-i Shah*," Mulla Shah, *Kulliyat*, fol. 129b. This chronogram actually corresponds to 1062 AH (1652/3), so either the mosque complex was finished after Shah Jahan's visit, or, which is not unlikely, the chronogram's date is imprecise.

105. Firdos Anwar, *Nobility Under the Mughals, 1628–58* (New Delhi: Manohar, 2001), 61–62.

106. Inayat Khan, *Mulakhkhas*, 536; translation, 459.

107. Inayat Khan, *Mulakhkhas*, 539–540; translation, 463.

108. For the gifts, see Qabil Khan, "Correspondence with Shah Jahan," *Adab-i Alamgiri*, 1: 21–253, §§10, 14, and 15; for Aurangzeb's efforts in procuring fruits, see §§5 and 22.

109. Qabil Khan, "Correspondence with Shah Jahan," *Adab-i Alamgiri*, 1: 21–25, 36–37, §10; Flynn, *An English Translation*, 34bis–35, §12. In many cases, I have modified Flynn's partial translation in my quotations.

110. Qabil Khan, *Adab-i Alamgiri*, 1: 37, §10; translation, 35, §12.

111. Qabil Khan, *Adab-i Alamgiri*, 1: 39, §16; translation, 50, §16.

112. Qabil Khan, *Adab-i Alamgiri*, 1: 65, §25; translation, 78, §25.

113. Qabil Khan, *Adab-i Alamgiri*, 86, §31; translation, 118, §31.

114. Qabil Khan, *Adab-i Alamgiri*, 90, §33; translation, 124, §33.

115. Qabil Khan, *Adab-i Alamgiri*, 96, §36; translation, 134–136, §36.

116. Qabil Khan, *Adab-i Alamgiri*, 98, §37; translation, 140–141, §37. For the proverb, see Inayatullah Shahrani, *Zarb-ul-masalha-yi Dari-yi Afghanistan* (Stockholm: Afghanistan Cultural Association, 2001), §5091.

6. Mission, 1652–1654

1. Munshi Shaikh Abu-l-Fath Qabil Khan, "Correspondence with Shah Jahan," *Adab-i Alamgiri*, ed. Abd-ul-Ghafur Chaudhari, 2 vols. (Lahore: Idara-i Tahq-iqat-i Pakistan, 1971), 1: 100–101, §38. Flynn assumes that they met during this leg of the journey on the basis of Aurangzeb's letter to Shah Jahan; Vincent Flynn, *An English Translation of the Ādāb-i-ʿĀlamgīrī. The Period before the War of Succession* (PhD thesis, Australian National University, 1974), 145: §38.

2. Qabil Khan, "Correspondence with Jahanara Begam," *Adab-i Alamgiri*, 2: 813, §10.

3. Qabil Khan, "Correspondence with Shahjahan," *Adab-i Alamgiri*, 1: 108–111, §44; translation, 162–170, §44. In this letter, Aurangzeb also includes a glowing, detailed description of the building activity in the palace-fort complex and associated structures.

4. Aqil Khan Razi (d. 1696/7), *Waqiat-i Alamgiri*, ed. Zafar Hasan (Delhi: Mercantile Print, 1946), 14–15. Aqil Khan does not mention Jahanara's role here though, simply mentioning that each brother played host to the other.

5. Qabil Khan, *Adab-i Alamgiri*, 1: 116, §47; translation, 181, §47.

6. Mirza Muhammad Tahir Inayat Khan (d. 1670), *Mulakhkhas-i Shahjahan-nama*, ed. Jamil-ur-Rahman (Delhi: Rayzani-i Farhangi-i Jumhuri-i Islami-i Iran, 2009), 548–549; translated as *The Shah Jahan Nama of ʿInayat Khan*, trans. A. R. Fuller, eds. W. E. Begley and Z. A. Desai (Delhi: Oxford University Press, 1990), 472–473.

7. Inayat Khan, *Mulakhkhas*, 553–554; translation, 477.

8. Muhammad Badi-uz-Zaman Rashid Khan, *Lataif-ul-akhbar,* British Library, MS Add. 8907, fols. 14a–14b.

9. Rashid Khan, *Lataif*, fol. 14a.

10. For the date of composition, see Diloram Yusupova, "History," in *The Treasury of Oriental Manuscripts: Abu Rayhan al-Biruni Institute of Oriental Studies of the Academy of Science of the Republic of Uzbekistan* (Taskhent: UNESCO, 2012), 17–26, 22 (no. 5400).

11. The date Rabi I 24, 1063 (February 22, 1653) is given in Rashid Khan, *Lataif*, fol. 7a; cf. Inayat Khan, *Mulakhkhas,* 554; translation, 478.

12. Rashid Khan, *Lataif*, fol. 15a.

13. *A Descriptive List of Farmans, Manshurs, and Nishans Addressed by the Imperial Mughals to the Princes of Rajasthan,* ed. and trans. Nathu Ram Khadgawat (Bikaner: Directorate of Archives, Rajasthan, 1962); translation, 82, §207, dated Jamadi I 11, 1063 (April 9, 1653).

14. *A Descriptive List of Farmans,* 82, §201, dated Shawwal 17, 1061 (October 3, 1651).

15. For instance, Dara Shukoh, *Diwan*, ed. Ahmad Nabi Khan (Lahore: Research Society of Pakistan, 1969), 71–72, §41.

16. See James Wescoat, "Introduction: The Mughal Gardens Project in Lahore," in *The Mughal Garden: Interpretation, Conservation, and Implications,* ed. Mahmood Hussain et al. (Rawalpindi: Ferozsons, 1996), 9–22; James

Wescoat and Joachim Wolschke-Bulmahn, "The Mughal Gardens of Lahore: History, Geography, and Conservation Issues," *Die Gartenkunst* 6 (1994): 19–33.

17. Farid-ud-Din Attar, *Tazkirat-ul-awliya*, ed. Reynold Nicholson, 2 vols. (London: Luzac, 1905–1907) 2: 145–146.

18. "*Guft an yar kaz u gasht sar-i dar buland/jurmash an bud kih asrar huwaida mi kard*," Shams-ud-Din Hafiz, *Diwan*, ed. Yahya Qarib (Tehran: Safi Ali Shah, 1978), 86.

19. Carl Ernst, *Words of Ecstasy in Sufism* (Kuala Lumpur: S. Abdul Majeed, 1994), 23–24.

20. Dara Shukoh, *Hasanat-i arifin*, ed. Makhdum Rahin (Tehran: Muassasa-i Visman, 1973), 2.

21. Dara Shukoh, *Hasanat*, 2–3. The infamous Abu Jahl (d. 624), uncle of the Prophet, is believed to be condemned to the fires of hell on the basis of Quran 96: 9–19.

22. On the role of Sufism in premodern Muslim societies see Nile Green, *Sufism, A Global History* (Malden, MA: Wiley-Blackwell, 2012), 126.

23. Ata Anzali, *"Mysticism" in Iran: The Safavid Roots of a Modern Concept* (Columbia: University of South Carolina Press, 2017), esp. 24–68.

24. "*Bihisht anja kih mullayi nabashad/zi mulla bahs o ghogayi nabashad/jahan khali shawad az shor-i mulla/zi fatwahash parwayi nabashad/ . . . dar an shahri kih mulla khana darad/dar inja hech danayi nabashad/mabin ay qadiri tu ruy-i mulla!/maro anja kih shaidayi nabashad*," Dara Shukoh, *Diwan*, 104–105, §94.

25. Muhammad Sadiq Kashmiri Hamdani (fl. 1636), *Tabaqat-i Shahjahani: Tabaqa-i Ashra* (Delhi: Danishgah-i Dihli, 1990), 34–35. On Afzal Khan, see also Rajeev Kinra, "The Learned Ideal of the Mughal *Wazīr*: The Life and Intellectual World of Prime Minister Afzal Khan Shirazi (d. 1639)," in *Secretaries and Statecraft in the Early Modern World,* ed. Paul Dover (Edinburgh: Edinburgh University Press, 2016), 177–205.

26. Hamdani, *Tabaqat*, 37.

27. Tawakkul Beg Kulabi, *Nuskha-i ahwal-i shahi,* British Library, MS Or. 3203, fol. 64a.

28. For a portrait of Dilruba, see the single-leaf folio housed in the Walters Art Museum, Baltimore, MS W. 696, which depicts six pirs: Shah Khayali, Miyan Abu-l-Maali, Mulla Shah, Miyan Shah Mir, Mulla Khwaja, and Shah Muhammad Dilruba. I am grateful to Murad Khan Mumtaz for discussing this painting with me.

29. Dara Shukoh, "Shah Dilruba," *Hasanat*, 72–75.

30. Dara Shukoh to Shah Dilruba, Letter 1, *Fayyaz-ul-qawanin*, British Library, MS Or. 9617, fol. 40a.

31. "*Bigana chira shudi tu az ma/ma o tu qadim ashnayim*," Dara Shukoh to Shah Dilruba, Letter 2, *Fayyaz*, fol. 41a.

32. Dara Shukoh to Shah Dilruba, Letter 3, *Fayyaz*, fol. 42a.

33. Dara Shukoh to Shah Dilruba, Letter 6, *Fayyaz*, fol. 45a.

34. Dara Shukoh to Shah Dilruba, Letter 4, *Fayyaz*, fol. 43a.

35. For an anachronistic treatment of the passage and its significance, see Iftikhar Ahmad Ghauri, *War of Succession: Between Sons of Shahjan (1657–1658)* (Lahore: Publishers United, 1964), 72–73.

36. Leonard Lewisohn, *Beyond Faith and Infidelity: The Sufi Poetry and Teachings of Mahmud Shabistarî* (Richmond, Surrey: Curzon Press, 1995), 279.

37. "*Agar kafir zi islam-i majazi gasht bezar/kira kufr-i haqiqi shud padidar/darun-i har buti janast panhan/bazer-i kufr imanast panhan,*" Mahmud Shabistari, *Gulshan-i raz,* ed. Kazim Dizfuliyan (Tehran: Talaya, 1382/2003–2004), 120. For an example of the extensive commentarial tradition on this poem, see, for instance, Sayin-ud-Din Ibn Turka (d. 1432), *Sharh-i Gulshan-i raz,* ed. Kazim Dizfuliyan (Tehran: Payk-i Iran, 1996), 212. For an earlier use of the dichotomy between *islam-i majazi* and *kufr-i haqiqi,* see Ain-i Quzat, *Tahmidat,* ed. Afif Usayran (Tehran: Chapkhana-i Danishgah, 1962), 349, and broadly, 205–254. The terms *haqiqa* and *majaz* have a long history in various Islamic hermeneutical discourses. On the origins of the categories in terms of literary criticism, see Wolfhart Heinrichs, "On the Genesis of the Ḥaqîqa-Majâz Dichotomy," *Studia Islamica* 59 (1984): 111–140.

38. For the topic of Akbar's religious reforms, see the still relevant survey by Makhanlal Roychoudhury, *The Din-i-Ilahi or the Religion of Akbar,* 2nd ed. (Calcutta: Das Gupta, 1952).

39. "*Az din-i islam-i majazi wa taqlidi kih az pidaran dida wa shanida,*" is part of the oath taken for Akbar's *din-i-ilahi,* as reported by Abd-ul-Qadir Badauni, *Muntakhab-ul-tavarikh,* ed. Sahib Ahmad Ali, 3 vols. (Tehran: Anjuman-i Asar, 2000), 2: 212. The date of 1580/1 for the enactment of the oath under Akbar is given in Roychoudhury, *Din-i-Ilahi,* 221, 240–241.

40. Reference later dialogues with Baba Lal.

41. See for instance, Muhammad Waris, *Badshah-nama,* British Library, MS I.O. Islamic 324, fols. 126b, 147a, 149a, and 154a. See also Muhammad Waris, *Badshahnamah of Muhammad Waris,* trans. Ishrat Husain Ansari and Hamid Afaq Qureshi (Delhi: Idara-i Adabiyat-i Dehli, 2017). 143, 151, 153, 162, 179, 182.

42. For the abridgment of the *Shah-nama,* see Tawakkul Beg, *Tarikh-i Dilgusha-yi Shamsher Khani,* ed. Tahira Parvin Akram (Islamabad: Markaz-i Tahqiqat-i Farsi-i Iran wa Pakistan, 2005).

43. For a discussion of the work and an enumeration of the many manuscripts see Charles Melville, "The *Shāhnāma* in India: The *Tārīkh-i Dilgushā-yi Shamshīr Khānī,*" in *The Layered Heart. Essays on Persian Poetry. A Celebration in Honor of Dick Davis,* ed. A. A. Seyed-Ghorab, Washington, DC: Mage, 2019), 411–41. I would like to thank the author for sharing this article with me prior to its publication. See also Pasha Khan, "Marvellous Histories: Reading the *Shāhnāmah* in India," *Indian Economic Social History Review* 49.4 (2012): 527–556; and Brittany Payeur, "The Lilly Shamshir-Khani in a Franco-Sikh Context: A Non-Islamic 'Islamic' Manuscript," in *The Islamic Manuscript Tradition: Ten Centuries of Book Arts in Indiana University Collections,* ed. Christiane Gruber (Bloomington: Indiana University Press, 2010), 221–250.

44. Augustus Le Messurier (d. 1916), *Kandahar in 1879: The Diary of Major Le Messurier* (London: W. H. Allen, 1880), 130–131. Quoted in Jadunath Sarkar, *History of Aurangzib,* 5 vols. (Calcutta: Sarkar and Sons, 1912–1924), 1: 142.

45. I have based my description of Qandahar on Jean-Baptiste Tavernier (d. 1689), *Les Six Voyages* (Paris: Gervais Clouzier, 1676), 516, 693–698 (bk. 5, ch. 1, 24); see, particularly, "Plan de la ville et de la forteresse de Candahar," translated as *The Six Voyages of John Baptista Tavernier,* trans. J. Phillips (London: M. P., 1678), 198, 257–258; Le Messurier, *Kandahar,* 69–72; T. J. Arne, "A Plan of Qandahar," *Imago Mundi* 4.1 (1947): 73; see also Sarkar, *History of Aurangzib,* 1: 126–169.

46. See, for instance, Sarkar, *History of Aurangzib,* 1: 166.

47. Inayat Khan, *Mulakhkhas,* 561; translation, 484.

48. Inayat Khan, *Mulakhkhas,* 562–563; translation, 486.

49. Henry G. Raverty, *Notes on Afghanistan and Part of Baluchistan* (London: G.E. Eyre & W. Spottiswoode, 1880), 25–26 (account based on Rashid Khan's *Lataif*).

50. Rashid Khan, *Lataif,* fol. 13a.

51. Rashid Khan, *Lataif,* fols. 61a–62a.

52. Rashid Khan, *Lataif,* fols. 65a, 66a.

53. Muhammad Salih Kamboh, *Amal-i Salih,* ed. Ghulam Yazdani, 3 vols. (Lahore: Majlis-i Taraqqi-i Adab, 1958–1960), 3: 124–125. Note that in the sources, the term for subjugating (*taskhir*) the citadel and subjugating demons in the service of that goal is the same, suggesting a further conceptual tie between the military and occult endeavors.

54. The honorific derives from a feted ancestor, the high-ranking leader Mirza Yar Ahmad Najm-i Sani (d. 1512), a commander-in-chief of the Safavid armies for the Persian Emperor Shah Ismail. On Muhammad Baqir Najm-i Sani, see Nawab Shahnawaz Khan, *Maasir-ul-umara,* ed. Maulvi Abd-ur-Rahim, 3 vols. (Calcutta: Asiatic Society of Bengal, 1888), 1: 180, 408–412. See also Gordon Mackenzie, *A Manual of the Kista District in the Presidency of Madras* (Madras: Lawrence Asylum Press, 1883), 293. See also Syed Hasan Askari, "Mirzā Muḥammad Bāqir Najm-i-Thānī, Author of the *Mauʿiza-i Jahāngīrī,*" in *ʿArshi Presentation Volume,* ed. Malik Ram and M. D. Ahmad (Delhi: Majlis-i Nazr-i ʿArshi, 1965), 103–122.

55. See Muhammad Baqir Najm-i Sani, *Mauiza-i Jahangiri,* edited and translated as *Advice on the Art of Governance: An Indo-Islamic Mirror for Princes,* ed. and trans. Sajida Sultana Alvi (Albany: State University of New York Press, 1989), fols. 56a–56b; see also, in particular, Alvi, "Introduction," 1–31.

56. For a treatise on physics and astronomy, see Muhammad Baqir Najm-i Sani, *Hayat,* Tehran Majlis Library, MS 10.7483, fols. 11a–48b.

57. For his grimoire, inspired in part by Fakhr-ud-Din Razi's *Sirr-ul-maktum,* see Muhammad Baqir, *Kashf-ul-asrar,* Bodleian Library, MS Ouseley Add. 14.

58. For instance, Muhammad Baqir's Persian translation of the Arabic talismanic collection ascribed to Aristotle, the so-called *Zakhira-i Iskandarani,* MS Whinfield 57, fols. 1b–77b. For more manuscripts of this particular text, see Raza

Library, Rampur, P. 1581 and P. 1582, and the references given in Barbara Schmitz and Ziyaud-Din Desai, *Mughal and Persian Paintings and Illustrated Manuscripts in the Raza Library, Rampur* (Delhi: Aryan Books International, 2006), 130–132, plates 209–210.

59. As recorded in Muhammad Baqir Najm-i Sani, *Siraj-ul-manahij*, Majlis-i Shura-i Islami, Tehran, MS 3797, 4–5. For more manuscripts, see *Fihrist-i nuskha-i khatti-i farsi kitabkhana-i Raza Rampur,* 3 vols. (Delhi: Diamond Printers, 1996), 3: 88–89.

60. For instance, the spectacular, illuminated Persian fragment of Fakhr-ud-Din Razi, *Sirr-ul-maktum*, originally produced in Akbar's court, Raza Library Rampur, Album 2, in Schmitz and Din Desai, *Mughal and Persian Paintings*, 20–27, plates 13–19; Yael Rice, "Cosmic Sympathies and Painting at Akbar's Court," *Marg* 68.2 (2016): 88–99. Also see the so-called Delhi collection, taken from the Mughal imperial, archives in 1858 during the British occupation of India, now housed in the British Library. The collection serves as a rough index for materials commonly held in the Mughal court. The holdings in the occult sciences are fairly rich. See, for instance, Sakkaki, *Ash-Shamil fi l-bahr-il-kamil*, which opens with an early Arabic redaction of the *Picatrix*, the famed book of spells (Delhi Arabic 1915). Collections of talismans are to be found (e.g., Delhi Arabic 361), among many others; see also Muhammad Sabzwari, *Tuhfat-ul-gharaib,* Delhi Persian 1183, dated 1095 AH (1684).

61. See Abu-l-Fazl, *Ain-i Akbari*, ed. Heinrich Blochmann, 2 vols. (Calcutta: Calcutta Baptist Mission Press, 1872–1877), 2: 57–58, 129; translated as *The Ā'in-i Akbarī*, trans. Heinrich Blochmann, ed. Douglas Craven Phillott, 3 vols. (Calcutta: Asiatic Society of Bengal, 1927–1949), 3: 239.

62. Ebba Koch, "*Diwan-i 'amm* and Chihil Sutun: The Audience Halls of Shah Jahan," *Muqarnas* 11 (1994): 143–165, 149.

63. For recent scholarship on Islamic talismans in the battlefield, see Christiane Gruber, "From Prayer to Protection: Amulets in the Islamic World," in *Power and Protection: Islamic Art and the Supernatural*, ed. Francesca Leoni (Oxford: Ashmolean Museum, 2016), 33–51; Rose Muravchick, "Objectifying the Occult: Studying an Islamic Talismanic Shirt as an Embodied Object," *Arabica* 64 (2017): 673–693. See also the online publication accompanying the exhibition curated by Maryam Ekhtiar and Rachel Parikh, "Power and Piety: Islamic Talismans on the Battlefield," (Metropolitan Museum of Art, New York, August 2016 February 2017), https://metmuseum.atavist.com/powerandpiety (accessed October 8, 2018). Further, Matthew Melvin Koushki's forthcoming *The Occult Science of Empire in Aqquyunlu-Safavid Iran* promises a pioneering intellectual history of "Timurid occult-scientific imperialism."

64. Rashid Khan, *Lataif,* fol. 62a. See also Kamboh, *Amal-i Salih*, 3: 131. On *jarr-i saqil*, see Muhammad Amin Tusi, *Farhang-i lughat-i adabi*, 2 vols. (Tabriz: Danishgah-i Adabiyat va Ulum-i Insani, 1967–1972), 2: 553–554. Cf. Kalika Ranjan Qanungo, *Dara Shukoh* (Calcutta: S. C. Sarkar and Sons, 1952), 40. Qanungo fundamentally misreads this passage on the Deccani engineers, nor does he fully grasp the significance of the occult within the context of military strategy.

65. Rashid Khan, *Lataif,* fol. 19a. On Jafar, who was appointed to "Barqandaz" Khan after the expedition to Qandahar and was one of Dara's favorites, see Kewal Ram, *Tazkirat-ul-umara,* translated as *The History of Nobles from Akbar to Aurangzeb's Reign, 1556–1707 AD,* trans. S. M. Azizuddin Husain (Delhi: Munshiram Manoharlal, 1985), 33. For an account of how Jafar was the subject of jealousy, see Niccolò Manucci, *Voyage et histoire du Mogol,* Staatsbibliothek, Berlin, MS Phillips 1945, part 1, fol. 75b (revised Portuguese version); translated in *Storia do Mogor or Mogul India 1653–1708,* trans. William Irvine, 4 vols. (London: John Murray, 1907), 1: 226–227.

66. Rashid Khan, *Lataif,* fols. 33b–34a. On earlier tensions between the two, see also fols. 31b–32a. For further information, see Qanungo, *Dara,* 65–66.

67. Rashid Khan, *Lataif,* fol. 9a. For Mirza Abdullah Beg Najm-i Sani, who was given the honorific Askar Khan after the Battle of Qandahar, see Shahnawaz Khan, *Maasir,* 2: 809. He is not to be confused with Fakhr Khan Najm-i Sani, who is explicitly identified as one of the sons of Muhammad Baqir Najm-i Sani and who was also in the service of Dara Shukoh during the Qandahar campaign, Shahnawaz Khan, *Maasir,* 3: 26–28.

68. For an analysis of the phenomenon, see Sanjay Subrahmanyam, "Iranians Abroad: Intra-Asian Elite Migration and Early Modern State Formation," *The Journal of Asian Studies* 51 (1992): 340–363.

69. Rashid Khan, *Lataif,* fol. 14b.

70. Rashid Khan, *Lataif,* fol. 96a; Qanungo, *Dara,* 57.

71. "*Mazhar-i sahibqirani, Shah Abbas-i duwwum / dar jihad-i akbar az farmandihan shud kamkar / bar-i digar az tah-i bal o par-i zaghan-i hind / baiza-i Islam, chun khurshid gardid ashkar … chun liwa-yi shah, ruy-i qiladaran shud safed / Hindiyan gashtand yaksar zardruy o sharmsar // az siyahi garcha balatar nabashad hech rang / zardruyi ghalib amad bar siyahan dar farar,*" Saib Tabrizi, *Diwan-i Saib Tabrizi,* ed. Parviz Natil Khanlari, 2 vols. (Tehran: Muassasa-i Intisharat-i Nigah, 1995 / 6), 2: 1386–1387, *qasida* §11. For more on Saib Tabrizi's poems celebrating the victory and a further panegyric to Shah Abbas, see Sunil Sharma, *Mughal Arcadia: Persian Literature in an Indian Court* (Cambridge, MA: Harvard University Press, 2017), 188.

72. John Renard, "Al-Jihād Al-Akbar: Notes on a Theme in Islamic Spirituality," *The Muslim World* 78.3 / 4 (1988): 225–242.

73. Annemarie Schimmel, "Turk and Hindu: A Poetical Image and its Application to Historical Fact," in *Islam and Cultural Change in the Middle Ages,* ed. Speros Vryoni (Wiesbaden: Harrassowitz, 1975), 107–126.

74. Sayyid Makhdum Rahin bases his edition of the *Hasanat* on a manuscript that according to him dates between 1654 and 1658, during Dara's lifetime. But Rahin curiously avoids mentioning in which private collection or library this manuscript, which he labels "MS A," might exist, though he provides details of other manuscripts used for comparison. Rahin, "Introduction," in Darah Shukoh, *Hasanat,* 37–38.

75. Dara Shukoh, *Hasanat-ul-arifin,* ed. Muhammad Abd-ul-Ahad (Delhi: Mujtabai, 1891).

76. For instance, Chandarbhan Brahman (attributed), *Gosht-i Baba Lal,* edited and translated as "Les entretiens de Lahore (entre le prince impérial Dârâ Shikûh et l'ascète hindou Baba La'l Das)," eds. and trans. Clément Huart and Louis Massignon, *Journal asiatique* 209 (1926): 285–334.

77. See www.bawalalji.org/web/biography.php (accessed October 8, 2018).

78. As Dhyanpur is east of Lahore, Dara Shukoh would not have had occasion to stop there on his return from Qandahar. Since it is also not on the direct route to Delhi, Dara would have had to either take a detour or summon the ascetic to Lahore.

79. "At first glance, I knew that it had been painted by Govardhan," Stuart Cary Welch, private written communication, April 26, 2008. Welch based his identification of Dara Shukoh on the resemblances with other identifiable portraits of the prince. The painting, for years on loan from Stuart Cary Welch to the Harvard University Art Museum, was labeled "Dara Shikoh with Hindu and Muslim Holy Men at the Peri Mahal." Printed with the same identification in Annemarie Schimmel, *Islam in India and Pakistan* (Leiden: E.J. Brill, 1982), Plate 24a. As does Welch, Schimmel entertains the possibility that the ascetic here represents Baba Lal. For more on the artist, see "Govardhan," *Grove Encyclopedia of Islamic Art and Architecture,* ed. Jonathan Bloom and Sheila Blair, 3 vols. (Oxford: Oxford University Press, 2009), 2: 119–120.

80. For an analysis of the gaze, see Gregory Minissale, "Seeing Eye-to-Eye with Mughal Miniatures: Some Observations on the Outward Gazing Figure in Mughal Art," *Marg* 58.3 (2007): 41–49.

81. These include "Prince and Ascetics," from the Late Shah Jahan Album, Cleveland Museum of Art, Andrew R. and Martha Holden Jennings Fund, 1971.9, attributed to Govardhan; and "Visit to Holy Man," Paris, Musée national des arts asiatiques Guimet, Ma 2471.

82. Painting by Nar Singh of the *Ibadat-khana,* folio from *Akbar-nama,* produced around 1605, Chester Beatty Library MS 3, fol. 263b.

83. "*Guftam kih khurak-i faqir dar gurusnagi chist/gufta kih gosht-i khud//guftam kih luqma dar halaq chist/gufta kih taam-i sabr//guftam kih wujud-i faqir/gufta kih dayim dar sujud," Sawal wa jawab-i badshahzada Dara Shukoh wa Baba Lal Das-Ji Bairagi,* ed. Chiranji Lal, lithograph (Delhi: Muhibb-ul-Hind, 1885), 3. For other translated extracts from this text, see Supriya Gandhi, "The Prince and the *Muvaḥḥid:* Dara Shikoh and Mughal Engagements with Vedanta," in *Religious Interactions in Mughal India,* eds. Vasudha Dalmia and Munis Faruqui (New Delhi: Oxford University Press, 2014), 65–101, 89–90.

84. Other versions mention these seven locations in Lahore as well. See, for instance, the dialogue between Baba Lal and Dara Shukoh in a miscellany of Dara's works, including the *Sirr-i Akbar* and the *Majma-ul-bahrain,* British Library, MS Add. 18,404, fols. 248–259.

85. See the manuscript uncovered by Vladimir Ivanow in Lucknow, designated as "MS E" in Chandarbhan Brahman (attributed), *Gosht-i Baba Lal,* 333–334.

86. See Sharif Husain Qasemi, "Čandra Bhān," in *Encyclopaedia Iranica,* ed. Ehsan Yarshater, 15 vols. (London: Routledge, 1982–), 4: 755–756. For more

on Chandarbhan and his life as a *munshi* in the court, see Rajeev Kinra, *Writing Self, Writing Empire: Chandar Bhan Brahman and the Cultural World of the Indo-Persian State Secretary* (Oakland: University of California Press, 2015). Kinra views with skepticism Chandarbhan Bhan's connections with Dara and dismisses the trip to Qandahar (241–258).

87. Rashid Khan, *Lataif*, fol. 64b, cf. fol. 18b. See also Qanungo, *Dara Shukoh*, 56n1.
88. Chandarbhan Brahman (attributed), *Gosht-i Baba Lal*, 291.
89. Chandarbhan Brahman (attributed), *Gosht-i Baba Lal*, 294.
90. Compare the different readings in the text edited by Huart and Massignon, Chandarbhan Brahman (attributed), *Gosht-i Baba Lal*, with the dialogues between Dara Shukoh and Baba Lal in Staatsbibliothek, Berlin, MS Sprenger 1659, fols. 176b–183a. The Sprenger manuscript is noted as "D" in Huart and Massignon.
91. Chandarbhan Brahman (attributed), *Gosht-i Baba Lal*, 303.
92. Quran 57: 3.
93. Dara Shukoh, *Hasanat*, 4.
94. Dara Shukoh, "Shaikh Bari," *Hasanat*, 67–72.
95. Dara Shukoh, "Muhammad Sharif," *Hasanat*, 58–59.
96. Dara Shukoh, "Miyan Mir," *Hasanat*, 50.
97. Dara Shukoh, "Baba Lal," *Hasanat*, 49.
98. Dara Shukoh, "Kabir," *Hasanat*, 53. For further information on the anecdote of Kabir's funeral, see the introduction to Kabir, *The Bijak of Kabir*, trans. Linda Hess (Oxford: Oxford Univeristy Press, 2002), 4.
99. Dara Shukoh, "Kabir," *Hasanat*, 54–55.
100. This quatrain is also collated in Dara's *Diwan*. See Dara Shukoh, *Diwan*, 'Rubaiyat,' § 59.
101. Abd-ul-Haqq Dihlawi, *Akhbar-ul-akhyar fi asrar-ul-abrar*, ed. Alim Ashraf Khan (Tehran: Danishgah-i Tihran, 2005), 599. Cited in M. Athar Ali, "Encounter and Efflorescence: Genesis of the Medieval Civilization," *Social Scientist* 18.1/2 (1990): 13–28, 25.
102. Qabil Khan, "Correspondence with Shah Jahan," *Adab-i Alamgiri*, 1: 116, §47; translation, 181, §47.
103. Qabil Khan, *Adab-i Alamgiri*, 1: 119, §48; translation, 185, §48.
104. Qabil Khan, *Adab-i Alamgiri*, 1: 119–120, §48; translation, 186, §48.
105. Ascribed to Hamid-ud-Din Khan, *Ahkam-i Alamgiri*, ed. Jadunath Sarkar, 2nd ed. (Calcutta: Sarkar and Sons, 1926), 6–9; translated as *Anecdotes of Aurangzib*, trans. Jadunath Sarkar (Calcutta: Sarkar and Sons, 1912), 28–30. See *Ahkam*'s inconsistencies when narrating the story of Aurangzeb's elephant fight, chap. 3, note 78.
106. Shahnawaz Khan, *Maasir*, 1: 790–791.
107. Qabil Khan, *Adab-i Alamgiri*, 1: 129, §53; translation, 201–202, §52.
108. Muzaffar Alam and Sanjay Subrahmanyam, "Love, Passion and Reason in Faizi's Nal-Daman," in *Love in South Asia: A Cultural History,* ed. Francesca Orsini (Cambridge: Cambridge University Press, 2006), 109–141.
109. Manucci, *Voyage*, fol. 82a; translation, 1: 231.

110. For a nuanced account of Aurangzeb's attitude toward music, a discussion of the Hira Bai story, and a critique of Manucci's reliability, see Katherine Butler Brown, "Did Aurangzeb Ban Music?" *Modern Asian Studies* 41.1 (2007): 77–120.

111. Qabil Khan, *Adab-i Alamgiri*, 1: 137, §56; translation, 219, §58.

112. Qabil Khan, *Adab-i Alamgiri*, 1: 163–164, §69; translation, 224–225, §60.

113. Qabil Khan, *Adab-i Alamgiri*, 2: 821–822, §18.

7. Confluence, 1654–1656

1. Stephen Blake, *Shahjahanabad: The Sovereign City in Mughal India 1639–1739* (Cambridge: Cambridge University Press, 1991), 31–32.

2. Blake, *Shahjahanabad*, 53–54.

3. For further information on Jahanara's architectural patronage, see Stephen Blake, "Contributors to the Urban Landscape: Women Builders in Safavid Isfahan and Mughal Shahjahanabad," in *Women in the Medieval Islamic World*, ed. Gavin R. G. Hambly (New York: St. Martin's Press, 1998), 407–428, 420–423.

4. Blake, "Contributors," 411, 422, table 1. Also see Mirza Muhammad Tahir Inayat Khan (d. 1670), *Mulakhkhas-i Shahjahan-nama*, ed. Jamil-ur-Rahman (Delhi: Rayzani-i Farhangi-i Jumhuri-i Islami-i Iran, 2009), 528; translated as *The Shah Jahan Nama of 'Inayat Khan*, trans. A. R. Fuller, eds. W. E. Begley and Z. A. Desai (Delhi: Oxford University Press, 1990), 451. In the translation Akbarabadi is identified as Shah Jahan's consort.

5. Blake, "Contributors," 411, table 1.

6. François Bernier, *Un libertin dans l'Inde moghole: les Voyages de François Bernier* (1656–1669), ed. Frédéric Tinguely, Adrien Paschoud, and Charles-Antoine Chamay (Paris: Chandeigne, 2008), 393–394, second letter to François Boysson, Seigneur de Merveilles, February 25, 1665. For further information, see Blake, *Shahjahanabad*, 67.

7. Chandarbhan Brahman, *Chahar Chaman*, ed. Muhammad Yunus Jaffery (Delhi: Rayzani-i Farhangi-i Jumhuri-i Islami-i Iran: 2004), 127.

8. Inayat Khan, *Mulakhkhas*, 573; translation, 496.

9. S. R. Sharma, *Mughal Empire in India*, 3 vols. (Bombay: Karnatak Printing Press, 1934), 2: 636. For an account of Juliana's life, see Taymiyya Zaman, "Visions of Juliana: A Portuguese Woman at the Court of the Mughals," *Journal of World History* 23.4 (2012): 761–791.

10. The British Library holds a painting of Ochterlony in his home, entertained by dancers and musicians, MS Add. Or. 2, published in William Dalrymple and Yuthika Sharma, *Princes and Painters: In Mughal Delhi, 1707–1857* (New York: Asia Society Museum, 2012), 102–103, plate 28.

11. François Bernier, *Voyages*, 242–244, Letter to Monsieur de La Mothe Le Vayer, July 1663.

12. Tawakkul Beg, *Nuskha*, fol. 72b.

13. Sayyid Akbarali Ibrahimali Tirmizi, *Mughal Documents*, 2 vols. (New Delhi: Manohar, 1989–1995), 2: 105.

14. Tirmizi, *Mughal Documents*, 2: 105.

15. Inayat Khan, *Mulakhkhas*, 575; translation, 497–498.

16. Inayat Khan, *Mulakhkhas*, 580–581; translation, 503. The English translation erroneously identifies Chandarbhan as the prince's *diwan* and Abd-ul-Karim as his *mir buyutat*. See also Muhammad Salih Kamboh, *Amal-i Salih*, ed. Ghulam Yazdani, 3 vols. (Lahore: Majlis-i Taraqqi-i Adab, 1958–1960), 3: 148. For Chandarbhan's report, see Shyamaladas, *Vir vinod*, 7 vols. (Udaipur: Rajayantralaya, 1886), 2.1: 403–408; cited in Tirmizi, *Mughal Documents*, 2: 108–109, §280.

17. Lahori, *Padshah-nama*, Royal Collection, Windsor Castle, MS 1367, fol. 205b; reproduced in Milo Cleveland Beach and Ebba Koch, *King of the World. The Padshahnama: An Imperial Mughal Manuscript, the Royal Library, Windsor Castle* (London: Thames and Hudson, 1997), plates 41–42.

18. Munshi Shaikh Abu-l-Fath Qabil Khan, "Correspondence with Shahjahan," in *Adab-i Alamgiri*, ed. Abd-ul-Ghafur Chaudhari, 2 vols. (Lahore: Idara-i Tahqiqat-i Pakistan, 1971), 1: 221, §97; translated in Vincent Flynn, *An English Translation of the Ādāb-i-ʿĀlamgīrī. The Period before the War of Succession* (PhD thesis, Australian National University, 1974), 254, §69.

19. Qabil Khan, *Adab-i Alamgiri*, 1: 193n1, §81; 1: 271n1, §73.

20. Tirmizi, *Mughal Documents*, 2: 106–107, §§269, 274.

21. Shyamaladas, *Vir vinod*, 2.1: 417–418, 419–421; summarized in Tirmizi, *Mughal Documents*, 2: 110–111, §§283, 284.

22. See chap. 5, note 66 and chap. 6, note 41.

23. Muhammad Waris, *Badshahnama*, British Library, MS I.O. Islamic 324, fol. 180a; translated as *Badshahnamah of Muhammad Waris*, trans. Ishrat Husain Ansari and Hamid Afaq Qureshi (Delhi: Idara-i Adabiyat-i Dehli, 2017), 226.

24. Waris mentions numerous occasions when Kavindracharya is rewarded at court, for instance: *Badshahnama*, fols. 112a, 116b, 119a, 126b, 147a, 149a, 154a, 180a, and 220a; translation, 132, 139, 143, 151, 153, 162, 179, 182, 190, 226, 269, 277, and 308.

25. Waris, *Badshahnama*, fol. 220a; translation, 269.

26. P.K. Gode points out that a letter of judgement from a pandit assembly dated 1657 CE, is signed by one Narasimha Ashrama also known as Brahmendra Saraswati. He also cites evidence from the *Kavindrachandrodaya* showing that Brahmendra Saraswati knew (and praised) Kavindracharya Saraswati. P.K. Gode, "The Identification of Gosvāmī Nṛsiṁhāśrama of Dara Shukoh's Sanskrit Letter with Brahmendra Sarasvatī of the Kavīndra-Candrodaya - Between AD 1628 and 1658," *Adyar Library Bulletin* 6 (1942): 172–177, 174–175.

27. C. Kunhan Raja, "A Sanskrit Letter of Mohamed Dārā Shukoh," *Brahmavidya: Adyar Library Bulletin*, 7.3 (1943): 192–204, 198–200.

28. V. A. Ramaswami Sastri, *Jagannātha Paṇḍita* (Annamalainagar: Annamalai University, 1942), 13–16.

29. Pullela Sri Ramachandrudu, *The Contribution of Paṇḍitarāja Jagannātha to Sanskrit Poetics* (Delhi: Nirajana, 1983), 22–23; Ramaswami Sastri, *Jagannātha Paṇḍita*, 17–18.

30. Panditaraja Jagannatha, *Rasagangadhara*, ed. Mathuranath Shastri (Bombay: Nirnaya Sagara Press, 1939). For an overview of Jagannatha's oeuvre, placing him in the larger context of Sanskrit literary history, see Sheldon Pollock, "Sanskrit Literary Culture from the Inside Out," in *Literary Cultures in History: Reconstructions from South Asia*, ed. Sheldon Pollock (Berkeley: University of California Press, 2003), 39–129, 96–99.

31. R. B. Athavale, "New Light on the Life of Paṇḍitarāja Jagannātha," *Annals of the Bhandarkar Oriental Research Institute* 48/49 (1968): 415–420, 418–419. Also cited in Sheldon Pollock, "Death of Sanskrit," *Society for Comparative Study of Society and History* 43.2 (2001): 392–426, 421n48.

32. Translation from Sheldon Pollock, "Death of Sanskrit," 409.

33. Kshitimohan Sen, *Medieval Mysticism of India* (London: Luzac, 1929), 189–190.

34. For instance, V. A. Ramaswamy Sastri, *Jagannātha Paṇḍita* (Annamalainagar: Annamalai University Press, 1942), 21; cited in Sheldon Pollock, "Sanskrit Literary Culture," 98n125.

35. François Bernier, *Voyages*, 337, letter to Jean Chapelain, October 4, 1667.

36. Inayat Khan, *Mulakhkhas,* 572; translation, 495. See also Visheshwar Sarup Bhargava, *Marwar and the Mughal Emperors, 1526–1748* (Delhi: Munshiram Manoharlal, 1966), 86.

37. For Jaswant Singh's writings, see Jaswant Singh, *Jasavantasimha granthavali,* ed. Vishwanathprasad Mishra (Varanasi: Nagari Pracarini Sabha, 1972); Chandramohan Singh Ravat, *Maharaj Jasvantasimh aur unka sahitya* (Delhi: Samuhik Prakashan, 2010).

38. Bernier, *Voyages*, 46–47, from his *Histoire de la dernière révolution de états du grand mogol* (Paris: Claude Barbin, 1670).

39. *Dabistan-i mazahib*, ed. Rahim Raza-zada Malik, 2 vols. (Tehran: Kitabkhana-i Tahuri, 1983), 1: 215.

40. Bernier, *Voyages*, 318, letter to Jean Chapelain, October 4, 1667.

41. "*Dar Kaaba o butkhana sang u shud o chob u shud/yakja hajar-ul-aswad yakja but-i Hindu shud,*" *Dabistan,* 1: 216.

42. "*Ma anchih khwanda-im faramosh karda-im/illa hadis-i dost kih takrar mikunim,*" Maulavi Abdul Wali, "Sketch of the Life of Sarmad," *Journal of the Asiatic Society of Bengal* 20 (1924): 111–122, 117–118. Abdul Wali translates this exchange, though the translations provided here are mine.

43. *Dabistan,* 1: 218–223.

44. See Christopher Minkowski, "Advaita Vedānta in Early Modern History," *South Asian History and Culture* 2.2 (2011): 205–231.

45. Inayat Khan, *Mulakhkhas,* 582; translation, 504.

46. My discussion of Roth draws on Arnulf Camps, "Introduction" in Heinrich Roth, *The Sanskrit Grammar and Manuscripts of Father Heinrich Roth S. J. (1620–1668)*, ed. Arnulf Camps and Jean-Claude Muller (Leiden: E.J. Brill, 1998), 1–25.

47. For the Vaisheshika in early modern India, see Jonardan Ganeri, *The Lost Age of Reason: Philosophy in Early Modern India 1450–1700* (New York: Oxford University Press, 2011), esp. chaps. 4 and 5.

48. Jan Gonda, *Der Religionen Indiens,* 3 vols. (Stuttgart: W. Kohlhammer, 1960–1964), 2: 91, cited in Camps, "Introduction," 18.

49. Another example of this genre is Dharmaraja's *Vedantaparibhasa,* composed in the seventeenth century.

50. Kamboh, *Amal-i Salih,* 3: 200.

51. "*[D]e sorte que c'estoit presque deux Roys ensemble,*" Bernier, *Voyages,* 53, from the *Histoire,* 31.

52. Dara Shukoh's colophon records the date of completion as 1065 AH (1064/5), noted as his forty-second year. As Dara was born on Safar 29, 1024 AH (March 30, 1615), his forty-second year would begin from the day he turned forty-one, which would date the completion of the work to some point after Safar 29, 1065 AH (January 8, 1655).

53. For the claim that Dara Shukoh's work "is an attempt to reconcile Hinduism and Islam," see Mahfuz al-Haq, "Introduction," in Dara Shukoh, *The Mingling of the Two Oceans,* ed. Mahfuz al-Haq (Calcutta: Asiatic Society of Bengal, 1929), 27.

54. Michael Sells, *Early Islamic Mysticism: Sufi, Quran, Miraj, Poetic and Theological Writings* (New York: Paulist Press, 1996), 39. On the early exegetical tradition and associations with the Ancient Near East, see Brannon Wheeler, *Moses in the Quran and Islamic Exegesis* (London: Routledge, 2002), 10–36.

55. On these connotations raised by the title of the *Majma-ul-bahrain,* I draw on Carl Ernst "Muslim Studies of Hinduism? A Reconstruction of Arabic and Persian Translations from Indian Languages," *Iranian Studies* 36.2 (2003): 173–195, 186.

56. "*Kufr o islam dar rahish puyan/wahdahu la sharika lahu guyan,*" Dara Shukoh, *Majma-ul-bahrain,* ed. Muhammad Reza Jalali-Naini (Tehran: Nashr-i Nuqrah, 1987/8), 1.

57. Noted by Ernst, "Muslim Studies," 187n54. See Abu-l-Majd Sanai, *Hadiqat-ul-haqaiq,* partial ed. and trans. John Stephenson (Calcutta: Baptist Mission Press, 1910), 1 (Persian); Jalal-ud-Din Rumi, *Fihi ma fi,* ed. Badi-uz-Zaman Furuzanfar (Tehran: Amir Kabir, 1969), 229; and for the variant "*kufr o islam,*" Ala-ud-Din Juwaini (d. 1283), *Tarikh-i Jahangusha,* ed. Mirza Muhammad Qazwini, 3 vols. (London: Luzac, 1912–1937), 1: 111.

58. "*Law kushshifa-l-ghita ma azdadtu yaqinan,*" quoted and translated in Reza Shah Kazemi, *Justice and Remembrance: Introducing the Spirituality of Imam 'Ali* (London: I. B. Tauris, 2007), 153.

59. Dara Shukoh, *Majma,* 2. The Sanskrit translation mentions specifically "Babalal," or Baba Lal Das, *Samudrasamgama,* Sanskrit 1.

60. The Arabic phrase at the end runs, "*at-tasawwufu [huwa] l-insafu wa-t-tasawwufu tarku-t-takalluf,*" Dara Shukoh, *Majma,* 2. Here *insaf* has the sense of both justice and equity, as in treating equitably two sides.

61. Dara Shukoh, *Majma,* 2.

62. The text of the *Samudrasangama* mentions that it was composed in 1655. This might just be a copy of the *Majma-ul-bahrain*'s date of composition. But given the deliberate nature of the *Samudrasangama*'s translation of the Persian text, I would argue that it was indeed composed concurrently with the *Majma.* The

manuscript tradition unfortunately does not provide further clues as to its date. The sole dated manuscript, located at the Bhandarkar Oriental Research Institute, MS 1043/1891–1895, is dated through its colophon to the Agrahayana month of Samvat 1765 or 1708 CE, that is, roughly half a century after Dara's death. It is this manuscript that forms the basis for subsequent editions of the text, including a translation and edition by Roma Chaudhuri and Jatindra Bimal Chaudhuri. Another, undated, manuscript of the *Samudrasangama* is located at the Deccan College, MS 7756. The Deccan College manuscript was identified by Christopher Minkowski, who presented an unpublished paper on it at the annual meeting of the American Oriental Society in 1997.

63. This last example is in the context of Quran 18:110, *"Qul innama ana basharun mithlakum,"* which Dara translates as "Say Muhammad, is it not that I too am human, like you?" The *Majma* interpolates into the translation the name of the Prophet Muhammad, who in traditional exegesis is understood to be the addressee of the verse. The *Samudrasamgama* has "Mahasiddha," meaning great adept, or perfect *yogin,* instead of Muhammad. Dara Shukoh, *A Critical Study of Dārā Shikūh's Samudra-Saṅgama,* eds. and trans. Roma Chaudhuri and Jatindra Bimal Chaudhuri (Calcutta: Sanskrita Siksa, 1954), Sanskrit, 3; translation, 131.

64. Dara Shukoh, *Samudrasamgama,* Sanskrit, 6; translation, 124.

65. For instance, Rosalind O'Hanlon, "Letters Home: Banaras Pandits and the Maratha Regions in Early Modern India," *Modern Asian Studies* 44: 2 (2010): 201–240.

66. Dara Shukoh, *Samudrasangama,* 8.

67. Chandarbhan Brahman (attributed), *Gosht-i Baba Lal,* edited and translated as "Les entretiens de Lahore (entre le prince impérial Dârâ Shikûh et l'ascète hindou Baba La'l Das)," eds. and trans. Clément Huart and Louis Massignon, *Journal asiatique* 209 (1926): 285–334, 307–308 (Persian text); Dara Shukoh, *Majma,* 3.

68. Dara Shukoh, *Majma,* on four worlds and sound, 15–18; on light, 19–21; on prophethood, 25–29; on liberation, 40–46. See also *Bhagavata Purana = The Bhagavata (Srimad Bhagavata Mahapurana),* ed. H. G. Shastri (Ahmedabad: B. J. Institute of Learning and Research, 1996), 156, verse 2.1.26.

69. *"Dunyadaran-i dakhin,"* Aurangzeb's letter to Qabil Khan, *Adab-i Alamgiri,* 1: 106, §43.

70. Ibrahim Adil Shah, *Kitab-i-Nauras,* ed. and trans. Nazir Ahmad (New Delhi: Bharatiya Kala Kendra, 1956), 95, translation, 128.

71. Françoise 'Nalini' Delvoye, "The Verbal Content of Dhrupad Songs from the Earliest Collections," *Dhrupad Annual* 5 (1990): 93–109, 99–101. The song collection has an anonymous Persian preface. There are multiple manuscripts of the text. I have consulted Sahas Ras, Cambridge University, MS Kings 218.

72. Nur-ud-Din Zuhuri, "Sih Nasr-i Zuhuri," ed. Muhammad Yunus Jaffery, in *Qand-i Parsi,* 63/64 (2014): 199–256, 222. I have altered the translation of the same text found in Muhammad Abdul Ghani, *A History of Persian Language and Literature at the Mughal Court* (Allahabad: The Indian Press, 1930), 366–367.

73. For a description of Nur-ud-din Muhammad Zuhuri, *Diwan*, see Hermann Ethé, *Catalogue of Persian Manuscripts in the Library of the India Office*, 2 vols. (Oxford: Horace Hart, 1903–1937), 1: 820–822.

8. The Greatest Secret, 1656–1657

1. For overviews of the topic of dreams in Islamic traditions, see Toufic Fahd, "The Dream in Medieval Islamic Society," in *The Dream and Human Societies*, ed. Gustave Edmund von Grunebaum (Berkeley: University of California Press, 1966), 351–363; John Lamoreaux, *The Early Muslim Tradition of Dream Interpretation* (Albany: State University of New York Press, 2002); and Nile Green, "The Religious and Cultural Role of Dreams and Visions in Islam," *Journal of the Royal Asiatic Society* 13.3 (2003): 287–313. For dreams in earlier Arabic writings of the self, see also Dwight Reynolds, "Arabic Autobiography and the Literary Portrayal of the Self," in *Interpreting the Self: Autobiography in the Arabic Literary Tradition*, ed. Dwight Reynolds (Berkeley: University of California Press, 2001), 72–103, 88–93.

2. For Busiri, see Suzanne Stetkevych, *The Mantle Odes, Arabic Praise Poems to the Prophet Muḥammad* (Bloomington: Indiana University Press, 2010), 82–88; for the caliph Mamun, see Dimitri Gutas, *Greek Thought, Arabic Culture, The Graeco-Arabic Translation Movement in Baghdad and Early ʿAbbāsid Society, 2nd–4th/8th–10th Centuries* (London: Routledge, 1998), 101–103.

3. Sufi Sharif, *Atwar fi hall-il-asrar,* British Library, MS Or. 1883, fol. 272a.

4. Abhinanda (attributed), *Laghuyogavasisthah*, ed. Vasudeva Sharma (Delhi: Motilal Banarsidass, 1985); Jürgen Hanneder, "*Mokṣopāya:* An Introduction," in *The Mokṣopāya, Yoga Vāsiṣṭha and Related Texts*, ed. Jürgen Hanneder (Aachen: Shaker Verlag, 2005), 9–21, 14; Walter Slaje, "Locating the *Mokṣopāya,*" in *The Mokṣopāya, Yogavāsiṣṭha and Related Texts,* ed. Jürgen Hanneder (Aachen: Shaker Verlag, 2005), 21–35; John Brockington and Anna King, *The Intimate Other: Love Divine in Indic Religions* (Delhi: Orient Longman, 2005), 40.

5. Peter Thomi, "The Yogavāsiṣṭha in its Longer and Shorter Version," *Journal of Indian Philosophy* 11.1 (1983): 107–116.

6. Dara Shukoh, *Jog Basisht,* eds. Sayyid Amir Hasan Abidi and Tara Chand (Aligarh: Aligarh Muslim University, 1998), 4.

7. Nizam Panipati, *Jog Basisht,* eds. Muhammad Reza Jalali-Naini and Narayan Shanker Shukla (Tehran: Iqbal, 1981). This translation of the *Yogavasishtha* is examined in Shankar Nair, *Translating Wisdom* (forthcoming).

8. Heike Franke, "Akbar's *Yogavāsiṣṭha* at the Chester Beatty Library," *Zeitschrift der Deutschen Morgenländischen Gesellschaft* 161.2 (2011): 359–375. For another examination of this question, see Muzaffar Alam, "In Search of a Sacred King: Dārā Shukoh and the Yogavāsiṣṭhas of Mughal India," *History of Religions* 55.4 (2016): 429–459.

9. For instance, Hermann Ethé, *Catalogue of Persian Manuscripts in the Library of the India Office,* 2 vols. (Oxford: India Office, 1903–1937), 1: 1100–1101,

§§1971–1973. See also MS 39 in the Aligarh Muslim University Library, microfilmed by the Noor International Microfilm Center, Delhi, as Microfilm no. 638, catalogued online at: www.indianislamicmanuscript.com (accessed October 8, 2018).

10. In his translation of the Sanskrit play *Prabodhacandrodaya*, titled *Gulzar-i Hal*, Banwalidas mentions relying on the help of one Bhawanidas, who helped him read the text in the vernacular of Gwalior. This translation, too, is thus based on a Hindavi translation of the Sanskrit and is not directly from the Sanskrit. See R. S. McGregor, "A Brajbhasa Adaptation of the Drama Prabodhacandrodaya by Nanddas of the Sect of Vallabha," in *Perspectives in Indian Religion, Papers in Honour of Karel Werner,* ed. Peter Connolly (New Delhi: Sri Satguru Publications, 1986), 135–144, 143.

11. See Aditya Behl and Simon Weightman, "Introduction" in Manjhan, *Madhumalati: An Indian Sufi Romance,* trans. Aditya Behl and Simon Weightman (Oxford: Oxford University Press, 2000), xi–xlvi.

12. "*Kunam ishq-i Manohar kitabi/diham az nam-i Mihr an ra khitabi/nawa-yi husn-i Madhumalat sarayam/dili dar parda-yi mahash numayam,*" quoted in Muhammad Amin Amir, "*Sahm-i Aqil Khan Razi dar adabiyat-i farsi ba ahd-i Aurangzeb,*" *Qand-i Parsi* 69/70 (2015): 109–127, 110.

13. See Hamid ibn Fazlullah Jamali (d. 1517), *Masnavi-i mihr va mah,* ed. Husamud-Din Rashidi (Ravalpindi: Markaz-i Tahqiqat-i Farsi-i Iran va Pakistan, 1974).

14. P. K. Gode, "Date of Nīlakaṇṭha, author of Cimanīcarita," *Annals of the Bhandarkar Oriental Research Institute* 9.2/4 (1928): 331–332.

15. Nilakantha Shukla, *Chimanicharitam: Premakavyam,* ed. Prabhat Shastri et al. (Prayagah: Devabhashaprakashanam, 1976), 25, verse 87.

16. "*Ut bhasha mahram sab koi/padhai jo matlab samjhe soi//tis karan yah premkahani/purab di bhasha bich ani,*" quoted in Moti Chand, "*Kavi Surdas krit Naldaman kavya,*" *Nagarini Pracharini Patrika* 43.2 (1938/9): 121–138, 122. This Surdas is not to be confused with the famed fifteenth-century poet-saint of the same name.

17. The date of composition is Samvat 1714, corresponding to 1656. See Rahurkar's introduction to Kavindracharya, *The Bhasayogavasisthasara (Jnanasara) of Kavindracarya Sarasvati,* ed. V. G. Rahurkar (Puna: Bharatavani-Prakashanamala, 1969), 33.

18. Rahurkar, for instance, speculates that this might have been the case; Kavindracharya, *Bhasayogavasisthasara,* 3.

19. *Ashtavakra Gita,* Staatsbibliothek, Berlin, MS Sprenger 1661 is an anonymous text. In 2009, I examined the Osmania University manuscript of the text attributed to Jadun Das, but was not permitted to obtain a digital copy for further study.

20. See Dara Shukoh, *Bhagvad Gita: Surud-i ilahi,* ed. Muhammad Reza Jalali Naini (Tehran: Kitabkhana-i Tahuri, 1970).

21. Abu-l-Faiz Faizi, *Shri Bhagvad gita farsi* (Jalandhar: Munshi Ram, 1901). For instance, the *Sirr-i akbar,* housed in the Khuda Bakhsh Library, Patna, MS HL 2747, is attributed to Faizi but authored by Dara Shukoh.

22. Abd-ur-Rahman Chishti, *Mirat-ul-haqaiq*, British Library, MS Or. 1883, fols. 257a–271a.

23. Victoria and Albert Museum, London, no. IS. 94–1965. Art historians have dated this to the first half of the 1650s on stylistic grounds. Elinor Gadon, "Note on Frontispiece," in *The Sants: Studies in a Devotional Tradition of India*, eds. Karine Schomer and W. H. Mcleod (Berkeley: Berkeley Religious Studies Series, 1987), 415–421, 420. In an in-person communication on September 18, 2008, Susan Stronge, curator at the Victoria and Albert Museum, noted that she agreed with Elinor Gadon's dating of the work.

24. For details regarding the writings of Varan Kavi and Sai, see D. N. Marshall, *Mughals in India: A Bibliographical Survey* (London: Mansell, 1985), 474, 562–563, §§1622A, 1824.

25. For instance, Sadiq Isfahani, *Shahid-i sadiq*, British Library, I.O. Islamic 1537, fols. 36a–38a. For the geographical section, see Sadiq Isfahani, *Khatima-i Shahid-i Sadiq: dar zabt-i asma-i jughrafiyai*, ed. Mir Hashim Muhaddis (Tehran: Majlis-i Shura-i Islami, 1998/9); the atlas is preserved in British Library, MS I.O. Egerton 1016, fols. 335a–359a. See broadly, Nazir Ahmad, "Muhammad Sadiq Isfahani, an Official of Bengal of Shah Jahan's Time," *Indo-Iranica* 24 (1972): 103–125; S. N. H. Rizvi, "Literary Extracts from *Kitab Subh Sadiq*," *Journal of the Asiatic Society of Pakistan* 16.1 (1971): 1–61. For more on Sadiq's contribution to geography, see Irfan Habib, "Cartography in Mughal India," *Proceedings of the Indian History Congress* 35 (1974): 150–162, 151–155.

26. Muhammad Bakhtawar Khan, *Mirat-ul-alam*, ed. Sajida Alvi, 2 vols. (Lahore: Research Society of Pakistan, University of Punjab, 1979), 2: 415.

27. "*Kamarikai mange baksis karai pamarike/hay mange hathi det hira det hansime*," Kavindracharya Sarasvati, *Kavindrakalpalata*, ed. Lakshmikumari Chundavat (Jaipur: Puratattvanveshana Mandir, 1958).

28. Tabatabai, *Dasturnama-i Kisrawi*, Oxford University, Bodleian Library, MS Ouseley 135; described in Eduard Sachau and Hermann Ethé, *Catalogue of the Persian, Turkish, Hindûstânî and Pushtû Manuscripts in the Bodleian Library* (Oxford: The Clarendon Press, 1889), 897–898, §1470.

29. For examples of Said's poetry, see Mohammad Quamruddin, *Life and Times of Murad Bakhsh, 1624–1661* (Calcutta: Quamruddin, 1974), 163 and 173.

30. Quamruddin, *Murad Bakhsh*, 168.

31. Marshall, *Mughals in India*, 467, §1797.

32. See chap. 9, 222.

33. Munshi Shaikh Abu-l-Fath Qabil Khan, *Adab-i Alamgiri*, ed. Abd-ul-Ghafur Chaudhari, 2 vols. (Lahore: Idara-i Tahqiqat-i Pakistan, 1971), 1: 232n4, §101; partial translation in Vincent Flynn, *An English Translation of the Ādāb-i-Ālamgīrī. The Period before the War of Succession* (PhD thesis, Australian National University, 1974), 341, §97.

34. Letter of Prince Sultan Dara Shikoh to Abdullah Qutb Shah, in K. K. Basu, "The Golconda Court Letters," *Journal of the Bihar Research Society* 26.4 (1940): 271–298, 294–295.

35. Qabil Khan, *Adab-i Alamgiri*, 1: 250–251, §116.

36. Sayyid Akbarali Ibrahimali Tirmizi, *Mughal Documents*, 2 vols. (New Delhi: Manohar, 1989–1995), 2: 113–114, §§295, 298, and 299.

37. Patrick Olivelle, "Introduction," in *The Early Upaniṣads: Annotated Text and Translation*, ed. and trans. Patrick Olivelle (Oxford: Oxford University Press, 1998), 3–27, 12.

38. Abd-ul-Qadir Badayuni, *Muntakhab-ut-tawarikh*, 3 vols. (Tehran: Anjuman-i Asar, 2000), 2: 146.

39. Dara Shukoh, *Sirr-i akbar*, eds. Tara Chand and Muhammad Reza Jalali-Naini (Tehran: Taban Printing Press, 1957), 490.

40. Quran 7: 1–2. For the argument that Dara Shukoh invokes the Timurid tradition of lettrism in the *Sirr-i akbar*, see Matthew Melvin-Koushki, "Timurid-Mughal Philosopher-Kings as Sultan-Scientists," forthcoming in Maribel Fierro, Sonja Brentjes and Tilman Seidensticker, eds., *Rulers as Authors in the Islamic World: Knowledge, Authority and Legitimacy* (Leiden: Brill, 2020). I am grateful to the author for sharing a draft of the article.

41. For this manuscript of the *Sirr-i akbar*, see British Library, MS I.O. Islamic 26, fol. 2a. Described in Hermann Ethé, *Catalogue of Persian Manuscripts in the Library of the India Office*, 2 vols. (Oxford: Horace Hart, 1903–1937), 1: 1102.

42. Dara Shukoh, *Sirr-i akbar*, iv.

43. Dara Shukoh, *Sirr-i akbar*, v.

44. Some manuscripts also refer to the collection as the *Sirr-i asrar*, "The Secret of all Secrets." For different perspectives on the *Sirr-i akbar* in modern scholarship, see Svevo D'Onofrio, "A Persian Commentary to the Upaniṣads: Dārā Šikōh's *Sirr-i Akbar*," in *Muslim Cultures in the Indo-Iranian World During the Early-Modern and Modern Periods*, eds. Fabrizio Speziale and Denis Hermann (Berlin: Klaus Schwarz, 2010): 533–563; for a detailed study of one Upanishad from the collection, the *Prashna Upanishad*, see Erhard Göbel-Gross, *Die persichen Upaniṣadenübersetzung des Moġulprinzen Dārā Šukoh* (PhD diss., Philipps-Universität, 1962). For the argument that the *Sirr-i akbar* was a political project for Dara Shukoh, see Munis Faruqui, "Dara Shukoh, Vedanta and the Politics of Mughal India," in *Religious Interactions in Mughal India, 16th–20th Centuries,* eds. Vasudha Dalmia and Munis D. Faruqui (New Delhi: Oxford University Press, 2014), 65–101.

45. For an overview of how these verses are treated by the early exegetical authorities, see Abu Jafar Tabari, *Jami-ul-bayan an tawil-il-Quran*, ed. Abdullah Turki, 26 vols. (Cairo: Dar Hajar, 2001), 22: 362–368. On the celestial origin of scripture as depicted in the Quran, see Daniel Madigan, *The Qurân's Self-Image: Writing and Authority in Islam's Scripture* (Princeton: Princeton University Press, 2001) 13–52.

46. Dara Shukoh, *Sirr-i akbar*, v–vi (Quran 56: 77–80).

47. Dara Shukoh, *Sirr-i akbar*, vi.

48. Adam is here identified as Brahma, though elsewhere in the *Sirr-i akbar*, Dara identifies Brahma with Gabriel. On the long association between Adam and India, see, for instance, Carl Ernst, "India as a Sacred Islamic Land," in *Religions of India in Practice*, ed. Donald S. Lopez (Princeton, NJ: Princeton University Press, 1995), 556–564, 557.

49. Dara Shukoh, *Sirr-i akbar*, iv–v. Notice the parallel account on the number of four Vedas, the role of Brahma as intermediary, and the antiquity of Sanskrit, in François Bernier, *Un libertin dans l'Inde moghole: les Voyages de François Bernier (1656–1669)*, ed. Frédéric Tinguely, Adrien Paschoud, and Charles-Antoine Chamay (Paris: Chandeigne, 2008), 332, Letter to Monsieur Chapelain, October 4, 1667. Bernier's knowledge derives from conversations with similar circles of pandits. The identification of Sanskrit as *langue pure* may explain Dara's use here of the common honorific for Adam as *Safiullah*, literally the pure one of God.

50. For the discovery of ancient prophetic writings as a Hermetic trope in the similarly titled work, see also pseudo-Apollonius, *Sirr-ul-khaliqa*, ed. Ursula Weisser (Aleppo: Mahad-ut-Turath, 1979), 5–7.

51. Mahmoud Manzalaoui, "The pseudo-Aristotelian *Kitab Sirr al-asrar*: Facts and Problems," *Oriens* 23/24 (1974): 146–257.

52. Muhammad Baqir, *Zakhira-i Iskandarani*, Bodleian Library, Oxford University, MS Whinfield 57, 3–10. For his work on Razi's *Sirr-i maktum*, see chap. 6, 161.

53. Olivelle, "Introduction," *Early Upaniṣads*, 24.

54. A perusal of the *New Catalogus Catalogorum*, a survey of the multitudinous Sanskrit manuscripts catalogued across the world, yields remarkably few Upanishad anthologies. The extant manuscript record does not indicate that there was an active textual practice of compiling Upanishad collections during Dara Shukoh's time. The most thorough scholarly treatment of Upanishad collections of which I am aware does not include any actual anthologies, as opposed to Upanishad lists, apart from Dara Shukoh's. See Joachim Sprockhoff, *Saṃnyāsa: Quellenstudien zur Askese im Hinduismus* (Marburg: Deutsche Morgenländische Gesellschaft, 1976), 13–26, 312, table 1.

55. *Early Upaniṣads*, 436–437.

56. Dara Shukoh, *Sirr-i akbar* (translation of *Mundaka* 1.1.1), 324.

57. Dara Shukoh, *Sirr-i akbar* (translation of *Mundaka* 1.1.8), 325.

58. *Early Upaniṣads*, 38–39.

59. Dara Shukoh *Sirr-i akbar* (translation of *Brihadaranyaka* 1.3.1), 6. The *Sirr-i akbar* echoes Shankara's commentary, which identifies the children of Prajapati as "the gods and the asuras, that is to say, the sensory organs, speech, and the rest of Prajapati himself." Shankara further elaborates that the sense organs become gods "under the influence of knowledge and karma born of the scriptures," as do the asuras "under the influence of knowledge and karma yielding visible results." V. Panoli, *Upanishads in Sankara's Own Words*, 4 vols. (Calicut: Mathrubhumi, 1993), 4: 62.

60. Olivelle, *Early Upanishads*, 460–461.

61. Dara Shukoh, *Sirr-i akbar* (translation of *Prashna* 1.15), 175. According to the *Ratishastra* 205 ("Doctrine of Conjugal Love"), "There are sixteen (days and) nights of the women's monthly fertile period. During it, (a man) should have intercourse on the even numbered (nights in order to have a son). But (acting) just (like) a *brahmacārin* (i.e., a celibate boy), he must avoid the first four days, and the (five) nights of the changing moon." *Conjugal Love in India: Ratisastra*

and *Ratiramana-Text, Translation and Notes*, trans. Kenneth Zysk (Leiden: Brill, 2002), 90.

62. Dara Shukoh, *Sirr-i akbar*, 1–2.

63. Bernier, *Voyages*, 324, 338–339, Letter to Monsieur Chapelain, October 4, 1667.

64. See above, note 49.

65. These are, respectively: *Kavindrachandrodaya*, eds. H. D. Sharma and M. M. Patkar (Poona: Bhandarkar Oriental Research Institute, 1939); and *Kavindra-chandrika*, ed. K. Divakar (Pune: Maharashtra Rashtrabhasha Sabha, 1966). For an examination of the *Kavindrachandrodaya* that also touches on the *Kavindrachandrika*, see Audrey Truschke, "Contested History: Brahmanical Memories of Relations with the Mughals," *Journal of the Economic and Social History of the Orient* 58.4 (2015): 419–452.

66. *Kavindrachandrodaya*, 24, line 170.

67. V. G. Rahurkar, "The *Bhasa-Yogavasisthasara* of Kavindracarya Sarasvati," *Proceedings and Transactions of the All-India Oriental Conference* (1955): 471–482, 477. Rahurkar is also of the opinion that the tax was lifted in 1657.

68. The date was Rabi-ul-Akhir 5, 1067 AH (January 21, 1657). Muhammad Waris, *Badshahnamah of Muhammad Waris*, trans. Ishrat Husain Ansari and Hamid Afaq Qureshi (Delhi: Idarah-i Adabiyat-i Delli, 2017), 308.

69. The relevant lines from the *Kavindrakalpalata* are discussed in Allison Busch, "Brajbhasha Poets at the Mughal Court," *Modern Asian Studies* (2009): 1–40, 25.

9. Succession, 1657–1659

1. Muhammad Salih Kamboh, *Amal-i Salih*, ed. Ghulam Yazdani, 3 vols. (Lahore: Majlis-i Taraqqi-i Adab, 1958–1960), 3: 264. I am grateful to Dr. Michael Rigsby, Director of Internal Medicine at Yale Health, for suggesting this in a personal communication, based on Kamboh's description of the emperor's symptoms (June 27, 2018). I mention this while aware, of course, of the problems associated with translating premodern conceptions of illness and the body into modern categories.

2. Kamboh, *Amal-i Salih*, 3: 264.

3. "*Ta sihhat ast unsur shah-i yagana ra/paidast itidal mizaj-i zamana ra,*" Mir Muhammad Masum, *Tarikh-i Shah Shujai*, ed. Muhammad Yunus Jaffery (Delhi: Rayzani-i Farhangi-i Jumhuri-i Islami-i Iran, 2007), 63.

4. Masum, *Tarikh*, 64.

5. One exception is the aforementioned *Amal-i Salih*, which Kamboh started while Shah Jahan was emperor, and completed after the results of the succession war were known.

6. Muhammad Faiz Bakhsh, *Tarikh-i Farahbakhsh*, translated as *Memoirs of Delhi and Faizabad*, trans. William Hoey, 2 vols. (Allahabad: Government Press, Northwestern Provinces and Oudh, 1888–1889), 1: 61.

7. Kamboh, *Amal-i Salih*, 3: 265–266.

8. Masum, *Tarikh*, 65.

9. Masum, *Tarikh*, 66–67.

10. Sayyid Akbarali Ibrahimali Tirmizi, *Mughal Documents,* 2 vols. (New Delhi: Manohar, 1989–1995), 2: 122. Dispatch dated Rabi-ul-Akhir 16, 1068 AH (January 21, 1658) in K. D. Bhargava, *A Descriptive List of Farmans, Manshurs and Nishans addressed by the Imperial Mughals to the Princes of Rajasthan* (Bikaner: Government of Rajasthan, 1962), 35, §231.

11. Tirmizi, *Mughal Documents*, 2: 124.

12. Jaipur records, quoted in Kalika Ranjan Qanungo, *Dara Shukoh* (Calcutta: S.C. Sarkar and Sons, 1952), 172.

13. Masum, *Tarikh*, 78.

14. Masum, *Tarikh*, 82–84.

15. Tirmizi, *Mughal Documents*, 2: 124.

16. Kalika Ranjan Qanungo, "Prince Muhammad Dara Shikoh and Mirza Rajah Jai Singh Kachhwaha," *Indian Historical Records Commission Proceedings of Meetings* 9 (1927): 86–94, 90.

17. Bihishti, *Ashob-i Hindustan*, ed. Syeda Khurshid Fatima Husaini (Delhi: Rayzani-i Farhangi-i Jumhuri-i Islami-i Iran, 2009), 87–102. On Bihishti's poem as an influential model for the later eighteenth-century *shahrashob* genre, and for a discussion of the poem's wide readership, see Sunil Sharma, *Mughal Arcadia: Persian Literature in an Indian Court* (Cambridge, MA: Harvard University Press, 2017), 167–168.

18. "*Dar an anjuman az kiran ta kiran / hawa gasht chun abr-i jauhar fishan // zar o gauhar o sim dar paytakht / furu rekhti hamchu gul az dirakht // zar o sim az baskih afshanda shud / zi bar chidanash dast ha manda shud,*" Bihishti, *Ashob*, 107.

19. Munshi Shaikh Abu-l-Fath Qabil Khan, "Correspondence with Murad," *Adab-i Alamgiri*, ed. Abd-ul-Ghafur Chaudhari, 2 vols. (Lahore: Idara-i Tahqiqat-i Pakistan, 1971), 2: 791–792, §2.

20. Aqil Khan Razi, *Waqiat-i Alamgiri*, ed. Zafar Hasan (Delhi: Publications of the Aligarh Historical Institute, 1945), 32–33. A concise English summary of these events can be found in Zafar Hasan, *The Waqiat-i-Alamgiri of Aqil Khan Razi: An Account of the War of Succession between the Sons of the Emperor Shah Jahan* (Delhi: Mercantile Press, 1946).

21. Jadunath Sarkar, *History of Aurangzib*, 5 vols. (Calcutta: Sarkar and Sons, 1912–1924), 1: 333–334.

22. Qabil Khan, *Adab-i Alamgiri*, 1: 374. For doubt concerning the authenticity of the agreement, see Sri Ram Sharma, *Studies in Medieval Indian History* (Sholapur: Institute of Public Administration, 1956), 254.

23. Qabil Khan, *Adab-i Alamgiri*, 1: 374–375; Sarkar, *History of Aurangzib*, 1: 336–337.

24. Aqil Khan, *Waqiat*, 34–35.

25. Qabil Khan, *Adab-i Alamgiri*, 1: 374–375.

26. See, for example, Iftikhar Ahmad Ghauri, *War of Succession: Between Sons of Shahjahan, 1657–1658* (Lahore: Publishers United, 1964), esp. 63–88.

27. Aurangzeb Alamgir, *Rukaat-i Alamgiri*, translated as *Letters of Aurungzebe with Historical and Explanatory Notes*, trans. Jamshid Bilimoria (London: Luzac and Co., 1908), 81–82.

28. Cross-reference chap. 7.

29. Muhammad Sadiq, *Tarikh-i Shah Jahani*, British Library, Or. 1671, fol. 96b. Compare the erroneous translation of the same passage in Ghauri, *War of Succession*, 78.

30. For the discrepancies in the accounts of Sadiq Khan and doubts cast on his authorship of the *Tarikh-i Shah Jahani*, see A. J. Syed, "A Note on Sadiq Khan and Mamuri," *Proceedings of the Indian History Congress* 37 (1976): 271–278.

31. Shyamaladas, *Vir Vinod*, 7 vols. (Udaipur: Rajayantralay, 1886), 1:419–420. The letter is also partially translated in M. Athar Ali, "Towards an Interpretation of the Mughal Empire," *Journal of the Royal Asiatic Society*, no. 1 (1978): 38–49, 42. My translation differs from Athar Ali's.

32. Sarkar, *History of Aurangzib*, 1: 368–369.

33. Aqil Khan, *Waqiat* , 38–42.

34. "*Saf-i rajputan-i ahan qaba / shikafanda az nok-i naiza hawa // shuda hamla bar hamchu sheran-i mast / ba suy-i mughal tegh-i hindi ba dast // rukh afrokhta ba atish-i kina-ha / zi nok-i sinan dokhta sina-ha // nadanista hargiz tariq-i gurez / kih inha nadarand bim az sitez . . . namudand jangi dar an pahn dasht / kazan Arjun o Bim sharminda gasht . . . musalman o hindu dar amekhtand / ba ham haqq o batil dar amekhtand,*" Masum, *Tarikh*, 80.

35. See, for example, letters of Murad Bakhsh in *Fayyaz-ul-qawanin*, British Library, Or 9617, fols. 77b–78a.

36. Aqil Khan, *Waqiat*, 46–47.

37. Aqil Khan, *Waqiat*, 48–49.

38. Aqil Khan, *Waqiat*, 53.

39. Masum, *Tarikh*, 82.

40. Sharing meals between Hindus and Muslims is often thought to be one of the last frontiers of intimacy in precolonial South Asia, though co-dining or inter-dining with Muslims would have been less incongruous for a Rajput than, say, for certain Brahmins.

41. Masum, *Tarikh*, 83–84.

42. For example, see Tirmizi, *Mughal Documents*, 2: 124, 126, 128, §§345, 359, 366.

43. Tirmizi, *Mughal Documents*, 2: 131, §378.

44. Qanungo, "Prince," 90.

45. Tirmizi, *Mughal Documents*, 2: 133, §§386, 388, 389.

46. Masum, *Tarikh*, 90.

47. Masum, *Tarikh*, 89.

48. Aqil Khan, *Waqiat*, 58.

49. For an overview of the complicated textual and linguistic history of Manucci's writings, see William Irvine, "Introduction," in Niccolò Manucci, *Storia do Mogor or Mogul India, 1653–1708*, trans. William Irvine, 4 vols. (London: John Murray, 1907–1908), 1: xviii–lvi. For doubts concerning the authenticity

of elements in Manucci's work, see Piero Falchetta, "Venezia, madre lontana: Vita e opere di Nicolò Manuzzi (1638–1717)," in the partial edition of the Italian redaction, Manucci, *Storia del Mogol di Nicolò Manuzzi Veneziano,* ed. Piero Falchetta, 2 vols. (Milano: Franco Maria Ricci, 1986), 1: 24–27. See also Sanjay Subrahmanyam, "Further Thoughts on an Enigma: The Tortuous Life of Nicolò Manucci, 1638–c. 1720," *The Indian Economic and Social History Review* 45.1 (2008): 35–76; and Sanjay Subrahmanyam, *Three Ways to be Alien: Travails and Encounters in the Early Modern World* (Waltham, MA: Brandeis University Press, 2011), 133–172. For a detailed study of the entirety of Manucci's corpus, including the paintings he commissioned while in India, see Marta Becherini, *Staging the Foreign: Niccolò Manucci (1638-ca. 1720) and Early Modern European Collections of Indian Paintings* (PhD diss., Columbia University, 2016).

50. Niccolò Manucci, *Voyage et histoire du Mogol,* Staatsbibliothek, Berlin, MS Phillips 1945, part 1, fol. 95a (revised Portuguese version); *Storia del Mogol,* 1: 122; translation, 1: 273–274. Here as in elsewhere, I have benefited from Irvine's translation when consulting the Portuguese version of the Berlin manuscript.

51. Aqil Khan, *Waqiat,* 59.

52. Aqil Khan, *Waqiat,* 60; summary, 10n2, 22nn2–3. For Daud Khan, see Nrip-endra Kumar Srivastava, "The Career of Daud Khan Quraishi and His Conquest of Palamau," *Proceedings of the Indian History Congress,* 60 (1999): 306–314, 306n7. For Rao Satarsal and Raja Rup Singh, see also Sarkar, *History of Aurangzib,* 2: 33, 51–52, 61–62.

53. Ghauri, *War of Succession,* 86.

54. M. Athar Ali, "The Religious Issue in the War of Succession, 1658–1659," in *Mughal India: Studies in Polity, Ideas, Society, and Culture* (Delhi: Oxford University Press, 2006), 245–252.

55. See the table, "Supporters of the Contending Princes in the War of Succession (1658–59)," in Muhammad Athar Ali, *The Mughal Nobility under Aurangzeb* (New York: Asia Publishing House for the Department of History, 1966), 96. Ghauri provides a less comprehensive enumeration of the Mughal nobility according to their rank and ethnic origin in *War of Succession,* 89–95. I have based my analysis on Athar Ali's table.

56. Amir Ahmad, "The Bundela Revolts during the Mughal Period: A Dynastic Affair," *Proceedings of the Indian History Congress* 66 (2005/6): 438–445, 440–441.

57. Athar Ali, *Mughal Nobility,* 96.

58. Tirmizi, *Mughal Documents,* 2: 127–128.

59. Nawab Shahnawaz Khan, *Maasir-ul-umara,* ed. Maulvi Abd-ur-Rahim, 3 vols. (Calcutta: Asiatic Society of Bengal, 1888), 1: 225.

60. Shahnawaz Khan, *Maasir,* 2: 686.

61. Shahnawaz Khan, *Maasir,* 2: 566–568.

62. Shahnawaz Khan, *Maasir,* 1: 235–241.

63. Shahnawaz Khan, *Maasir,* 3: 943–946.

64. Shahnawaz Khan, *Maasir,* 1: 252–253.

65. Manucci, *Voyage,* fol. 95a; *Storia,* 1: 122; translation, 1: 273–274.

66. Manucci, *Voyage*, fol. 96a; *Storia*, 1: 126; translation, 1: 276–277.

67. Masum, *Tarikh*, 92.

68. Masum, *Tarikh*, 93.

69. Manucci, *Voyage*, fol. 95b; *Storia*, 1: 128; translation, 1: 278.

70. Manucci, *Voyage*, fol. 97b; *Storia*, 1: 132–133; translation, 1: 281–282.

71. Masum, *Tarikh*, 94.

72. Payag (attributed), Harvard University Art Museums, 1999.298.

73. Masum, *Tarikh*, 94–95.

74. Masum, *Tarikh*, 137.

75. Masum, *Tarikh*, 96; Manucci, *Voyage*, fol. 100a; translation, 1: 288. This section is not included in the partial Italian edition.

76. Aqil Khan, *Waqiat*, 67–68.

77. Aqil Khan, *Waqiat*, 69–75.

78. Masum, *Tarikh*, 97–99.

79. Aqil Khan, *Waqiat*, 80–81.

80. Masum, *Tarikh*, 100.

81. Victoria and Albert Museum, London, no. IS. 12–1962. For further information, see Robert Skelton, *The Shah Jahan Cup* (London: Victoria and Albert Museum, 1969).

82. Aqil Khan, *Waqiat*, 81.

83. Aqil Khan, *Waqiat*, 84.

84. Bihishti, *Ashob*, 166.

85. Jonathan Scott (d. 1829), *Tales, Anecdotes, and Letters* (Shrewsbury: T. Cadell and W. Davies, 1800), 389–390.

86. Tirmizi, *Mughal Documents*, 2: 136.

87. Qanungo, *Dara Shukoh*, 192.

88. Masum, *Tarikh*, 109.

89. Bihishti, *Ashob*, 161.

90. Aqil Khan, *Waqiat*, 87–88.

91. Aqil Khan, *Waqiat*, 90.

92. Masum, *Tarikh*, 111; Bihishti, *Ashob*, 180–181. According to Manucci, though, he resisted the slave girl's attentions and instead got his own eunuch, Shahbaz Khan, to rub his feet. Manucci, *Voyage*, fol. 104a; translation, 1: 302.

93. Aqil Khan, *Waqiat*, 93.

94. Manucci, *Voyage*, fol. 104b; translation, 1: 303.

95. Masum, *Tarikh*, 112–113.

96. Manucci, *Voyage*, fol. 105b; translation 1: 306; Aqil Khan, *Waqiat*, 98.

97. Qanungo, "Prince Muhammad Dara Shikoh," 93. I am reading Chetpur for Jitpur as transcribed by Qanungo.

98. Manucci, *Voyage*, fol. 106b; translation, 1: 309.

99. Manucci, *Voyage*, fol. 107a; translation, 1: 310.

100. Masum mentions two daughters with Dara during his exile. For the possibility of another daughter named Amal-un-Nisa Begam, see Qanungo, *Dara Shukoh*, 166.

101. Manucci, *Voyage*, fol. 114a; *Storia*, translation, 1: 326.

102. Masum, *Tarikh*, 116, 118.
103. Manucci, *Voyage*, fols. 107a–b; translation, 1: 311. Manucci cites two successive letters.
104. Masum, *Tarikh*, 119.
105. Masum, *Tarikh*, 122. Masum states here that Daud Khan murdered the women of his harem in a show of his loyalty to Dara, but it was to no avail.
106. Masum, *Tarikh*, 123–133.
107. Manucci, *Voyage*, fol. 111b; translation, 1: 320.
108. Manucci, *Storia*, fol. 114b; translation, 1: 325n2. See the portrayal of Shahnawaz Khan as betraying Dara in François Bernier, *Un libertin dans l'Inde moghole: les Voyages de François Bernier (1656–1669)*, ed. Frédéric Tinguely, Adrien Paschoud, and Charles-Antoine Chamay (Paris: Chandeigne, 2008), 101–102.
109. Masum, *Tarikh*, 162.
110. Aqil Khan, *Waqiat*, 113.
111. Syamaladas, *Vira vinod*, 2: 432–433.
112. Aqil Khan, *Waqiat*, 114–115.
113. This battle position was "admirably chosen" according to Sarkar, *History of Aurangzib*, 2: 152.
114. See Bernier, *Voyages*, 114–115.
115. Masum, *Tarikh*, 163.
116. Masum, *Tarikh*, 164.
117. Masum, *Tarikh*, 164–165.
118. "*Chu an gul kih bar khak uftad zi bad / bidan guna dar pay-i Jivan uftad . . . mara ba zar o zewar-i be shumar / ba silk-i kanizan-i matbakh dar ar // mara dukht-i Parwez Shah madar ast / pidar al-i Taimur sahib-i farr ast / ba dunya ba jay-i kanizam numay / zi pa band-i zanjir-i Dara gushay,*" Bihishti, *Ashob*, 214–215.
119. Masum, *Tarikh*, 166.
120. Bernier, *Voyages*, 120–121.
121. Bernier, *Voyages*, 122.
122. "*Bidinsan chu shud dakhil-i paytakht / siyah ruy shud Jivan-i shor bakht // zi har barzan o bam o dar be dirang / giriftand u ra ba dushnam o sang / zi afghan-i bad tinat-i ru siyah / basi sar zi tan rekht dar khak-i rah // zi bas shud zi har gosha ghogha buland / shahinshah ra dar tawahhum fikand // bipursid kin shor o ghoghay chist / tirazanda-yi in hama fitna kist // ba arzash risandand kay shahryar / zi Dara shud in shor o sharr ashkar // mar u ra sitayand khalqan tamam / shahinshah ba zishti bar awurda nam / chun bishanid Aurang Shah in sukhan / zi ghairat balarzid bar khweshtan // ba khud guft Darast ta dar hayat / jahanbani-yi ma nadarad sabat // zi dil aks-i mihr o wafa ra zibud / hamandam ba qatlash isharat namud,*" Bihishti, *Ashob*, 216–217.
123. Masum, *Tarikh*, 166.
124. "*Qu'il n'estoit point Musulman, qu'il y avoit long-temps qu'il estoit devenu Kafier, Idolatre, sans Religion,*" Bernier, *Histoire*, 240–241; *Voyages*, 122–123.

125. That is, the Vedas. The shift from /v/ to /b/ was a characteristic of some North Indian forms of Hindavi. This form was commonly used in Indic words transliterated in the Perso-Arabic script, suggesting the role of Hindavi in mediating the translation of Sanskrit learning into Persian. Muhammad Kazim's reference to the Vedas most likely refers to Dara Shukoh's translation of roughly fifty Upanisads, conflated here with the Vedas. A similar misidentification is found in the manuscript tradition of the Upanisad translations. For instance, I have seen manuscripts in the Andhra Pradesh Government Oriental Manuscripts Library purport to be translations of the Rig Veda, Sama Veda, and Atharva Veda; however, upon inspection, they appear to be compilations of Persian Upanishad translations from Dara's *Sirr-i Akbar*, rearranged according to their associated Vedas.

126. Muhammad Kazim, *Alamgir-nama*, eds. Khadim Husain and Abd al-Hayy (Calcutta: College Press, 1868), 34–35.

127. For the use of rings in Akbar's court for imperial discipleship, see Makhanlal Roychoudhury, *The Din-i-Ilahi or The Religion of Akbar*, 2nd ed. (Calcutta: Das Gupta, 1952), *Din-i Ilahi*, 285–287.

128. Kazim, *Alamgir-nama*, 432.

129. "*Risanid chun qatilash jam-i zahar/kih dar kish ba hukm-i shahinshah-i dahar//aba kard o gufta mara az nakhust/buwad ba khuda itiqad-i durust//musalmanam o payrow-i Mustafa/chu kuffar jan ra siparam chira/shuda sard az zindagani dilam//ba har nau dani bokun bismilam*," Bihishti, *Ashob*, 217.

130. "*Badi ra badi sahl bashad jaza/agar mardi ahsin ila man asa*," Masum, *Tarikh*, 168.

131. However, contra Masum, Manucci notes that Sipihr Shukoh was already taken to the Gwalior prison. Manucci, *Voyage*, fol. 129b; *Storia*, 1: 154; translation, 1: 356.

132. Masum, *Tarikh*, 169.

133. To lend veracity to the account, Manucci provides a Persian transcription of what he purports to be Dara's last words, which he translates into Portuguese with a subtle pun on Dara's name, "*Mahamed me mata, e o Filho de Deos me dara a vida*," Manucci, *Voyage*, fol. 129b; *Storia*, 1: 154; translation 1: 357.

134. Shuja's death is discussed in Rishad Choudhury, "An Eventful Politics of Difference and Its Afterlife: Chittagong Frontier, Bengal, c. 1657–1757," *The Indian Economic and Social History Review* 52.3 (2015): 271–296.

135. Saqi Mustad Khan, *Maasir-i Alamgiri*, trans. Jadunath Sarkar (Calcutta: Royal Asiatic Society of Bengal, 1947), 323.

136. *Maasir-i Alamgiri*, 77.

137. *Maasir-i Alamgiri*, 73.

138. *Maasir-i Alamgiri*, 49.

139. Jahanara, *Ayat-i bayyinat*, Aligarh Muslim University, Maulana Azad Library, Habibganj Collection, MS 1/55, fols. 38b–39b (Quran 17: 23–24). Completed at the end of Rajab 1073 AH (March 1663). See Travis Zadeh, *The Vernacular Qur'an: Translation and the Rise of Persian Exegesis* (Oxford: Oxford University, 2012), 589n75. Compare with the autograph colophon of Jahanara, *Munis-ul-arwah*, British Library, Or. 5637, fols. 122b–123a.

Conclusion

1. Muhammad Fayz Bakhsh, *Tarikh-i Farahbakhsh,* translated as *Memoirs of Delhi and Faizabad,* trans. William Hoey, 2 vols. (Allahabad: Government Press, Northwestern Provinces and Oudh, 1888–1889), 1: 114.
2. Muhammad Kazim, *Alamgir-nama,* 1: 433.
3. For instance, the grave is identified as Dara Shukoh's in Waldemar Hansen, *The Peacock Throne* (New York: Holt, Rinehart and Winston, 1972), Figure 24. It also comes up in Google searches for the prince's grave.
4. Yunus Jaffery holds this view, in Yunus Jaffery, "Shahzada Dara Shukoh," *Qand-i Parsi* 67–68 (March-April 2015):82–111, 88.
5. *Memoirs of Delhi and Faizabad,* 114; Quran, 59:2: *"Fa-tabiru ya-ula l-absar."*
6. *"Subh dil-i man chun gul-i khurshid shiguft/haqq zahir shud ghubar-i batil ra girift//tarikh-i julus-i shah-i aurang mara/'zill-ul-haqq' guft, in ra haq guft,"* Tawakkul Beg, *Nuskha-i ahwal-i shahi,* British Library, MS Or. 3203, fol. 75a.
7. These letters are translated in Rajeev Kinra, *Writing Self, Writing Empire: Chandar Bhan Brahman and the Cultural World of the Indo-Persian State Secretary* (Berkeley: University of California Press, 2015), 54–55.
8. Yunus Jaffery also makes a similar point about Dara's omission in his edition of the Chahar Chaman; Chandarbhan Brahman, *Chahar Chaman,* ed. Mohammad Yunus Jaffery (New Delhi: Centre of Persian Research, 2007), 16.
9. Kinra, *Writing Self,* 56.
10. *"Uryani-i tan buwad ghubar-i rah-i dust/an niz ba tegh az sar-i ma wa kardand,"* Aqil Khan Razi, *Waqiat-i Alamgiri,* ed. Zafar Hasan (Delhi: Publications of the Aligarh Historical Institute, 1945), 121.
11. I draw on the reading of these chronicles presented in Vikas Rathee, *Narratives of the 1658 War of Succession for the Mughal Throne, 1658–1707* (unpublished PhD diss., University of Arizona, 2015). Rathee also casts doubt on the attribution of the *Khulasa* to Sujan Rai Bhandari. See also Sujan Rai Bhandari, *Khulasat-ut-tawarikh,* ed. M. Zafar Hasan (Delhi: J. and Sons, 1917).
12. Francois Bernier, *Histoire de la dernière révolution des états du Grand Mogol,* 4 vols. (Paris: Claude Barbin, 1671–1672), 1: 8.
13. Vincent Arthur Smith and Stephen Meredyth Edwardes, *The Oxford History of India, from the Earliest Times to the End of 1911* (Oxford: Clarendon Press, 1928), 408.
14. I draw here on the concepts of cultural memory and archive elucidated by Aleida Assmann, "Canon and Archive," in *Cultural Memory Studies: An International and Interdisciplinary Handbook,* eds. Astrid Erll and Ansgar Nünning (Berlin: Walter de Gruyter, 2008), 98–107.
15. Muhammad Fayz Bakhsh, *Tarikh-i Farahbakhsh,* 98.
16. Athar Ali, *Mughal Nobility under Aurangzeb* (Delhi: Oxford University Press, 1997), 31.
17. For more on Persophone Hindus as well as the circulation of brief soteriological texts, see my unpublished doctoral dissertation: Supriya Gandhi, *Mughal Self-Fashioning, Indic Self-Realization: Dara Shikoh and Persian Textual Cultures in Early Modern South Asia* (PhD diss., Harvard University, 2011).

18. For reflections on Persian textual production in early modern India, see Nile Green, "The Uses of Books in a Late Mughal Takiyya: Persianate Knowledge between Person and Paper," *Modern Asian Studies* 44 (2010): 241–265.

19. I refer to the date of composition and not the date that the manuscript was copied; Debi Das ibn-i Bal Chand Sandilwi, *Khulasat-ul-khulasa,* Aligarh University, MS Ḥabibganj 24/3.

20. National Library, Kolkata, Buhar collection, MS Arabic 133, Dara Shukoh, *Majma-ul-bahrain.*

21. These names include a certain Ibn Mulla Muhammad Tutanji, whose patronymic means "tobacconist" in Turkish, pointing to an Ottoman connection. The translator is Muhammad Salih, son of the late Shaykh Ahmad Misri, whose patronymic suggests his Egyptian ancestry.

22. For a list of seventy-four of these, see Gandhi, *Mughal Self-Fashioning,* Appendix 2.

23. Carmichael Lib. Varanasi, P2029, cited in Mahesh Prasad, "The Unpublished Translation of the Upanishads by Prince Dara Shikoh," in *Dr. Modi Memorial Volume: Papers on Indo-Iranian and Other Subjects,* ed. Darab Peshotan Sanjana (Bombay: Fort Printing Press, 1930), 622–638.

24. For instance, Asiatic Society, MS Curzon 678, *Sirr-i Akbar.*

25. Khuda Bakhsh Library, Patna, HL 3662, *Sirr-i Akbar.*

26. Girdharilal Tikku, *Persian Poetry in Kashmir, 1339–1846: An Introduction* (Berkeley: University of California Publications, 1971), 266.

27. Rosane Rocher, "Nathaniel Brassey Halhed on the Upaniṣads (1787)," *Annals of the Bhandarkar Oriental Research Institute* 58/9 (1977/8): 279–289, 282.

28. Nathaniel Brassey Halhed, *A Code of Gentoo Laws or Ordinations of the Pundits from a Persian Translation from the Original Written in the Shanscrit Language* (London: s.n., 1776), xxi.

29. William Jones, "On the Musical Modes of the Hindus: Written in 1784, and Since Much Enlarged," *Asiatick Researches* 3 (1792): 55–87, 65.

30. It is not clear which particular version of the *Jog Basisht* that Sir John Shore translated. See Sir Leslie Stephen, *Dictionary of National Biography* (London: Smith, Elder, and Co., 1897), 52: 151.

31. Abraham Hyacinthe Anquetil-Duperron, *Oupnek'hat (id est, secretum tegendum),* 2 vols. (Strasbourg: Levrault, 1801), 2: x–xi.

32. Anquetil-Duperron has a particularly sustained attack aimed at Montesquieu's arguments on Oriental despotism developed in *De l'esprit des lois* (1748). See Lucette Valensi, "Éloge de l'orient, éloge de l'orientalism: Le jeu d'échecs d'Anquetil-Duperron," *Revue de L'histoire Des Religions* 212 (1995): 419–452.

33. Anquetil-Duperron, *Description Historique et Géographique de L'Inde* (Berlin: C. S. Spener, 1786–1789), 562.

34. "[N]ous n'aurions aucune traduction des Livres Indiens," Anquetil-Duperron, *Législation Orientale* (Amsterdam: Marc-Michel Rey, 1778), 140, cf. 21.

35. See his comments about conversion to Christianity in Anquetil's second preface, *Oupnek'hat.*

36. "[I]dem dogma, unicum universitatis parentem, unicum principium spirituale invenies,"Anquetil-Duperron, *Oupnek'hat,* 1: viii.

37. "An Account of Books for the Year 1802," anonymous review of *Oupnek'hat, The Asiatic Annual Register* (1803): 13–18.

38. For questions regarding the influence of Indic thought on Schopenhauer's philosophy, see Douglas Berger, *The Veil of Māyā: Schopenhauer's System and Early Indian Thought* (Binghamton: Global Academic Publishing, 2004). For an amusing account of a misunderstanding arising out of one of Schopenhauer's scribbled notes on his copy of the *Oupnek'hat,* which stated that this work talked of Amida, the bodhisattva Amitabha, see Urs App, "How Amida got into the Upanishads: An Orientalist's Nightmare," in *Essays on East Asian Religion and Culture,* ed. Christian Wittern and Lishan Shi (Kyoto: Editorial Committee for the Festschrift in Honour of Nishiwaki Tsuneki, 2007), 11–33. For more on Anquetil-Duperron, see App, *The Birth of Orientalism* (Philadelphia: University of Pennsylvania Press, 2010), 363–439.

39. Urs App, "Schopenhauer's Initial Encounter with Indian Thought," *Schopenhauer-Jahrbuch* 87 (2006): 35–76, esp. 53–56.

40. Tara Chand, "Rafi al-Khilaf of Sita Ram Kayastha Saksena," *The Journal of the Ganganatha Jha Research Institute,* 11 (1944): 7–12.

41. *"Ba nam-i ankih nami nadarad / Ba har nami kih khwani sar bar arad,"* Dara Shukoh, *Majma-ul-bahrain,* 2.

42. Chandrabhan Brahman, *Nazuk Khayalat* (Lahore, 1901), 3–4. There is no such text attributed to Shankara in the Sanskrit tradition. The *Nazuk Khayalat* is probably referring to *Atma Bodha* (Self-Wisdom), a work credited to Shankara's authorship.

43. Dara Shukoh (attributed), *Tariqat al-Haqiqat* (Gujranwala: Qaumi Press, 1895).

44. Dara Shukoh (attributed), *Rumuz-i tasawwuf* (Lahore: Mashhur-i Alam Press, 1923).

45. Nik Akhtar Timuri Dihlawi, *Sirat-i wahdat,* Hyderabad, Salar Jung Library, MS Tasawwuf 3476.

46. Dara Shukoh (attributed), *Ima al-muhaqqiqin,* Hyderabad, Salar Jung Library, MS Tasawwuf 25.

47. For instance, Rammohun Roy, *Tuhfat al-Muwahhidin* (Calcutta: Sadharan Brahmo Samaj, 1950).

48. Included in Rammohun Roy, *Translation of Several Principal Books, Passages and Texts of the Veds, and of Some Controversial Works on Brahmunical Theology* (London: Parbury, Allen, and Co., 1832).

49. Kanhaiyalal Alakhdhari, *Alakh Prakash* (Sialkot: Gyan Press, 1876), 23–24.

ACKNOWLEDGMENTS

Though writing is a seemingly solitary exercise, the leisure to research and write relies on the generosity and labor of others. My research on Dara Shukoh began at Harvard University, where I completed my PhD. I am grateful to my advisor, Ali Asani, as well as Parimal Patil, and Wheeler Thackston for their advice and encouragement. At the University of Pennsylvania, where I was a visiting student and a postdoctoral fellow, I thank Daud Ali, Jamal Elias, and Tajmah Assefi-Shirazi. I have shared many adventures in the Indo-Persian world with Sunil Sharma, from Sufi dargahs in Delhi to seminars at Harvard, and he kindly read the whole manuscript. Other scholars, including Muzaffar Alam, Carl Ernst, Jack Hawley, and Francesca Orsini, have always encouraged my research. Fellowships from the Andrew Mellon Foundation and the Fulbright Hays facilitated my initial forays into the visual and manuscript cultures of Mughal India.

Some of those who have helped plant the seeds of this book are sadly no longer with us. Yunus Jaffery and Majid Ahmady were my first teachers of Persian and always took an interest in my work. Ahmed Reza Jalali Naini and Daryush Shayegan gifted me their books before I knew I would write on Dara Shukoh. Madiha Gauhar gave me a CD of her play on Dara with Shahid Nadeem. I wish I could have shared the finished version of the book with Ankit Chadha.

I presented material from this book at Kashmir University, Yale University, Columbia University, the University of Virginia, and Indiana University

Bloomington. At Oxford University, Cornell University, and the University of Pennsylvania I gave talks that touched upon some of the themes in this book. I am grateful to the many who invited me and engaged with my work at these venues.

My research has drawn on the holdings of several libraries. I am especially indebted to the staff of the British Library, the Bodleian Library, Cambridge University Library, the Maulana Azad Library at Aligarh Muslim University, and the Allama Iqbal Library at Kashmir University, as well as to Imtiaz Ahmad, former director of the Khuda Bakhsh Oriental Library, Abdul Moid Khan, director of the Maulana Azad Arabic and Persian Research Centre in Tonk, and Mehdi Khajeh Piri of the Iran Culture House, New Delhi. Research on premodern South Asia is greatly eased when repositories allow scholars to take photographs of manuscripts or otherwise make digital images available. I am thankful for those that do, and I hope that more libraries will facilitate the availability of their resources.

I completed this book while at Yale University. My department chair, Kathryn Lofton, offered much support and hospitality and so did colleagues in Religious Studies, including Gerhard Bowering, Phyllis Granoff, Frank Griffel, Noreen Khawaja, and Nancy Levene. Elsewhere at Yale, I thank Abbas Amanat, Rohit De, Kasturi Gupta, Karuna Mantena, Swapna Sharma, and Shawkat Toorawa. Funding from the MacMillan Center for International and Area Studies at Yale helped with expenses incurred during the book's production. Outside Yale, I benefited from discussing aspects of this book with many colleagues, including Afshan Bokhari, Munis Faruqui, Rajeev Kinra, Matt Melvin Koushki, Murad Khan Mumtaz, Shankar Nair, Dan Sheffield, and Audrey Truschke.

I feel fortunate to have been able to work with Sharmila Sen of Harvard University Press. Heather Hughes shepherded me through the publication process. John Hoey of Westchester Publishing Services ensured that the production of the book ran efficiently. In addition, Valerie Joy Turner helped smooth out some of the manuscript's rough edges.

This book was composed over the course of moves and travels across three continents, with a small child in tow. My parents, Usha and Rajmohan Gandhi, made crucial visits during school holidays, enabling me to get writing done. In India, where I began writing this book, the generous support of Jayashree and Ravindra Rao was indispensable, and Pramila Kamble provided much-needed childcare. Several friends helped sustain me, including Neeti Nair and Sarah Quraishi. I am also grateful to my brother Debu Gandhi, sister-in-law, Sandra Snabb, and mother-in-law, Cynthia Eastman. My partner, Travis Zadeh, championed my work and read the book with a critical eye. I dedicate this book to our son Anoush, who has seen it take shape since he could walk and talk.

ILLUSTRATION CREDITS

Page x. Map ocourtesy of the author.

Page 13. Submission of Rana Amar Singh to Prince Khurram. Painted by Nanha. Lahori, *Padshah-nama*. © The Royal Collection, Royal Library, Windsor Castle, MS 1367, fol. 46b, 1005025.g.

Page 29. Jahangir converses with Chidrup. Detached folio from a *Jahangir-nama*, circa 1620. Courtesy of the Musée des Arts asiatiques-Guimet, Paris, 85EE1944.

Page 33. Portrait of Shuja as a child. The Art and History Collection, courtesy of the Freer Gallery of Art and Arthur M. Sackler Gallery, Smithsonian Institution, Washington, D.C., LTS1995.2.98.

Page 35. Khurram with young Dara Shukoh. Album folio, painted by Nanha, circa 1618. Courtesy of the Metropolitan Museum of Art, New York, 55.121.10.36.

Page 36. Khurram with young son, circa 1620. © Victoria and Albert Museum, London, IS 90–1965.

Page 63. Shah Jahan at his accession meeting sons accompanied by Asaf Khan, March 1632. Painted by Bichitr. Lahori, *Padshah-nama*. © The Royal Collection, Royal Library, Windsor Castle, MS 1367, fol.50b, 1005025.k.

Page 84. Aurangzeb facing the elephant Sudhakar, June 1632. Lahori, *Padshah-nama*. © The Royal Collection, Royal Library, Windsor Castle, MS 1367, fol. 134a, 1005025.ad.

Page 110. Portrait of Mulla Shah Badakhshi. Album folio. The Art and History Collection, courtesy of the Freer Gallery of Art and Arthur M. Sackler Gallery, Smithsonian Institution, Washington, D.C., LTS2002.2.4.

Page 112. Portrait of Mulla Shah Badakhshi. Album folio misidentified. Courtesy of the Boston Museum of Fine Arts, 14.664.

Page 113. Portrait of Mulla Shah Badakhshi under tree. Album folio. © Trustees of the British Museum, London, 1949,0212,0.5.

Page 165. Mughal prince converses with Hindu ascetic and other holy men. Private collection, image courtesy of Stuart Cary Welch.

Page 178. Shah Jahan and Dara Shukoh meet Khizr en route to the Chishti shrine at Ajmer. *Padshah-nama.* © The Royal Collection, Royal Library, Windsor Castle, MS 1367, fol. 205b, 1005025.ap.

Page 200. Gathering of Holy Men. Album folio, circa 1650. © Victoria and Albert Museum, London, IS 94–1965.

Pages 228–229. Battle of Samugarh. Attributed to Payag, circa 1658. Harvard Art Museums/Arthur M. Sackler Museum. © President and Fellows of Harvard College, 1999.298.

Page 242. Portrait of Dara Shukoh's head brought to Aurangzeb. Niccolò Manucci, *Histoire de l'Inde,* also known as the *Libro rosso,* late seventeenth-century painting in the Deccani style. Bibliothèque Nationale de France, Paris, Estampes, Rés., Codex Od. 45, no. 14, pet. fol., fol. 31a.

Page 243. Colophon of Jahanara, *Ayat-ul-bayyinat,* dated 1663, autograph copy. Author's photo. Aligarh Muslim University, Maulana Azad Library, Habibganj Collection, MS 1/55, fol. 74b.

Pages 252–253. Dara Shukoh with pandits. Illustrated in the *Sirr-i akbar,* late eighteenth-century manuscript. Author's photo. Khuda Bakhsh Oriental Public Library, Patna, MS HL 3662, fol. 2a.

Page 256. Om/Allah, opening to early twentieth-century lithograph edition of Dara Shukoh, *Sirr-i akbar,* Jaipur: Hiralal Press, n.d. Author's photo, private collection.

INDEX

Bernier, François, 175, 176, 181, 182, 183, 186, 212, 224, 235–236, 237, 238, 247–248

Bihishti of Shiraz, 215, 217–218, 231, 232, 236–237

Bihzad, Kamal-ud-Din, 28

Bir Singh Bundela, 100

blasphemy, 246. *See also* apostasy

book knowledge, 131, 133, 168, 188, 190. *See also* religious studies, Dara Shukoh's

books, Dara Shukoh's. *See* writings, Dara Shukoh's

Brahma, 209–210

bureaucracy, Mughal, 21, 248–249

Burhanpur, 26, 65

Busée, Henri (Henricus Busaeu), 182

calendar system, 106

calligraphy, 74–76

Central Asian campaign, 131–132, 138

Central Asian nobility, 144

certainty, 107

Chadha, Ankit, 5

chakras, 134

Chandarbhan Brahman, 136, 167, 175, 177, 246–247, 254

charismatic transference, 96, 108

Chaudhuri, Jatindra Bimal, 190

Chidrup, 27–30, 31–32

child mortality, 31, 43

children: in Khurram's rebellion, 49; raising of, 26

Chishtis: Abd-ur-Rahman Chishti, 69–70, 71, 72, 129, 199; Ahmad Sirhindi, 38–39, 70–71, 73, 74; Dara Shukoh's association with, 129–131; eclecticism of, 72; engagement with Indic thought, 69–70; Jahanara's association with, 105, 122; Khwaja Muin-ud-Din Chishti, 12, 14, 22, 70, 104–105, 122, 201; Nizam-ud-Din, 37, 72; Qutb-ud-Din Bakhtiyar Kaki, 201; relationship with state, 71–72; Shaikh Muhibbullah Mubariz, 129–131; tombs of, 175. *See also* Sufis

Christianity: Dara Shukoh as martyr, 241; Jesuits, 182–183, 184–185; trinity, 210

chronicles, of Akbar's reign, 8, 106, 137, 156

chronicles, of Aurangzeb's reign, 238–239

chronicles/chroniclers, of Shah Jahan's reign, 220; Lahori, 67, 73, 80, 82, 86, 87, 106, 124, 126; Muhammad Salih Kamboh, 214; Orchha campaign in, 100;

Padshah-nama, 62, 64, 67, 73, 80, 82, 177, 178; Tabatabai, 79, 99, 202; tax on Hindu pilgrims and, 212. *See also* Qazwini, Mirza Amin; *individual chroniclers*

circumcision, 43

civil war. *See* war of succession

Colebrooke, Henry Thomas, 251

colonial rule, 255, 257

conservatives, religious: Dara's censure of, 154; in Shah Jahan's rule, 8–9, 106. *See also* orthodoxy; piety

corpses, transfer of, 43

Coryate, Thomas, 19, 20, 22–23, 24, 25, 57

Dabistan-i mazahib (The School of Religious Sects; Mubad Shah), 94, 183, 184, 191

Dara Shukoh, 105; aesthetic sensibilities of, 74; after Jahangir's death, 59; after war of succession, 231–232, 233; birth of, 15, 17; children of, 85–86, 97, 102, 126, 233, 236–237, 242, 244 (*see also* Sipihr Shukoh; Sulaiman Shukoh); context of, 9–10; depictions of in art, 32, 34, 35, 77; execution of, 3, 4, 240–241; grave of, 245–246; health of, 86–87; historical/cultural memory of, 167, 248; as hostage, 52–53, 55–59; image of, 4, 136–137, 247–248; known as Shah Buland Iqbal, 185; legacy of, 5; military experience of, 104, 117, 144, 145, 147, 151, 157–163, 235; as mythical character, 2, 4; Qadiri life and, 88; rank of, 85, 216; redemption of, 4; relationship with brothers, 82; relationship with Jahanara, 26, 97–98; religious and intellectual interests of, 7 (*see also* religious studies, Dara Shukoh's); responsibilities of, 103–104; reunion with parents, 62–64; scholarship on, 6–7; siblings of, 26, 43, 66 (*see also* Aurangzeb; Jahanara; Shah Shuja); sympathy for, 248; trial of, 1–2; visions/dreams of, 128–129, 150, 194–195, 196; visits to Mulla Shah, 94, 128; wives of, 77 (*see also* Nadira Bano Begam)

dastan, 5

Dawar Bakhsh, 32, 43, 58, 59, 60, 61–62

death, law and, 43

Debi Das, 249

Delhi, 144. *See also* Shahjahanabad

della Valle, Pietro, 42